David Philipp Lorenz

The Application of Sustainable Development Principles to the Theory and Practice of Property Valuation

**Karlsruher Schriften zur
Bau-, Wohnungs- und Immobilienwirtschaft**

Band 1

Herausgeber

Universität Karlsruhe (TH)

Lehrstuhl Ökonomie und Ökologie des Wohnungsbaus

Prof. Dr.-Ing. habil. Thomas Lützkendorf

The Application of Sustainable Development Principles to the Theory and Practice of Property Valuation

von
David Philipp Lorenz

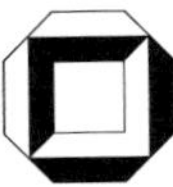

universitätsverlag karlsruhe

Dissertation, genehmigt von der Fakultät für Wirtschaftswissenschaften der Universität Fridericiana zu Karlsruhe, 2006

Referenten: Prof. Dr. Thomas Lützkendorf, Prof. Dr. Hermann Göppl

Impressum

Universitätsverlag Karlsruhe
c/o Universitätsbibliothek
Straße am Forum 2
D-76131 Karlsruhe
www.uvka.de

Universitätsverlag Karlsruhe 2006
Print on Demand

ISSN: 1863-8694
ISBN-13: 978-3-86644-089-0
ISBN-10: 3-86644-089-8

Vorwort des Herausgebers

Die Reihe von Karlsruher Schriften zur Bau-, Wohnungs- und Immobilienwirtschaft wird vom Stiftungslehrstuhl Ökonomie und Ökologie des Wohnungsbaus an der wirtschaftswissenschaftlichen Fakultät der Universität Karlsruhe (TH) herausgegeben. Einrichtung, Aufbau und Betrieb des Lehrstuhls werden seit dem Jahr 2000 in großzügiger Weise durch die Schwäbisch Hall-Stiftung „bauen – wohnen – leben" unterstützt.

Die Schriftenreihe versteht sich als ein Medium zur Vorstellung von Ergebnissen der wissenschaftlichen Auseinandersetzung u.a. mit Fragen der Planung, Errichtung und Bewirtschaftung von Gebäuden, der Bewertung, Finanzierung und Versicherung von Immobilien, der dynamischen Entwicklung von Gebäudebeständen oder von Trends im Bedürfnisfeld Bauen und Wohnen. Durch die Beiträge soll die Weiterentwicklung von Grundlagen und Ansätzen u.a. der integralen Planung, der Lebenszyklusanalyse, der Investitions- und Wirtschaftlichkeitsrechnung sowie insbesondere der Umsetzung von Prinzipien einer nachhaltigen Entwicklung im Immobilienbereich unterstützt und befördert werden.

Mit dem Band 1 wird die am Lehrstuhl entstandene und betreute Dissertationsschrift von Herrn David Lorenz vorgestellt. Sie leistet einen Beitrag zur Integration von mit der Umsetzung von Prinzipien einer nachhaltigen Entwicklung verbundenen Aufgaben und Zielen in den Arbeits- und Verantwortungsbereich von Akteuren der Immobilienbranche. Ausgehend von einer intensiven Auseinandersetzung mit den Wurzeln, Grundlagen und Trends der Nachhaltigkeitsdiskussion stellt Herr Lorenz am Beispiel von Vorschlägen zur Weiterentwicklung der Immobilienwertermittlung Ansätze vor, wie u.a. die funktionale, technische und ökologische Qualität von Immobilien in die Beschreibung, Bewertung und Berücksichtigung einer hieraus resultierenden ökonomischen Vorteilhaftigkeit einfließen kann. Die Ergebnisse der Arbeit stellen eine Grundlage für die Entwicklung und Beurteilung von sich an den Prinzipien einer nachhaltigen Entwicklung orientierenden Investmentprodukten im Immobilienbereich und die Formulierung entsprechender Anlagestrategien dar und liefern so einen Beitrag zu einer hochaktuellen Diskussion in der Finanz- und Immobilienbranche.

Karlsruhe, im Dezember 2006

Prof. Dr.-Ing. habil. Thomas Lützkendorf
Leiter des Lehrstuhls für Ökonomie und
Ökologie des Wohnungsbaus

Editor's Preface

This series of publications on the construction, housing, and property industry (Karlsruher Schriften zur Bau-, Wohnungs- und Immobilienwirtschaft) is issued by the Chair of Sustainable Management of Housing and Real Estate at the School of Economics and Business Engineering at the University of Karlsruhe. The Chair's formation, installation as well as its current operation are generously supported since the year 2000 through the foundation Schwäbisch Hall-Stiftung "bauen – wohnen – leben".

The intention of this series of publications consists in presenting research results concerning, amongst other issues, questions related to the planning, construction and management of buildings; the valuation, financing and insurance of property assets; the dynamic development of building stocks or of trends in the area of housing and living. The publications shall support and promote the further development of basics and approaches concerning, for example, integral planning, life cycle assessment, investment and economic appraisal as well as the implementation of the principles of sustainable development within the property sector.

The first issue of this series presents the dissertation written by Mr. David Lorenz which has been developed and supervised at the Chair of Sustainable Management of Housing and Real Estate. The dissertation contributes to the integration of duties and goals associated with the implementation of the principles of sustainable development into the fields of work and areas of responsibility of actors from within the property sector. Starting from an intense examination of the roots, basics and trends of the sustainable development discourse Mr. Lorenz introduces proposals for the further development of property valuation practice and shows, amongst other issues, how the functional, technical and ecological quality of buildings can be taken into consideration for the description and evaluation of resulting economic benefits. The findings of this work also contribute to a highly topical discussion within the finance and property sector since they provide a basis for the development and assessment of property investment products and respective investment strategies that are aligned with the principles of sustainable development.

Karlsruhe, December 2006

Prof. Dr.-Ing. habil. Thomas Lützkendorf
Head of the Chair of Sustainable Management
of Housing and Real Estate

The Application of Sustainable Development Principles to the Theory and Practice of Property Valuation

DISSERTATION

Submitted to achieve the scientific degree of a Doctor in Economics
(Dr. rer. pol.)

Approved by the School of Economics and Business Engineering,
Universität Fridericiana of Karlsruhe

Dipl. Bw. (BA) David Philipp Lorenz B.A. M.Sc. MRICS

Date of the examination: 31 October 2006
Referee: Prof. Dr. Thomas Lützkendorf
Co-referee: Prof. Dr. Hermann Göppl

Acknowledgements

This dissertation is the result of my work as a research assistant at the Chair of Sustainable Management of Housing and Real Estate at the University of Karlsruhe.

First of all, I would like to express my sincere gratitude to Prof. Dr. Thomas Lützkendorf, my supervisor, for providing me with the right balance of intellectual guidance and freedom necessary to complete this dissertation. In particular, I thank him for his ongoing willingness to spend time for discussion and critical debate.

In addition, I thank Prof. Dr. Hermann Göppl for acting as the co-referee as well as Prof. Dr. Ute Werner and Prof. Dr. Christof Weinhardt for their participation in the examination.

I also want to thank Richard Lorch for reviewing the manuscript and for helping me to bypass the pitfalls of the English language. Additionally, I thank him for very useful comments and constructive critique.

Furthermore, I am grateful to Dr. Stefan Trück for critical comments on the statistical part of the dissertation and to John Mansfield for continuing exchange of ideas on property valuation theory.

I also thank Martin Weller from the valuation expert committee of the city of Stuttgart for his generosity of providing the property transaction dataset.

Finally, my thanks go to all the members of the Chair of Sustainable Management of Housing and Real Estate for creating a friendly and productive working environment.

Dedicated

*to my parents, Elli and Werner, for always supporting me
and for enabling me to study in freedom,*

and

to Mieke, for all her love and encouragement.

Table of Contents

List of Figures

List of Tables

List of Boxes

1. Introduction

1.1 Motivation and focus

Within property markets several actors such as constructors, designers, engineers, researchers, governmental authorities, or certain occupiers and clients have been concerned with aspects of sustainable development since decades. Also within investment markets efforts are being made to include issues of social responsibility and environmental protection into investment and business policies since over a decade. However, actors within global property investment markets[1] such as fund and asset managers, institutional and private investors, estate agents, valuers and analysts have responded more slowly to the challenges imposed by sustainable development. For example, the first full commitment to environmental protection and social responsibility in property investment and management was issued in February 2006 by the UK-based fund company Hermes (2006).

Sustainable development means development that meets the needs of the present without comprising the ability of future generations to meet their own needs (WCED, 1987). This concept comprises two strong elements: (1) the element of satisfying human needs and requirements (i.e. quality of life), and (2) an element of intra- and intergenerational ethics which is required due to the strains imposed by both intensive technologies and social organizations on nature's ability to provide essential ecosystem services for present and future generations. However, environmental and social concerns have not been on property investment agendas until very recently. This is an urgent issue because within efforts undertaken by the global community to achieve more sustainable development, probably no industrial sector has as great a potential role as property and construction; and it is the property investment sector that drives the market and determines 'best practice' in planning, construction, management, and demolition of buildings. In OECD countries the built environment is responsible for around 25-40% of total energy use, 30% of raw material use, 30-40% of global greenhouse gas emissions and for 30 to 40% of solid waste generation (OECD, 2003 and UNEP, 2006). Thus, property and construction has the largest single share in global environmental degradation and impairment of human well-being.

The Earth's ecosystems are now at a critical stage: they are not only being severely damaged but human activity currently leads to *irreversible* losses of critical (i.e. life-supporting) eco-

---

[1] The total market value of the global investible property universe was estimated to be around US\$ 6.2 trillion by the end of 2003 representing 14% of the global investment market (see Chen and Mills, 2004 and Section 2.4.2 below).

system functions (MA, 2006). A dreadful example for this is the recent rupturing of the Ward Hunt ice shelf which took place without almost any coverage in the media.[2] 'By any measure, we are destroying the most productive systems ever seen on earth while statistically blinding ourselves to the problem' (Hawken et al., 1999, p. 61). In doing so, human activity seriously restricts the Earth System's capability to self-regulate the planet's climate and chemistry in order to be as favourable as possible for contemporary life.[3] The Earth System dynamics are characterised by critical thresholds and abrupt changes and the system is already struggling to maintain the desired temperature (ADGC, 2001). By adding ever more greenhouse gases to the air while at the same time destroying or replacing natural ecosystems (like forests with farmland), the Earth is hit twice: 'We are interfering with temperature regulation by turning up the heat and then simultaneously removing the natural systems that help to regulate it' (Lovelock, 2006, p. 45). Several groups of reputable scientists have recently argued that environmental degradation caused by human activity has reached levels at which the ability of the Earth's ecosystems to sustain future generations can no longer be taken for granted (MA, 2005; see also IPCC, 2001a; ADGC, 2001; WI, 2006 and MA, 2006).

In response to this situation the present dissertation aims motivating more sustainable patterns of behaviour within property investment markets. Due to the interconnectedness of property investment and construction markets, the dissertation outlines both the property investment and construction industries' challenges caused by the pressing need for more sustainable development as well as the industries' possible contribution to major environmental release and gains in individual and collective well-being. However, the major argument is not that sustainable behaviour in property and construction markets should be pursued only because it is

---

[2] The Ward Hunt ice shelf has lost 90% of its mass in less than a century and is now melting away along with the unique ecosystem of ice-nourished bacteria that it supports. Its recent rupturing ended another ecosystem by allowing a rare freshwater lake to drain into the ocean: 'In September 2003, almost exactly two years after the massacres in New York City and Washington, DC, an even more ominous event occurred, although it featured on no front pages and inspired no rousing speeches from our leaders. The Ward Hunt ice shelf – the largest ice shelf in the Arctic [a 450-square-kilometre ledge that's 25 metres thick and reaches up into the Arctic Ocean from the mouth of Ellesmere Island's Disraeli Fiord], which had been in place for tens of thousands of years – suddenly ruptured and began to collapse. Warwick Vincent, a professor of biology at Laval University in Quebec, explained: 'We'd been measuring the incremental changes in the Arctic ice each year. Suddenly everything changed.' The scientists witnessing the event later admitted to weeping with the same shock and grief felt by those who watched the Twin Towers fall to dust: this was global warming happening far more quickly than anyone had anticipated' (The Independent, 19 September 2005).
[3] The notion that the Earth self-regulates its climate and chemistry was publicly announced by over 1,500 scientists from over 100 countries on 13 July 2001 in the Amsterdam Declaration on Global Change: 'The Earth System behaves as a single, self-regulating system comprised of physical, chemical, biological and human components. The interactions and feedbacks between the component parts are complex and exhibit multi-scale temporal and spatial variability' (ADGC, 2001, p. 1). The notion that this self-regulating system has the goal of being as favourable or habitable as possible for contemporary life is one central element of so-called Gaia theory, named after the Greek goddess and introduced by James Lovelock in 1979 (see Lovelock, 1979, 2005 and 2006).

good for people and the environment and because environmental legislation requires to do so, but because it significantly increases financial profit and long-term competitiveness.

There are no adverse side effects of applying sustainable development thinking to the investment in, development and management of property assets. Indeed, sustainable development thinking particularly lends itself to cope with the nature of property investments which traditionally require pursuing medium- to long-term investment strategies. Taking sustainability issues into consideration results in countless win-win situations for the actors of property markets. Sustainable buildings squeeze the maximum utility for owners, users and the wider public out of the lowest possible use of land and throughput of energy and raw materials. These buildings are not more expensive to build from the outset than conventional ones but their ownership results in various benefits for investors, ranging from drastically lower operating costs to improved marketability, longer useful life-spans, more stable cash flows and significantly increased occupant productivity and well-being (Wilson et al., 1998; Yates, 2001; Heerwagen, 2002; Kats et al., 2003 and RICS, 2005). Thus, the working hypothesis of this dissertation is that increasing economic return, sustaining the natural environment and protecting social values are not incompatible; at least not within property and construction markets.

However, while various forces such as governmental policies and regulations, changes in consumer behaviour and in corporate governance and accounting practices are currently reshaping the 'rules of the property game' to further promote the business case for more sustainable development, the application of sustainable property investment strategies is far from being a mainstream activity. The reason for this is seen in the circumstance that property investors are cut off from feedback on the environmental and social performance of the buildings they own, manage, trade or occupy. Property investors are cut off from this feedback because contemporary property valuation practice neglects the benefits of sustainable design as well as the risks associated with conventional buildings that increasingly fail to attract market demand and that are increasingly exposed to ever more stringent environmental legislation. Evidence for these shortcomings in property valuation practice is found in the lack of valuation literature on this issue. The only known published contributions that provide initial proposals to reflect sustainability issues in property market valuations are Lützkendorf and Bachofner (2002); McNamara (2002); Guidry (2004); Lorenz and Lützkendorf (2004); Lützkendorf and Lorenz (2005); McNamara (2005a); Lorenz et al. (2006); and Kimmet (2006).[4]

Given that the literature on this issue is sparse, it is likely that contemporary property valuation practice fails to account for all the factors that determine the competitive position of property assets in the marketplace. As a consequence, contemporary valuation practice bears the risk that estimates of property values are being distorted and that uninformed and harmful decisions are made on the basis of these valuations. For this reason, the primary focus of this dissertation is on property values, on how they are created and destroyed and, most importantly, on how they are estimated.

1.2 Research objectives, information sources and research strategy

This dissertation is an exploration into the fields of sustainable development, property investment and valuation. The two primary research objectives are: (1) to explore the rationale for both immediately and rigorously integrating sustainability issues into property investment strategies as well as into property valuation theory and practice; and (2), to offer a property valuation framework that allows valuers simultaneously responding to the urgent need of expressing property risk and valuation uncertainty more explicitly within valuation reports *and* to account for sustainability issues when estimating market value. In order to achieve this, four main research questions need to be addressed at four different strategic levels or areas of interest respectively. These main research questions as well as resulting sub-questions are depict in Figure 1.

In order to answer these questions and to accomplish the two primary research objectives, the author draws upon information obtained through: (1) literature research; (2) internet research; (3) participation in various property and construction related conferences (e.g. World Building Congress, Toronto, May 2004; European Real Estate Society Conference, Milan, June 2004; Central and Eastern European Conference on Sustainable Building (SB04), Warsaw, October 2004; World Sustainable Building Conference (SB05), Tokyo, September 2005); (4) participation in several workshops and meetings relating to this topic (e.g. the Architects' Council of Europe Taskforce meeting on Environment and Sustainable Architecture, Strasbourg, October 2004; United Nations Environment Programme's EU-Asia Cross-Learning Seminar on Mainstreaming Sustainable Building and Construction in China, Shanghai, May 2005; the Royal Institution of Chartered Surveyors' Great George Street Debate on Sustainable Property Investment, London, March 2005; United Nations Environment Programme's launching event of the Sustainable Buildings and Construction Initiative, Paris, February 2006); (5) an empirical analysis of a property transaction dataset covering more than 20,000 transactions that appeared during 1995 and 2005 within the city of Suttgart, Germany; and (6) own practical experiences in the fields of property valuation and investment advisory.

Figure 1: *Main research questions and resulting sub-questions*

Strategic level	Main research questions	Resulting sub-questions
Society	**What is sustainable development and why is it necessary?**	➢ Why is there an urgent need for ethical and economic re-evaluation and what is the deeper cause of the modern ecological crisis? ➢ Which ‚schools of thought' or ‚worldviews' have led to the contemporary understanding of the concept of sustainable development? ➢ What are the management principles of a sustainable society and how to measure progress in achieving sustainability?
Property and construction market	**What is sustainable property investment and what are sustainable property investment products?**	➢ What is the role of the property and construction sector within the struggle towards sustainability? ➢ What are appropriate strategies for different actors in order to move purposefully towards success? ➢ Which forces currently shape the property market and alter the competitive position of buildings in the marketplace?
Single Buildings	**What are the constituents of sustainable buildings and how to measure their performance?**	➢ What are sustainability key performance indicators and which methods and tools can be used to assess them? ➢ What are the links between sustainable design features and economic benefits?
Property Valuation	**What are theoretical and practical options for valuers to account for sustainability issues within their estimates of market value and to express risk and uncertainty within valuation reports at the same time?**	➢ What determines property value and which methods can be used to estimate it? ➢ Which data requirements need to be met in order to reflect sustainability issues in property valuation? ➢ What is property risk and valuation uncertainty and why is it necessary to express it in valuation reports?

The research strategy pursued in this dissertation follows a 'strategic sustainable development model' for integrating environmental, social and financial factors into business decision-making that has recently been proposed by Waage et al. (2005) in an article published in the Journal of Cleaner Production. This model relies on continual consideration of the broader system in which specific actions are embedded. 'The core argument is that without a sustainability vision of the future – based on principles to achieve success – it is possible to invest in measures that provide short-term benefits without addressing the long-term sustainability of systems' (Waage et al., 2005, p. 1147). For the purpose of this dissertation the proposed model is particularly useful but it had to be slightly modified or re-interpreted in order to comply with the specific aim if this dissertation. Having said this, the dissertation's research strategy can be generally described as follows:

Step 1: Defining the system (i.e. understanding the basic functions of the ecosystem's services and the constitutional principles of this system, including both ecological and social principles).

Step 2: Identifying outcomes and success (i.e. defining sustainable development and drafting a vision for the future).

Step 3: Articulating strategies for forward movement (i.e. understanding the crucial role of property and construction within the struggle towards sustainability and explaining different strategies for different actors of property and construction markets to move purposefully towards success).

Step 4: Determining action (i.e. identifying concrete actions that need to be undertaken within the property and construction sector in order to reach success. In this regard, two actions have been identified which are considered critical: (1) organising loops of feedback and adaptation through continuous sustainability assessment of property assets, and (2) integrating this information into the processes of property investment, management and property valuation).

Step 5: Identifying, developing and proposing appropriate methodological basics and procedures (i.e. frameworks for building performance assessment, sustainable property investment, and property valuation).

1.3   Summary

The dissertation is divided into three main parts (Chapter 2, 3 and 4). The second Chapter deals with sustainable development in general and with the role of the property and construction sector. The third Chapter looks at the changing business environment for property investments and discusses progress and responses made by the property and construction industry to meet the challenges imposed by sustainable development. The fourth Chapter builds upon the previous chapters and deals exclusively with property valuation. These three chapters are summarized in the following:

Chapter 2 starts off with a brief explanation of current environmental problems, of basic ecosystem functions and of the links between ecosystem services and human well-being. This is followed by a broad introduction into the field of sustainable development. Section 2.2 traces sustainable development thinking back to its roots and explains the contemporary understanding of the concept of sustainable development as well as its goal and principles. Within this, the attempt is made to set the philosophical foundations of a more poetical economy which can be seen as the broader framework in which sustainable patterns of behaviour can flourish and prosper. In doing so, a sustainability vision of the future is drafted. Section 2.3 explains how progresses in achieving sustainability can be measured and why this is important. Basic forms of assessment are explained and different approaches to sustainability assessment (i.e. environmental, social, and economics driven approaches) are critically discussed. Section 2.4 identifies buildings and construction activity as the cornerstone of sustainability and highlights the property and construction sectors' significant environmental, social and economic impacts as well as its major potential for environmental release and increases in collective and individual well-being. Furthermore, recommendations for different groups of actors in property and construction markets are given in order to collectively move towards sustainability. Finally, the critical roles of information and trust within property markets are explained and it is shown why success in property and construction depends as much on information as it depends on integrity, intact inter-human connections, social networks, and agreeable behaviour.

Chapter 3 begins with a short discussion of the 'anatomy' of property transactions and of the 'rules of the property game'. This is followed by a detailed analysis of forces that further promote the business case for sustainable development in property and construction, and thus, alter the competitive position of property assets in the marketplace (Section 3.2). These forces can generally be described as changes in: governmental policy and regulation; consumer behaviour; investment, corporate governance and accounting practices; as well as in banking and insurance practices. This chapter also contains an estimation of the current, untapped market potential for sustainable property investment products. It is shown that from the perspective of optimal asset allocation, the Socially Responsible Investment (SRI) sector is significantly underallocated in property assets. Based on the size of the global SRI sector the market for sustainable property investment products is estimated to equal to approximately 1/3 of the current free-float market capitalization of the FTSE EPRA/NAREIT[5] global listed real estate index which was at US$ 644 billion by the end of 2005. Subsequent to this analysis of the wider business environment for property investments, Section 3.3 looks at the property

---

[5] On 21 February 2005 the global index provider FTSE took over the calculations of this index series designed to track the performance of listed real estate companies and real estate investment trusts (REITs) worldwide. The index was formerly calculated by the European Public Real Estate Association (EPRA) and the U.S. National Association of Real Estate Investment Trusts (NAREIT).

and construction industry itself and pinpoints two key successes and two key failures in achieving more sustainable development. Also, the concept of sustainable development is translated to construction works and the constituents of sustainable buildings are explained. In addition, an integrated building performance assessment framework, as well as respective sustainability key performance indicators for property assets, is introduced. Section 3.3 concludes with a brief outline of the evolution of building assessment tools and with recommendations for the further development of these tools so that a new and desirable quality of support can be provided for design and decision making processes. Section 3.4 introduces the notion of property investing in pursuit of sustainability. A framework for sustainable property investing is proposed and respective investment strategies are explained. Finally, the role of property valuation is discussed and it is argued that successes in achieving more sustainable development in property and construction largely depends on progresses in integrating sustainability issues into property valuation theory and practice.

Chapter 4 looks at property valuation in detail. The chapter begins with a review of the basic goal of property valuation, its main purposes and of the history of the valuation profession. Furthermore, the introductory part outlines two challenges – besides accounting for sustainability issues – that need to be met by the valuation profession in order to improve the quality of valuation services and the standing of the profession in the business world. These are: reporting of risk and accounting for uncertainty within valuation reports; i.e. to increase the transparency of valuation processes. Section 4.2 outlines the theoretical and methodological basics of property valuation. This includes: (1) an investigation into the theory of value which has been identified as a neglected area of property valuation research. The theory of value as put forward in this dissertation is based on the works of Xenophon, Aristotle and the Austrian School of economics (notably the works of Carl Menger and Ludwig van Mises); (2) a critical discussion of the main concepts of value used in property valuation; and (3), a brief description of all available property valuation methods. Section 4.3 explains how property valuers can reflect sustainability issues within their estimates of market value and calculations of worth. Section 4.3 begins with a discussion of both general options for valuers to reflect sustainability issues in valuation reports and of the suitability of particular valuation methods to accomplish this task. This is followed by a hedonic pricing case study. The goal of this case study is to test the applicability of hedonic regression and index construction methodology in revealing insights into the value market participants place on particular sustainable design features. Subsequently, a proposal is offered for the extension of the most widespread valuation method – the income approach. This proposal for a property valuation framework is designed in a way that allows valuers to meet three challenges of the valuation profession at the same time; i.e. reporting property risk, accounting for valuation uncertainty, and reflecting sustainability issues within estimates of market value. Finally, within Section 4.4 it is argued that the valuation profession can only become part of the sustainability vision of the future if it manages to re-design educational programmes for valuers to include elements of education for sustainable development and if it can provide clients with real feedback on the environmental, social and economic performance of the buildings they own, sell or wish to buy.

In summary, the dissertation's main contribution consists in the provision of the methodological and conceptual basis for integrating sustainability issues into property investment processes, products and property valuation theory and practice. In order to achieve this, it was necessary to solve research questions at four different strategic levels. The major outcomes are summarized in the following Figure 2.

Figure 2: *Major contributions of this dissertation*

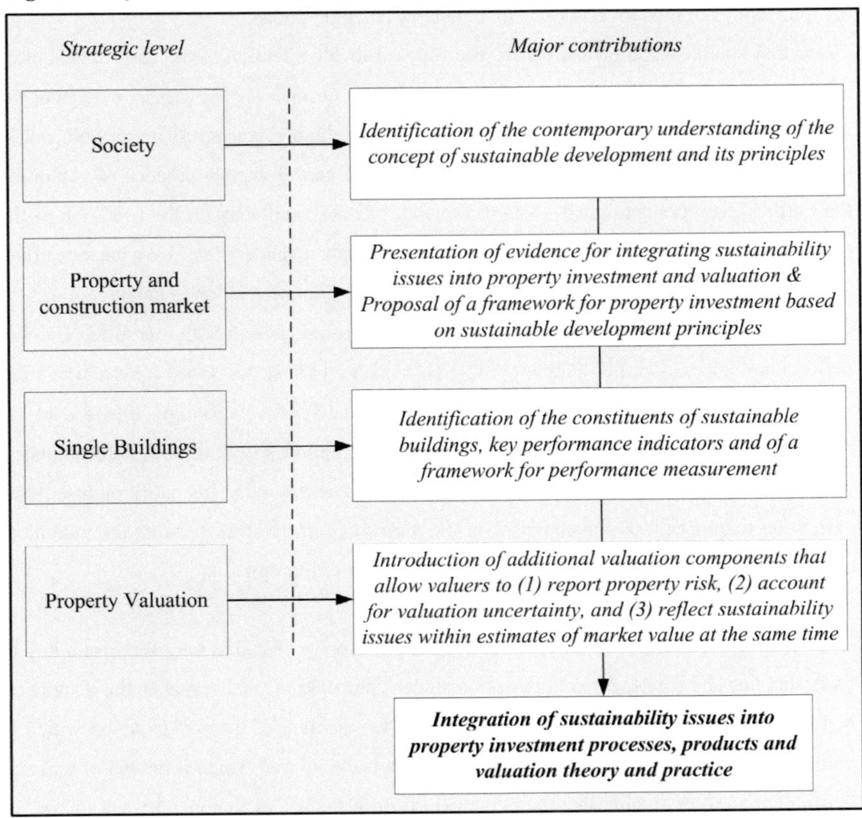

2.   Sustainable development and the role of property and construction

2.1   Introduction

The current state of the Earth's ecosystems gives rise for more than serious concern. The board of the Millennium Ecosystem Assessment (MA) – which was called for by United Nations Secretary-General Kofi Annan in 2000 and was published in 2005 involving the work of more than 1.360 experts worldwide – stated that:

> *'Human activity is putting such strain on the natural functions of Earth that the ability of the planet's ecosystems to sustain future generations can no longer be taken for granted.' (MA, 2005, p. 2)*

Warnings on the adverse and degrading effects of human activity on nature have been formulated already at the beginning of the 19th century: Wordsworth (1814) saw nature fundamentally endangered as a result of humankind's alienation from nature grounded in the ideological foundations of modern economic thought (Becker et al., 2005).

Given that similar warnings have also received worldwide attention in the early seventies of the last century – Meadows' et al. book *The Limits to Growth* (1972) took into account the various interactions between human activity and nature and predicted a catastrophic fall in worldwide-standard of living within 50 to 100 years if current human practice of exploiting the Earth's resources continued – this recent and 'official' testimony on the condition of the planet can be surprising. But it is not as surprising if one considers that there has been (and still is) a tendency in humankind to misunderstand its position in relation to nature.

This tendency and the resulting consequences can be traced back in literature to the German philosopher Johann Gottlieb Fichte (1762-1814). Fichte (1794) developed a system of transcendental philosophy, called *Grundlage der gesamten Wissenschaftslehre,* intended to lay the foundations of all theoretical science (including the philosophy of science, ethical theory, philosophy of law and the philosophy of religion). Fichte grounded his entire philosophical system on the concept of subjectivity; i.e. the *pure I* or *self*. He believed that the individual ego alone exists and that all manifestation is a reflection of this ego.

According to Becker and Manstetten (2004) the philosophy of Fichte may serve as a key to understanding the fundamental attitudes of modern humankind: Fichte makes the distinction between the *self* and the *nonself* and argues that the essence of the *self* is action which is guided by will and reason. The object of all actions is the *nonself* which is devoid of will and reason. He goes on arguing that the perpetual effort of the *self* is to transform the *nonself* as far as possible. Independent of the *self*, the *nonself* has no identity. Whatever the *nonself* may be, it is nothing but the result of the action of the *self*. Furthermore, according to Fichte's philosophy nature is nothing but the absence of the *self*, it is the *nonself*. This interpretation of the relationship between human mind (ego or self) and nature as being two separate and opposed entities, whereby the human mind represents the higher principle, can also be found in the work of Thomas R. Malthus (1766-1834), Francis Bacon (1596-1650) and Rene Descartes (1596-1650) and is central to the understanding of the modern ecological crisis (Becker and Manstetten, 2004; and Becker et al., 2005).

Becker and Manstetten (2004) show that viewing nature from the perspective of the individual ego only has far-reaching theoretical and practical implications for the relationship between humans and nature since it implies that nature has to be acquired and used by humans for the purposes of humanity without any restrictions. Fichte states that:

> *'The attempt to master the forces of nature is based in the essence of humanity.*
> *[...] The relationship between mankind and nature be it living or non-living can*
> *be characterised as follows: Humankind aims to modify nature according to its*
> *purposes ... (Fichte, [1795], 1966, p. 99)*

This view 'brings to light the philosophical roots of the anthropocentric positions expressed in the procedures of modern western science, technology and the economy' (Becker and Manstetten, 2004, p. 104).

The implications of these 'procedures' for the Earth's ecosystems can be circumscribed by – mentioning the most striking trends only – a growing rate of biodiversity loss and exorbitant rates of species extinction, increasing pollution, detoxification and waste, oversupply of nutrients, climate change, increasing impact of extreme weather events, overexploitation of natural resources, habitat loss, increasing poverty and hunger, emergence or resurgence of several infectious diseases, water scarcity, rapid loss of culturally valued landscapes and a dramatic loss of forests (see Box 1).

Box 1: *Millennium Ecosystem Assessment (MA, 2006) – selected findings*

> *Nearly two thirds of the services provided by nature to humankind are found to be in decline worldwide.*
>
> *Significant areas of forest, cultivated land, dryland rangelands, and costal and marine systems are now degraded, and the degraded area continues to grow.*
>
> *Since 1945 more land (such as forests, savanna and natural grassland) was converted to cropland than in the eighteen and nineteenth centuries combined, and now approximately one quarter of Earth's terrestrial surface has been transformed to cultivated systems.*

While the Millennium Ecosystem Assessment also revealed that human well-being (including basic material for good life, freedom of choice and action, health, good social relations and security), by several measures and on average across and within many societies, has improved substantially over the past two centuries, the report clearly states that 'the gains in human well-being are not distributed evenly among individuals or social groups, nor among the countries they live in or the ecosystems of the world. The gap between the advantaged and the disadvantaged is increasing' (MA, 2006, p.16).

This finding clearly conflicts with one of the foundations of the modern western economy as well as of modern economic thought; i.e. self-interest as the only guiding principle and creator of wealth. It questions Adam Smith's view – formulated in *Inquiry into the Nature and Causes of the Wealth of Nations* (1776) – that egoistic individual economic behaviour leads automatically (through the 'invisible hand') to the greatest possible accumulation of wealth for all:

The individual economic actor 'intends only his own security ...[and] he in-
tends only his own gain; and he is in this, as in many other cases, led by an in-
visible hand to promote an end which was no part of his intention. Nor is it al-
ways the worse for the society that it was no part of it. By pursuing his own in-
terest, he frequently promotes that of the society more effectually than when he
really intends to promote it. [...] The natural effort of every individual to better
his own condition, when suffered to exert itself with freedom and security, is so
powerful a principle that it is alone, and without any assistance, capable of
carrying on the society to wealth and prosperity...' (Smith, 1776, Book IV, Ch.
2 and Ch. 5).[6]

This idea has been one of the most influential principles in Western economic theory up until today (Becker and Manstetten, 2004). As a consequence, 'neoclassical welfare economics continue to offer bad advice in dealing with some the most pressing environmental and social issues faced in the twenty-first century, including growing income disparity, global climate change and biodiversity loss' (Gowdy and Erickson, 2005, p. 208).

Ecosystems have been defined in the Millennium Ecosystem Assessment as a dynamic complex of plant, animal, and microorganism communities and the nonliving environment interacting as a functional unit. Humans are an integral part of ecosystems. Ecosystems vary enormously in size; a temporary pond in a tree hollow and an ocean basin can both be ecosystems. Ecosystem services are defined as the benefits people obtain from ecosystems including provisioning services such as food and water; regulating services such as regulation of floods, drought, land degradation, and disease; supporting services such as soil formation and nutrient cycles; and cultural services such as recreational, spiritual, religious and other nonmaterial benefits. Changes in these services impact on human well-being in many ways and the demand for them is now so great that it became ultimately clear that healthy ecosystems are central to the aspirations of humankind. (MA, 2005 and 2006). This can be pinpointed through Figure 3 which depicts the strength of linkages between categories of ecosystem services and components of human well-being that are commonly encountered. The figure also includes indications of the extent to which it is possible for socioeconomic factors to mediate the link-

---

[6] It has to be noted that Adam Smith also wrote that the extent to which individuals shall be free to pursue their self-interest has its limits: 'those exertions of the natural liberty of a few individuals, which might endanger the security of the whole society, are, and ought to be, restrained by the laws of all governments, of the most free as well as of the most despotical. [...] The sovereign has [...] the duty of protecting, as far as possible, every member of the society from the injustice or oppression of every other member of it' (Smith 1776, Book IV, Ch. 9 and Book II, Ch. 2). But such warnings were by and large ignored and Smith's ideas have often been reduced to the single principle that self-interested behaviour automatically leads to wealth for all.

age (e.g. for example, if it is possible to purchase a substitute for a degraded ecosystem service, then there is a high potential for mediation).

Figure 3: *Linkages between Ecosystem Services and Human Well-being (adopted from MA, 2006)*

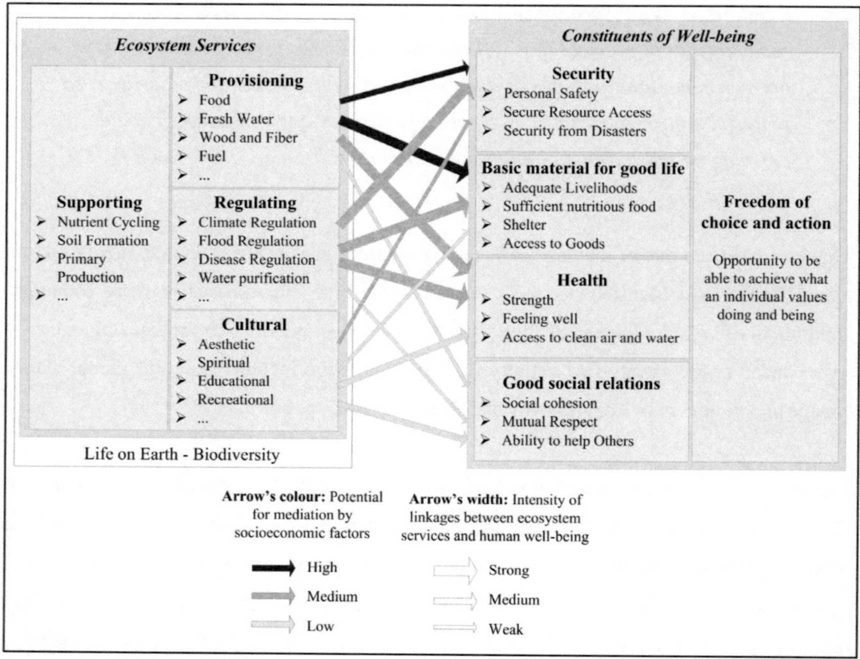

Protecting, maintaining and mitigating the further loss of ecosystem services requires both collaborative action and radical, ethical and economic re-evaluation since the 'protection of nature's services is unlikely to be a priority as long as they are perceived to be free and limitless by those using them' (MA, 2005, p. 18).

If the economic discipline – i.e. 'the science which studies human behaviour as a relationship between ends and scarce means which have alternative uses' (Robbins, 1932, p. 15) – aspires contributing to the protection of Earth and to improvements in collective human well-being, a reform of the understanding of individual's and humankind's position in relation to nature is now urgently required. Ruth (2006) expressed it this way:

'... should economics continue along the path it has followed throughout much of the last century, it will not only risk failing to contribute to the sustainability debate, but may itself not be sustainable. A society faced with allocating scarce resources to meet its needs may eventually decide to allocate fewer resources to

the discipline that claimed to study the best use of scarce resources but failed to deliver its promising valuable insights.' (Ruth, 2006, p. 336)

Since the last three decades have generally been consistent with the predicted scenarios outlined in *The Limits to Growth* (Meadows et al., 1972 and 2004), the need for radical, ethical and economic re-evaluation or for changing the structure of the system[7] respectively is currently expressed in a number of different approaches and 'worldviews' that jointly shape the contemporary understanding and interpretation of the concept of sustainable development (see for example Sen, 1999; Princen, 2003; Newman, 2005; Sneddon et al., 2005; Gowdy and Erickson, 2005; Porritt, 2006). The corresponding theoretical and philosophical underpinning can be found in the works of David Hume (1711-1776), William Wordsworth (1770-1850), Novalis (1772-1801) and Henry David Thoreau (1817-1862). Within this dissertation the concept of sustainable development is interpreted as a process or journey towards the end goal sustainability (see the following Section 2.2.1). The author takes the view that humankind can act 'rationally' and change unsustainable behaviour in order to overcome the current ecological crisis by jointly organising a deliberate turnaround.[8]

---

[7] A word of caution is necessary when terms like *radical re-evaluation* or *structural change* are used. This has best been expressed by Meadows et al. (2004, p. 236-237): 'The phrase *changing structure* often has ominous connotations. It has been used by revolutionaries to mean throwing people out of power, sometimes throwing bombs in the process. People may think that changing structure means changing physical structures, tearing down the old buildings and building new ones. [...] Given those interpretations, changing structure appears be difficult, dangerous and threatening to those with economic and political power. In systems language, however, *changing structure* has little to do with throwing people out, tearing things down, or demolishing bureaucracies. In fact, doing any of those things without real changes in structure will just result in different people spending as much or more time and money pursuing the same goals in new buildings or organizations, producing the same old results. In systems terms, changing structure means changing the *feedback structure, the information links* in a system: the content and timeliness of the data that actors in the system have to work with, and ideas, goals, incentives, costs, and feedbacks that motivate our constrain behaviour. The same combination of people, organizations, and physical structures can behave completely different, if the system's actors can see a good reason for doing so, and if they have the freedom, perhaps even the incentive, to change.'

[8] However, it needs to be noted that some ecologists (notably James Lovelock) have recently taken a dark view about humankind's inability to implement the necessary changes to reduce societies' major environmental impacts such as climate change. Lovelock (2006) predicts famine, war, and disease on an unprecedented scale over the next 100 years with 5/6 of the world's population not surviving. So instead of advocating sustainable development, he suggests considering survival concepts for the few, not the many.

2.2   Sustainable development

2.2.1   The concept of sustainable development

2.2.1.1   The renaissance of sustainable development thinking

In most of contemporary 'sustainability' literature the origins of the term and concept of sustainable development are often dated to the 80s and 90s of the last century; namely to the United Nations Conference on the Human Environment held 1972 in Stockholm (know as the Stockholm Conference), to the follow-up installation of the World Commission on Environment and Development (WCED) in 1983 (known as the Brundtland Commission) and to the resulting publication of the book *Our Common Future* in 1987 (know as the Brundtland Report). While this dating holds true for the beginning of earnest, large-scale sustainable development thinking, the concept of sustainable development or, to be more precise, some of its basic underlying principles were already inherent in the thoughts of the ancients, e.g. Aristotle (384-322 BC), Cato (234-149 BC), Cicero (106-43 BC), and Caesar (100-44 BC). 'To sustain and to abstain, that is, to be patient and continent, appeared to some of the ancients a summary comprehension of all morals' (Hume, 1751, Appendix IV).[9]

It appears that within the German language the term 'sustainable' ('nachhaltig') and its underlying concept have first been framed by Hannß Carl von Carlowitz (1645-1714), a mining engineer responsible for the forestry in Freiberg (Saxony) during 1711 and 1714 (at that time forestry was a sub-supplier to the mining industry). In his guideline concerning the cultivation and conservation of timber called *Sylvicultura oeconomica* he argued as follows: 'The most difficult art, science, and effort as well as the greatest feature of countries will lie in safeguarding that the manner of conserving and cultivating timber enables a continuous, durable and sustainable use of this resource; this is an essential issue without which a country cannot remain its character or even existence' (Carlowitz, 1713, p. 106, author's translation). A much broader interpretation of the concept is offered by the English philosopher David Hume who appears to be the first that used the term (in its current meaning) within the English language:

> *'We may observe, that, in displaying the praises of any humane, beneficent man, there is one circumstance which never fails to be amply insisted on, namely, the happiness and satisfaction, derived to society from his intercourse and good offices. [...] With him, the ties of love are consolidated by beneficence and friendship. [...] His domestics and dependants have in him a sure resource; and no longer dread the power of fortune, but so far as she exercises it over*

---

⁹ Most non-Western cultures also have a rich tradition of conceptualizing humankind's interrelationship with the natural environment. However, this falls outside the boundary of this dissertation.

*him. From him the hungry receive food, the naked clothing, the ignorant and
slothful skill and industry. Like the sun, an inferior minister of providence, he
cheers, invigorates, and sustains the surrounding world. [...] If confined to private life, the sphere of his activity is narrower; but his influence is all benign
and gentle. If exalted into a higher station, mankind and prosperity reap the
fruit of his labours.' (Hume, 1751, Section I, Part II)*

It is, indeed, astonishing but from the early 18th century until the 1970s or 1980s sustainable development thinking has apparently only been an important issue within the forestry of some European countries (see for example: Oesten, 2004). Thus, if one takes a closer look at Hume's and other philosophers' writings (which will be done below) it seems that sustainable development thinking has been an almost lost, but fortunately re-invented achievement or re-discovered 'inner sense'.

It's renaissance started somewhere in the 1950s and the Stockholm Conference in 1972 stands as a landmark for the beginning of international cooperation directed towards more sustainable development in policy making and in many other aspects of human activity. Today, a large number of formal definitions of sustainable development can be found in literature; Parkin (2000) refers to more than two hundred. However, the most prominent and universal definition is contained within the *Brundtland Report* as an outcome of 4 years of study and debate by the WCED led by the former Prime Minister of Norway, Gro Harlem Brundtland. The Commission defined sustainable development as follows:

*'Sustainable development is development that meets the needs of the present
without compromising the ability of future generations to meet their own needs.
(WCED, 1987, p. 54)*

Thus, this concept comprises two strong elements: (1) the element of satisfying human needs and requirements (i.e. quality of life or human well-being) and (2) an element of intra- and intergenerational ethics ('don't cheat your fellow citizens and children'). The latter element is required due to the strains imposed by both intensive technologies and social organizations on nature's ability to provide essential ecosystem services for present and future generations.
The concept of sustainable development (intentionally defined rather vaguely by the Brundtland Commission) evolved over time and still is further evolving; the following Box 2 provides an overview on major steps at the global level that helped consolidating its understanding as well as setting the agenda for its practical implementation.

Box 2: *Sustainable development – Important steps*

> ***1948: Foundation of The World Conservation Union*** *IUCN (formerly: International Union for Conservation of Nature and Natural Resources, since 1988: The World Conservation Union), the world's largest organisation for environmental protection*
>
> ***1968: International Conference for Rational Use and Conservation of the Biosphere*** *(Paris, France), United Nations Educational, Scientific, and Cultural Organization (UNESCO)'s pioneering event for discussing ecologically sustainable development*
>
> ***1972: United Nations Conference on the Human Environment*** *(Stockholm, Sweden), Addressed economic, social and environmental issues and led to the United Nations Environment Program (UNEP) and its mission to 'provide leadership and encourage partnership in caring for the environment by inspiring, informing, and enabling nations and peoples to improve their quality of life without compromising that of future generations.'*
>
> ***1983: World Commission on Environment and Development****, Prime Minister of Norway (Gro Harlem Brundtland) asked by Secretary General of United Nations to lead a special commission addressing how the world could develop a long-term environmental strategy for achieving sustainable development by the year 2000 and beyond as well as to define a shared perception of long-term environmental issues and appropriate efforts to deal with them effectively.*
>
> ***1983: International Conference on Environment and Economics,*** *concluded that environment and economics should be mutually reinforcing. Helped shape 'Our Common Future'.*
>
> ***1987: Our Common Future****, published report of the World Commission on Environment and Development that popularized the term 'sustainable development.'*
>
> ***1992: United Nations Conference on Environment and Development*** *(Rio de Janeiro, Brazil; known as Earth Summit), Established 'sustainable development' as a common goal of human development. Set out Agenda 21 as a blueprint for action in the 21st century.*
>
> ***1997: United Nations General Assembly Special Session,*** *(New York; US; known as Earth Summit II), Reviewed the progresses made since the first Earth Summit meeting; revitalized and energized the nations' commitments to sustainable development and frankly recognised that little progress has been made since the first Earth Summit meeting.*
>
> ***2000: United Nations Millennium Declaration,*** *was adopted by countries of the United Nations during the Millennium Summit to reaffirm their commitment to 'a more peaceful, prosperous and just world.' Declaration identifies eliminating poverty as highest priority; and includes related Millennium Development Goals. The section on 'Protecting our common environment' emphasizes need to adopt a new ethic of conservation and stewardship.*
>
> ***2002: World Summit on Sustainable Development*** *(Johannesburg, South Africa), resulted in two negotiated documents: Johannesburg Declaration on Sustainable Development and Johannesburg Plan of Implementation. The summit also focused implementation of Agenda 21 set out at the Rio conference but was more concerned with integrated and cross-sectoral solutions through voluntary public/private partnerships for sustainable development.*
>
> ***2005: United Nations World Summit*** *(New York; US), all 191 member States agreed to achieve the Millennium Development Goals by 2015.*

Of particular importance were the four so-called environmental mega-conferences (Stockholm, Rio, New York and Johannesburg) mainly because they addressed the overall course of human development and its relationship to the environment as a whole (Seyfang, 2003). Although, these conferences have been generally criticised for several reason – e.g. for being unmanageable, attracting agendas beyond their brief, creating delays in diplomatic agreement, and for failing to deal seriously with the important environmental problems but to pursue a variety of ideological and economic disputes (Jordan and O'Riordan, 2003; Meadows et al., 2004) – they served (and will do so the in the future) six important core functions which have been identified by Seyfang and Jordan (2002). These are:

- setting global agendas,
- facilitating 'joined-up' thinking on environment and development,
- endorsing common principles,
- providing global leadership for national and local governments,
- building institutional capacity, and
- legitimising global governance by making the processes more inclusive.

The conferences' contribution to the understanding of sustainable development is summarized in core function 2, facilitating 'joined-up' thinking; i.e. replacing usual short-termism of political reality with a long-range vision (Seyfang, 2003). By focussing on the interface between the environment, social and economic development the conferences helped viewing sustainable development as a dynamic, long-term *multi-level* and *multi-actor* process based on three *mutually reinforcing* pillars or on the reconciliation of three imperatives respectively (commonly referred to as the 'triple bottom line' of sustainable development):

- social equity or the improvement of human well-being (i.e. a social imperative to effectively propagate and safeguard the values that people wish to live by),
- economic security or more equitable distribution of resource use benefits across and within societies (i.e. an economic imperative to ensure that resources are used efficiently *and* effectively for the benefits of all people worldwide),
- ecological integrity or the protection of nature's capability to provide ecosystem services over intra- and intergenerational scales (i.e. an ecological imperative to respect global biophysical carrying capacities and to maintain biodiversity).

A large body of literature – see for example Enquete-Kommission (1998) and Rogall (2004) – now support the view that these pillars are 'interdependent and mutually reinforcing' (UN, 2005a, p. 12), and that all pillars have to be taken into account to achieve sustainable development and that none of them dominates or is 'more important' than the others (see also Parkin, 2000; Doughty and Hammond, 2004; Newman, 2005; Sneddon et al., 2005; Lützkendorf and Lorenz, 2005 and 2006a; and Turner, 2006a). However, Sneddon et al. (2005, p.4) note that while this interpretation may 'serve a useful heuristic purpose the actual interrelations of these three ideals are complex and often contradictory in practice.' For this reason, the interpretation of the triple bottom line has been an issue of intense debate (Dresner, 2002). For example, it has been argued that the environmental dimension is the dominant or prior one because ecological integrity (or the protection of the value in nature in the form of ecosystem services) is a pre-condition for the existence of other values (Gren et al., 1994 and Turner et al., 2003). Also, some writers – for example, David Pearce (1941-2005) who introduced the idea that environmental damage was not due to people's greed, indifference, or malevolence but to the environment's being under-priced (Barret, 2005); Pearce argued that adequate pricing of externalities will have impact on both people's behaviour and the improvement of the environment – believe that 'individuals have a right to pursue their lives without an excess of moralising about how they should pursue their lives. [...] His [Pearce's] view was that human freedom is more important than human survival' (Turner, 2006b, p. 3).

While in contrast, others have stated that a triumvirate view of the triple bottom line bears the danger of considering any amount of environmental protection or any social gain as sufficient to offset any amount of economic activity which 'clearly runs the risk of tokenism' (Rydin, 2003, p. 4). In order to resolve this conflict the following view or line of reasoning might be useful: Improving human well-being is the overarching goal while ecological integrity is the precondition and economic activity the instrument to achieve it. This view ties the three pillars together and is in line with seeing them as mutually interdependent and reinforcing. Similarly, Porritt (2006, p. 19) argues that profound change in the face of today's gathering ecological crisis can only be realised while 'working with the grain of markets and free choice. It means embracing capitalism as the only overarching system capable of achieving any kind of reconciliation between ecological sustainability, on the one hand, and the pursuit of prosperity and personal wellbeing, on the other'.

Besides the triple bottom line the concept or notion of sustainable development itself has been open to criticism. For example, the term has been called an oxymoron by arguing that development *per se* cannot be sustainable. However, this argument is only valid as long as *development* is interpreted solely as economic growth (defined as per capita growth of gross domestic product (GDP) or income). More harshly, the Brundtland Report and much of the sustainable development debate were termed 'a tale that the disenchanted (modern) world tells itself about its sad condition' (Escobar, 1996, pp. 53-54). This view is based on the assumption that sustainable development is 'unforgivably anthropocentric and thus unable to dissolve the false barriers between the human sphere of economic and social activities and the ecological sphere that sustains these activities' (Sneddon et al., 2005, p. 8). Nonetheless, Sneddon et al. (2005, p. 9) conclude that both advocates and critics would agree that 'a socially just and ecologically sustainable world, or even an approximation, would be a desirable end.'

In order to circumscribe this *desirable end* the term *sustainability* is used. Although, it is difficult to define sustainability from a scientific perspective, the realization of sustainability can be measured – following Porritt (2000) – against a set of four basic[10] 'system conditions'. These are:

- Finite materials (including fossil fuels) are not extracted at a faster rate than they can be redeposited in the Earth's crust.
- Artificial materials (including plastics) are not produced at a faster rate than they can be broken down by natural processes.
- The biodiversity of ecosystems is maintained, whilst renewable resources are only consumed at a slower rate than they can be naturally replenished.
- Human needs are met worldwide in an equitable and efficient manner.

The difficulties of defining the destination of sustainable development are, amongst other reasons, due to the circumstance that the end-goal bears in it both static and dynamic elements. On the one hand, sustainability circumscribes a steady or durable state of Earth's ability to vest humankind with the capability to do valuable things. On the other hand, ecosystems and social-ecological systems as well as human needs do change over time. With a focus on such systems, Holling (2001, p. 390) provided alternative definitions of sustainability – i.e. the capacity to create, test, and maintain adaptive capability – and of development – i.e. the process of creating, testing, and maintaining opportunity – in order to derive at an understanding of a further facet of sustainable development: 'the goal of fostering adaptive capabilities and creating opportunities. It is therefore not an oxymoron but a term that describes a logical partnership.'

According to Holling (2001) the basis of ecosystems and social-ecological systems across scales is comprised by a nested set of adaptive cycles, a so-called panarchy. 'The panarchy describes how a healthy system can invent and experiment, benefiting from inventions that create opportunity while being kept safe from those that destabilize because of their nature or excessive exuberance' (Holling, 2001, p. 390). Figure 4 shows a stylized representation of the ecosystem as an adaptive cycle.

---

[10] Section 2.2.2 below contains a more detailed description of further 'system conditions' that are also referred to in the literature as principles of sustainable development or management rules for a sustainable society.

Figure 4: *Representation of the four basic ecosystem functions, r: Exploitation; K: Conservation; α: Reorganisation; and Ω: Release (Holling, 2001, p. 395)*

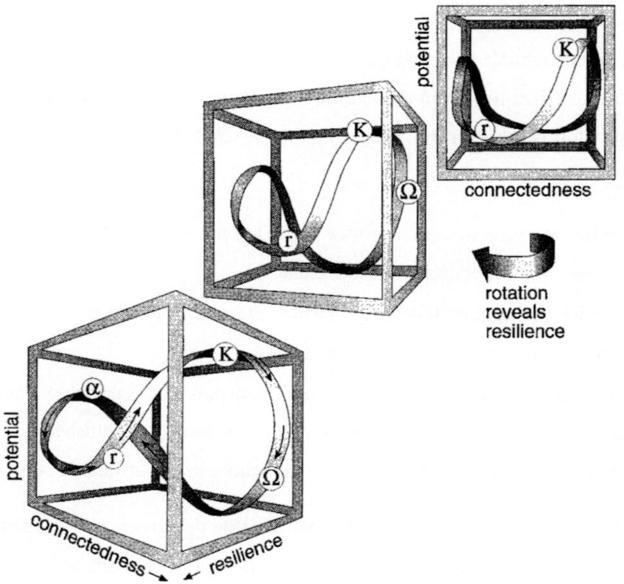

Adaptive cycles can collapse if their potential and diversity have been eradicated due to misuse or an external force; the result has been termed a 'poverty trap'. An example is the productive savannah that flips into an irreversible, eroding state, beginning with sparse vegetation as a result of human overuse and misuse (Holling, 2001).

The Earth's interconnected ecosystems are incredibly complex and human intervention can and does have unforeseen long-term consequences. For example, 'the story of stratospheric ozone depletion and humanity's response now appears to be a success,[11] but its final chapter won't be written for several more decades. So it is also a cautionary tale, an illustration of how perplexing it can be to guide the complex human enterprise toward sustainability within the interwoven systems of the planet while relying on imperfect understanding, delayed signals, and a system with enormous momentum' (Meadows et al., 2004, p. 10). A further example for the destabilizing impact of human intervention and the Earth System's momentum is

---

[11] The international response to the news in the 1980s of a deteriorating stratospheric ozone layer – which has been associated with rising levels of skin cancer and other harmful effects on living species – can be used as a strong counterexample to the pervasive and cynical belief that people, governments, and corporations can never cooperate to solve global problems. The use of chlorofluorocarbons, the most widespread ozone-depleting substances, has been reduced dramatically. In developed regions the ozone-depleting potential has been reduced from 618.000 metric tons in 1990 to 1.000 metric tons in 2002 (UN, 2005b). However, the damage to the ozone layer is already evident and recovery is expected within the next 50 years.

the rise in CO_2 concentration, temperature and sea level *after* emissions have been reduced. According to the Assessment Report[12] of the Intergovernmental Panel on Climate Change (IPCC, 2001a) stabilisation of carbon dioxide (CO_2) emissions at near-current levels will not lead to a stabilisation of CO_2 atmospheric concentrations; instead stabilisation at any level requires eventual reduction of global CO_2 net emissions to a small fraction of the current emission level. The lower the chosen level for stabilisation, the sooner the decline in global net CO_2 emissions needs to begin (see Figure 5).

Figure 5: *Rise in CO_2 concentration, temperature and sea level after emissions are reduced (adopted from IPCC, 2001a, p. 17)*

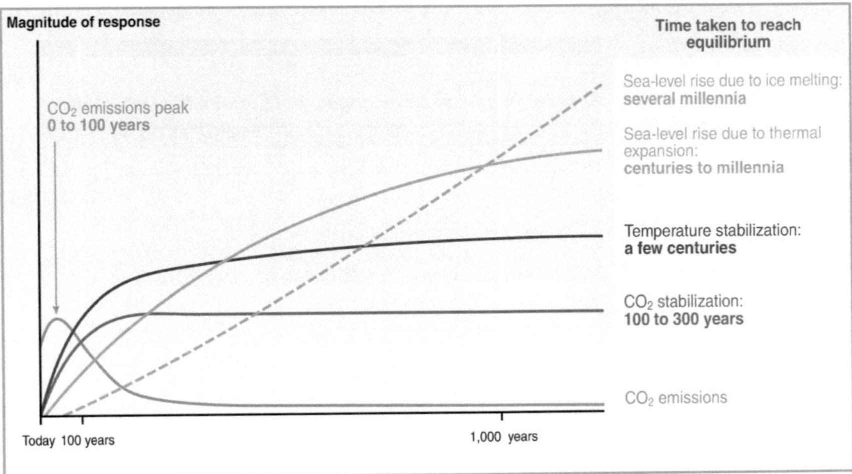

Advances in understanding the dynamics and functioning of the Earth System led to the conclusion that the system has moved well outside the range of the natural variability over the last half million years at least. 'The nature of changes now occurring simultaneously in the Earth System, their magnitudes and rates of change are unprecedented. The Earth is currently operating in a no-analogue state' (ADGC, 2001, p. 2).

Since the accelerating human transformation of the Earth System is not sustainable, a new ethical framework as well as adaptive strategies and actions to respond to the challenge of global change are required. For this reason and due to the circumstance that change is the norm and driving force in ecosystems and social-ecological system, sustainable development

---

[12] The three-volume Assessment Report was prepared by over 600 authors from around the world and was reviewed by approximately 500 technical experts and government officials. The report was unanimously accepted within the scope of a meeting in Shanghai in January 2001 by 99 IPCC member governments.

has recently been termed 'a moving target; each successful adaptation is only a temporary 'solution' to changing selective conditions' (Newman, 2005, p. 3).

In order to capture this moving target, the author's understanding of the concept of sustainable development will be further explained by referring to a combination of the following approaches or 'worldviews': *natural economics, development as freedom, political ecology* and the *poetical economy* (see Figure 6). These four approaches make up the interpretation of sustainable development offered within this dissertation. They are expressive of the different strands of research and schools of thought from which a new understanding of sustainable development evolves. A rather detailed explanation of these approaches is necessary because they are critical for altering the understanding of economics and of humankind's position in relation to nature.

Figure 6: *Different approaches leading to an understanding of Sustainable Development*

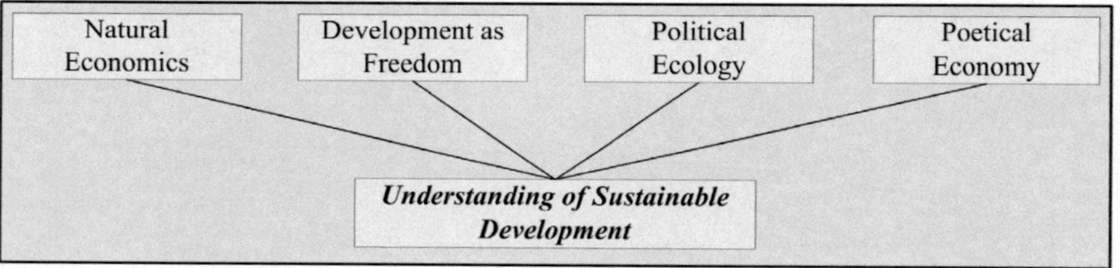

2.2.1.2   Natural Economics

Natural economics is a rather new but enlightening approach to economics that represents a further development of several other strands of economic research. The term first appeared in a speech titled *New Economics for the 21st Century: Natural Economics* held by Tachi Kiuchi on 1 May 2004 in Kuala Lumpur. Kiuchi argued that a reformulated economic discipline is required, which takes nature as its framework, measure and model. 'We need a new discipline of Natural Economics which in detail spells out the why's and how's of a sound economy operating within the basic framework laid down by nature. It is not only possible to create such an economic system; it is also our only choice' (Kiuchi, 2004).

According to Ruth (2006) who first framed the concept from a more scientific perspective, natural economics synthesises the key insights from the following strands in an effort to identify and apply their major contributions to the understanding and promotion of sustainable development:

- *Natural resource economics* – concerned with the optimal extraction of non-renewable resources the discipline has identified conditions for inter-temporally optimal extraction but ultimately faces the problem that the optimal extraction path results in over-exploitation and depletion when prices reach levels where demand is choked off (Ruth, 2006 and Dasgupta and Heal, 1974).

- *Environmental economics* – concerned with the incorporation of external costs of environmental damages caused by production and consumption into the pricing of goods and services and into cost-benefit analysis (CBA)[13].

- *Industrial Ecology* – a rather technocratic approach that focuses mainly on the assessment of energy and mass flows (i.e. life cycle assessments of products) in order to develop and guide environmental friendly production and (to some extent) consumption processes as well as to influence investment and policy strategies in order to reduce adverse environmental impact.

- *Ecological Economics* – a transdisciplinary approach based on the principle that all economic systems (like any other man-made system) must be regarded and treated as sub-systems of nature as the main system. This is necessary because if the 'main system and sub-system collide, the sub-system cannot win, it will lose. If the mother company [i.e. nature] goes bankrupt, all subsidiaries will go bankrupt along with it' (Kiuchi, 2004).

Before the building blocks of natural economics are briefly outlined in the following, Ruth's (2006) critique and suggestions for the further development of these four strands of economic research are briefly summarized. Concerning natural resource and environmental economics (as modified versions of the neo-classical paradigm) he argues that market-driven approaches to resource and environmental problems are often 'greeted with deep scepticism by those having to balance economic efficiency with issues of effectiveness, fairness and justice' (Ruth, 2006, p. 334).

Although the insights from these disciplines can be regarded as an important starting point to address issues of sustainable development in economics, Ruth (2006) has formulated six major challenges that have to be met by these two disciplines if they aim further contributing to the sustainable development discourse. These are:

---

[13] CBA is a technique which seeks to bring greater objectivity into decision-making by identifying all the relevant benefits and costs of a particular scheme or project and quantifying them in money terms so that each can be aggregated and then compared. A good explanation of CBA, including its role, methods and limitations can be found in Harvey (2000, pp. 139-166).

- *Integration of resource and environmental economics* because continuing to separate research on resource extraction from issues of environmental damage will only provide partial answers and solutions.

- *Consistency with physical and biological principles* because human activities are subject to the self-enforcing, self-organising and self-regulating laws of nature. For example, natural resources will deteriorate and finally be 'mined' if they are harvested at a faster rate than they can be naturally redeposited or replenished. Since this is not a new insight Ruth (2006) refers to Marshall (1898) who has – more than a hundred years ago – called for economics that are guided by biological principles rather than treating Earth like a mechanistic system.

- *Development of a systems perspective* because the analysis of partial systems can lead to theories that are meaningless from a broader perspective.

- *Recognition of interdependencies of allocation, distribution and scale* because economics has focused too much on the issue of optimal allocation only; while optimal allocation implies efficiency, problems of distribution and scale call for measure of effectiveness.

- *Demonstration of policy relevance* because mathematically sophisticated modelling or extensive econometric analyses only, will not be sufficient to make a difference in real-world decisions.

To a large extent these challenges have already been met or addressed by the discipline of ecological economics. This is described in detail in a recent research paper by Gowdy and Erickson (2005) and can be summarized by referring to their portrayal of the key conceptual differences between neo-classical economics and ecological economics. This is displayed in the following Table 1.

Table 1: *Key conceptual differences in economic approaches (adopted from Gowdy and Erickson, 2005)*

Conceptual issue	Neo-classical economics	Ecological economics
Value Monism	Reduces value to commensurable monetary units; based on utility functions	Separates value into incommensurable categories based on multi-criteria assessments
The Rational Actor	Individual consumers and firms are at the centre of the analysis	Analyses humans as social actors
Marginal Analysis	Assumes comparative statics of marginal changes	Recognises discontinuous change and total effects
Evolutionary change	Perceives evolution as constrained optimisation; believes in 'survival of the fittest' and individual based selection	Recognises the importance of contingency, historical accidents, and path dependency. Considers altruism and group selection as well as selfishness; believes in 'survival for all who fit'[14]
Uncertainty	Reduces uncertainty to risk; adopts a 'market outcome' approach to decision-making	Adopts a precautionary principle to deal with pure uncertainty; adopts a process oriented and co-evolutionary approach to decision-making
Decision Criteria	Efficiency as the sole criterion, usually based on potential Pareto improvements	Efficiency and effectiveness, equity, stability, resilience of environmental and social systems
Production Process	Sees production as allocation of fixed resources; based on production functions	Sees production as a biophysical process
Discounting	Straight-line discounting of future costs and benefits	Recognises the difference between individual and collective valuation of the future; applies hyperbolic discount rates[15]

One very popular field of ecological economics is concerned with the contribution of ecosystem services to the overall economy. Because most of ecosystem services are perceived to be free and limitless to use there is no market for these service. For this reason ecological economists argue that ascribing a monetary value to ecosystem services would appropriately reflect their contribution to the economy as a whole. For example, Costanza et al. (1997) have estimated that the value of Earth's ecosystems or its contribution to the economy respectively ranges between US\$ 16–54 trillion (10^{12}) per year, with an average of US\$ 33 trillion. However, Ruth (2006) refers to Toman (1998), Turner et al. (1998) and to Sagoff (2004) and argues that pricing ecosystem services is hampered by empirical and conceptual problems that arise from the sheer complexity of ecosystems. In addition, the applied valuation approach is

---

[14] This statement was not contained within the table from Gowdy and Erickson (2005) but was adopted from Kiuchi (2005) because it describes the ecological economics' approach of evolutionary change quite well.

[15] Hyperbolic discounting is a way of accounting in a model for the difference in the preferences an agent has over consumption now versus consumption in the future. Hyperbolic discounting means that our discount rates do not remain constant, but are greater in the short run than the long run (Dupree, 2001).

similar to the traditional economic approach based on the concept of marginal value (i.e. the value of an extra unit of a good or service) which only makes sense when ecosystems are far from their limits. However, this is not the case anymore. Therefore, Ruth (2006, p. 336) argues that pursuing this research further is not likely to help solving current conflicts surrounding the use of scarce resources because 'calculating the value of losing another hectare of forest ... from interpolated data makes little sense if we are left with little of these systems and if we do not know were ecological thresholds are.'

This is certainly true, but the approach of valuing ecosystem services can be used to clearly demonstrate – to those that are not yet worried about losing another hectare of forest – why it makes sense financially to invest in maintaining ecosystem functions. For example, James et al. (1999) estimated that the potential costs to society for a properly funded global conservation strategy amount up to US$ 300 billion per year. Given that the global society already spends between US$ 950 billion and US$ 1,400 billion on perverse subsidies (to farmers, energy producers, fisheries, etc.), the amount for conserving ecosystem services does not sound too much (Myers, 1998 and Porritt, 2006). 'In effect, what this shows us is that we need annual investments around $300 billion to secure $33 trillion worth of natural services – not a bad return on investment, all things considered' (Porritt, 2006, p. 132). In order to put this figure of $300 billion for a properly funded global conservations strategy into another perspective, the net fiscal income of the world's largest public companies can be calculated on the basis of data[16] provided by the Wall Street Journal Market Data Group: in 2003 this figure was at $465.1 billion.

Concerning the field of industrial ecology Ruth (2006) puts forward the argument that this discipline has focused too much on engineering solutions to increase material and energy efficiencies while comparatively little attention has been paid to consumption processes. However, consumption processes determine overall environmental impact to a very large extent. Thus, Ruth (2006, p. 337) argues that a better understanding of consumption is necessary which requires a larger system context; 'one in which socioeconomic (behavioural), biophysical and engineering insights are combined.'

In an effort to overcome these problems and to synthesise the major insights from these fields of economic research outlined above, Ruth (2006) sketches the vision of natural economics which:

---

[16] Available here: http://www.globalpolicy.org/soccon/tncs/2004/biggestcorp.pdf

- builds on concepts from nature (because natural processes do favour the long-term viability of populations and communities over the short-term gain of individuals, humans must ultimately follow principles similar to those ensuring sustainability in nature),

- takes into account the roles of efficiency (i.e. the highest productivity per unit of a resource) *and* effectiveness (i.e. the highest utility from what is used) in decision making,

- applies adaptive and anticipatory management and decision making approaches (because biophysical, technological, and socioeconomic conditions always change, people typically lack all the information needed to identify the best decisions; therefore an iterative process of data collection, interpretation and adjustments of management decisions is necessary), and

- recognises the need for holistic impact assessments (because an engineering or economic solution that does not take into account ethical, legal, institutional and environmental constraints is not a real solution).

In sum: 'To develop and select system designs that are sustainable will require a natural economics – one that builds on the fundamental insights from the natural sciences for sustainable system behaviour and, on the basis of these insights, establishes the economic, legal, institutional and ethical basis for humans to interact with their environment (Ruth, 2006, p. 339).

2.2.1.3   Political Ecology

In a generalised sense, political ecology can be defined as a field of research that studies the various relationships between the environment, politics and society. However, this definition is so broad that it becomes difficult to grasp what it is all about (for example, political ecology can embrace common property theory, green materialism, peasant studies, critical environmental history, postcolonial studies, cultural ecology, human ecology, ecological anthropology and geography, etc.). Therefore, Wolford (2005) argued that political ecology can best be understood through an examination of what it argues against; or, as Robbins (2004, p.13) suggests, through 'what political ecologists do.' What political ecologists do can be summarized as follows; they investigate, explain and (if possible) attempt to affect:

- *Political influences on human-environment relationships* since people's ideas about ecological systems are directed through political and economic processes (Robbins, 2004),

- *Political and economic influences on environmental change* caused by the exercise of power and struggles for control over and access to natural resources (see for example Moore, 1998 and McCarthy, 2001),

- *Issues concerning social justice* since some political ecologists view human communities as contributors to ecological sustainability instead of viewing them as environmental threats (Walker, 2005; see for example Leach and Mearns, 1996 and Forsyth, 2003),

- *Issues concerning threats* for both people and humankind caused by major environmental problems (Forsyth, 2003),

- *Environmental change dynamics* (including research on biodiversity and natural resource exploitation) and its interrelationship with social processes (e.g. Turner (1993 and 1998) investigated the factors that determine livestock populations or rangeland productivity while Zimmerer (1991) explained how ecological conditions contribute to the persistence of peasant agriculture).

While this summary gives only a brief overview it must be noted that the discipline of political ecology is currently expanding and further developing; mainly as a reaction to the increased concerns about human activities' malicious impacts on the Earth's ecosystems. This leads to the examination of what political ecologist argue against. In short, political ecology stands against 'apolitical' environmental theories such as environmental determinism and market optimism (Wolford, 2005). A more detailed insight that exemplifies the importance of this discipline within the struggle towards sustainability is provided by Sneddon et al. (2005) who argue that political ecologists radically criticise current global political economy and its ecological effects while at the same time demand for sensitivity to structural forces impeding sustainability transformation, attention to discourse and power, incorporation of ecological concerns into critical social theory, social justice, equity and ecological integrity, and finally radical changes in existing institution.

2.2.1.4   Development as Freedom

Until recently, the sustainable development discourse focused much more on the 'sustainable side' of the term than on the 'development side'. While much has been done to understand and define the former, the latter has not received too much attention. Successful human development is very often seen as GDP and real income growth which is assumed to increase people's happiness (Prendergast, 2005). This is, however, not the case (see Figure 7). Tim Kasser (2002) argued that people who are highly focused on materialistic values have lower personal well-being and psychological health than those who believe that materialistic pursuits are relatively unimportant. And people believe in materialism because society is so materialistic, and society is so materialistic because many people believe that materialistic pursuits are paths to happiness (see also Porritt, 2006, p. 317-318).

The viewpoint that materialism pursuits lead to happiness can be circumscribed by what has been termed the 'opulence-oriented approach' to development (see Anand and Sen, 2000; Brekke and Howarth, 2002). Understood in this sense, sustainable development is indeed an oxymoron because the maxim or principle to 'produce more, earn more, and consume more in order to be happier' has not turned out to be a sustainable path.

Figure 7: Life satisfaction in the UK and GDP per capita 1973-1997 (Donovan and Halpern, 2002, p. 17)

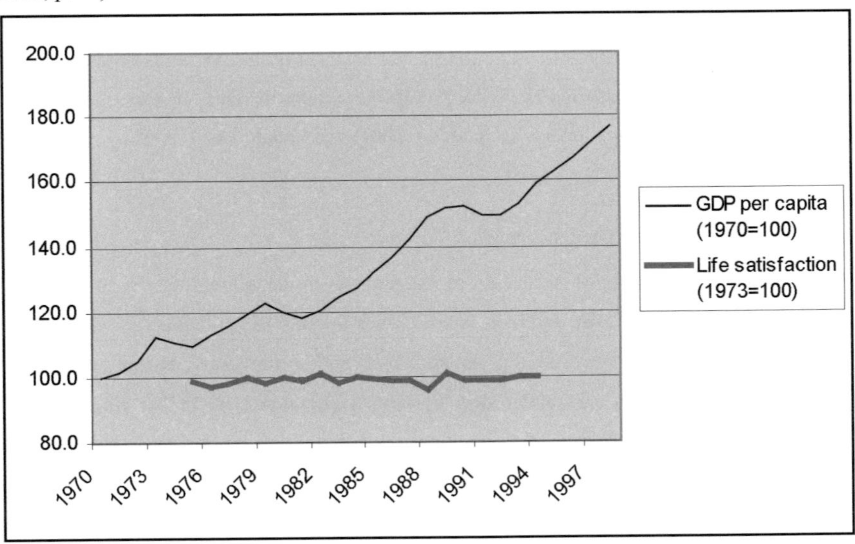

Lewis (1955) has pointed out that the case for economic growth is not that wealth increases happiness but that 'it gives man greater control over his environment and thereby increases his freedom' (Lewis, 1955, p. 420). More recently, Amartya Sen has put forward the argument that human development should be seen as a process of expanding people's freedom (e.g. political rights, economic and social opportunities, transparency guarantees and security) which contrasts with the 'widely prevalent concentration on the expansion of real income and on economic growth as the characteristics of successful development' (Sen, 1990, p. 41). In the book *Development as Freedom* (1999) Sen outlines his vision of better and more acceptable societies and attempts to integrate the idea of development as freedom into mainstream economic thinking. His work beautifully supports the argument that the linkage of sustainability with development needs 'not to be the death-knell of sustainable development that many have taken it to be' (Sneddon et al., 2005, p. 10).

By highlighting the relationship between collective economic wealth and people's capability to do and be things of value (e.g. to be educated or to produce useful goods and services), Sen stresses the crucial role of economics and economic research to address and improve individual and collective well-being. 'Sen has broadened our understanding of how to do descriptive, positive and normative analysis, and by doing this he enriched – but not at all abandoned – economics' (Tungodden, 2001, p. 20).

Sen's most appealing argument (and summary of his internal 'development' critique) is that the expansion of human freedom should not only be the primary *end* of development but also among its principle *means* (Sen, 1999). 'In Sen we can begin to see a way to radically alter the general orientation of development, away from its obsession with an aggregate, ill-defined wealth towards a rigorously defined notion of freedom that builds on ideals of social justice and human dignity' (Sneddon et al., 2005, p. 10). For a more detailed analysis of Sen's writings and lines of argumentation see Tungodden (2001) and Prendergast (2005).

2.2.1.5   Envisioning the poetical economy

Policy makers (including policy makers in national governments, multilateral organisations *and* global corporations[17]) use and look to economics in order to guide policy. Since policies – outlining and guiding humankind's, governments' and corporations' overall strategy and actions – are so vital for sustainable development, the economic discipline plays a crucial role. The increasing extent to which policy making bears on economics raises the methodological question about the relationship between a *positive* science concerning 'facts' and a *normative* investigation into what ought to be or what is estimable.

> *'Most economists and methodologists believe that there is a reasonably clear distinction between facts and values, between what is and what ought to be, and they believe that most of economics should be regarded as a positive science that helps policy makers choose means to accomplish their ends, though it does not bear on the choice of ends itself.' (Hausman, 2003, Chapter 2)*

---

[17] Of the 100 largest economic entities in the world, 51 are now global corporations; only 49 are countries; e.g. Mitsubishi is larger than the fourth most populous nation on earth: Indonesia; General Motors is bigger than Denmark; Ford is bigger than South Africa and Toyota is bigger than Norway (Anderson and Cavanagh, 2000). 'There is a powerful school of thought which argues that multinationals … have systematically increased their reach, scope and influence so that they are now *the* dominant social institution anywhere in the world.' (Porritt, 2006, p. 101)

This view is questionable, mainly because economics is a scientific discipline; and thus a human activity that is guided by values or by individual's views of what is *right* and *wrong*. Consequently, economics is greatly influenced by economic scientists' beliefs how people in fact behave (Hausman, 2003, Chapter 2). There is evidence that studying theories that are based on the assumption or principle that individuals are 'self-interested' (masters of nature) leads to people – and thus, to societies – that regard self-interested behaviour more favourable and to become even more self-interested (Marwell and Ames, 1981, Frank et al., 1993). This points out why it is so important to address and set sound philosophical foundations of the concept of sustainable development. This concept is, in essence, based on and guided by both, the fundamental understanding of the relationship between nature and humankind and peoples' moral attitudes, i.e. their views of what ought to be or what is *right* and *wrong*. For this reason, the vision of the *poetical economy* is laid down in the following.

In order to understand the limitations of this vision, it is important to consider the principles of envisioning. These have been identified by Robert Costanza (2003) in a recent research paper on *a vision of the future of science*. The principles are:

- In order to effectively envision, it is necessary to focus on what one really wants (e.g. self-esteem, health, human happiness), and not on what one will settle for (e.g. a fancy car, medicine, unsustainable growth).
- A vision should be judged by the clarity of its values, not by the clarity of its implementation path. Holding the vision and being flexible about the path is often the only way to find the path.
- Responsible vision must acknowledge, but not be crushed by, the physical constraints of the real world.
- It is critical for visions to be shared because only shared visions can be responsible.
- Visions must be flexible and evolving.

Having said this, the vision of the poetical economy can be based on the work of David Hume: In his book *An Enquiry Concerning the Principles of Morals* the English philosopher David Hume – generally regarded as the most important philosopher ever to write in English (Morris, 2001) – has questioned and heavily criticised approaches of reasoning that are based on *a-priori* formulated general principles (such as the principle of self-interest as the only creator of wealth and prosperity): 'I am sensible, that nothing can be more unphilosophical than to be positive or dogmatical on any subject; and that, even if excessive scepticism could be maintained, it would not be more destructive to all just reasoning and enquiry. I am convinced, that, where men are the most sure and arrogant, they are commonly the most mistaken, and have there given reins to passion, without that proper deliberation and suspense, which can alone secure them from the grossest absurdities' (Hume, 1751, Section IX, Part I). As a consequence of this attitude, Hume's view was that the guiding principles of human action should be derived from sentiment. Although he posed the question whether these guiding principles (i.e. the principles of morals) derive from reason (i.e. a chain or argument and induction) or from sentiment (i.e. an immediate feeling and finer internal sense), he stated that the final judgement which 'pronounces characters and actions amiable or odious, praiseworthy or blameable; that which stamps on the mark of honour or infamy, approbation or censure; that which renders morality and active principle, and constitutes virtue our happiness, and vice our misery … depends on the internal sense or feeling, which nature has made universal in the whole species' (1751, Section I). Nonetheless, Hume called for reasoning or science in the form of making nice distinctions, drawing just conclusions, forming distant comparisons, examining complicated relations and fixing and ascertaining general facts in order to 'pave the way for such sentiment, and give a proper discernment of its object' (Hume 1751, Section I).

Box 3: *Quotes of David Hume*

David Hume
1711-1776

It may be esteemed, perhaps, a superfluous task to prove, that the benevolent or softer affections are ESTIMABLE; and wherever they appear, engage the approbation and good-will of mankind. The epithets, sociable, good-natured, humane, merciful, grateful, friendly, generous, beneficent, or their equivalents, are known in all languages, and universally express the highest merit, which human nature is capable of attaining. Where these amiable qualities are attended with birth and power and eminent abilities, and display themselves in the good government or useful instruction of mankind, they seem even to raise the possessors of them above the rank of human nature, and make them approach in some measure to the divine. Exalted capacity, undaunted courage, prosperous success; these may only expose a hero or politician to the envy and ill-will of the public: But as soon as the praises are added of humane and beneficent; when instances are displayed of lenity, tenderness, or friendship: envy itself is silent, or joins the general voice of approbation and applause.

*

But I forget that it is not my present business to recommend generosity and benevolence, or to paint, in their true colours, all the genuine charms of the social virtues. These, indeed, sufficiently engage every heart, on the first apprehension of them; and it is difficult to abstain from some sally of panegyric, as often as they occur in discourse or reasoning. But our object here being more the speculative, than the practical part of morals, it will suffice to remark, (what will readily, I believe, be allowed) that no qualities are more entitled to the general good-will and approbation of mankind than beneficence and humanity, friendship and gratitude, natural affection and public spirit, or whatever proceeds from a tender sympathy with others, and a generous concern for our kind and species.

1751, An Enquiry Concerning the Principles of Morals, Section II, Part I

In order to identify these guiding principles of human action, he formulated – more than 250 years ago – a 'research agenda and strategy' that is still up-to-date these days. According to

Hume, the only object of reasoning is to discover and analyse what 'we call PERSONAL MERIT … and thence, reach the foundation of ethics, and find those universal principles, from which all censure or approbation is ultimately derived' (Hume, 1751, Section I). He went on arguing that the question of personal merit can only be satisfactorily solved by following an 'experimental research method' and by deducing general maxims from the comparison of particular instances while in contrast, the other research or scientific method 'where a general abstract principle is first established, and is afterwards branched out into a variety of inferences and conclusions, may be more perfect in itself, but suits less the imperfection of human nature, and is a common source of illusion and mistake in this as well as in other subjects' (Hume, 1751, Section I).

According to Hume, personal merit 'consists altogether in the possession of mental qualities, useful or agreeable to the person himself, or to others …' (Hume, 1751, Section IX, Part I). This theory of *utility* and *agreeableness* appears to be an easy moral theory to follow in order to guide any kind of human action: 'It might be expected, that this principle would have occurred even to the first rude, unpracticed enquirers concerning morals, and been received from its own evidence, without any argument or disputation. Whatever is valuable in any kind, so naturally classes itself under the division of useful or agreeable … that it is not easy to imagine, why we should ever seek farther, or consider the question as a matter of nice research or enquiry. […] And it seems a reasonable presumption, that systems and hypotheses have perverted our natural understanding; when a theory, so simple and obvious, could so long have escaped the most elaborate examination' (Hume, 1751, Section IX, Part I). Finally, Hume identifies what he perceives to be the guiding principles of human action; i.e. the principles of morals. These are *benevolence, justice,* and *allegiance* (to governments and the laws of nations, of modesty, and of good manners); simply because we approve these principles for their utility and agreeableness. 'We approve them in all times and places, even where our own interest is not at stake, solely for their tendency to benefit the whole society of that time or place' (Cohen, 2004, Chapter 7).

In contrast to Hume, the writers Henry David Thoreau and William Wordsworth were more concerned with the relationship between nature and humankind or, to be more precise, between mental and material life. While both saw nature as an individual mysterious other (i.e. they draw a clear distinction between humans and nature), they believed in the 'initial unity of nature and humankind in a common divine origin' (Becker et al., 2005); i.e. the opposite of Fichte's (1794) *self* and *nonself.*

Thoreau was an American philosopher, poet, and environmental scientist whose major work *Walden* (1854) addressed these several disciplines by focussing on the concrete problems of living in the world as a human being (Furtak, 2005). Thoreau became frustrated with society and therefore turned 'to the woods': 'I went to the woods because I wished to live deliberately, to front only the essential facts of life, and see if I could not learn what it had to teach, and not, when I came to die, discover that I had not lived. I did not wish to live what was not life, living is so dear; [...] I wanted to live deep and suck out all the marrow of life ...' (Thoreau, 1854, Ch. 2). While *Walden* has been criticised for being a work of many gaps and contradictions, it explains Thoreau's approach of integrating nature and the human mind. Thoreau recognised its original unity but also its clear distinction (Becker and Manstetten, 2004). His view was that nature's physical outward appearance is symbolic of invisible yet discernible spiritual facts. He believed that humans can translate and transform nature's symbols into their rational mind if they will allow it. Thoreau argued that the only reason why humans cannot always determine the right 'path' is because they are not completely tuned into their inner voice (Brulator, 1999). 'What is it that makes it so hard sometimes to determine whither we will walk? I believe that there is a subtile magnetism in Nature, which, if we unconsciously yield to it, will direct us aright. It is not indifferent to us which way we walk. There is a right way; but we are very liable from heedlessness and stupidity to take the wrong one. We would fain take that walk, never yet taken by us through this actual world, which is perfectly symbolical of the path which we love to travel in the interior and ideal world; and sometimes, no doubt, we find it difficult to choose our direction, because it does not yet exist distinctly in our idea' (Thoreau, 1862).

Box 4: *Quotes of Henry David Thoreau*

<table>
<tr><td>

Henry David Thoreau
1817-1862

'The finest qualities of our nature, like the bloom on fruits, can be preserved only by the most delicate handling. Yet we do not treat ourselves nor one another thus tenderly.' 1854, Walden, Chapter One

'Nature is a personality so vast and universal that we have never seen one of her features.' 1862, Walking

'I perceive that, when an acorn and a chestnut fall side by side, the one does not remain inert to make way for the other, but both obey their own laws, and spring and grow and flourish as best they can, till one, perchance, overshadows and destroys the other. If a plant cannot live according to nature, it dies; and so a man.' 1849, Resistance to Civil Government, article 27

'While almost all men feel an attraction drawing them to Society, few are attracted strongly to Nature. In their relation to Nature men appear to me for the most part, notwithstanding their arts, lower than the animals. It is not often a beautiful relation, as in the case of the animals. How little appreciation of the beauty of the landscape there is among us! We have to be told that the Greeks called the world Kosmos Beauty - or Order, but we do not see clearly why they did so, and we esteem it at best only a curious philological fact.' 1862, Walking

</td></tr>
</table>

Similarly, the English poet William Wordsworth – a leader of the Romantic Movement in England – believed that a divine spiritual principle is inherent in both, nature and the human being and that this principle (upon which both are founded) is directly connected to the soul of the child:

> *'To every Form of being is assigned [...] / An 'active' Principle: --howe'er removed / From sense and observation, it subsists / In all things, in all natures; in the stars / Of azure heaven, the unenduring clouds, / In flower and tree, in every pebbly stone / That paves the brooks, the stationary rocks, / The moving waters, and the invisible air. / Whate'er exists hath properties that spread / Beyond itself, communicating good / A simple blessing, or with evil mixed; / Spirit that knows no insulated spot, / No chasm, no solitude; from link to link / It circulates, the Soul of all the worlds. / This is the freedom of the universe; / Unfolded still the more, more visible, / The more we know; and yet is reverenced least, / And least respected in the human Mind, / Its most apparent home.' (Wordsworth, 1814, Book IX)*

Wordsworth view was that humans remove themselves from the original divine source through the development of reason and that it is only possible to re-approach this principle once more on a new level of reflection through both, memorizing one's childhood and interacting with nature. Following Wordsworth, humans' creative productivity is therefore an expression of this initial unity with nature; however, its perfected realisation is only possible through a close interrelation with nature. This describes the inner mutuality between nature and humankind (Becker et al., 2005). 'Humans and nature are one, and are different as well. Both approaches represent two sides of the same coin. Isolating either one leads to shortcomings' (Becker and Manstetten, 2004, p. 112).

All this can be summarized in the notion of the *poetical economy*. Apparently, the term was first used by French artist Robert Filliou in 1966: 'A *Principles of Poetical Economy* must be written. Write it' (cited in Filliou, 1996, p. 21). The term re-appeared in 1996 as the title of a video exhibition called *From Political to Poetical Economy* showing works of Filliou at the Morris and Helen Belkin Art Gallery, Vancouver (see also Box 5).

More recently, Becker and Manstetten (2004) grounded their understanding of the poetical economy on the ideas and writings of German philosopher Novalis, who was part of a literature movement called 'Jena Romanticism'. According to Novalis, the 'poet' overcomes the separation from nature since he is able to experience both, nature as a counterpart or partner in true dialogue (nature as a 'You') *and* unity with nature. However, it is important to note that

Novalis' understanding of poetry is not restricted to people that are the authors of poems, novels, etc., but is rather an 'essential trait of humanity in general' (Becker and Manstetten, p. 108).

> *'It is too bad [...] that [poetry] has a special name and that poets make up a special guild. It is not anything special at all. It is the peculiar mode of activity of the human mind. Does not everybody use his mind and his imagination all the time?' (Novalis, [1842] 1964, cited in Becker and Manstetten, p. 107)*

Following Novalis (or other German Romantics), poetry represents the integration of two essential dimensions of what makes humanity human: (1) creativity or inventiveness, and (2) love. As a consequence, poetry is the unifying link between humankind and nature (Becker and Manstetten, 2004). By referring to Novalis, Becker and Manstetten (2004) argue that to 'be human in its proper sense does not mean to dominate nature, but to be in poetical communication with nature, something which would lead to a universal harmony':

> *'Poetry elevates each single thing through a particular combination with the rest of the whole. [...P]oetry is as it were the key to philosophy, its purpose and meaning; for poetry shapes the beautiful society – the world family – the beautiful household of the universe.' (Novalis, 1997, cited in Becker and Manstetten, p. 109)*

Within this 'beautiful household' humankind plays a crucial role; i.e. humans have to take care that all things are in their proper place and can exist in harmony with 'the rest of the whole'. The term household is understood here in its original Greek meaning; the Greek expression 'oikonomia' (economy) originally meant 'the art of good housekeeping' (Becker and Manstetten, 2004). Or expressed in the words of Tachi Kiuchi[18]: 'Economy means household management – society's household or the household of the earth' (Kiuchi, 2004).

The notion of a more poetical economy has been introduced here to provide the philosophical and moral foundations for a more symbiotic relationship between humans and nature or between human economic activity and the Earth System respectively. A symbiotic relationship is necessary because 'we have grown in number to the point where our presence is perceptibly disabling the planet like a disease. As in human diseases there are four possible outcomes: destruction of the invading disease organisms; chronic infection; destruction of the host; or

---

[18] Tachi Kiuchi is the current Chairman of the Future 500 group of companies (see: www.future500.org); he was Chairman and CEO of Mitsubishi Electric America and Managing Director of Mitsubishi Electric Corporation.

symbiosis – a lasting relationship of mutual benefit to the host and the invader (Lovelock, 2006, p. XII-XIII).

Box 5: *Art meets science and spirituality in a changing economy (Wijers, 2002)*

<table><tr><td>

'The collection of quotes presented here is meant to strengthen our motivation to make the world a success.'

Joseph Beuys *(artist, 1921-1986):*
'We have to create the world as a living sculpture. In the social body money should flow like a bloodstream. This method can only succeed if all people work together.'

'Quality will spring from this and will heal the damages and deformations of man and nature.'

Robert Filliou *(artist, 1926-1987):*
'Prostitution is the driving force of our economic system. We do not sell goods so much as we sell ourselves. We need an international network of people refusing the Economics of Prostitution, to further the ideas of Poetical Economy. The aim of Poetical Economy is to make people happy.'

Rupert Sheldrake *(biologist and author):*
'Obviously one ideal, which is already perfectly apparent to many people, is that the development of the earth should be sustainable. We should think not just three years ahead, or five years ahead, but a hundred or two hundred years ahead.'

Fritjof Capra *(physicist):*
'Are we talking about global partnership, global interdependence, or are we talking about global exploitation? Most economic policies and most business policies today, as we know, are more in the direction of global exploitation than global partnership. The model of the economy that we need has to be a systems approach. Economists, ecologists, scientists, psychologists, people in all these fields have to work together to deal with economics from a systematic point of view.'

'There needs to be a shift in values, together with a shift in thinking. A shift from fragmentation to wholeness, from quantity to quality, from growth to sustainability, from domination to partnership.'

David Bohm *(physicist, 1917-1992):*
'The first thing we have to do, is to look at our whole way of thinking. That means that people have to make a co-operative effort to have a dialogue, in which we will not merely exchange opinions, but actually listen deeply to the views of other people without resistance.'

'We have to understand each other even if we are different, then a coherent consciousness may arise which is capable of peace and the decrease of suffering over the whole world.'

'What we need is dialogues in the real sense of the word 'dialogue', which means 'flowing through'. The spirit of dialogue is not competition, but it means that everybody wins.'

Francisco Varela *(biologist and philosopher, 1946-2001):*
'You actually have a whole set of behavioural processes, genetic processes and ecological phenomena that can only be accounted for on the basis of co-operation. Behavioural processes on the basis of co-operation can be called love.'

J.C.J. Vanderheyden *(artist):*
'Human love is the only opposite of fear. There is no fear in a moment of love. Love is the energy for surviving.'

</td></tr></table>

The understanding of the concept of sustainable development that has been explained above by referring to four different approaches or 'worldviews', is summarized in the following Figure 8. It shows that sustainable development means a continuous effort to reach ecological integrity, social equity and economic security through managing the household of the Earth by operating within the basic framework laid down by nature, by understanding development as an effort to expand people's freedom and through incorporating ecological concerns into social theory and existing institutions.

Figure 8: *Understanding Sustainable Development*

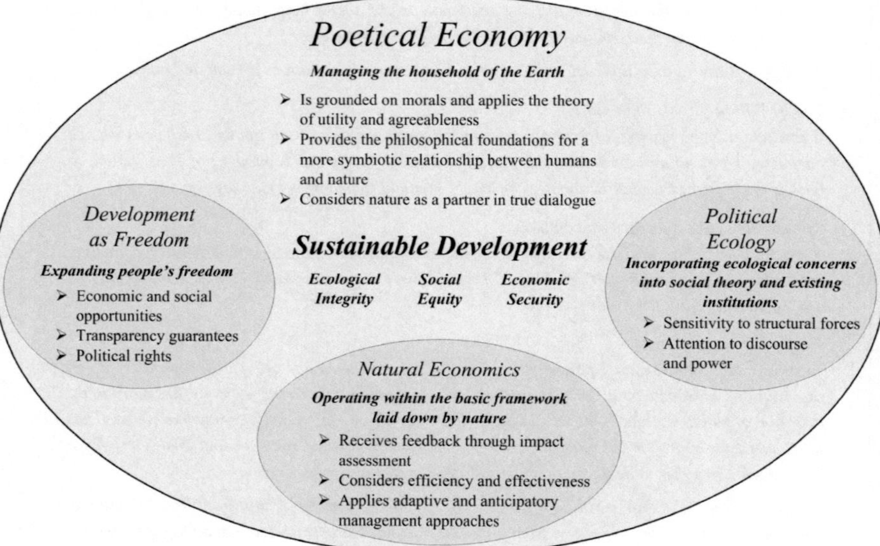

This rather detailed explanation of the concept of sustainable development now serves as a starting point for deducing the operating principles or management rules for a sustainable society. These principles are then subsequently used to formulate the constituents of sustainable buildings as well as to draft a framework for sustainable property investment. Furthermore, the natural economics' approach of informing and guiding economic activity through impact assessment will deserve further attention.

2.2.2 The principles of sustainable development

The term principle is derived from the Latin expression *principium* – which means beginning. The Encyclopaedia Britannica (2004) defines a principle as (1) a comprehensive and fundamental law, doctrine, or assumption; (2) as a rule or code of conduct; (3) as a habitual devotion to right principles; or (4) as the laws or facts of nature underlying the working of an artificial device.

Carrying out an internet search on the term 'principles of sustainable development' leads to millions of hits (more precisely, in April 2006 Google counted more than 42 million). Nearly every larger company, organisation or government has now formulated and committed themselves (at least on paper) to the 'principles of sustainable development'. However, most of these sets of principles differ from each other since no common 'reference'-set exists. This is mainly due to the circumstance that sustainable development is perceived to be an ambiguous concept with a complex meaning. Carter (2001) has argued that this elusiveness is both, strength and weakness: it allows a multitude of diverging interests to unite under one banner, while attracting the criticism that sustainable development is nothing more than an empty slogan. Consequently, formulating the principles of sustainable development is a difficult and intricate exercise. These principles strongly depend on the understanding of the concept of sustainable development and thus, on different 'worldviews'. For example, the neo-classical interpretation of sustainable development as the maximisation of welfare over time – which is usually further simplified by equating the maximisation of welfare with the maximisation of utility derived from consumption – may result in only one principle of sustainable development: maximise GDP growth through efficient resource allocation (i.e. market mechanisms) to maximise income in order to maximise consumption. As it was shown above, other approaches to sustainable development take the view that only some problems can be appropriately dealt with through market efficiency, while others require the application of different measures (such as a 'safe minimal standard' approach) in order to protect essential resources and environmental functions. This, in return, involves normative analyses, the formulation of moral imperatives and social values as well as public decision making (Harris, 2000).

According to Princen (2003) the two dominant classes of principles for sustainable resource use – *efficiency* (including division of labour, economies of scale, specialization, streamlining, intensification and conservation) and *cooperation* (including equal representation, public participation, full disclosure, information sharing and consensus) – are no longer appropriate in order to meet current challenges since they take the status quo environment as the starting point and aim for environmental improvement; i.e. doing better than present conditions, even if better is only slowing down the rate of degradation. Princen (2003, p.34) argues that other principles are now urgently required since 'many environmental threats are of a wholly different order from that presumed in many environmental and economic institutions. Critical environmental threats entail irreversibilities and non-substitutabilities; they threaten vital life-support systems.' For this reason, Princen (2003) opts for a different class of principles (including *restraint, precautionary, polluter pays, zero,* and *reverse onus*) which he subsumes under the term *sufficiency*. Sufficiency describes the simple and *intuitive* idea that as one does more and more of an activity, there can be enough, and finally, there can be too much. Although Princen (2003) acknowledges that implementing sufficiency principles in practice may be a difficult exercise, he refers to the ecological economist Herman Daly who stated that: 'It will be very difficult to define sufficiency and build the concept [of sufficiency] into economic theory and practice. But I think it will prove far more difficult to continue to operate [as if] there is no such thing as enough' (Daly, 1993, pp. 360-361). However, sufficiency principles form only one part of a comprehensive normative framework for sustainable development; other important principles include those oriented to democratic values such as human rights and justice (Princen, 2003).

Furthermore, principles have been defined as fundamental laws or assumptions or as general rules of conduct (e.g. management rules for a sustainable society). But rules need to be carefully defined for whom or what: society as whole, individuals, policy makers, businesses, the functioning of artificial or natural systems. Therefore, it is not easy to group principles of sustainable development into clearly defined categories since substantial overlapping exist. For example, the sufficiency principle of *restraint* applies for individuals and businesses while other sufficiency principles (such as *reverse onus*) apply for policy makers since they appear to be the only ones capable of enforcing them.

The attempt is made in the following to draft a normative framework for sustainable development by providing a list of relevant principles. Hereby, the principles are based on the understanding of the concept of sustainable development as outlined in the previous chapter; the principles are grouped under five main headings. These are: moral and social principles, policy principles, ecological principles, business principles, and system principles.

Moral and social principles: Within a sustainable society, people
- follow Hume's (1751) theory of utility and agreeableness;
- are 'human' in its proper sense and do not attempt to dominate nature (Thoreau, 1854 and 1862; Wordsworth, 1814; Novalis, 1842; Becker and Manstetten, 2004; and Kiuchi, 2004);

- assume a custodian's accountability for resources essential to meeting their needs and take a steward's responsibility for the resources required for meeting their wants (Ruth, 2006);

- show the behavioural tendency to use less than what is physically, technically, legally or financially possible; i.e. adopt the sufficiency principle (Princen, 2003);

- increase contributions to meeting the needs[19] of other people within their society and worldwide (Waage et al., 2005); and

- promote and protect other peoples' capability to do and be things of value (Sen, 1999).

Policy principles: Within a sustainable society, policies

- enforce warrant corrective action in the face of environmental or human threats even if science is not yet conclusive; i.e. adopt the precautionary principle[20] (Princen, 2003; Turner and Hartzell, 2004; Newman, 2005);

- make polluters pay; i.e. ensure that those actors primarily responsible for degradation pay for clean-up and amelioration (Princen, 2003);

- make sure that the burden of proof is on those who would intervene into critical life support systems; i.e. adopt the reverse onus principle[21] (Princen, 2003);

- ban (*ex ante*) human interventions that are incompatible with ecosystem functioning; i.e. adopt the zero principle (Princen, 2003);

- encourage new foundations[22] for renewal that build and sustain the capacity of people, economies, and nature to deal with change (Holling, 2001);

- identify and reduce destructive constraints and inhibitions on constructive change, such as perverse subsidies (Holling, 2001);

---

[19] Includes basic needs such as food, clothing, housing, health, etc. (Harris, 2000) as well as social achievement goals such as advanced technology and safe conveniences in housing, mobility, leisure time, advanced education and safe working conditions, etc. (Schmidt-Bleek, 2004); this can be summarized as follows: access to resources, use of resources, flow of benefits and accrual of impacts. All these terms should be interpreted in the broadest sense; for an explanation see: Waage et al., (2005, p. 1151).

[20] The precautionary principle and the ambiguity that surrounds it has been the issue of intense debate concerning environmental policy; for example, the precautionary principle has found support only if it is subject to a 'cost-benefit' filter (Turner, 2006b). For this reason, Turner and Hartzell (2004, p. 458) have developed the definition of a *cost conscious precautionary principle* which is as follows: 'When an activity A raises threats of harm to the environment or human health, whoever is doing or contributing to A should take the *most cost effective* precautionary measures available, even where there is ignorance concerning the likelihood of harm and/or the seriousness of harm.'

[21] The reverse ones principle as well as the make polluters pay principle directly address the issues of increasing 'risk export' and 'responsibility evasion'; i.e. in the global economy, too many risks as well as the resulting costs are externalized to people OTHER than customers and shareholders, and never show up on financial statements (Princen, 2003 and Kiuchi, 2003).

[22] Amongst other issues, this includes encouraging programs to expand an understanding of change and communicate it to citizens, businesses, as well as to people at different levels of administration and governance (Holling, 2001).

- increase the economic value of natural resources (Carnoules Appeal, 2000);

- enforce the adoption of the no net loss principle in order to maintain natural resources at current levels (Dalal-Clayton and Sadler, 2004);

- promote and protect people's rights, intra- and intergenerational equity as well as political accountability and participation (Harris, 2000); and

- integrate economic, social and environmental considerations through holistic impact assessments (Sneddon et al., 2005; Ruth, 2006).

Ecological principles: Within a sustainable society,

- nature's adaptive capability (including biodiversity) is maintained and nature's carrying capacity[23] is respected through eliminating contribution to systematic increases in (1) concentrations of substances produced by society; (2) concentrations of substances extracted from the Earth's crust; and (3) physical degradation of nature through over-harvesting and other forms of modification (Holling, 2001; Schmidt-Bleek, 2004; Waage et al., 2005; Porritt, 2006).

Business principles: Within a sustainable society, businesses

- produce *useful* goods and services (Hume, 1751);

- provide solutions instead of products (Schmidt-Bleek, 2004);

- consider the roles of effectiveness and efficiency (adopt the efficiency principle) in decision making (Ruth, 2006);

- operate in an environmentally compatible state of industrial material flows and energy use; i.e. produce goods and use production technologies only that are consistent with nature's metabolism (adopt the consistency principle) (Huber, 1995 and 2000);

- apply adaptive and anticipatory management approaches (Ruth, 2006); and

- integrate economic, environmental and social considerations in decision-making processes through holistic impact assessments of both, the goods and services produced as well as the actions required to produce them (Ruth, 2006).

System principles: Within a sustainable society,

- measures and actions are adjusted and re-calibrated through feedback loops and adaptation (Kiuchi, 2003 and 2005).

---

[23] Current appropriations of natural resources and services already exceed Earth's long term carrying capacity. Enabling everybody to enjoy the same ecological standards as North Americans would (using prevailing technology) require three Earths to satisfy aggregate material demand (Meadows et al., 2004 and Porritt, 2006).

It may sound surprising but the last-named principle (feedback and adaptation) may be the one that most powerfully drives sustainable development. Why this is the case has been explained in two speeches held by Tachi Kiuchi at the GreenBuilding 2003 conference in Pittsburgh and more recently, at the UN Global Compact Symposium in San Francisco. Kiuchi (2003 and 2005) argued that everything in nature emerges from an organic process of feedback and adaptation (see also Figure 2 above). According to Kiuchi this principle best illustrates its power in the rainforest, the most effective value creating system in the world. 'The vitality of nature – its capacity to cultivate ever more advanced forms of life, and to support them, for billions of years, on finite resources and a fixed flow of energy from the sun – this capacity comes from the process of feedback-and-adaptation through which nature evolves' (Kiuchi, 2003). This is also true for the capitalist system which *has* been successful through its capacity to harness marketplace feedback and adaptation. The problem is, however, that companies increasingly cut themselves off feedback. As companies extend their influence across nations they become less and less tied to the communities they serve. 'They know nothing of their impacts on people, culture, health, or the environment. They subsist only on the shallowest feedback: direct internal financial returns' (Kiuchi, 2003).

This is dangerous and leads to a false statement of corporate accounts since huge and growing external cost categories are ignored. Kiuchi (2003) goes on arguing that shareholders may not notice these unstated costs while in contrast stakeholders do. Thus, companies *and* economies that systematically cut themselves off from feedback of the larger marketplace (i.e. the economic, social, and environmental feedback of the triple bottom line) 'will ultimately doom themselves ...' (Kiuchi, 2003).

As it was said before, some of these principles mentioned above are currently being implemented in practice by governments and corporations. For example, the Future 500 companies have recently agreed on the installation of a software called the 'Corporate Accountability Gap Audit' in order to receive feedback from the larger marketplace[24]. In addition, the European Commission has recently announced a set of guiding principles for sustainable development that address much of what has been explained above. The EU's principles can be found in Box 6.

---

[24] For more information on the Corporate Accountability Gap Audit, see: http://www.future500.org/press/5/

Box 6: *European Union's Guiding Principles for Sustainable Development (European Commission, 2005)*

> ***Promotion and protection of fundamental rights***
> *Place human beings at the centre of the European Union's policies, by promoting fundamental rights, by combating all forms of discrimination and contributing to the reduction of poverty worldwide.*
>
> ***Intra- and intergenerational equity***
> *Address the needs of current generations without compromising the ability of future generations to meet their needs in the EU and elsewhere.*
>
> ***Open and democratic society***
> *Guarantee citizens' rights of access to information and ensure access to justice. Develop adequate consultation and participatory channels for all interested parties and associations.*
>
> ***Involvement of citizens***
> *Enhance the participation of citizens in decision making. Promote education and public awareness of sustainable development. Inform citizens about their impact on the environment and their options for making more sustainable choices.*
>
> ***Involvement of businesses and social partners***
> *Enhance the social dialogue, corporate social responsibility and private-public partnerships to foster cooperation and common responsibilities to achieve sustainable production and consumption.*
>
> ***Policy coherence and governance***
> *Promote coherence between all European Union policies and coherence between local, regional, national and global actions in order to increase their contribution to sustainable development.*
>
> ***Policy integration***
> *Promote integration of economic, social and environmental considerations so that they are coherent and mutually reinforce each other by making full use of instruments for better regulation, such as balanced impact assessment and stakeholder consultations.*
>
> ***Use best available knowledge***
> *Ensure that policies are developed, assessed and implemented on the basis of the best available knowledge and that they are economically sound and cost-effective.*
>
> ***Precautionary principle***
> *Take a precautionary approach where there is objective scientific uncertainty in order to avoid potential damage to people's health or to the environment and take preventive action.*
>
> ***Make polluters pay***
> *Ensure that prices reflect the real costs to society of production and consumption activities and that polluters pay for the damage they cause to human health and the environment.*

The principles of sustainable development or the management rules for a sustainable society respectively which have been formulated above have been deduced form the contemporary understanding of the concept of sustainable development. It is clear that these principles cannot be implemented at once and that trade-offs between them exist at the moment. For example, in order to respect nature's carrying capacity businesses need to operate in an environmentally compatible state of industrial material flows and energy use; this however, requires changing existing production technologies which takes time. Furthermore, these principles are now formulated in a generalised manner. For this reason, they need to be translated and integrated into the areas of responsibility and action of individual and institutional actors within different business sectors and at all levels of society. Furthermore, the principles need to serve as a starting point to derive at sustainability requirements for different assessment objects (e.g. products, services and processes). With a focus on property and construction this will be pursued within Section 2.4.3 and the subsequent parts of this dissertation. But before this is done, it will be analysed and discussed how contributions to sustainable development can be measured.

2.3 Measuring contributions to sustainable development

2.3.1 Basic forms of assessment

Measuring the contributions to sustainable development is often described as a process by which the ecological, social and economic implications of an activity are evaluated. Here the term activity has to be interpreted in a broad sense; i.e. an activity can encompass existing policies, a plan or program, a project, or a particular practice such as the production of goods and services. In order to term this process, a variety of expressions can be found in literature; e.g. sustainability assessment, sustainability appraisal, corporate sustainability assessment, strategic sustainability analysis, integrated or holistic impact assessment, and so on. This process is of critical importance because what is not measured cannot be improved.

Whatever the process is called and irregardless of the disputes concerning the appropriate methodology it has (or should have) one common goal: to detect whether or not an economy, a nation, a corporation, an economic sector, a city, the world as a whole, etc. is on a sustainable development path (Pearce and Barbier, 2000). If the assessment results are positive, the assessment object is colloquially named 'sustainable'. While in reality, human activities currently do (and will do so for the foreseeable future) only contribute (more or less) to sustainable development. Indeed, recent assessments have shown that 'humanity is *already* in unsustainable territory' (Meadows et al., 2004, p. XIV).

Humanity is in *overshoot*. This is can be indicated, for example, by humanity's ecological footprint which has already exceeded the Earth's carrying capacity (see Box 7) and by the Living Planet Index published by WWF (2004, p. 1); the index shows average trends in populations of terrestrial, freshwater, and marine species worldwide. The index declined by about 40% from 1970 to 2000.

Box 7: *Ecological footprint vs. carrying capacity of the Earth (Wackernagel et al., 2002 and Wackernagel et al., n.d.)*

The "ecological footprint" methodology provides a natural capital account that can determine at each scale, from the global down to the household, how much of nature's services are appropriated for supporting these entities. The benchmark is calculated as follows: Adding up the biologically productive land per capita world-wide of 0.25 hectares of arable land, 0.6 hectares of pasture, 0.6 hectares of forest and 0.03 hectares of built-up land shows that there exist 1.5 hectares per global citizen; and 2 hectares once we also include the sea space. Not all that space is available to human use as this area should also give room to the 30 million fellow species with whom humanity shares this planet. According to the Brundtland Report, at least 12% of the ecological capacity, representing all ecosystem types, should be preserved for biodiversity protection. This 12% may not be enough for securing biodiversity, but conserving more may not be politically feasible. Accepting 12% as the magic number for biodiversity preservation, one can calculate that from the approximately 2 hectares per capita of biologically productive area that exists on our planet, only **1.7 hectares per capita are available for human use.** *These 1.7 hectares become the ecological benchmark figure for comparing people's ecological footprints. It is the mathematical average of the current ecological reality.*

The following graph shows that human activities have exceeded the biosphere's capacity since the 1980s. This overshoot can be expressed as the extent to which human area demand exceeds nature's supply. Human demand overshoots nature's supply by some 20% in 1999. An overshoot of 20% means that it would require 1.2 earths to regenerate what humanity used in the year 1999. However, it needs to be noted that this calculation is based on the Earth's total ecological capacity for each year. Reserving 12% of the biologically productive area for conservation (following the Brundtland Report's suggestion) moves the crossing-over point from the 1980s to the early 1970s and increases the current overshoot from 20% to nearly 40%. The global average per capita area demand for 1999 was up to 2.3 hectares.

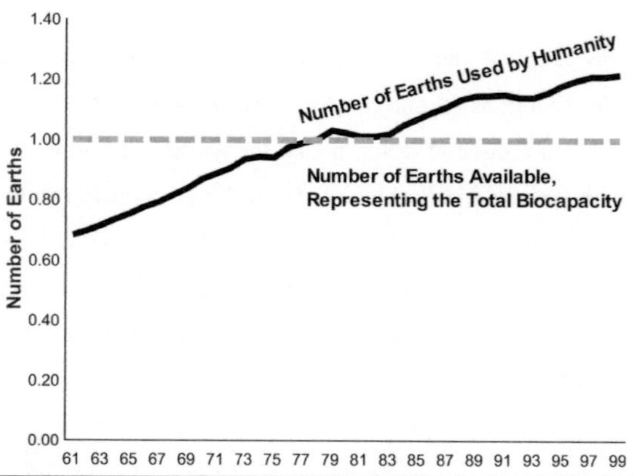

Meadows et al. (2004, p. 1) have identified three causes of overshoot which are always the same, at any scale from personal to planetary. These are: (1) Growth, acceleration, or rapid change (concerning the world as a whole, such change is driven mainly by exponential growth in both human population[25] and the material economy[26]). (2) Some form of limit or barrier, beyond which the moving system may not safely go, and (3) a delay or mistake in the perceptions and the responses that strive to keep the system within its limits.

Given this, the time may be right to redefine intention and role of sustainability assessments which are, in most cases, seen as a nice add-on to, but not yet as an integral part of decision-making processes. By making reference to a number of other researchers and writers, Pope et al. (2004, p. 609) have stated that sustainability assessments must be applied within a structured framework:

- to existing practices across all sectors;
- to proposed new initiatives at all levels of decision-making;
- to the prevailing policy and legislative paradigm;
- to any decision with the potential to impact on patterns of production and consumption, governance and settlement; and
- by all sectors of society.

There is nothing that could be added to this enumeration since sustainability assessment is the *only* instrument or tool capable of providing feedback from the larger marketplace (i.e. the economic, social, and environmental feedback of the triple bottom line) in order to reduce or correct for *'delay or mistake in the perceptions and the responses that strive to keep the system within its limits.'* This is necessary in order to organise a deliberate turnaround, a correction, a careful easing down; or expressed in other words: to avoid collapse (Meadows et al., 2004).

Sustainability assessment combines decision-making, evaluation and reporting processes and is, therefore, an interdisciplinary activity and such a broad field of research that exploring the issue in depth and attempting to deliver a full picture appears to be impossible within the limited scope of this dissertation (however, a good overview can be found in Dalal-Clayton and Sadler, 2004). Many streams of research and 'schools of thought' can and will contribute to this relatively new and challenging field, including economics, ecology, systems theory, the

---

[25] Current population numbers around 6.4 billion and is expected to reach 9 billion by 2050 (UNFPA, 2005).

[26] For example, the global consumption of five important metals (copper, lead, zinc, tin, and nickel) grew more than four-fold between the years 1950 and 2000. In summary: 'Over the past half century human beings have multiplied their own population, their physical possession, and the material and energy flows they utilize by factors of 2, 4, 10, or even more, and they are hoping for more growth in the future' (Meadows et al., 2004, p. 101-102). In order to achieve genuine environmental sustainability by about 2050 the environmental impact per unit of consumption would need to fall by at least 90%; i.e. the necessary 'Factor10' improvement in resource productivity (Ekins, 2000; Schmidt-Bleek, 2001; Porritt, 2006).

health and social sciences, engineering and applied sciences, community planning, law, business management, performance measurement, IT-development, and so on.

The basic principles of sustainability assessments are laid down in the so-called *Bellagio Principles* (IISD, 1997); the principles address the following ten key aspects: guiding vision and goals; holistic perspective; essential elements; adequate scope; practical focus; openness; effective communication; broad participation; ongoing assessment; and institutional capacity. According to Dalal-Clayton and Sadler (2004) sustainability assessments can take three basic forms (their strengths and weaknesses are summarized in Table 2). These are:

- *Accounts-based approaches* draw on constructions of raw data and provide assessment results in a converted, common unit (such as money, area, or energy). Most approaches address important but small aspects of sustainability while other, more complex accounts sum many aspects of the economy, society and the environment into a single statement. In general, accounts based approaches refer to one or a narrow set of indicators and can include the system of national accounts (covering the market economy), the ecological footprint and the ecological 'rucksack' (covering resource consumption and its efficiency), and energy and material accounts (covering physical exchanges between the economy, society, and the environment)[27]. Examples are the Genuine Progress Indicator (GPI)[28], the Genuine Savings Indicator[29], Schmidt-Bleek's (1994) Material Input Per Service unit (MIPS); and David Pearce's posthumously published sustainability account of the UK construction industry (Pearce, 2006).

- *Narrative assessments* combine text, maps, satellite images, graphics, and tabular data, etc. They may use indicators but they are not built around them and the indicators used may change from one reporting period to another. Examples are the *Millennium Ecosystem Assessment* (MA, 2006), the 23rd edition of the Worldwatch Institute's *State of the World Report* (WI, 2006), the *UN Millennium Development Goals Report* (UN, 2005b), and UNEP's impressive collection of past and contemporary satellite images contained within *One Planet Many People: Atlas of our Changing Environment* (UNEP, 2005).

- *Indicator based assessments* are organized around a broader set of indicators but can also include narrative elements. Indicators can be classified as driving-force-, pres-

---

[27] For more information on ecological rucksacks, material intensity measures and strategies for efficient resource use, see: http://www.factor10-institute.org/ and http://www.wupperinst.org/FactorFour/FactorFour_FAQ.html

[28] See: http://www.gpiatlantic.org or http://www.gpionline.net/index.htm

[29] An explanation is contained in Pearce and Barbier (2000, pp. 92-96) and in World Bank (2006). The Genuine Savings Indicator (now called Adjusted Net Savings Indicator) is calculated by the World Bank for 140 countries (see also Figure 5 below).

sure-, response-, state- and impact-indicators.[30] They enable assessments to be selective; therefore, they are equipped to cover the wide array of issues necessary for an adequate portrayal of human and environmental conditions. 'Indicator-based assessments are potentially more transparent, consistent and useful for decision-making than other approaches; but whether they fulfil their potential depends on how well they are designed and executed' (Dalal-Clayton and Sadler, 2004, p. 27). Examples are the Dashboard of Sustainability, WWF's Living Planet Index and the Dow Jones Sustainability Group Indexes.[31]

Table 2: *Strengths and weaknesses of different sustainability assessment approaches (based on Dalal-Clayton and Sadler, 2004, pp. 23-33)*

Assessment approach	Strengths	Weaknesses
Accounts-based	Directly comparable with the GDP, the most widely used measurement of national performance High potential for consistency	Many aspects (such as the costs of loosing biodiversity) are so difficult to evaluate and to convert in monetary units that they are omitted Low potential for transparency (the construction of the accounts, including assumptions, judgements and omissions, is very difficult for non-specialists to follow) Highly aggregate accounts do not clearly reveal the constituents of overall performance which limits their usefulness for strategy development
Narrative	Familiarity, flexibility; easy to understand Huge potential for participation since the assessment can be tailored to the skills of participants	Unsystematic choice of topics together with uneven treatment can mask gaps in coverage and obscure assessment priorities Can prevent the identification of trends since the topics covered can change between reporting periods
Indicator-based	High usefulness for decision-making High potential for transparency and consistency: procedures for choosing indicators lay bare the selection and arrangement of issues covered by the assessment and the values involved; by employing the same set of indicators over time, benchmarking and trend identification becomes possible	Growing complexity: the growing understanding of the complexity of sustainability leads to the question of how to manage the huge amount of data required to monitor it? Difficulty of presenting assessment results in ways that are simple, elegant and effective without comprising the underlying complexity[32]

---

[30] For a more detailed explanation of different indicator types, see the Europen Environment Agency's Typology of indicators: http://reports.eea.europa.eu/TEC25/en

[31] A compendium of indicator initiatives is provided by the International Institute for Sustainable Development (IISD) and can be found here: http://www.iisd.org/measure/compendium/searchinitiatives.aspx

[32] Dalal-Clayton and Sadler (2004, p. 29) argue that the best way to overcome the weaknesses of indicator-based assessments is to combine the indicators into indices. 'When indicators are combined into indices, they can provide a clear picture of the entire system, reveal key relationships between subsystems and between major components, and facilitate analysis of critical strengths and weaknesses. No information is lost, because the constituent indicators and underlying data are always there to be queried.'

In practice, sustainability assessment approaches can be classified under four major groups; these are environmental, economics, and social driven approaches as well as integrated assessments for sustainability. The first three approaches developed relatively independent from each other while the latter one represents a further development or synthesis of the former three.

2.3.2   Environmental driven approaches

Environmental driven assessment approaches have been developed as a response to many reputable scientists' concerns that environmental degradation may reach critical thresholds beyond which there could be irreversible loss of ecosystem functions. In short, they have been developed to provide greater environmental sustainability assurance[33]. In principle, environmental driven assessment approaches are used for three different purposes: (1) to support decision-making process by evaluating environmental impacts of technologies, policies, products, etc. before they are realized, implemented or agreed upon; (2) to accompany the stages of planning and implementation in pursuit of continuous improvement; and (3) to evaluate existing products, technologies, processes, etc. in order to communicate the assessment results towards third parties.

In the literature a distinction is sometimes made between retrospective and proactive approaches. Popular retrospective approaches are ecological footprints and rucksacks. Assessments like these 'allow humanity, using existing data, to monitor its performance regarding a necessary ecological condition for sustainability: the need to keep human demand within the amount that nature can supply' (Wackernagel et al., 2002, p. 9270). Popular proactive approaches include environmental impact assessment (EIA) and strategic environmental assessment (SEA). EIAs focus on single projects such as roads, municipal buildings, farming, windmill parks, etc. and are carried out at the end of the design stage, while in contrast, SEAs are applied to plans, programs and policies in order to ensure that assessments of consequences and analyses of environmentally friendly alternatives take place while plans, programs and policies are being prepared and *before* they are agreed upon. EIAs and SEAs are usually applied by authorities; they require carrying out similar procedures; an authority (e.g. a municipality) has to go through more or less the same phases but the level of detail and the scope of the investigation can be different (Larsen, 2004). An explanation of these basic pro-

---

[33] Environmental sustainability assurance means that critical resource stocks and ecosystem functions must be safeguarded, depletion and deterioration of sources and sinks must be kept within acceptable levels or safe margins, and losses of natural capital must be made good (Dalal-Clayton and Sadler, 2004).

cedures is contained within Annex 1 of the EU Strategic Environmental Assessment Directive. As a consequence of this directive, conducting SEAs is now a mandatory activity within EU member countries[34] since July 2004; the directive covers all plans and programmes which are likely to have significant effects on the environment (2001/42/EC, Article 1). Pope et al. (2004) provide an overview on the development of SEA- and EIA-procedures and argue that these assessment approaches have been further extended to incorporate social and economic considerations in order to reflect a triple bottom line approach to sustainability. According to Pope et al. (2004) EIAs and SEAs are now better described by the terms 'EIA-driven integrated assessments' and 'objectives-led integrated assessments'. The former approach aims to identify the environmental, social and economic impacts of a proposal after the proposal has been designed, and compares these impacts with baseline conditions in order to determine whether they are acceptable or not. While in contrast, the latter approach determines the extent to which a proposal contributes to defined environmental, social and economic goals, before the proposal has been designed and identifies the 'best' available option in terms of meeting these goals or vision. However, both approaches 'tend to limit themselves to measuring whether or not a proposal represents a positive or negative contribution to sustainability. In other words, they consider 'direction to target', where the target is a sustainable society. [...] while this may be useful, it may not be sufficient to drive the kind of change required in the pursuit of this goal. [Instead,] processes are needed that actually assess whether an initiative is, or is not, sustainable' (Pope et al., 2004, p. 614).

2.3.3   Economics driven approaches

Environmental economists' approaches to sustainability assessment are based on the valuation of a range of 'capital' stocks. They have defined sustainability as improving the capital stock and the range of opportunities that it represents for the next generation; i.e. rising individual well-being over time. Consequently, there are two basic rules for achieving sustainability: (1) An intact or improved capital stock must be passed on from one generation to the next. In doing so, generations meet the test of inter-generational equity. (2) Proceeds of resource booms must be reinvested in other assets or in other forms of capital respectively; i.e. savings must exceed depreciation and the accumulated capital stock must proceed at a faster rate than population growth (Pearce, 2006).

---

[34] For example, the German construction law (Baugesetzbuch – BauGB) has been revised in 2004 and in 2005 respectively. Ensuring sustainable development is now the prime objective of any construction or community related planning activity (§1 Abs. 5 and §2 Abs. 4, BauGB).

But what is the capital stock? Capital can be defined as 'a stock of anything that has the capacity to generate a flow of benefits which are valued by humans. It is this flow … that makes the capital stock an asset, and the value of the asset is derived directly form the lifetime value of the flows to which it gives rise' (Porritt, 2006, p. 112). According to Pearce (2006) the capital stock (or wealth) consists of four 'capitals': man-made (or manufactured), human, natural, and social. The only existing measure of wealth comes from the World Bank and is depicted in Table 3 (intangible capital as defined by the World Bank means human capital and the quality of formal and informal social institutions).

Table 3: *Wealth per Capita by Region and Income Group in 2000 (World Bank, 2006)*

Region	in $ per capita				% share of total wealth		
	Total wealth	Natural capital	Produced capital	Intangible capital	Natural capital	Produced capital	Intangible capital
Latin America and the Caribbean	67,955	8,059	10,83	49,066	12	16	72
Sub-Saharan Africa	10,73	2,535	1,449	6,746	24	13	63
South Asia	6,906	1,749	1,115	4,043	25	16	59
East Asia and the Pacifc	11,958	2,511	3,189	6,258	21	27	52
Middle East and North Africa	22,186	7,989	4,448	9,749	36	20	44
Europe and Central Asia	40,209	11,031	12,229	16,88	27	31	42
Income Group							
Low-income countries	7,216	2,075	1,15	3,991	29	16	55
Lower-middle-income countries	23,612	4,398	4,962	14,253	19	21	60
Upper-middle-income countries	72,897	10,921	16,481	45,495	15	23	62
High-income OECD countries	439,063	9,531	76,193	353,339	2	17	80
World	90,21	4,681	16,16	69,369	5	18	77

However, the Forum for the Future (a UK-based sustainable development charity) has added a fifth form of capital – financial capital – because the issues regarding ownership and use of this form of capital go *'right to the heart of what sustainability means.'* This makes a lot of sense although most economists would strongly disagree with the inclusion of financial capital in any 'capital model' because financial capital has no *intrinsic* value; it is not a capital stock in its own right. Porritt (2006, p. 177) explains why financial capital should be included within the capitals framework anyway:

> *'... the uses to which financial capital are put have a huge impact upon the prospects of us ever achieving a genuinely sustainable society – from the role money plays in our lives, all the way through to the way today's capital markets operate, with their increasingly destructive emphasise on short-term profit maximisation in the service of disloyal and footloose investors. [...] And there are still those, of course, who believe that money is indeed the roots of all evil – the principal source of psychological alienation and unsustainable lifestyles in today's consumer capitalism.'*

According to Porritt (2006), financial capital needs good stewardship[35] in order to continue to provide the flow of services required because, like any other form of capital, financial capital depreciates as it is used and can be degraded if it is abused. The flow of services provided by financial capital is portrayed in Figure 9. Porritt argues that exchange of money today for a promise of money in the future – i.e. 'inter-temporal' trade and the risk associated with it – is the essence of financial markets. Financial institutions such as banks, asset managers and insurers have accumulated specialist knowledge on how to attract the resources from savers to provide them to borrowers, on how to select and monitor projects or businesses to lend to, and how to transfer, share, pool or diversify the risk associated with granting a loan that may not be repaid. Within a 'perfect market' this would not be necessary.

Figure 9: *Stocks of financial capital (based on Porritt, 2006, p. 179)*

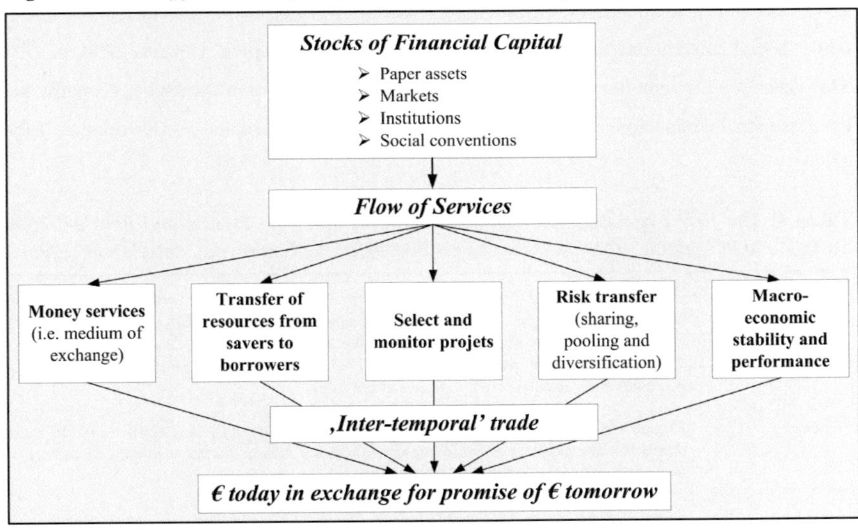

Assuming that rational behaviour underpins decision-making, if businesses and consumers have access toth 'perfect information' and if there would be close social relationships between them, then the exchange of goods and services in the marketplace would be an easy matter

---

[35] The idea of good stewardship of the financial capital stock is closely related to the idea of a 'citizens' income'. There are now groups of distinguished and reputable researchers in many countries (including those from the Institute for Entrepreneurship, Universität Karlsruhe (TH), Germany) that promote a citizens' income which is defined in *A Citizens' Income: A Foundation for a Sustainable World*: 'The citizens' income is the principle that every man, woman and child should receive a weekly sum sufficient to cover the basic needs of food, fuel, clothing and accommodation. It will be tax-free, paid to individuals and unconditional. So everyone will keep it whether they are working or not, or even whether they need it nor not. The citizens' income will replace all existing social security benefits and income tax allowance for the able bodied. In short, the citizens' income is the unconditional provision of basic necessities for all from a common fund, provided by members of the community as a whole according to their ability to pay' (Lord, 2003, cited in Porritt, 2006, p. 192).

because money would 'flow like a bloodstream' (see the quote of Joseph Beuys, Box 5). Investors would know who had surplus funds and the lenders would know that the borrowers would be able to repay the loans. No transaction costs would occur associated with combining the other forms of capital in order to produce goods and services, and there would be no need for banks to collect surplus funds, or to select and monitor projects and businesses to which they lend (Porritt, 2006).

However, the world does not work this way and there are mainly two issues that hamper the 'performance' of human economic interaction: The first one is the imperfection of information; i.e. unequal distribution of and access to it (see Castells, 1996, 1997a, 1997b and Rifkin, 2000). The second one is a lack of trust[36] or of useful and agreeable (i.e. morally acceptable) behaviour (see Axelrod, 1981 and Hume, 1751). 'Imperfect information [and a lack of trust] gives economic and social value to the paper assets, markets, institutions and, most importantly, social conventions that make up the stock of financial capital' (Porritt, 2006, p. 178). This describes the important roles of morals and information within the global economy and gave rise for the inclusion of a fifth form of capital within the 'capitals' framework (see Table 4).

Table 4: *The Five Capitals (four capitals-framework based on Pearce and Barbier, 2000; extension to five capitals-framework based on Forum for the Future, n.d. and Porritt, 2006)*

Forms of Capital	Explanation
Natural	*Natural Capital is any stock or flow of energy and material that produces goods and services. It includes: Resources - renewable and non-renewable materials; Sinks - that absorb, neutralise or recycle wastes; and Processes - climate regulation. Natural capital is the basis not only of production but of life itself!*
Human	*Human Capital consists of people's health, knowledge, skills and motivation. All these things are needed for productive work. Enhancing human capital through education and training is central to a flourishing economy.*
Social	*Social Capital concerns the institutions that help maintaining and developing human capital in partnership with others; e.g. families, communities, businesses, trade unions, schools, and voluntary organisations.*
Manufactured	*Manufactured Capital comprises material goods or fixed assets which contribute to the production process rather than being the output itself – e.g. tools, machines and buildings.*
Financial	*Financial Capital plays an important role within the economy, enabling the other types of Capital to be owned and traded. But unlike the other types, it has no real value itself but is representative of natural, human, social or manufactured capital; e.g. shares, bonds or banknotes.*

---

[36] The economic consequences of a lack of trust are best described by what has been termed the 'prisoner's dilemma': 'A group whose members pursue rational self-interest may all end up worse off than a group whose members act contrary to rational self-interest.' This is described in detail in Kuhn (2003).

An understanding of the relationships between these five forms of capital is critical for the understanding of economics driven approaches to sustainability assessment. Porritt (2006, p. 114) argues that these five capitals are the essential ingredients of modern industrial productivity: 'Natural capital … is … required to maintain a functioning biosphere, supply resources to the economy and dispose its wastes. Human capital provides the knowledge and skills which create manufactured capital and operate it effectively. Social capital creates the institutions that provide the stable context and conditions within and through which economic activity can take place, and which enables individuals to be vastly more productive. Financial capital provides the lubricant to keep the whole system operating.'

The question is: Are these forms of capital substitutable? Some environmental economists believe that they are, while ecological economists argue that they are not; in particular, they argue that there is nothing that can substitute for the loss of natural capital. The different views on the degree of substitutability of forms of capital can be expressed through the following notions of sustainability (Seragelding and Steer, 1994, cited in Dalal-Clayton and Sadler, 2004, p. 52):

- *Weak sustainability* involves maintaining the total capital stock intact without regard to its composition. Natural capital can and should continue to be converted into economic capital and output (goods and services) governed only by existing environmental policies, regulations and guidelines. Thus, from the weak sustainability position, one form of capital can be run down (or depleted) provided that proceeds are re-invested in other forms of capital (Turner, 2006a).
- *Moderate sustainability* requires that some attention is given to the level of capital as well. Natural capital is considered to be substitutable only up to certain critical limits – thresholds that are not yet know.
- *Strong sustainability* means maintaining natural capital at current levels (no net loss). This implies resource losses and ecological damages resulting from development must be replaced or offset.
- *Absolute sustainability* means non-depleting and non-damaging use of natural resources. This would allow only net annual increment of renewable resources could be used.

Diverging perceptions on these four notions of sustainability (particularly on the operationalisation of the strong position) are the cause of various debates on the superiority or appropriateness of economics driven approaches to sustainability assessment. Environmental economics' literature (e.g. *Blueprint for a Green Economy* by Pearce et al., 1989) formulates strong sustainability as maintenance of natural capital with additional critical natural capital constraints. In contrast, the formulation that usually appears in ecological economics' literature refers to preserving physical stocks of critical natural capital. Consequently, the operationalisation of the strong sustainability position is different: While environmental economists rarely discus issues of critical natural capital – the thresholds are never specified or stressed (Özkaynak et al., 2004) – they focus on the economic value of the entire natural capital stock, on the development of environmental valuation techniques, and on their proper application. In contrast, ecological economists insist on the concept of incommensurability and on the necessity of non-monetary indicators in order to evaluate critical natural capital directly in physical terms. Both approaches have their pitfalls and most of them have been identified by Özkaynak et al. (2004):

Environmental economics' approaches: Since these approaches focus on monetising the value of environmental resources and systems and on incorporating the costs of environmental damages into cost-benefit analysis (CBA) or the pricing of goods and services their, limitations (or criticisms) can be reduced to the technical and conceptual problems of assigning monetary values to environmental resources: Is it possible to adequately express environmental concerns through one single common unit of measurement (i.e. money)? Köhn et al. (1999) have argued that the basic concept of monetary valuation of natural resources may be questioned because there can, in principle, be no meaningful monetary values for such resources. Furthermore, the valuation techniques – usually contingent valuation surveys or conjoint analyses that aim measuring peoples' preferences for changes in the state of their environment, and their preferences for changes in the level of risk to their lives (Pearce, 1993) – are criticised for three reasons: (1) Vatn and Bromley (1995) have argued that one metric (price) is unable to capture all relevant information about the different kinds of values assigned by an individual to the environment because of the moral aspect of environmental choices. (2) The economic value assigned by an individual to environmental resources strongly depends on the distribution of income, wealth and power. Willingness to pay is a function of both, individual preferences and income. 'This means that the use of the constancy of the monetary value of the stock of natural resources as an indicator of sustainability is misleading in a very precise way; it has no relation to the viability of the biophysical condition of the planet' (Özkaynak et al., 2004). (3) The whole environmental valuation process is built on the idea of rational, optimising agents who have exogenously determined preference functions (Hodgson, 1997). However, preferences need to be treated as endogenous, with their characteristics largely shaped by the context in which they are formed. Therefore, participants of contingent valuation surveys have no real a priori value for particular environmental resources and goods but create one during the survey process. 'If this is the case, then accepting contingent valuation, or any other hypothetical valuation technique, as a legitimate decision-making tool for environmental issues implies acceptance of an underlying model that is even less appropriate for public goods than it is for private goods' (Özkaynak et al., 2004 with reference to Jacobs, 1997).

Ecological economics' approaches: these approaches focus explicitly on physical indicators of critical natural capital and situate economic analysis in a thermodynamic and co-evolutionary framework. They are based on a variety of different multi-criteria evaluation models and various aggregation procedures characterised by different philosophical and mathematical underpinnings can be found in the literature (Martinez-Alier et al., 1998). Thus, ecological economics approaches to sustainability assessment attempt to 'bring together the range of information and viewpoints necessary for informed deliberative decision making ...' (Özkaynak et al., 2004, p. 292). However, these approaches still have restrictions: (1) The extent to which ecological economics is currently able to influence real world policy is small; this is due to a separation of the development of indicators from the analysis of the economic and political context in which they can effectively be used. (2) It may be possible that 'the distribution of economic and political power within capitalist society is incompatible with the procedurally rational decision-making processes that ecological economics correctly argues are necessary for socially acceptable environmental policies to be made' (Özkaynak et al., 2004, p. 294). (3) Ekins et al. (2003) have proposed a practical framework for the analysis of critical natural capital and strong sustainability; the analysis is based on the identification of what they called the *sustainability gap.* 'The difference between the current situation, the state of the natural capital stock or the pressure being put upon it and the sustainability standard, may be described as the 'sustainability gap' (SGAP). SGAPs will be expressed in physical terms and may be interpreted as the physical 'distance' to environmental sustainability in relation to the present situation and practices' (Ekins et al., 2003, p. 181). These physical distances then indicate that critical natural capital is actually being depleted. However, sustainability standards[37] are not yet defined; Turner (2006a) argues that the precise definition and measurement of critical natural capital is still an open scientific question.

---

[37] According to Ekins et al. (2003) and important part of critical natural capital analysis is the derivation of specific sustainability standards which define the minimum conditions for the critical natural capital to perform its critical environmental functions. The standards may be expressed as indicators of the state of the critical natural capital (e.g. quality of air or water, concentration of greenhouse gases) or of the pressure upon it (e.g. emissions into air or water). These sustainability standards 'need to be as firmly grounded as possible in natural science, with assumptions and the elements of uncertainty clearly defined' (Ekins et al., 2003, p. 166).

Irrespective of these unsolved questions and technical problems (both approaches are, of course still under development), they both serve a common goal and their major strength is the extent of integration that they can achieve between the different dimensions, particularly between environmental and economic variables.[38] If they are combined they can reveal deep insights into the functioning and interplay of economic and ecological systems; in particular, they pinpoint the *limits* of what nature can supply and the *limitations* of the current capitalistic system. 'The rise of China and India illustrates more clearly than any development in recent memory that western, resource-intensive economic model is simply not capable of meeting the growing needs of more than 8 billion people in the twenty-first century. Major shifts in resource use, technologies, policies, and even basic values are needed' (WI, 2006, p. 21). Both environmental and ecological economics' approaches to sustainability assessment can be used to create a powerful picture of global imbalances (see Tables 5-6 and Figure 10).

Table 5: *Global imbalances I (Source: WI, 2006)*

Country or Region	Population, 2004 (million)	GDP, 2004 (trillion)	GDP per person (dollars)	Human Development Index, 2003	Carbon emissions[39] (million tons)	Carbon emissions[38] per person (tons)	Increase in carbon emissions (1990-04)
China	1,297	7.2	4,600	0.76	1,021	0.8	+ 67 %
India	1,080	3.3	2,500	0.60	301	0.3	+ 88%
Europe	457	11.7	26,900	0.92	955	2.5	+ 6%
Japan	128	3.6	29,400	0.94	338	2.7	+ 23%
US	294	11.8	40,100	0.94	1,616	5.5	+ 19%

Table 6: *Global imbalances II (Source: WI, 2006 and World Bank, 2006)*

Country or Region	Total Footprint, 2002, (million global hectares)	Footprint per person, 2002 (global hectares)	Footprint as share of country's biocapacity	Growth in Footprint (1992-2002)	Genuine Savings Indicator
China	2,049	1.6	201 %	24 %	25.5
India	784	0.8	210 %	17 %	12.9
Europe	2,164	4.7	207 %	14 %	14.1[40]
Japan	544	4.8	569 %	6 %	15.1
US	2,810	9.7	205 %	21%	8.2

---

[38] No valuation or assessment approach is perfect and it needs to be noted that despite their rather harsh critique of environmental economists' approaches to sustainability assessment, Özkaynak et al. (2004) acknowledge that the discipline of environmental economics has been able to expand the horizons of neoclassical economic theory by accommodating environmental concerns in its analysis. In particular, they acknowledge the contributions of the London School of environmental economists (notably David Pearce) who developed the concept of the maintenance of the natural capital stock as a condition of the strong version of sustainability. 'In this regard, *Blueprint for a Green Economy* (1989) by Pearce, Markandya and Barbier represents a milestone in the environmental economics and sustainable development literature' (Özkaynak et al., 2004, p. 281).

[39] These numbers refer to carbon (in terms of the mass of the C), rather than to carbon dioxide (CO_2). Carbon dioxide is 3.67 times heavier than carbon. Emissions expressed in units of C can be converted to emissions in CO_2 units by adjusting for the mass of the attached oxygen atoms, that is by multiplying by the ratios of the molecular weights, i.e. 3.67. For more information on carbon dioxide emission, see the FAQ of the Carbon Dioxide Information Analysis Center: http://cdiac.ornl.gov/pns/faq.html

[40] Average of genuine savings indicator of the following countries: Denmark, Finland, France, Germany, Ireland, Italy, the Netherlands, Norway, Portugal, Spain, Sweden, and the UK.

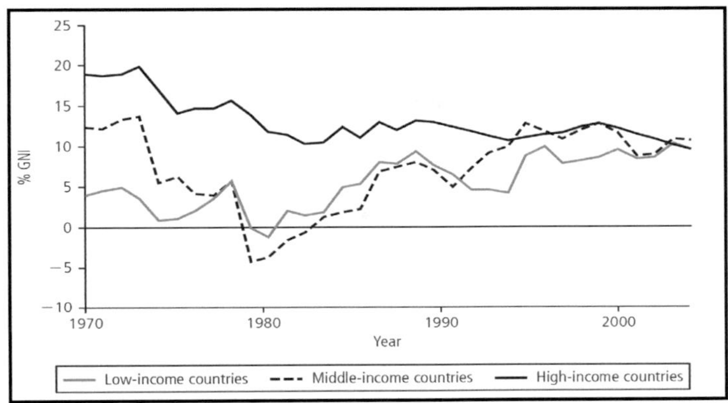

Furthermore, environmental and ecological economics' approaches to sustainability assessment can serve as strategic and operational business management tools since they can be applied at a number of stages in decision-making (*ex-post* or *ex-ante*) and at different levels (macro, sub-national, sectoral and project level). 'Where economic assessments are transparent about the assumptions made, they can provide useful information for stakeholders on the tradeoffs between different types of variables and the effects on different groups' (Grieg-Gran and Dufey, 2004, p. 94). However, less progress has been made in integrating the social dimension into economics driven approaches to sustainability assessment.

2.3.4   Social driven approaches

The problem with social driven approaches to sustainability assessment is that no real assessment approaches are described in the literature. 'The literature on the social dimension of sustainability generally does not discuss approaches to integrate different dimensions of sustainability in assessment procedures – they involve distinctly separate bodies of literature' (Baines and Morgan, 2004, p. 96). Practical attempts to integrate the social dimension into an overall framework of sustainability assessment appear to very experimental and in an emergent stage. Furthermore, very little published experience exists that describes such processes and practices (particularly at the macro-level). This may indicate that (1) lessons from moni-

---

[41] Adjusted net or genuine saving measures the true level of saving in a country after depreciation of produced capital; investments in human capital (as measured by education expenditures); depletion of minerals, energy, and forests; and damages from local and global air pollutants are taken into account. The development of the genuine savings measure shows if overall wealth is actually declining or rising.

toring and evaluation of new approaches are yet to emerge, or (2) reflect a *de facto* absence of conscious, formalised, systematic efforts to record and reflect 'the procedural and analytical processes that are being adopted in pursuit of substantive integration of the environmental, economic, and social dimensions of sustainability' (Baines and Morgan, 2004, p. 96). However, Sinner et al. (2004, p. 16) have identified some broadly accepted ingredients of the social dimension. These are:

- meeting basic needs (i.e. fostering individual and community well-being);
- overcoming disadvantage attributable to personal disability;
- fostering personal responsibility, including social responsibility and regard for the needs of future generations;
- maintaining and developing the stock of social capital, in order to foster the trusting, harmonious and co-operative behaviours that underpin a civil society;
- attention to the equitable distribution of opportunities in development, in the present and in the future;
- acknowledging cultural community diversity and fostering tolerance; and
- empowering people to participate on mutually agreeable terms in influencing choices for development and decision-making.

However, these ingredients are all interlinked and overlap to some extent. Furthermore, tensions and conflicts exist between them; for a more detailed explanation of this issue, see Sinner et al., 2004 and Baines and Morgan, 2004). In order to address these ingredients into sustainability assessments, the available literature focuses on three main issues: (1) the appropriate role of position of social objectives within the overall sustainable development paradigm; (2) the systematic relationship between social, economic and environmental variables; and (3) particular objectives within the broader social sustainability goal which should be emphasised (Baines and Morgan, 2004). For example, UNEP (2004) views social sustainability objectives as a layer of normative values that provides direction to processes of change. Consequently, the integration of the social dimension depends on ethical principles; therefore processes of social performance measurement (including reporting and the choice of indicators) are much more than a 'technical matter'; instead they are directly linked to the meaning and ethics of sustainable development for a community (Baines and Morgan, 2004). This implies that meaningful indicators for social performance measurement can only be defined through a process of public participation which leads us to the notion of integrated assessments for sustainability.

2.3.5 Integrated assessments for sustainability

Due to a range of technical and conceptual difficulties and unsolved ethical questions the notion of integrated assessments for sustainability has only been recently defined in theory but is not yet evident in practice. For example, Pope et al. (2004) have argued that sustainability assessments are only truly integrated if the interrelations between the three dimensions of impacts are considered. This is because the combined impacts (positive and negative) are likely to be much more than simply the sum of impacts of their constituent measures because of *synergetic effects*. If sustainability assessments are not integrated effectively, then this form of 'integrated' assessment 'is reduced to the three separate impact assessments, each generating data relating to the potential environmental, social and economic impacts of the proposal [, project, action] or initiative. The three sets of data must then be 'integrated' in some way after it has been collected in order to reach a decision as to whether or not the proposal [, project, action] or initiative is acceptable within a sustainability context' (Pope et al., 2004, p. 602-603). But what means integrated? And what has to be integrated? According to Milner et al. (2005) the term integrated assessment has been used from within a number of contexts, including the development of cross disciplinary insights and methodological guidelines on how to give equal weight to different types of assessments as well as related to considerations of how to undertake a number of assessments at similar points in time. Following Lee (2006, p. 58), integrated assessments cover three types of integration. These are:

- Vertical integration of assessments i.e. linking together separate impact assessments, which are undertaken at different strategic levels or stages in the policy, planning and project cycle; an example for this is the integration of assessments of construction materials, building products and single buildings in order to derive at an assessment of the national building stock (see for example, Kohler and Hassler, 2002; and Kohler and Lützkendorf, 2002).
- Horizontal integration of assessments i.e. bringing together different types of impacts – economic, environmental and social– into a single, overall assessment at one or more stages in the planning cycle. It may also involve horizontal co-ordination between contemporaneous assessments for separate, but inter-related, policy, planning and project cycles.
- Integration of assessments into decision-making i.e. integrating assessment findings into different decision-making stages.

Scrase and Sheate (2002) went even further and identified 14 different types of integration in the context of sustainability assessment (see Table 7). They argue that 'integration is a matter of value judgements concerning assessment design in specific historical and social contexts. Far from providing a panacea, integration would appear to create as many challenges as it might resolve in seeking to achieve more sustainable development' (Scrase and Sheate, 2002, p. 275).

Table 7: *Different forms of integration in sustainability assessment (adopted form Scrase and Sheate, 2002, p. 278)*

Meaning	Main focus
Integrated information sources	*Facts and data*
Integration of environmental concerns into governance	*Environmental values*
Vertically integrated planning and management	*Tiers of governance*
Integration across environmental media	*Air, land and water*
Integrated environmental management (regions)	*Ecosystems*
Integrated environmental management (production)	*Engineering systems*
Integration of business concerns into governance	*Capitalist values*
The environment, economy and society	*Development values*
Integration across policy domains	*Functions of governance*
Integrated environmental-economic modelling	*Computer modelling*
Integration of stakeholders into governance	*Participation*
Integration among assessment tools	*Methodologies and procedures*
Integration of equity concerns into governance	*Equity and socialist values*
Integration of assessment into governance	*Decision and policy context*

Also, indicator sets for integrated assessments have been developed. These can be found, for example, in Pope et al. (2004), Schmidt-Bleek (2004), and in Dalal-Clayton and Sadler (2004). In summary, there is a growing support for the use of integrated assessment approaches for policy-making and planning in order to promote sustainable development. 'However, delivering good quality [integrated assessments] in the near future will be challenging. [...] This is [due to] the potential gap between the kinds of contributions, which researchers and technical experts are making to the development of assessment methodologies, and the types of assessment methods that planning practitioners seem most able/willing to use' (Lee, 2006, p. 74). Yet, there is one fundamental question that remains unsolved and that is rarely addressed in sustainability assessment literature: how to ensure public participation? According to Pope et al. (2004, p. 608)

> *integrated assessments for sustainability need to 'allow society to define what is meant by 'sustainability' and then compare initiatives against this definition.'*

This view can also be found in Noël and O'Conner (1998) who stated that threshold levels chosen for critical natural capital should be both scientifically plausible and socially acceptable; thus, the selection of the levels of environmental functions to be sustained amount to a choice process that is as much political as technical in nature. In addition, Özkaynak et al. (2004, p. 292) argue that the operationalisation of the strong sustainability position 'must involve a wider socio-economic policy design, with the new challenge of combining scientific understanding with social values and responsibilities towards absent parties.' Following this logic would ultimately result in the application of Hume's (1751) theory of utility and agreeableness at the global scale. However, the challenges facing us today in order to realise this vision appear to be daunting.

Within the following sections of this dissertation, the overall concept of sustainable development, its principles and assessment methods will now be discussed with a focus on property and construction. This means that the overall concept and its principles will be translated and adjusted to the assessment object; i.e. buildings and associated plots of land, and to the areas of responsibility and action of individual actors; i.e. participants of the property and construction industry in general, and property investors and valuation professionals in particular.

2.4 Buildings and construction - the cornerstone of sustainability

2.4.1 Environmental, social and economic impacts

Within efforts undertaken by the global community to achieve sustainability, probably no industrial sector has as great a potential role as buildings and construction (UNEP, 2003; OECD, 2003 and Bakens, 2003). For this reason, buildings and the construction industry have been termed the *cornerstone of sustainability*. However, 'coming to grips with the building and construction sector and its many economic, environmental and social impacts can seem like wrestling with an octopus' (UNEP, 2003, p. 3). In addition, buildings can be viewed and assessed from a number of different perspectives; e.g. as an industry sector, as physical/material assets representing embodied resources, as a factor of production or investment vehicle, or as a provider of human needs like protection, identity and culture.

Estimates vary but it can be assumed that investment volume in new and existing buildings per annum is in Europe around US$ 1.2 trillion, in the USA around US$ 1.1 trillion and in Asia around US$ 0.9 trillion. Construction represents over 50% of national gross fixed capital formation in most countries. Investments in construction account for approximately 10 % of global GDP and 111 million people are directly employed within this sector (UNEP, 2003 and 2006; European Commission, 2004a). Furthermore, the share of the built environment in global resource use and pollution emission is immense: For example, in OECD countries the built environment is responsible for around 25-40% of total energy use, 30% of raw material use, 30-40% of global greenhouse gas emissions and for 30 to 40% of solid waste generation (OECD, 2003 and UNEP, 2006).

The environmental impact of the built environment is expected to grow rapidly. For example, in low-income OECD countries the share of unpaved roads is on the order of 71% and the share of population without sanitation amounts up to 25.4%; while in contrast, this share in high-income OECD countries is only 15.6% and 1.1% respectively (UNEP, 2003). As these low-income countries aspire achieving similar standards and 'if current patterns do not change, expansion of the built environment will destroy or disturb natural habitats and wild-life on over 70% of the Earth's land surface by 2032, driven mainly by increases in population, economic activity and urbanisation' (UNEP, 2003, p. 5).

Property investment decisions and the ways that buildings and the built environment are designed, constructed, operated, renovated and demolished significantly impact on the economic performance of towns, cities and regions and on the quality of life of urban and rural citizens because:

- almost 50 % of all humans live in cities, and this figure is expected to rise up to 60% by 2030; around 9% of the world's urban population – about 280 million people – currently live in megacities, and this figure is likely to rise to 350 million over the next ten years; approximately 80 % of Europe's citizens live in urban areas;
- people spend almost 90 % of their time inside buildings;
- the built environment represents a substantial and relatively stable resource. Most buildings survive for several decades, and very many survive for centuries; and
- buildings require spending between approximately 6.5% (for housing estates) and 30% (for schools and hospitals) of initial construction costs for repair and maintenance activities each year (OECD, 2003; Bruhns, 2003; European Commission, 2004b; Munich Re, 2005 and Porrit, 2006).

As a consequence, implementing the principles of sustainable development in the property and construction sector is of paramount importance for creating more sustainable communities and economies. This has been explicitly recognized by the European Commission, by many national governments around the world, as well as by many major international organisations that are capable of executing institutional power (e.g. by the United Nations, the Organisation for Economic Co-operation and Development, and the World Health Organisation). A huge responsibility exists for all those groups of actors who jointly shape and design the built environment; this is particularly true for institutions because of their traditional role in society. There is much room for both, reducing the property and construction sector's negative impacts and for dramatically increasing its positive effects. But the current global situation regarding sustainability in property and construction has been characterised by UNEP (2006) as follows[42]:

- Building practices are largely guided by short-term economic considerations.
- Legislation and building standards primarily refer to the technical function of buildings, while sustainability considerations are at best provided as voluntary guidelines, but are normally not taken into account at all.
- Environmental aspects, if considered, are often limited to the immediate problem in the construction phase, such as workplace waste management, while the functioning of the building is not considered.
- There is a lack of governmental policies and incentives supporting sustainable building practices.
- Investors, insurance companies, property developers and buyers / tenants of buildings are normally unaware of the long-term economic, social and environmental benefits of sustainable building practices.

Under such circumstances government policies are expected to play an important role (OECD, 2003). However, this is not yet completely recognized and accepted at all levels and areas of policy making. Buildings and associated construction and property markets fall within different sectors or areas of political and institutional responsibility (i.e. environment, economy, health and welfare) at global, national and local level. As a consequence, efforts to foster sustainable development in property and construction are sectoral and made by using many different instruments and measures. This does not always lead to satisfactory results.

2.4.2   Property as an asset class

The building and construction sector is not only the world's largest and most influential industry in terms of environmental, economic and social impact, the market on which buildings are traded also represents one of the world's largest investment markets. Property investment has become an increasingly important component of global mixed asset-portfolios and by the end of 2003 the total market value of the global investible property universe was estimated to be around US$ 6.2 trillion and thus, represented 14% of the global investment universe (see

---

[42] There are, however, many exceptions from this rather pessimistic appraisement. They will be analysed in more detail in the following chapters.

Figure 11). Cross-border property / real estate[43] investment has become a mainstream activity during the last decade; mainly due to diversification benefits, higher and more stable yields, the development and maturing of return benchmarks in a number of countries (such as the Investment Property Databank (IPD) Indices), the proliferation of REIT-structures, and the growth of non-listed investment vehicles (Chen and Mills, 2004).

Figure 11: *Global market capitalisation: US$ 43.8 trillion (based on Chen and Mills, 2004)*

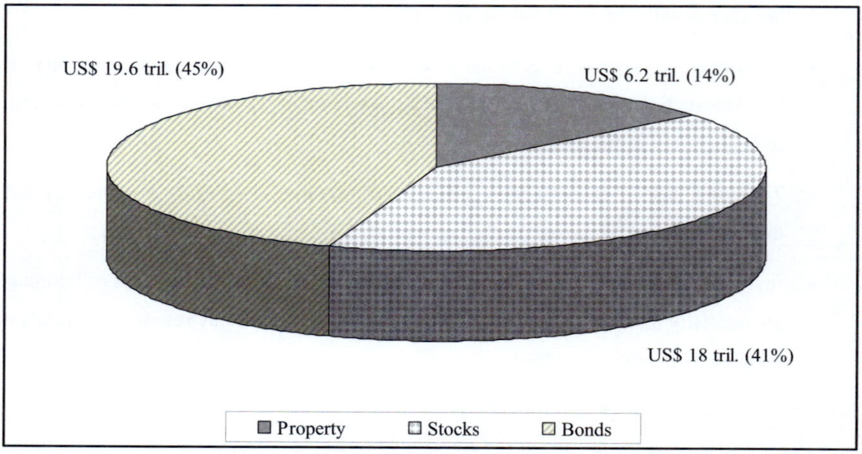

The amount of US$ 6.2 trillion roughly equals to the market capitalization of the stock exchanges of Europe or of the Asia-Pacific region and has even grown up to US$ 6.6 trillion by the end of 2004 (see Table 8). This figure is based on the estimated property market size in 26 core countries which have been considered suitable for property investment, based on a set of criteria including size of economy, level of economic prosperity, economic diversity, and political stability (Chen and Mills, 2006). The figures presented in Table 8 on the size of the property investment market in single countries must not be confused with the current values of the national building stock which is considerably higher. For example, in Germany alone the net value (at current replacement costs) of the national building stock has been estimated by the Federal Statistical Office to be on the order of € 5.9 trillion at the beginning of 2006, representing almost 90% of the net stock of fixed assets of the country. This figure is comprised of € 3.5 trillion for dwellings and € 2.4 trillion for other buildings and constructed assets.[44]

---

[43] The terms property and real estate are often used interchangeably; while the term property is more common in a UK context, the term real estate is preferred in the US. For the remainder of this dissertation the term property is used; except for those cases where a direct quote contains the term real estate.

[44] See: www.destatis.de/basis/e/vgr/vgrtab13.htm

Table 8: *Investment property market size by country in US$ billions*[45] *(based on Chen and Mills, 2006)*

Country	Property market size	Share of total market	Country	Property market size	Share of total market
United States	*2,612*	*39.5%*	*Singapore*	*94*	*1.4%*
Japan	*752*	*11.4%*	*Belgium*	*63*	*1.0%*
UK	*481*	*7.3%*	*Sweden*	*53*	*0.8%*
Germany	*453*	*6.9%*	*Austria*	*51*	*0.8%*
France	*360*	*5.4%*	*Switzerland*	*50*	*0.8%*
Italy	*306*	*4.6%*	*Greece*	*41*	*0.6%*
Canada	*219*	*3.3%*	*Norway*	*39*	*0.6%*
Spain	*188*	*2.8%*	*Denmark*	*34*	*0.5%*
South Korea	*182*	*2.8%*	*Portugal*	*34*	*0.5%*
Hong Kong	*150*	*2.3%*	*Ireland*	*31*	*0.5%*
Australia	*124*	*1.9%*	*Finland*	*30*	*0.5%*
Taiwan	*116*	*1.8%*	*Czech Republic*	*29*	*0.4%*
Netherlands	*98*	*1.5%*	*New Zealand*	*19*	*0.3%*
Total market size				**6,609**	*100.0%*

Property is now seen as a distinct asset class (as opposed to grouping property investments together with small cap stocks) since it fulfils the three key criteria for the designation of a separate asset class; these criteria are: sufficient market size, competitive risk-adjusted returns compared to other established asset classes such as stocks and bonds, and unique return characteristics. Property adequately meets these criteria since the market is deep enough to support a 10% or greater property allocation in an efficient mixed-asset portfolio, property has historically provided 4 to 6% average annual real rates of returns (i.e. net of inflation), the low volatility of property returns leads to competitive risk-adjusted performance over time, and property exhibits a very low correlation with other major asset classes (Chen and Mills, 2004). The latter argument can be supported with research undertaken by Sirmans and Worzala (2003) and by Worzala and Sirmans (2003) who reviewed research results and studies carried out during the past 20 years on this issue. They argued that international property investments (direct or indirect) improve the risk-return-ratio of any mixed-asset portfolio. Therefore, investors should not ignore this asset class when making asset allocation decisions. Hereby the optimum share of property assets within the portfolio appears to be between 10 and 20% (Sirmans and Worzola, 2003).

Despite the significant growth of property markets around the world – the growth in market capitalization of publicly traded property assets and REIT-structures has been quite dramatic: in 2005 alone the total free-float market capitalization of the FTSE EPRA/NAREIT global

---

[45] Chen and Mills (2006, p. 16-17) state that 'the estimation of real estate market size for any country remains largely a work of art. Even if an appraisal were performed on every property in the universe, almost inevitably appraisers would arrive at different values, and methodological differences in estimation can lead to varying results.'

listed real estate index rose by 27.5% from US$ 505 billion to US$ 644 billion – Chen and Mills (2006) believe that this has only been an early phase of a larger growth cycle. In order to underpin this assumption, they provide two arguments. (1) Property as a distinct asset class has only very recently begun to gather wider recognition from institutional and private investors worldwide; particularly large investors in emerging economies (e.g. China and India) as well as in Japan or in South Korea are expected to follow their European and American counterparts and start investing a substantial amount of capital in property (e.g. the average share of property assets contained within Japanese private pension funds is estimated to be less than 2%). (2) From the perspective of optimal asset allocation, many investors are significantly under-allocated (even in the US, many investors hope that the values of their actual property investments increases in order to match their allocation targets which are on the order of 10% or more). Chen and Mills (2006, p. 19) conclude that 'the breadth and depth of the global real estate investible universe are so substantial that it is likely to take several more years before we should start to be concerned about oversupply of private investment vehicles, especially those that are structured to invest on a global basis, or become concerned about saturation of public real estate markets.'

Given the current size of the property investment market and the prospects for further growth, it is, indeed, worrying that sustainability issues are completely missing on most property investment agendas. Apparently, the property investment sector is not yet fully aware of the potential contribution it can make for achieving more sustainable development. The contribution could be a powerful one and would not only result in major environmental release but also in a win-win situation for all stakeholders involved. The economic benefits – in terms of improved short- and long-term cash-flow – as well as the risk reduction potential and the social gains of sustainable buildings can be immense (see Section 3.3.1). Unfortunately, there are very few indirect property investment options (such as sustainable property funds or REITs) available that offer investors the opportunity to invest in environmentally and socially friendly buildings. In contrast to the stock market, no rating agencies or indexes track the environmental and social performance of property investment vehicles, no guidelines for sustainable property investing are available to the public, and the development of appropriate investment strategies is, at best, in an emerging stage. In summary, the issue of sustainability in property investing has been addressed in theory (see: McNamara, 2002; Sayce et al., 2004a and 2004b; Lorenz and Lützkendorf, 2004; McNamara, 2005a; Pivo and McNamara, 2005; RICS, 2005; Lützkendorf and Lorenz, 2005; and Lützkendorf et al., 2006) but its practical evidence is very limited and sustainable property investing is far from being a stream and even less a mainstream. However, there are exceptions which are worthwhile mentioning here; some of the pioneers in sustainable property investing and management are listed in Table 9.

Table 9: *Pioneers in sustainable property investing and management*[46]

Company name, country	Est. size of property portfolio	Explanation
Hermes, UK	£8bn	*Hermes is an institutional fund management company. It operates on behalf of over 230 clients including pension funds, insurance companies, government entities and financial institutions, as well as charities and endowments. Hermes published and adopted a set of responsible property investment principles in February 2006[47]. The principles serve as an operational framework against which the company's fund managers can measure performance. This is unique in the property investment sector. http://www.hermes.co.uk/*
Wereldhave, NL	€2.3bn	*Wereldhave is a property company with an internationally diversified property portfolio in Europe and the United States. Wereldhave attaches great importance to construction and management measures which lower total costs and raise tenant flexibility, whilst simultaneously relieving pressure on the environment. http://www.wereldhave.nl/*
British Land, UK	£14.6bn	*Investors in UK property, focused on managing, financing and developing prime commercial property. Britsh Land has adopted a Corporate Responsibility Policy that requires the company, amongst other issues, to take a property's environmental and social performance aspects into account when deciding to buy or sell a particular asset. http://www.britishland.com/crhandbook/*
Land Securities, UK	£11bn	*The company owns and manages over 7 million m^2 of commercial property space and provides property services to more than 2,500 private and public sector clients. The company strives to minimise any harm caused to the environment and to meet best practice in non-regulated areas; e.g., integrating biodiversity considerations into its activities, working in partnership with clients, agents, contractors and other suppliers. http://www.landsecurities.co.uk/ls03.asp?PageID=204*
Prudential Property Investment Managers, UK	£17.2bn	*With over £17.2bn invested in the UK property market and overseas, PruPIM is responsible for nearly 1,000 properties. The company has made a strong commitment to Corporate Responsibility and has recently stated that 'We will take actions that lessen the environmental and social impact of our properties without detracting from investment performance.' http://www.prupim.com/documents/7a_Factsheet.pdf*
Rose Smart Growth Investors, US	$0.1bn	*The company is an affiliate of the Jonathan Rose Companies, a New York based network of planning and development firms, whose mission is to repair the fabric of cities, towns and villages, while preserving the land around them. In April 2006 the company launched the Rose Smart Growth Investment Fund. The fund is investing in a diverse pool of environmentally and socially responsible real estate. http://www.rose-network.com/*
Klépierre, F	€7.4bn	*Klépierre is a real estate specialist focused on the two segments of the commercial property market: shopping centres and office properties. Amongst other issues, Klépierre seeks for property investments that preserve the environment and support local communities. http://www.klepierre.com*
Mitsubishi Estate, JP	not known	*Mitsubishi Estate is listed on the Tokyo Stock Exchange. With a core activity in property development, the Mitsubishi Estate Group considers protection of the global environment as a cornerstone of its efforts to fulfil its corporate social responsibility. http://www.mec.co.jp/e/group/investor/annual/pdf/ar2005_e.pdf*

---

[46] This list is neither complete nor exhaustive. The author is thankful for any suggestions that help extending and updating the list of pioneers in sustainable property investing and management.

[47] The document entitled *Responsible Property Investment – defining the challenge* can be downloaded here: http://www.hermes.co.uk/real_estate/real_estate_rpi_challenges.htm

CalSTRS, US	$8.6bn	*CalSTRS is the third-largest public pension fund in the United States, with a current market value of $115 billion. CalSTRS has set up a Clean Technology Advisory Board to develop responsible and environmentally friendly investment and asset management strategies. The fund has recently built a new headquarters equipped with various sustainable design features.* http://www.calstrs.com/newsroom/archive/news102104.aspx
CalPERS, US	$9.3bn	*CalPERS is the largest public pension fund in US with assets totalling $207.1 billion as of February 28, 2006. CalPERS investments span domestic and international markets. Their property investment strategy is focussed on generating attractive investment returns while adopting environmental and green building technologies. CalPERS has set an energy reduction goal of 20 percent in its core property portfolio over the next five years.* http://www.calpers.ca.gov/
VicSuper, AU	*not known*	*VicSuper Fund is one of Australia's largest public offer superannuation funds with over 207,000 members and $4.2 billion in assets. VicSuper also invests in property and has set up sustainable investing and corporate governance policies.* http://www.vicsuper.com.au/www/html/157-vicsuper-investments.asp

2.4.3   Challenging the actors of property and construction markets

Given the significance of the built environment and the huge potential of contributing to sustainable development, it can be argued that concerted and carefully coordinated approaches that involve major groups of stakeholders are required. The principles of sustainable development need to be translated or operationalised to the areas of responsibility of the different actors concerned. However, the multitude of activities with relevance for the property and construction sector reflects the complex nature of buildings and of property markets which involve a huge number of social, political, economic and physical factors, impacts and processes as well as many different groups of actors, each group with different motivations, goals and perceptions.

Concerning the variety of actors in property and construction markets a 'top-down approach' can be observed on the one hand; this approach is imposed by the European Commission and other multinational organisation consisting of a number of guidelines, directives and initiatives. Furthermore, certain states have adopted a national strategy on sustainable development by creating and introducing national codes of best practice, legislation and programmes in order to support sustainable development in property construction. On the other hand, a 'bottom-up approach' can be observed which is driven by a group of academics, practitioners and others. The tension between these two approaches involves the process of understanding existing barriers and why certain actions need to be taken. Furthermore, it can be argued that the success of implementing principles of sustainable development in the property and construction sector strongly depends on the progress made with respect to several dimensions. The first is a cultural / ethical one of getting sustainability issues accepted and incorporated within the built environment (this involves clients, policy makers, financial institutions, users, practitioners, etc.). The second dimension is a more technical one of understanding how sustainability issues relate to a set of specific circumstances; (i.e. the business and economic environment, the legacy of the existing building stock, social values and aspirations, environmental damage and human well-being, etc). This is an urgent issue since over-reliance on free market forces within this particular economic sector can lead to aberrations which are very difficult to remediate; this is mainly due to the long-term impacts of building- and construction-related decisions (Lorenz et al., 2005). In order to better understand both existing barriers concerning different groups of actors as well as actions required in order to make change easy, the EU Expert Working Group Sustainable Construction Methods & Techniques (2004) has identified five clusters of relevant property and construction markets' participants and proposed a variety of recommendations for each group of actors. The five clusters are: (1) ownership-related actors, (2), production-related actors, (3) policy-related actors, (4) market-related actors, and (5) finance-related actors. The following Table 10 is based on the EU Expert Working Groups' publications (particularly on Annex 1 (pp. 3-26) of the final report); however a sixth cluster of actors – design and consultancy – has been formed in order to pinpoint the importance of this group of actors. Further modifications, extensions and omissions have been made wherever regarded appropriate.

Table 10: *Challenges for actors of property and construction markets (based on EU Expert Working Group Sustainable Construction Methods & Techniques, 2004)*

Clusters	Major barriers	Main recommendations
Ownership *- Property management companies*	*Cost-reduction potential of managing buildings in a sustainable way is not fully understood*	*Incentives for efficient operation and maintenance could be created through tax reductions*
	These companies can represent one more bureaucracy filter for information *When managing several properties, a single solution could be chosen without making the effort of adapting it to each specific / local situation*	*Enhancing staff's capability (through education and training) to interpret early symptoms of future failures in buildings; and adoption of preventive property management approaches* *Increased monitoring, benchmarking and communication of building performance*
- Owners and Investors (not end-users)	*Unawareness of buildings' key performance characteristics* *Limited incentives for choosing sustainable buildings since running costs are usually paid by end-users* *Believe in the myth that sustainable construction is more expensive* *Limited motivation to cut future maintenance costs since these are discounted*	*Various incentives could be created by other actors; including CO_2-credits, tax incentives, preferential insurance and financing conditions* *Targeting this actor by education and awareness raising campaigns* *Adoption of life-cycle-cost approaches* *Changing the current contractual tradition; i.e. sharing running costs between owners and end-users*

Design and consultancy		
- Design team	In professional education, sustainability is, generally a vertical subject, making the approach to sustainability and isolated rather than an integrated one	Other actors can reward and encourage design teams to produce more sustainable solutions
	Lack of integration within the design team	Increasing the capacity of the design team to work together from an early design stage
	Guidelines for architects and technical engineers for making sustainable choices are not yet easily accessible for all	Create awareness that the environmental, social and economic performance of the building is no less important than the mere aesthetic result
	Clients' perception of sustainable construction as more expensive can limit the scope of measures, techniques and components the specialists are permitted to implement	Create and adopt design tools that allow for a combined assessment of design solutions, life-cycle-costs, and life-cycle impacts on the environment
	Incorporating new solutions may require more design time	Full integration of sustainability issues into all aspects of architects' and engineers' education and training
	When a design does not incorporate the state of the art in sustainable construction it is often a '100 year missed' opportunity	Integration of post-occupancy evaluation and monitoring into the project in order to provide the design team with feedback from the later stage of occupation
	Adoption of design approaches that aim improving environmental performance rather than adopting cradle-to-cradle or closed-loop solutions	
- Property agents, valuers, advisors and analysts	Information on buildings' key performance characteristics are usually unavailable	Other actors could ask for real building performance data
	Unawareness of the positive effects of sustainable buildings	Awareness raising and training programmes
		Development and publication of guidelines on how to address sustainability issues in property valuation and investment analysis processes

Production		
- Developers and contractors	Initial changes in the building brief and the processes required to achieve more sustainable construction represent an added risk; no incentives available to compensate for this perceived risk	Various incentives could be created by other actors: performance-based building regulations, tax incentives, preferential insurance and financing conditions, faster granting of building permissions, increased responsibility for building performance documentation
	Poorly informed developers and constructors believe in the myth that sustainable construction is more expensive	Provision of extensive user manuals explaining to end-users how to make the most of the comfort, systems and services the building can offer
	No clear advantage to invest in the long-term quality of the building	
	Authorities involved in the granting of building permissions are largely unable to recognise the added value of more sustainable construction	Awareness raising and training; particularly concerning the best available construction methods and techniques
- Manufacturers	Low rate of recovery from demolitions' waste due to a lack of separation of materials via planned deconstruction as opposed to 'ball-and-chain' type demolition. Deconstruction is viewed by many as uneconomic and its adoption is slow	Voluntary agreements between governments and industry on reducing construction and demolition waste that goes to landfills
	No widespread use of Environmental Product Declarations (EPDs)	Tax reduction for research and development on sustainable construction products
		Performance-based design and construction require information on the perform-

| | | *ance of different building components and on how these are produces; thus, it is necessary to increase the manufacturers' responsibility for the information required; i.e. EPDs* |
| | | *User manuals should accompany materials and building components in order to encourage good practice in use* |

Policy

- Urban planners	*Values and indicators that classify the quality of the built environment are neither consensual nor widely available*	*Other actors must define sets of sustainability indicators which can be adapted to each different local context (including thresholds and integrated objectives for quality of life)*
	The objectives of sustainable urban planning are unclear	*Increase people's participation*
	Urban planning is focused on 'what not do do' rather than on defining targets and goals for the qualitative performance of the built environment	*A common language needs to be established*
	When urban planning does not incorporate the appropriate flexibility for implementing more sustainable construction, it is a missed opportunity for improving the quality of life of many generations	*Building physics and the performance of the built environment need to become part of the know-how of urban planners* *Integration and harmonisation of existing planning and assessment tools and development of tools in areas where there are none in existence*
- Governments, municipalities and local authorities	*Links between the environment and the economy are unclear*	*Send a clear top down message through incentives and through positive as well as penalty tax tools*
	Lack of international co-operation relating to sustainability in the property and construction sector	*Adopt responsibility by quantifying clear targets for CO_2-reduction, etc. and set building performance targets which then can be transformed into incentives*
	Insufficient effort of the public sector to set an example in public building projects; this sends a negative top-down message to the market	*Encourage other actors (such as banks and insurance companies) to provide respective incentives as well*
	Building regulations in some countries are very prescriptive; this creates severe constraints to the design team's creative role	*Link the granting of building permissions with sustainability considerations*
	The technical working team in governments and municipalities is not always willing to implement change	*Set an example through public buildings* *Integrate impact assessments in the property and construction-related policy-making process*
	Often the role of preservation of the quality of the built environment is a barrier for implementing sustainable construction in refurbishment	*Create an agency for the promotion of sustainable construction*
	Tools for sustainable urban design and management are available but not sufficiently harmonised and don't cover all relevant areas resulting in the fact that they are therefore not generally used	*Create observatories which will monitor the meeting of environmental commitments and of the established targets; make sure that the information flows to the actors that need to work towards achieving these targets*
	Nobody is held liable for indoor air quality; it has not yet been possible to create an institutional connection between indoor air quality and peoples' health which has far reaching cost-implications for the health care systems	*Provide sustainability in building codes and technical regulations, focussing on performance rather than on prescriptive rules* *Define acceptable thresholds for indoor air quality; then transform the costs of ill-health into a penalty tax for buildings that prove to have low indoor air quality*

- Inter-governmental institutions	*The top-down messages arriving at national states and multinational organisations (e.g. banks, utility suppliers, insurance companies) is unclear about moving towards sustainability; thus, there is no collaboration of these very influential actors. For these institutions there is no clear connection between their responsibilities in every day practice and the environment and public well-being*	*Stricter and quantified results must be required from single states if any considerable improvements in the performance of buildings are to be expected*
	A lack of co-ordination causes redundancies, gaps and incoherence in different laws and does not promote synergies	*A common assessment methodology for buildings needs to established, which can then be adapted to the specific cultural and climatic reality of each single state* *Facilitate better co-ordination and co-operation*
	A lack of commercial and technical systems to ensure the availability of materials, products, tools and standards to categorise them (e.g. labelling and rating systems) in order to create conditions to kick start a genuine market for more sustainable construction	*Create an observatory (on European and international level) to monitor the performance of the property and construction sector; then disseminate its findings to the key actors involved (i.e. provide feedback)* *Set up more funding for research relating to sustainability in property and construction*

Market

- Occupiers	*Issues of comfort, health and energy consumption are easy to understand since they have an expression in daily life; but the message of long-term targets (such as CO2-emission levels or ecological footprint limits) has not yet reached the end-user*	*Other actors can make the end-user aware of the benefits and responsible for the correct use of buildings*
	Lack of knowledge on how to improve building performance	*Promote awareness raising and education programmes*
	Lack of interest to use buildings efficiently since the benefits are not clear enough	*Install adequate procedures for feedback from and to the end-users*
	Complexity and user-unfriendliness of modern, technical building systems can hamper efficient and effective use of buildings	*Focus on constructive improvements of the built environment by defining a set of occupier-specific indicators and targets*
	Lack of pro-activity and participation in public decision-making processes makes the adopted solutions less tailored for the end-user	
	Due to a lack of knowledge and awareness, the specific contributions to the public decision-making processes are not always adequate, nor in the interest of future generations or absent parties	
- Researchers and teachers	*On the one hand, the academic sector can be far removed from the day to day reality of the business world; therefore, there may be no clear message as to the relevant tendencies to follow.*	*Indicators and tools for sustainable construction need to be further developed and construction- related databases need to be harmonised*
	On the other hand, the rigorous analysis of the academy may find little sympathy in a marketplace distorted by unequal competition and other failures	*Sustainability should be a topic addressed at all levels of education, reaching across all subject areas; raising awareness to form a more sustainable attitude should also be included in primary and secondary education: the younger the child, the more open the mind is to take into consideration alternative patterns of behaviour*
	Lack of both resources and co-ordination of existing information	
	Lack of dissemination of research results; this hampers the creation of an advance	*Universities should include sustainability as a horizontal theme in all the disciplines*

	platform for future sustainability research	*in order to allow the professionals to internalise sustainability as a permanent, holistic and integrating process*
	Sustainability issues are not yet fully integrated and are taught as a vertical subject	*Universities should encourage multi-thematic and multi-disciplinary approaches in education and life-long learning of professionals*
		A lot of information exists from previous research. This information needs to be made available in a way that is attractive to the actor that benefits from it; re-packaging and marketing existing information is one way to make the investment in research worthwhile
- Property index and data providers	*Lack of awareness that many actors could greatly benefit from an inclusion of environmental and social building performance data in existing property indexes and databases*	*Benchmarks and greater availability of building performance data are of vital importance for informed decision making and for more rigorous property investment analyses. Therefore, existing indexes should be extended and new ones should be created*
- Media	*The complex interrelations between the environment, society and the property and construction sector are difficult communicate*	*The media message can change the value given to sustainability by making sustainability issues 'fashionable' and by disseminating sustainability indicators and targets as well as examples of good practice*
	Too much information versus little 'technical' knowledge in these areas	*Other actors can raise awareness of the local media through information, education and training*
	The general public is stimulated by the media to give more importance to life-style and design than to sustainability issues, especially because sustainability issues are perceived to be not 'fashionable'	*Campaigns to increase public awareness for sustainability issues should be part of the obligations of the global media*

Finance

- Banks and mortgage institutions	*Ignorance and unawareness of the need for sustainable construction (e.g. the vast majority of banks does not distinguish between sustainable buildings and unsustainable ones when approving a mortgage)*	*Banks and mortgage institutions should be made co-responsible for the potential building performance failures and their negative impact on the environment*
	Unawareness of the risk-reduction potential of sustainable buildings; no link has yet been established between environmental and social building performance and the probability of default of property loans	*The interest rates for sustainable buildings and construction projects should be lower, reflecting the reduced probability of default (e.g. lower running costs provide the owner with more flexibility to repay his mortgage completely and in time)*
		Banks should send out information on the positive effects of sustainable construction in order to increase motivation among their clients
- Insurance companies	*In the traditional construction process, the way in which liability is insured tends not to encourage innovation nor improvement of sustainability in construction*	*Insurance companies should distinguish between sustainable buildings and unsustainable ones; this should be reflected in the pricing of existing insurance services and through the development of new insurance products that foster more sustainable construction*
	The majority of insurance companies is completely unaware of the added value of more sustainable construction and of its risk-reduction potential	*National administrations, public awarding authorities as well as private clients and*
	Lack of holistic perspectives: it has not yet	

been recognised that the property and construction sector can contribute to major environmental release; this can reduce both extent and likelihood of natural disasters like flooding which in return can reduce the costs of such events for the insurance sector. Such considerations are not yet included in the pricing of insurance services for the property and construction sector	*their advisors should be made aware of the advantages of single point liability insurance arrangements* *Insurance companies should be encouraged to play a significant role in promoting the introduction and widespread use of single point liability insurance policies*

What becomes clear from the enumeration of the various barriers and recommendation contained in Table 10 is, that organising change in the property and construction sector will not be an easy matter. Realising these recommendation would mean changing the rules of the property game; it would mean installing loops of feedback and adaptation; it would mean changing the ways of negotiating and concluding contractual arrangements; it would mean creating new professions and institutions; and it would even mean changing the ways children's are educated at school in order to help them better understand the built environment.

The EU Expert Working Group Sustainable Construction Methods & Techniques (2004, p. 8) stated that 'although the scope and intensity of the barriers is as far-reaching as the impact of the construction sector on our society, they can be collectively and individually addressed and overcome.' In order to achieve this and to reveal the property and construction sector's powerful contribution to a more sustainable society, to fundamental keys have been identified. The first key is information, the second one is trust.

The role of information: Feedback loops and adaptation to changing conditions works only if there is a sufficient amount of information available (see Holling, 2001 and Kiuchi, 2005). Thus, the role of information is a fundamental one; in nature, society and economy. The role of information in the global economy has been examined in detail by Manuel Castells in his trilogy 'The Information Age: Economy, Society and Culture' (Castells, 1996, 1997a and 1997b). Castells argued that the global economy is undergoing major changes caused by a myriad of socio-cultural, technological and political transformations around the world. Castells explained that a new form of capitalism or economic environment – he called it an 'informational economy' – has emerged at the end of the last century: global in its character, hardened in its goals and much more flexible than any of its predecessors. The economy is informational because the sources of productivity and the competitiveness of its central actors (corporations, regions and nations) depend, more than ever, on knowledge and information and on the technology of their processing, including the technology of management and the management of technology (Castells, 1996). This is particularly true for the actors of property and construction markets. Information and feedback are not only essential to motivate more sustainable behaviour; they are also the essence of financial success in global property and construction markets. For example, investors and their professional advisors are now forced to analyse and evaluate various aspects of building performance and the attractiveness of a particular location in great detail while they are simultaneously required to take into account a variety of complex institutional influences and externalities at global, regional and national level (Seabrook et al., 2004; Lorenz and Lützkendorf, 2005a). The mere amount of information and data which has to be generated, analyzed and processed in order to provide adequate feedback is enormous and requires powerful analytical tools and information systems. As a consequence, progress towards a more sustainable – and thus, financially sound – property and construction sector strongly depends upon knowledge and on the capabilities and sophistication to assess, interpret and understand the increasing complexity of factors from diverse sources of property-related information.

The role of trust: There remains a great lack of information in property and construction markets. Appropriate benchmarks for the variety of important aspects of a building's performance simply do not yet exist and reliable sources of building-related information such as building files which could flow between the various actors involved and which could be used as a basis for informed decision making are not yet widely available. If construction companies, investors or occupiers know nothing or very little about the real performance of the buildings they construct, buy, use and operate, i.e. if they are cut off from feedback, these buildings cannot be improved systematically in pursuit of both individual and collective well-being. In addition, uninformed decision-making leads to adverse selection and finally to a loss in the quality of buildings that are offered in the marketplace (Lützkendorf and Speer, 2005). Also, within property markets certain factors not only make it difficult to obtain up-to-date information but lead to transaction costs being relative high (Harvey, 2000). For example, millions are spent for costly due diligence processes in order to gain information assurance within the scope of large-scale property transactions.

Confronted with the absence of reliable and easily accessible information, actors of property and construction markets need to trust each other. Their success depends as much on information as it depends on integrity, intact inter-human connections, social networks, agreeable behaviour. Actors in property and construction markets operate in a permanent prisoners' dilemma. For example, investors need to trust their professional advisors and asset managers that they will assist them in making beneficial decisions, that they will take good care of the buildings they own and that they do not act in favour of their own, short-term financial interests; developers and awarding authorities need to trust the designers, contractors and project managers that they will deliver good value for money; private and commercial end-users need to trust their estate agents that they will deliver reliable and useful information on the buildings or premises they wish to buy or occupy; fund managers, banks, insurance companies, accountants and many other actors such as national financial supervisory authorities need to trust the property valuers that they will deliver useful estimates of a building's market value. Put simply, if actors in property and construction markets cannot trust each other, then there is substantial loss of performance and waste of resources. But actors in property and construction markets can escape the prisoners' dilemma by willingly pursuing the interests of the group in addition to pursuing their own interests. For this reason, buildings and associated markets are not only the cornerstone of sustainability, property and construction markets are also the ideal 'test-filed' to see if a vision of a sustainable society that is grounded on moral principles could work out in practice.

3. A survey of the development towards sustainable property markets

3.1   Introduction

Due to the property and construction sectors' many environmental, social and economic impacts, the markets on which buildings or other real property rights are traded and construction activity takes place are incredibly complex.[48] They are shaped by a relatively high degree of governmental regulation and intervention as well as by a variety of other strong institutional influences or external forces such as banks' and insurance companies' financing and insurance polices. Property markets reveal different conventions and practices depending on both the types of property being traded or constructed and the regional or local cultural and climatic context. For example, due to historical reasons nearly every country or region has its own codes, guidelines or habits concerned with the measurement of building specifications, land, rent, etc., whether for planning, taxation, sale and letting, property valuation or other purposes.[49] Furthermore, construction techniques vary significantly between different climatic regions and a particular building solution may be sustainable in one area while inappropriate in another.

The term *real property* refers to a particular type of good – land or resources embodied in land. Neither is physically movable. This characteristic distinguishes it from other goods and explains why it is actually the property rights which are dealt with; land or buildings simply cannot be handed over in the same way as movable goods. But what is *the property market*? Modern economies are often described as 'exchange economies'. In exchange economies people do not only produce directly for their own wants, but specialise in production in order to increase total output. Consequently, both factors of production and final products are exchanged. Exchange takes place because buyers and sellers benefit from it. In order to exchange factors of production and final products, buyers and sellers must be put in touch with one another. Any arrangement for doing this can be described as 'a market'. Exchanges take place on the basis of prices determined in the market by the interaction of supply and demand. Therefore, the property market is the arrangement by which buyers and sellers of land, build-

---

[48] In the following, the term *property market* is used as an umbrella term for both exchange of factors of production and final products. Thus, the construction market is considered as one of the property market's submarkets. Although the construction market reveals a range of industry-specific particularities and mechanisms which cannot be reviewed here in detail, it can be argued that the construction market and its practices are mainly driven and determined by excesses of supply or demand and the prevailing preferences in the wider property market.

[49] For instance, the value of land in India may be quoted at a price per ground, which is a unit of 223 square metres; in Japan traditional units are sometimes used instead of square metres such as a *tsubo* which is equal to 3.3 square metres while in contrast in El Salvador, land is measured in terms of the square *vara* which is equal to 0.6984 square metres (Mackmin, 1999).

ings or any other forms of property rights are brought together to determine a price at which the particular property right can be exchanged. In other words, *the property market* is an abstract term aggregating all transactions in real property throughout a given local area, country or region (Harvey, 2000).

However, the mechanisms and the 'anatomy' of property transactions are much more complicated than for most other classes of goods and services. Property transactions function according to a variety of rules (imposed by governments, financial institutions, professional bodies, etc.), conventions, social norms, customs and practices, sometimes referred to collectively as 'rules regime' or 'rules of the game' which are often taken for granted by investors or their professional advisors when appraising value or advising on investment decisions in familiar markets. However, property investment analyses – particularly concerning investments in foreign markets – can require mapping information deficits and constructing profiles of potential opportunities and threats by addressing several key questions that arise for any given transaction (Seabrook et al., 2004, p. 45):

- Which rules regimes apply?
- What is the relative influence or impact of a given rule regime?
- What is the nature of the institutional arrangements that arise from relevant rule regimes?
- To what extent should they be reflected in the terms of the transaction?

A detailed investigation of the rules of the 'property game' and of the extent to which these rules are currently being changed in order to respond to the need of more sustainable development would lead beyond purpose and scope of this dissertation. However, major developments and tendencies (at the global and European level) in areas that are likely to direct and guide the property market on a more sustainable course will be reviewed in the next chapter. The areas that are likely to further promote the so-called 'business case' for more sustainable development in property and construction are:

- Governmental policy and legislation (Section 3.2.1);
- Consumer behaviour (Section 3.2.2);
- Investment, corporate governance and accounting practices (Section 3.2.3);
- Banking practices (Section 3.2.4); and
- Insurance practices (Section 3.2.5).

The analysis of these external forces is followed by an investigation of the major successes and failures in achieving sustainability within the property and construction sector itself. It is argued that the knowledge and the technology necessary to produce sustainable buildings is available and that the economic benefits of sustainable construction are described in the literature but that the production of sustainable buildings and the mainstreaming of sustainable construction and property investment practices is still hampered by a so-called 'vicious circle of blame'. However, according to David Pearce (2005, p. 481) the property and construction industry 'can be forgiven if it struggles to take sustainable development, or sustainability, on board since there is a shortage of sound guidance on just what the concept means [for property and construction] and what the industry would have to do to achieve it.' For this reason, the constituents of and requirements for sustainable buildings are deduced in Section 3.3.2 and a framework for measuring sustainability performance along the life-cycle of buildings is introduced. Finally, Section 3.4 contains a framework for sustainable property investment based on the concept and the principles of sustainable development.

3.2   The business case for more sustainable development in property markets

3.2.1   Governmental policy and legislation

In most developed countries, a variety of governmental initiatives and programmes are being implemented to provide sustainable development within planning, construction, management, refurbishment and demolition of buildings. This includes the introduction of performance-based building regulations which are now in use or under development in numerous countries worldwide, the introduction of building related energy efficiency codes as well as the use of economic instruments such as subsidy programmes, heavier fiscal burdens for unsustainable construction and tax credit schemes in order to create more sustainable property markets (e.g. first experiences are made in the EU, the United States, Canada, Japan and Australia). For an overview on these activities see DCAT (2001); Beyer (2002); OECD (2003); Drouet (2003) and Meacham et al. (2005). Even in Russia efforts are made to implement regional and federal building energy performance codes (Matrosov et al., 2003). Furthermore, governments start introducing guidelines for sustainable building which bring together best practice in a measurable way and which will raise standards over time. First examples can be observed in the UK and in Germany; see Sustainable Buildings Task Group (2004) and Federal Ministry of Transport, Building and Housing (2001).

Countries that exhibited a traditionally high degree of state involvement are now facing pressure to deregulate markets by reducing the number and scope of laws and regulations. But deregulation implies the need to strengthen market actors' capacity for responsibility. This in return requires that actors are vested with appropriate information and decision support. For this reason a trends towards strengthening consumer rights can be observed in Europe. The aim of recent EU legislation is to safeguard consumers by providing them with information and thereby allow more responsible and informed decisions. This is to overcome information asymmetries and the interconnected problems of adverse selection. An example of this is the introduction of energy performance certificates. From 2006 onwards, these certificates are required for each building that is constructed, sold or rented (European Commission, 2002). It is obvious that this directive will have a significant impact on the EU property market (e.g. tenants will be able to compare buildings on that basis) and even the Royal Institution of Chartered Surveyors (RICS), UK's major valuation organisation, reported that the energy efficiency directive is likely to have influence on property values and building design, renovation and investment decisions (RICS, 2003a). The certificate shall be clearly displayed in public buildings over 1,000 m² and shall be issued for all buildings on completion or whenever there is a change of owner or tenant. The certificate shall include references to the building's current energy performance[50], to current legal minimum standards and benchmarks regarding energy performance as well as accompanying recommendations on how the building can be cost-effectively improved to meet these standards if necessary (European Commission, 2002, Article 7).

Furthermore, within the scope of 'the thematic strategy on the urban environment', the European Commission has explicitly expressed its future strategy in order to achieve an area-wide implementation of the principles of sustainable development in the property and construction sector (European Commission, 2004b). An analysis of this strategic document leads to the assumption that forthcoming EU legislation will require building owners, construction project developers and other market participants to gather and process an even wider array of building-related information and data, for example on the building's life cycle costs, environmental performance and on characteristics and attributes related to occupants' health and safety. In summary, it can be assumed that the EU is striving towards what can be called an 'integrated building performance certification approach' (see Figure 12 and Box 8).

---

[50] The energy performance of a building is defined as 'the amount of energy actually consumed or estimated to meet the different needs associated with a standardised use of the building, which may include, *inter alia*, heating, hot water heating, cooling, ventilation and lighting. This amount shall be reflected in one or more numeric indicators which have been calculated, taking into account insulation, technical and installation characteristics, design and positioning in relation to climatic aspects, solar exposure and influence of neighbouring structures, own-energy generation and other factors, including indoor climate, that influence the energy demand' (European Commission, 2002, Article 2).

Figure 12: *From energy performance to integrated building performance certification (Lorenz et al., 2005)*

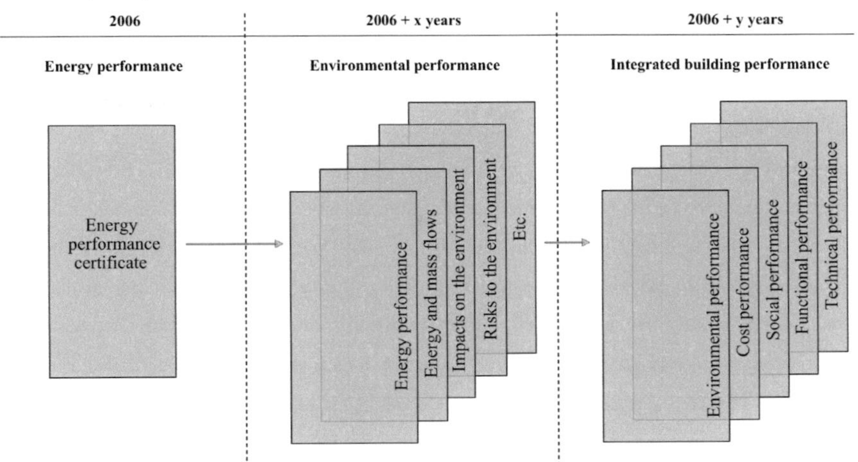

A shift in numerous countries' legal frameworks towards requiring more sustainable practices can not only be observed with regard to the property and construction sector but also concerning the wider business environment. An overview on recent legislative developments (until September 2002) concerning sustainability reporting and transparency requirements can be found in Loew (2002). A more recent and far reaching legislative act is the EU accounts modernisation directive which came into effect in June 2003 (European Commission, 2003). The directive requires that corporate accounts include (from January 2005 onwards) an analysis of environmental and social aspects necessary for an understanding of the company's development, performance or position wherever this is appropriate (see Box 8). Such legislative acts represent a response to the fact that corporations tend to externalize as high a proportion of costs as they are legally permitted to do (Porritt, 2006). The reason for this behavioural tendency lies in the legal status of corporations and in their fiduciary duties to shareholders. Bakan (2004) described the modern corporation as an 'externalizing machine' and argued that corporations are literally bound to maximise profit for shareholders as long as it stays within the law:

> *The corporation can neither recognize nor act upon moral reasons to refrain from harming others. Nothing in its legal makeup limits what it can do to others in pursuit of its selfish ends, and it is compelled to cause harm where the benefits of doing so outweigh the costs. Only pragmatic concern for its own interests in the laws of the land constrain the corporation's predatory instincts, and often that is not enough to stop it from destroying lives, damaging communities*

and endangering the planet as a whole. These tend to be viewed as inevitable and acceptable consequences of corporate activity – 'externalities' in the coolly technical jargon of economics' (Bakan, 2004, cited in Porritt, 2006, p. 72).

This pinpoints the importance of proper company law and governmental regulation – despite all those calls for deregulation and more liberalization of markets. Furthermore, the same or even stronger behavioural tendency to disregard externalities and to maximise profit for beneficiaries or shareholders as long as its stays within the law applies for institutional investors. For this reason, certain countries (including Australia, France, Germany, Italy, and the UK) have legislation in place (or are expected to do so shortly) to require investment decision-makers, particularly in the pensions context, to disclose the extent to which they take environmental, social and governance (ESG) considerations into account. This finding is one of the results of a recent study commissioned and published by UNEP FI (2005) in order to investigate if the integration of ESG issues into investment policy (including asset allocation, portfolio construction and stock-picking or bond-picking) is voluntarily permitted, legally required or hampered by law and regulation. The study covered the jurisdictions of the following regions or countries: Australia, Canada, EU, France, Germany, Italy, Japan, Spain, the UK, and the US. The study's authors confirm that the links between ESG factors and financial performance are increasingly being recognised and state that:

> *'In our view, decision-makers are required to have regard (at some level) to ESG considerations in every decision they make. This is because there is a body of credible evidence demonstrating that such considerations often have a role to play in the proper analysis of investment value. As such they cannot be ignored, because doing so may result in investments being given an inappropriate value' (UNEP FI, 2005, p. 10-11).*

Regarding the jurisdictions under investigation the study concludes that 'integrating ESG considerations into an investment analysis so as to more reliably predict financial performance is clearly permissible and is arguably required in all jurisdictions. It is also arguable that ESG considerations must be integrated into an investment decision where a consensus (expressed or in certain circumstances implied) amongst the beneficiaries mandates a particular investment strategy and may be integrated into an investment decision where a decision-maker is required to decide between a number of value-neutral alternatives' (UNEP FI, 2005, p. 13). However, within all jurisdictions the weight that the decision-maker gives to ESG considerations is left to the discretion of the investment manager alone.

EU Directive on the energy performance of buildings (2002/91/EC):
'Member States shall ensure that, when buildings are constructed, sold or rented out, an energy per-formance certificate is made available to the owner or by the owner to the prospective buyer or ten-ant, as the case might be.' (Article 7, sentence 1)

EU Thematic strategy on the urban environment (COM(2004)60):
'[The EU directive on the energy performance of buildings] should be extended to include other key environmental and sustainability elements, such as indoor air quality, accessibility, noise levels, com-fort, environmental quality of the materials and the life-cycle cost of the building. It should also in-clude the ability of the building to resist environmental risks, such as flooding, storms or earthquakes, depending on their location.' (p. 22)

'The common [assessment] methodology [...] and the resulting evaluations and life-cycle costing should then be used to promote best practice linked to a range of incentives. For example, a high level of sustainability might lead to lower tax rates; insurance companies and lending institutions might of-fer more favourable conditions. Once the appropriate methodology is well established, the Commis-sion will then propose further non-energy-related environmental performance requirements to com-plement Directive 2002/91.' (p. 23)

EU Working Group on Sustainable Construction Methods & Techniques, Final Report 2004:
'Taxes and all other regulatory mechanisms at global, regional and local political levels need to be adapted (transformed into incentives) and used to help motivate the actors in contributing to achieve more sustainable construction.' (p. 23)

EU Accounts modernisation directive (2003/51/EC):
'The information [within the annual report and the annual consolidated report] should not be re-stricted to the financial aspects of the company's business. It is expected that, where appropriate, this should lead to an analysis of environmental and social aspects necessary for an understanding of the company's development, performance or position.' (Article 9)

EU Corporate Governance Action Plan (COM (2003)284):
'Well managed companies, with strong corporate governance records and sensitive social and envi-ronmental performance, outperform their competitors. Europe needs more of them to generate em-ployment and higher long term sustainable growth.' (p. 3)

3.2.2 Consumer behaviour

The role of consumer behaviour and its potential for driving change towards a more sustain-able economy in general and a more sustainable property market in particular can be dis-cussed from, at least, three different viewpoints:

(1) Those who trust in free market forces and who object any increase in the power of gov-ernments believe that the only way to achieve a genuinely sustainable economy is through consumers using their purchasing power (or withholding it) in order to make sure that markets deliver sustainable development as a by-product of consumer sovereignty. This is 'a wonder-ful notion *if* one believes that we live in a world of perfect information' (Porritt, 2006, p. 265). Given that consumer's preferences do not develop 'outside the system' but are created,

reinforced and deceived by the system (e.g. through the media, corporate manipulation or prices that do not reflect true costs), consumer sovereignty is a myth (Hamilton, 2003).

(2) Then there are those who also take the view that consumer behaviour has an important role to play for achieving a sustainable economy, but who acknowledge that sustainable consumer behaviour demands a more sophisticated and creative policy approach. Views like this can be found in the work of Jackson (2005) who produced a comprehensive and well-documented report on how to motivate sustainable consumption (examples of such consumption include: purchase of sustainable products such as energy efficient household appliances or buildings, choosing green energy tariffs, recycling of household wastes, investing in 'ethical' funds, changing travel behaviour, reducing material consumption, buying organic food, pursuing 'voluntary simplicity' and so on). Jackson (2005) argued that the rhetoric of 'consumer sovereignty' and 'hands-off' governance is inaccurate and unhelpful because policy-makers are not innocent bystanders in the negotiation of consumer choice. Instead, policy intervenes continually in consumer behaviour both directly (e.g. through regulation and taxes) and more importantly through its extensive influence over the social context within which people act. Therefore, 'a concerted strategy is needed to make behaviour change easy: ensuring that *incentives structures and institutional rules* favour pro-environmental behaviour, *enabling access* to pro-environmental choice, *engaging people* in initiatives to help themselves, and *exemplifying the desired changes* within the Government's own policies and practices' (Jackson, 2005, p. iii). This is, however, a very difficult exercise and well-balanced strategies are needed. For example, in one extreme case a California utility provider spent more money on advertising the benefits of home insulation that it would have cost to install the installation itself in the targeted homes (McKenzie-Mohr, 2000).

(3) And finally there are those who believe that consumers are currently unable to drive change towards a sustainable economy because the media discourage people from doing so. They take the view that 'corporate-dominated media shield [people] from the reality of what is really happening, and an active propaganda machine seduces people into comatose consumerism as a substitute for real life and active engagement in the world around us' (Porritt, 2006, p. 101). Similar views and more detailed explanations of the role and power of the media in the global economy can be found in the works of Noam Chomsky (e.g. 2002 and 2003). Chomsky views the private media as businesses selling a product (i.e. readers and audiences, rather than news) to other businesses (i.e. corporations and advertisers).

In summary, the role of consumer behaviour is a controversial one. However, the second viewpoint – as an intermediate between the most extreme positions – appears to be realistic and useful; i.e. consumers are increasingly willing to take action (through both the support of companies that show sustainable behaviour patterns and through various initiatives to stop companies' from damaging the natural and social environment) but further encouragement through government intervention is needed in order to make sure that sustainable consumption continues to grow. That consumers are, indeed, willing to take action and to change behaviour can be evidenced by a number of developments concerning both the economy in general as well as the property market in particular: Today, 'civil society creates pressures for businesses to be more open and transparent in the way it deals with the public, government, other businesses, and local communities. International NGOs [non-governmental organisations] ensure that corporate activities anywhere in the world are under stakeholder and shareholder scrutiny. Failure to perform responsibly in a distant market along the supply chain or in the launch of new products and technologies may erode corporate reputation and harm competitive position in core markets and equity markets' (WRI, 2002, p. 53). Currently more than 2,000 (NGOs) hold consultative status at the United Nations compared to 928 in 1991 and just 41 in 1948. Furthermore, access to information through the internet[51] has led to increased shareholder activism, pressure for corporate disclosures, and new stock investment strategies. For example, the Investor Responsibility Research Center has tracked shareholder resolutions in the United States since 1973 on social issues (e.g. diversity, human rights, environment, equal employment, and labour standards) and the number of resolutions that received the 3% support needed to submit the resolution: The average level of support for these shareholder resolutions has risen steadily form 5% in the 1970s to today's level of about 9% (WRI, 2002). Other examples for a change in consumer behaviour can be found in the Co-operative Bank's Ethical Consumerism Report – an overview on the extent and spread of ethical purchasing power in the UK. The 2005 report reveals that overall market share of ethical consumerism in the UK has increased by 22% within the last 6 years; however, market share for ethical products and services remained under 2% of total sales. 'In effect, the role of the ethical consumer is to support and pioneer the early development of ethical products and services. Subsequently, with the help of Government intervention, they can make the next step' (Co-operative Bank, 2005, p. 6).

Evidence for more sustainable consumption within the property market can be found in the following publications: St. Lawrence (2004); Sayce et al. (2004a and 2004b) and Kraus (2005). It is argued that private as well as corporate market participants are becoming more aware and informed of the quality and performance of the space they use and occupy and that

---

[51] Examples of relevant information sources are: www.ethicalconsumer.org; www.irn.org; www.corpwatch.org; www.globalpolicy.org; and www.eiris.org

they are beginning to want more sustainable buildings. Furthermore, poor environmental and social building performance is increasingly being seen as an investment risk or as a reason for not buying or renting a particular premise (Filose, 2005). The awareness for environmental problems is high and constantly growing among the general public within a number of countries. For example, 92 % of German citizens consider environmental protection important (BMU, 2004). This clearly has an impact on the residential property market and on the success-factors of its central actors. Recent research from the German Energy Agency (Dena) indicates that a large proportion (72 %) of residential property market participants consider the building's energy consumption as an important criteria when deciding to buy or rent a flat (Dena, 2005). Furthermore, between 80 and 90 % of building owners in Germany (including owner-occupiers, landlords and housing companies) are interested in questions related to housing health, energy performance and environmentally friendly design and take the view that an improvement of their buildings' energy performance will lead to increase in the buildings' Market Value (Kraus, 2005). For more information on the interrelation between people's attitudes concerning environmental protection and the residential property market in other countries, see: Li and Shen (2002), Sunikka and Boon (2003), Chiu (2004), Lundqvist (2004), and Klunder (2004).

3.2.3   Investment, corporate governance and accounting practices

The issues of Socially Responsible Investing (SRI) and Corporate Social Responsibility (CSR) appear to attract a growing number of corporations, financial institutions and private investors (Eurosif, 2003, SiRi Group, 2005 and US SIF, 2006; see also Figure 13). SRI can be defined as 'an investment process that considers the social and environmental consequences of investments, both positive and negative, within the context of rigorous financial analysis' (O'Rourke, 2003, p. 684). It is a process of identifying and investing in assets and/or companies that meet certain baseline standards or criteria of CSR which includes issues such as environment, health and safety, diversity, human resource policies, human rights and the supply chain. In April 2006, UN Secretary-General Kofi Annan released the Principles for Responsible Investment (PRI, 2006) and stated as follows: 'Developed by leading institutional investors in a process overseen by the UN Environment Programme Finance Initiative and the UN Global Compact, the Principles include environmental, social and governance criteria, and provide a framework for achieving better long-term investment returns and more sustainable markets. It is my hope that the Principles will help to align investment practices with the goals of the United Nations, thereby contributing to a more stable and inclusive global economy. I invite institutional investors and their financial partners everywhere to embrace the Principles and bring them to life in their daily activities and decision-making. By acting collectively on the basis of the Principles for Responsible Investment, we can help protect all the world's precious assets.'

Box 9: *The Principles for Responsible Investment (PRI, 2006)*

> *1. We will incorporate ESG issues into investment analysis and decision-making processes.*
>
> *2. We will be active owners and incorporate ESG issues into our ownership policies and practices.*
>
> *3. We will seek appropriate disclosure on ESG issues by the entities in which we invest.*
>
> *4. We will promote acceptance and implementation of the Principles within the investment industry.*
>
> *5. We will work together to enhance our effectiveness in implementing the Principles.*
>
> *6. We will each report on our activities and progress towards implementing the Principles.*

CSR (sometimes referred to as 'good' corporate governance) can be defined as an open and transparent business practice that is based on ethical values and respect for employees, communities, and the environment. It is designed to deliver sustainable value to society at large, as well as to shareholders (US SIF, 2006).

Figure 13: *Key finding – Global Investor Opinion Survey[52] (McKinsey, 2002)*

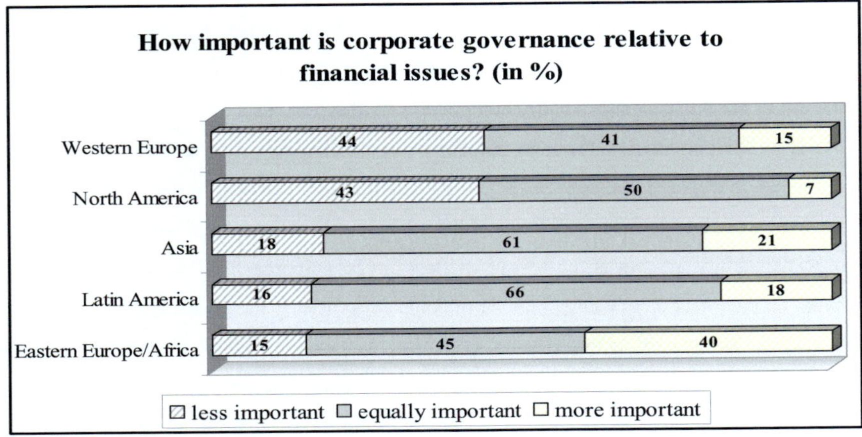

---

[52] McKinsey's survey was undertaken between April and May 2002. The survey is based on responses from over 200 institutional investors, collectively responsible for some US$ 2 trillion of assets under management (their organizations manage an estimated US$ 9 trillion assets under management). Corporate governance is defined here as effective boards of directors, broad disclosure, and strong rights and equal treatment for shareholders; financial issues are, for example, profit performance and growth potential.

A detailed explanation of the concept of CSR is offered by Wilenius (2005). Examples for CSR leadership are the World Economic Forum's self-commitment on 'Global Corporate Citizenship' (WEF, 2002) or the World Bank's 'Equator Principles', an agreement of the world's biggest banks to provide credit only to large-scale projects (>$50 million) that are neither environmentally nor socially harmful and for which the borrower has completed an extensive environmental assessment (Equator Principles, 2003). Other examples for good and bad corporate governance are presented in CORE (2005); an overview on recent developments within the SRI market can be found in IFC (2005).

Although no common definition exists for the SRI market, nevertheless it can be circumscribed by referring to its central actors and to the four prevailing investment strategies. Besides private and institutional investors the SRI market's central actors are: (1) financial institutions and fund companies that develop, market, trade and manage environmentally and socially advantageous investment products; (2) agencies and services providers that screen companies' environmental and social performance (i.e. sustainability screening or positive screening); and (3) companies which voluntarily exhibit themselves as well as their products to such screening processes and which publish relevant information. The four prevailing investment strategies which are sometimes applied in combination are:

Selection through sustainability rating / positive screening: Rating or screening practices involve the evaluation of retail investment funds and of single companies or assets based on social, environmental and/or corporate governance criteria. Sustainability ratings can involve the use of checklists, questionnaires and multi-criteria assessments based on information published by the company or the fund initiator or by stakeholders such as NGOs. Investments grounded on elaborate rating or positive screening practices can be assigned to the 'core' SRI market. A variant of sustainability rating that is often used in connection with the construction of sustainability indexes is the so-called 'Best-in-Class-Approach'. This rating approach is based on the selection of a large number of companies (usually the largest and most important ones) from all industry sectors. The companies are then examined through screening practices and those companies scoring best are subsequently included in the index. However, no standardised assessment processes and criteria exist; choice and weighting of assessment criteria are subject only to the rating agencies' or index providers' decisions. Furthermore, Best-in-Class-Approaches usually do not pick out 'critical' industries or branches. Therefore, certain sustainability index providers (such as FTSE and Dow Jones) apply a combination of Best-in-Class-Approaches and negative screenings.

Negative screening: Within the scope of negative screenings several companies or branches (e.g. tobacco, alcohol, weapons, nuclear energy, etc.) whose business practices or products are perceived to be harmful to individuals, communities, or the environment are categorically defined as 'not sustainable' and are ruled out as a possible investment option.

Shareholder Engagement / Advocacy: This investment strategy involves dialoguing with companies on issue of social or environmental concern as well as filing, co-filing, and voting on shareholder resolutions. These efforts generally aim to improve company or investment polices and practices by encouraging management to exercise good corporate governance while promoting long-term shareholder value and financial performance (US SIF, 2006).

Community investing: This investment strategy directs capital from investors and lenders to communities that are underserved by traditional financial services. Community investing provides access to capital that these communities would otherwise lack. It enables local organisations to provide financial services to low-income individuals and to supply capital for small businesses and vital community services such as affordable housing, childcare and healthcare (US SIF, 2006). Unlike making a donation, community investing requires that the original investment can be returned.

Given this rather broad definition of the SRI market, estimates of its size can vary significantly. The most recent estimates on the volume of the European SRI market report a market size of up to €360 billion in 2003/2005. This figure comprises a total of €24.1 billion of assets under management within 375 retail SRI funds[53] at the end of the second quarter of 2005 and a total of €336 billion of assets attributable to the institutional SRI market in 2003 (Eurosif, 2003; SiRi Group, 2005). While the retail market consists of funds only that use elaborate screens for portfolio selection, the institutional market also comprises investments that are subject to negative screens and/or shareholder engagement. An overview on the European SRI market can be found in Figure 14.

---

[53] For comparison: The amount of SRI assets grew from €11 billion in 1999 (managed by 159 funds) to the today's figure of € 24.1 billion which represents a share of 0.6% of all assets managed by European retail funds.

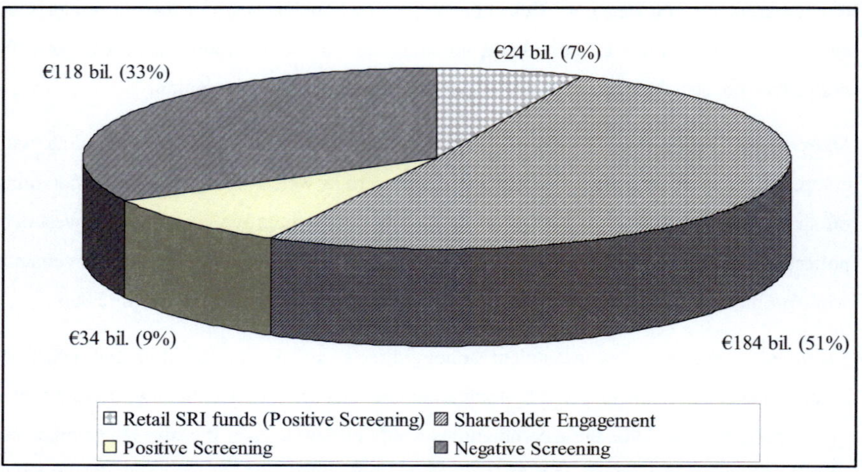

Thus, a total of €58 billion worth of assets (retail and core institutional SRI market) can be identified in professionally managed portfolios that use ethical, social and environmental screening as the basic element of their investment philosophy. This number represents the most conservative view of the European SRI market, while the €360 billion mentioned above represent a rather optimistic view.

While SRI in Europe is a small but growing niche market, the US market is in a much more matured stage. According to the US Social Investment Forum (US SIF, 2006) SRI assets in the US grew more than 258% from US$ 639 billion in 1995 to US$ 2.29 trillion in 2005 (representing 9.4% of all assets) while the broader investment universe of assets under professional management increased less than 249% from US$ 7 trillion to US$ 24.4 trillion over the same time period. The largest share of SRI assets (US$ 1.5 trillion) in the US were found in separate accounts (i.e. portfolios privately managed for individuals and institutions); assets in screened retailed funds and other pooled products rose to US$ 179 billion in 2005; this represents a 15-fold increase compared to US$ 12 billion in 1995. Figure 15 presents an overview on the US SRI market; it needs, however, to be noted that a designation of assets to the core SRI market is not possible since the US SIF does not distinguish between positive and negative screening.

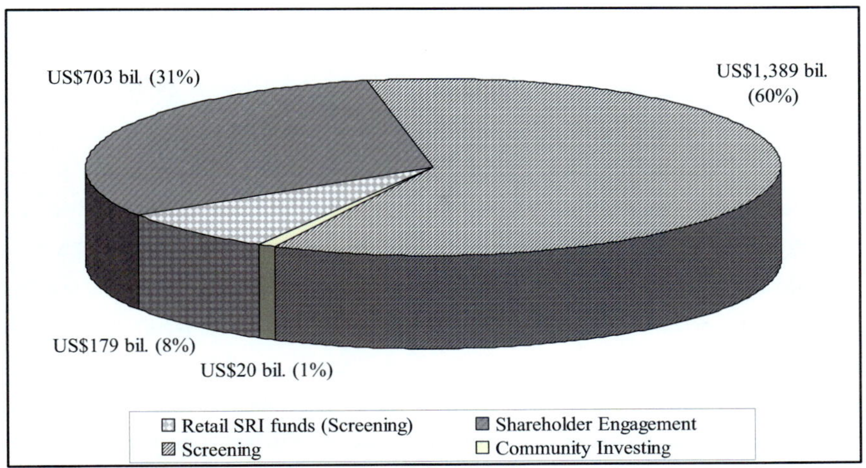

SRI markets within other countries or world regions[54] have also grown fast during the last few years and it is expected that the global SRI market will further expand rapidly. This assumption can be underpinned by referring to the variety of research studies carried out during the last decade investigating the correlation between corporate profitability or investment performance on the one hand, and environmental and social performance of businesses and investment products on the other hand. In particular, three publications need to be mentioned that contain reviews of a large number of relevant studies on this issue:

(1) Murphy (2002) concluded – based on an extensive literature review – that companies that score well according to objective environmental criteria realise stronger financial returns than the overall market, and companies that score poorly have weaker returns. Furthermore, Murphy stated that companies that go beyond legal compliance realise stronger stock price gains and market value growth than the S&P 500. In contrast, laggard companies that are threatened by actual or impending environmental laws have been shown to experience weaker returns.

(2) Schröder (2003) reviewed literature on the comparison between the financial performance of SRI funds and indexes and the performance of conventional funds and stock indexes. He concluded that SRI assets do not show weaker returns in comparison to other assets. (3) The investment management company Phillips, Hager & North (2005) reviewed literature on the performance of sustainability indexes versus traditional stock indexes, of SRI funds versus conventional funds, as well as of the financial performance of companies that score high on

---

[54] Information sources are: www.eia.org.au and www.ethicalinvestor.com.au for Australia; www.asria.org for the Asia Pacific region; and www.socialinvestment.ca for Canada.

one or more measures of good corporate governance versus those that do not. Their main finding is that the literature does not provide any evidence that socially responsible investing or the adoption of good corporate governance policies result in lower investment returns or financial performance respectively.

In summary, a vast body of credible evidence now indicates that there are no financial disadvantages, and in some cases, positive financial effects associated with the adoption of SRI and CSR polices. Furthermore, it is likely that the range of environmental and social advantages of such policies are not yet fully expressed in investment value since they cannot yet be truly reflected through the traditional approaches to investment analysis that focus on internal financial returns only and neglect external costs and benefits. Consequently, the question is no longer if, but when will it be possible to clearly demonstrate that SRI and CSR approaches that are adopted properly and not only seen as having mere alibi function, outperform the conventional modes of business and investment practice from any relevant point of view; i.e. economically, environmentally and socially? In addition, it can be concluded that it is now generally agreed that environmental, social and CSR issues need to be integrated into the investment analysis process in order to appropriately determine investment value and to minimize investment risk. Recently, Klaus Töpfer (former Executive Director of UNEP) stated in the foreword of a report commissioned by UNEP FI (2004, p. 3) that 'long term protection of shareholder value rests upon rigorous integration of environmental, social and corporate governance issues in the valuation process. Too many analysts and financial institutions tend to insufficiently acknowledge and appreciate environmental, social and corporate governance issues. [...] such bias may expose investors and companies to unnecessary risk. Environmental, social and corporate governance thinking must therefore be fully integrated into our market, investment and board room considerations by those that wish to create the foundation for, and then realise, long-term shareholder value.' Also, a survey of 195 fund managers from around the world conducted by Mercer Investment Consulting in 2005 revealed that 'the use of positive screening for environmental, social and ethical factors is entering mainstream investment analysis particularly where such screening may potentially yield superior financial performance by targeting companies that adopt socially responsible practices and thereby avoid future liabilities and losses' (Ambachtsheer, 2005).

Astonishingly, the SRI community has not yet fully recognised the diversification benefits offered through investments in property assets. Apparently, none of the over 200 stated retail SRI funds in the US as well as none of the 375 funds in Europe offer investors a screened and professionally managed property portfolio. Furthermore, Gary Pivo (2005) stated that none of the over 300 REITs in the US makes social responsibility or sustainability and explicit goal.

He goes on arguing 'that neither the real estate research firms that evaluate real estate funds nor the SRI screening firms that evaluate all kinds of companies collect or distribute information on the social or environmental practices of the many retail or institutional real estate investments that are offered in the USA. This is not to say that no real estate investment firms may be constructively engaged in these issues. But if they do exist, they're simply too hard to find' (Pivo, 2005, p. 17). The situation is very similar in Europe; the only known property investment firms or funds that make sustainability an explicit goal are listed in Table 9 above. Given that an optimal share of property (direct or indirect investment) within a mixed-asset portfolio lies between 10 and 20% (Sirmans and Worzala, 2003; Worzala and Sirmans, 2003), the retail SRI market as a whole is significantly under-allocated from the perspective of optimal asset allocation. Consequently, the untapped market potential for publicly offered sustainable property investment products is huge and can be easily calculated: it is simply 10 to 20% of the volume of the current retail SRI market; i.e. between US$17.9 and US$35.8 billion in the US and between €2.4 and €4.8 billion in Europe. Table 11 gives an overview on the market potential within single countries.

Table 11: *Untapped market potential for publicly offered sustainable property investment products in million € (based on data provided by SiRi Group, 2005 and US SIF, 2006)*

US	22,000 – 44,000	Europe	2,410 – 4,820
UK	800 – 1,600	Netherlands	176 - 352
France	310 - 620	Swiss	160 - 320
Italy	268 - 536	Germany	116 - 232
Sweden	250 - 500	Austria	110 - 220
Belgium	213 - 426	Spain	7 - 14

Exactly the same calculation cannot be made for the institutional SRI market because little is known on the share of property owned by SRI engaged institutional investors. However, given the worldwide lack of sustainable property investment products and given the fact that sustainable building is not yet a mainstream activity, it may be reasonable to assume that those buildings or property investment products owned by institutional investors may not be the most sustainable ones. Thus, if only 10% of the more than US$ 2 trillion now in SRI would be moved to sustainable property assets it would equal to approximately 1/3 of the current free-float market capitalization of the FTSE EPRA/NAREIT global listed real estate index which was at US$ 644 billion by the end of 2005. A possible reason for this lack of appropriate investment products might be the absence of both knowledge and common understanding of the benefits and constituents of sustainable buildings in general and of sustainable property investment products in particular as well as of appropriate systems or frameworks to assess and report their performance.

The issue of assessing and reporting environmental and social performance of corporations, products, or processes – commonly referred to as sustainability accounting – is closely linked to the concepts of SRI and CSR. Sustainability accounts or reports are the key sources of information for investors, sustainability rating agencies as well as for the wider public to decide whether ore not a company or an investment product meets certain environmental and social criteria. Sustainability accounts may include the presentation of relevant information in the following formats (Lamberton, 2005, p. 22):

- Tables of performance indicators which measure actual values of pre-defined indicators for a specified accounting period;
- Inventories of stocks of natural capital segregated into various categories;
- Cost estimates of sustainable alternatives to current business practice;
- Input-output analysis;
- Life-cycle analysis;
- Lists of non compliance with relevant legislation incidents; and
- Narratives of environmental and social impacts.

Sustainability accounting has received attention in the academic accounting literature since the late 1980s (see for example: Gray et al., 1988 and Gray, 1992). Lamberton (2005) described the history and contemporary understanding of sustainability accounting (i.e. its conceptual framework) and stated that sustainability accounting represents an enormous challenge to business organisations and requires a significant commitment of resources to achieve widespread implementation.

> *'Failure to meet this challenge enables business organisations to continue to avoid accountability for their continuing unsustainability.' (Lamberton, 2005, p. 7)*

Insights into the interrelationships between sustainability accounting and conventional financial accounting can be found in Gray (2002). According to Gray (2002, p. 358), 'social and environmental accounting *and finance* offer a way to recover a moral and productive accounting and finance that places survival of the species at its very heart.' Thus, sustainability accounting is important, also from a mere pragmatic perspective: it is increasingly required by legislators and it can bring financial benefits. Concerning property and construction firms, this can be exemplified by referring to the introduction and growing acceptance of stock indices that track the financial performance of 'sustainability driven' companies (e.g. the 'Dow Jones Sustainability Index' and the 'FTSE4Good Index series'). Inclusion in one of these indexes is perceived to be highly beneficial for long-term company stock performance and thus for company shareholders. For example, to become included in the FTSE4Good Index (FTSE, 2006), companies are assigned a 'high', 'medium' or 'low' impact weighting according to their industry sector (e.g. construction companies are ranked among the 'high', property developers among the 'medium' impact sectors). The higher the environmental impact of the company's operations, the more stringent the inclusion criteria are. Companies must meet certain environmental and social/stakeholder requirements (e.g. strategic moves towards sustainability, identification of significant environmental impacts, environmental performance measured against targets) from three core areas: corporate policy, management and reporting. Thus, construction companies or property firms that want to be included within the index must *identify, describe, assess and report* the impacts of their actions and business processes (e.g. the environmental and social performance of the buildings they develop, construct, operate or sell).

Principles, standards and guidelines for sustainability accounting and reporting have been developed by the Institute of Social and Ethical AccountAbility (AccountAbility, 2006) and by the Global Reporting Initiative (GRI, 2005). The latter possess high international profile and influences while the former reveal a unique focus on the processes of accountability (Adams, 2004). Currently, 84 organisations (including businesses, NGOs and governmental institutions)[55] use the framework offered by AccountAbility while approximately 250 corporations and organisations[56] use the GRI guidelines.

But these reporting guidelines and standards do not yet contain any rules on how to report on the performance of property assets. In fact there exists a general 'ethical, social and environmental reporting-performance portrayal gap'. This gap has been identified by Adams (2004) and by Hummels and Timmer (2004). It is argued that current ethical and social reporting practice does not provide investors and other stakeholders with appropriate information 'to assess the material consequences of company activities and behaviour in socially or politically sensitive areas. Companies should therefore reconsider their current SEE [social, ethical and environmental] information processing and start to disclose information that is geared to the needs of the (financially oriented) investor' (Hummels and Timmer, 2004, p. 83). The problem with sustainability accounting and reporting standards is, that they do not yet appropriately specify data collection processes, calculations methods or reporting units; i.e. key performance indicators are not yet established. For example, SAM's Sustainability Yearbook

---

[55] See: www.accountability.org.uk/aa1000/default.asp?pageid=122
[56] See: http://www.globalreporting.org/about/Pamphlet.pdf

2005 (SAM, 2005) ranks companies in almost 60 sectors but performance data are not presented.

> *'Until reports that compare sustainability performance are freely available, as ubiquitous as financial reports, we will remain lost in the quagmire of intriguing anecdotes, unable to determine who performs better, or even what indicators really matter in the quest for sustainability. [...] In a world with comparable reports, sustainability reporting can fulfil its true potential: providing concise, transparent information that clearly reflects the reality of environmental and social issues, allows for benchmarking, highlights long-term risk and opportunities, and contributes to improved levels of public and investor confidence. [...] Otherwise sustainability reporting will remain an exercise in creative writing ...' (Rogers, 2005, p. 39)*

One recent development in the area of financial accounting needs to be mentioned here since it serves as an example for the convergence of sustainability and financial accounting frameworks: Recently, the US Financial Accounting Standards Board (FASB) issued Financial Interpretation No. 47 (FIN 47 – Accounting for Conditional Asset Retirement Obligations). FIN 47 became effective in December 2005 and requires companies to identify and estimate environmental pollution clean-up obligations and report them as liabilities. This has far reaching consequences not only for companies[57] but also for property valuers. Most property valuation reports prepared today contain environmental disclaimers in which the valuers claims no knowledge of environmental conditions and states that the valuation of the property is made as 'clean' (Lipscomb et al., 2006). This disclaimer is now inappropriate for valuation assignments covered by generally accepted accounting principles (GAAP) in the US. Since the FASB is collaborating with the International Accounting Standards Board (IASB) to reach convergence between International Financial Reporting Standards (IFRSs) and US-GAAP it is likely that similar accounting requirements will become reality also for European companies that are obliged to use IFRSs.

---

[57] See: http://www.advancedenvironmentaldimensions.com/fin47_adoption.htm

3.2.4 Banking practices

Since financial services organisations considered themselves as being part of a 'clean' industry (in terms of resource use, emissions and pollutions), banks started relatively late to recognise the need for more sustainable development or to care about their – and much more importantly, their clients' – environmental and social impacts and associated risks.

Marcel Jeucken (2001, 2002 and 2004) has investigated in depth the role banks play within sustainable development as well as their responses and actions to meet the challenges that sustainability represents. According to Jeucken (2002), banks were not interested in their own environmental situation or that of their clients until the late 1980s. Then, banks in the US realised that they are exposed to mainly three sources of risk associated with environmental and social issues: (1) the enforcement of a client's security interests; (2) the influencing of the client's business policy; and (3) non-disclosure of environmental and social risks (known to the bank) towards the client. When these sources of risk are accompanied with environmental or social damage, banks can be held directly liable for the damage and for the remediation costs by governments and third parties. This first happened in the US after the Comprehensive Environmental Response, Compensation and Liability Act (CERCLA) was passed in 1980; for example, a bank had been held liable for the costs of decontaminating their client company's soil because the bank participated in the financial management of the company and had the 'capacity to influence' the decision that resulted in the pollution, *even though* the bank had no actual influence on their client's activities. Banks even went bankrupt under this scheme (Jeucken, 2001 and 2002).

Because European banks were not exposed to such liabilities, they first started in the mid 1990s to focus on issues of internal environmental care in order to decrease costs and to demonstrate environmentally friendly business practices; i.e. downsizing the throughput of the bank's own business activities (e.g. paper, water and energy use, waste production, etc.). An example for internal environmental care in the banking business is the German Association for Environmental Management in Banks, Savings Banks, and Insurance Companies (Verein für Umweltmanagement in Banken, Sparkassen und Versicherungen, VfU) which was founded in 1994. The association has developed principles, guidelines and indicators for environmental accounting and reporting within the financial services sector.[58] The association has also published a survey of developments concerning principles and guidelines for in-house eco-balances of financial services providers (VfU, n.d.).

---

[58] These can be obtained through the associations website: http://www.vfu.de/ver%F6ffentlichungen.htm

Later, banks extended their focus on the introduction of environmental risk management processes into credit management and on the development of new products such as socially and environmentally responsible investment funds (Weber, 2005). But already in 1992 many of the largest members of the financial services industry issued the Statement by Financial Institutions on the Environment & Sustainable Development within the scope of UNEP: 'We recognize that identifying and quantifying environmental risks should be part of the normal process of risk assessment and management, both in domestic and international operations. [...] We encourage the financial services sector to develop products and services which will promote environmental protection' (UNEP FI, 1997)[59].

Nine years later, Jeucken (2001) conducted a survey exploring the state-of-the-art on sustainability among 34 mainstream banks. The survey – based on studying the banks' environmental and annual reports – did not look at banks known to be actively involved in sustainability issues but has selected banks according to their size in terms of total assets. The survey revealed that the majority of the banks adopted a defensive position towards the environment (53%). The areas under investigation included: adoption or availability of respective codes of conduct, environmental reporting and management systems, environmental policy statements; environmental risk assessment and guidelines; financial products for environmental care as well as socio-economic activities and sponsoring. In total, a group of ten 'front runners' or very proactive banks were identified, a group of six followers and a group of 18 stragglers. In summary, Jeucken (2002) argued that the majority of banks still do not see the role they can play and maybe should play towards a sustainable development.

Following Jeucken (2004) four major phases, stances or strategic concepts can be distinguished from the point of view of a bank's drive towards sustainability. These are (1) defensive banking, (2) preventive banking, (3) offensive banking, and (4) sustainable banking. A brief explanation of these concepts is contained in Figure 16.

---

[59] The quotes are taken from a revised version of the original statement of 1992. For a description of the history of this initiative, see: http://www.unepfi.org/about/background/index.html

Figure 16: *Four different concepts of banking in relation to sustainable development (based on Jeucken, 2004, pp. 130-141)*

Defensive Banking	Preventive Banking	Offensive Banking	Sustainable Banking
➢ The bank is a follower and contests every government measure concerning sustainable development only because its direct or indirect self-interest is threatened ➢ Cost savings in its internal environmental care are not considered ➢ All environmental laws and regulations are thought to be threats to business ➢ Only curative measures are taken ➢ View: sustainability is not an isse at all; care for the environment only adds to cost and there is certainly no money to be earned from it	➢ The bank identifies potential costs savings ➢ Focus on internal environmental care (e.g. downsizing of paper and water use, waste, etc.) ➢ The bank also aims to limit external risks and investment losses related to environmental and social issues (e.g. through environmental risk assessment) ➢ The bank does not go beyond existing or expected laws and regulations ➢ View: Sustainability is an issue; however, only in terms of saving costs through fewer loss items as a result of social and environmental risks in credit extension	➢ Includes the elements of the preventive phase; but the bank goes a significant step further ➢ The bank is proactive and creative since it sees potential for increased profits through new financial products and through financing new sustainability related markets ➢ View: Sustainability can pay; extra actions are taken when there are win-win situations that have a pay-off period within a required time frame and when the level of risk is deemed acceptable ➢ The fact that the bank's activities are sustainable is coincidental	➢ Includes the elements of the offensive phase but the bank lays down pre-conditions so that all its activities are sustainable ➢ The bank's activities are visionary originated ➢ The bank refrains from certain forms of lending and participation ➢ The bank is prepared to accept lower margins and/or higher risks to stimulate sustainability at large ➢ Examples for activities are: micro-finance; debt-for-nature-swaps; innovation funds for sustainability, etc. ➢ The bank aims to position itself as a sustainability leader in the business world

According to Jeucken (2004, p. 132) a large group of developed countries' banks have made it as far as the preventive banking phase since 'preventive banking is inevitable for most banks because politicians and interest groups are directly or indirectly stipulating preconditions for bank activities through environmental laws, jurisprudence and regulations.' The offensive phase has been achieved by a limited number of banks only (examples are: ABN AMRO, Bank Austria, Bank of America, Barclays Bank, Credit Suisse, Deutsche Bank, ING, NatWest Bank, Rabobank, and UBS), and the 'goal of pure sustainable banking appears to be feasible for only a few niche players, such as the Triados Bank in The Netherlands or the Co-operative Bank in the UK' because society does not yet price all the negative and positive environmental and social 'externalities'; i.e. within the current socio-economic paradigm the risks of sustainable banking are considered to be too large, the profit margins too low, or the pay-off periods too long (Jeucken, 2004, p. 134).

Recently, Weber (2005) conducted a benchmark study of European banks inquiring the extent to which they have integrated sustainability into their policies, strategies, products, services and processes. He started with the 129 European signatories of the UNEP Statement by Financial Institutions on the Environment & Sustainable Development. The banks were then screened by making use of their business reports; areas under investigation were (1) internal operations, (2) investment business, and (3) credit business. As a result, 20 European banks were identified that integrate sustainability issues into their business strategies and practices. Unfortunately, the names of the banks were – in contrast to the study carried out by Jeucken (2001) – not published. However, Weber (2005) identified five models or motives for integrating sustainability into the banking business. These are briefly explained in Table 12.

Table 12: *Models of integrating sustainability into the banking business (based on Weber, 2005, pp. 81-85)*

Model	Explanation
Event related integration of sustainability	*Includes the creation of socially and environmentally friendly investment funds or the offering of new sustainability driven products in response to a particular environmental accident, the introduction of an environmental tax or a conference on sustainability. The banks' motivation stems from the desire to build up positive reputation among those who are interested in sustainability issues.*
Sustainability as a new banking strategy	*Originated in the 1980's from a group of banking specialists with an anthroposophical background and the willingness to handle money in an environmentally and socially friendly way. This model is based on holistically integrating sustainability into all the banks' activities (i.e. sustainable banking). This can lead to a unique niche position and to certain competitive advantages.*
Sustainability as a value driver	*Evolved from the viewpoint that environmental and social issues are not only business risks but can present an opportunity and have a positive influence on shareholder value. This model includes the creation of sustainable products in the fields of asset or credit management but does note represent the banks' core business. This is seen to be beneficial in terms of creating a better banks' image.*
Sustainability as a public mission	*Mainly applies for banks that officially perform their business on behalf of a public body such as a state or local authority. If this public body has a mission of sustainability, the banks generally integrate this mission into their own mission in order to contribute to the public body's sustainable development goals. This model can involve creating sustainable products and services; investing in socially and environmentally friendly funds; granting 'green' loans and mortgages; and engaging in public projects.*
Sustainability as a requirement of clients	*Evolved from a desire to create a socially responsible image because the banks found out that this is increasingly being requested or valued by clients. This model can lead to the adoption of an ethical policy covering environmental and social aspects as well as to the adoption of the criteria of the banks' policy to their clients' needs.*

Weber (2005, p. 86) concluded that sustainability driven banking products and services are mainly in their infancy but that alternative banks (i.e. those that view sustainability as their main business goal) can 'also be financially successful and have growth rates similar to, or even better than, those of their conventional competitors.'

Studies like this are, indeed, important in order to show that sustainable banking can be a profitable alternative to conventional banking approaches; however, they show half the truth only. The other half has recently been investigated by ten leading UK based NGOs; they published a report that exposed the damaging impacts of the European finance sector on the environment, human rights and development (see Box 10). The report was compiled in response to the UK Government's failure to exercise leadership to ensure that the finance sector does not continue to undermine global policy objectives in areas ranging from climate change to corruption and the Millennium Development Goals. Approximately ten years after the publication of the Statement by Financial Institutions on the Environment & Sustainable Development, this report shows that most banks have completely failed to meet their self-imposed targets and clearly demonstrates the finance sector's inability to embed corporate responsibility on a voluntary basis (CORE, 2005).

Box 10: *CSR within the European finance sector? (CORE, 2005, p. 1)*

The European finance sector:

- *provides a haven to siphon off much-needed tax revenues from cash-strapped developing countries, benefiting only a wealthy minority who avoid paying tax altogether;*

- *has abjectly failed to internalise the financial risks of climate change, which may ultimately lead to a global economic breakdown as the costs of climate change begin to outstrip any benefits generated by the global economy, especially for the world's most vulnerable people;*

- *is a primary conduit for bribery and corruption, providing billions of dollars in loans to repressive governments;*

- *perpetuates poverty and social exclusion in Europe by providing unscrupulous levels of debt at high rates to those least able to afford it, all the while bringing in record-level profits;*

- *regularly undermines human rights protection by financing projects which pose a threat to the implementation of human rights laws in developing countries, in breach of some companies' own codes of conduct; and*

- *often fails to assess adequately the environmental impacts of projects and to address issues raised before releasing project finance, yet continues to reap the reputational benefits of participation in voluntary CSR initiatives.*

These findings are accompanied with a call for a Europe-wide approach to enact laws that guarantee corporate responsibility right from the outset (CORE, 2005, p. 2). For a similarly harsh critique of the banking business and for rather unconventional but comprehensive and appealing approaches to solve the huge problems that confront benefits and welfare systems, see Porritt (2006, p. 190-194) and Robertson and Bunzl (2003).

In order to come back to the issue of sustainable development within property markets, two interrelated aspects of day-to-day banking practice deserve attention: (1) How do banks usually assess and monitor the risks associated with property lending, and (2) how do they calculate credit conditions for property loans and do these conditions stimulate more sustainable behaviour within property markets?

Property risk assessment

The methodologies and processes by which banks assess and monitor the risks associated with property lending are currently undergoing major changes. Until very recently banks' internal risk assessments did not distinguish between sustainable buildings and unsustainable ones. However, this is no longer the case anymore. The application of new, international banking capital adequacy rules called Basel II requires banks to take a much more sophisticated approach with regard to the risks they take in lending (BCBS, 2004). As a consequence, so-called property ratings will increasingly be conducted for lending purposes. In a very general sense, a rating can be defined as a procedure which illustrates the assessment of a thing, a person or situation, etc. on a scale in order to improve the informational basis for the prediction of future outcomes. Rating is not a new concept; it is has been used since the beginning of the 20th century by companies like Moody's and Standard & Poors in order to provide information on the financial strengths and willingness of companies to comply with liabilities completely and in time (TEGoVA, 2003a). The European Group of Valuers Associations (TEGoVA) has recently developed a property and market rating system which is likely to become influential for European property lending practice. TEGoVA's rating system contains four different criteria classes (market, location, property and quality of the property cash flow), up to 4 levels of sub-criteria classes and employs a rating scale that ranges from 1 (excellent) to 10 (disastrous). The following Table 13 shows that the criteria class 3 'property' contains the rating criterion 'ecological sustainability'.

Table 13: *TEGoVA's property and market rating, criteria class 3 'property' (TEGoVA, 2003a)*

Sub-criteria		Weighting (sub-criterion)	Weighting (criteria class)
3.1	*Architecture*	*20%*	
3.2	*Fitout*	*10%*	
3.3	*Structural condition*	*15%*	*Criteria class 3*
3.4	*Plot situation*	*25%*	*20%*
3.5	***Ecological sustainability***	***10%***	
3.6	*Profitability of the building concept*	*20%*	
Result for the property rating		*100%*	

Unfortunately, what is meant by ecological sustainability and the issue of how to assess it is neither defined nor explained within TEGoVA's publications. However, the rating proposal of the German association of public banks (VÖB), currently being implemented by public banks across Germany, defines three sub-criteria of ecological sustainability which will have to be assessed: building materials, energy performance and emissions. Critics may argue that 10 out of 20% is a very modest start. However, both rating approaches contain (slightly different) 'dynamic risk weight functions'; i.e. the basic weighting assigned to each indicator or sub-criteria class is flexible; the more the rating score deviates from the average, the more significantly it impacts on the overall rating results. This is done to reflect the circumstance that a high level of exposure to one particular hazard is usually perceived to have a greater impact on the outcome of a property investment or on the property's selling or letting prospects respectively (e.g. a property with very good overall structural condition and fitout, etc. would achieve a good rating for the criteria class 'property'; however, if the property's location is 'disastrous' then this circumstance deserves more attention). As a result of applying dynamic risk weights, a particular indicator that is originally assigned secondary importance can have a great impact on the overall rating result. For example, a 'disastrous' or 'excellent' rating of the criterion ecological sustainability can change the overall result by several points. Given that the rating scale ranges from 1 to 10, sustainability issues can, indeed, have a strong impact on the banks' assessment of the risks associated with property lending and thus, on lending decisions as well as conditions (this will be dealt with more fully in Section 4.3.3.3).

Credit conditions for property financing

In general, it can be stated that the better the rating is, the better the credit conditions will be. However, it is not yet ultimately clear how property rating results and the conditions offered for granting a property loan or for financing a particular project are interrelated. Indeed, the interrelation between ratings (of companies, individuals, projects or property assets) and the calculation of credit conditions (including loan amount and interest rate) is probably one of the best kept secrets in the banking business. For this reason it cannot yet be argued that sustainable buildings or building projects will deserve preferential credit conditions in general, but it is likely that this will be the case. However, at the moment, most banks do not distinguish between sustainable buildings and unsustainable ones when it comes down to the calculation of credit and mortgage conditions; nonetheless, there are some banks that already do, particularly in Switzerland. Here most of the smaller county banks offer 'green' or 'energy-efficient' mortgages (see: Energia, 2005, p. 5). Table 14 provides some examples of banks that offer preferential credit conditions for sustainable buildings or for financing measures to improve building performance.

In summary, although the majority of banks do not yet offer these products, some bankers increasingly see preferential credit conditions for sustainable buildings as a business opportunity. Recently, the following two statements could be found in the American Banker's online journal (Berg, 2006): (1) 'There's significant profit opportunity for lenders that understand these issues and can appropriately value the costs and benefits.' and (2) 'This is the ultimate niche market. You've got something better than kryptonite here, and nobody knows about it.'

Table 14: *Preferential credit conditions for sustainable buildings*

Country	Bank	Explanation
Germany	*Kreditanstalt für Wiederaufbau (KfW)*	*Lower interests rates for measures to reduce energy consumption in buildings; covers new and existing buildings.* http://www.kfw-foerderbank.de
Germany	*SEB-Bank Hannover*	*Higher loan amount for energy efficient houses made of wood.* http://www.seb-bank.de
Switzerland	*Various Banks*	*Almost all smaller county banks offer green or energy-efficient mortgages; including reduced interest rates and higher loan amounts (see: Energia, 2005, p. 5).*
US	*Fannie Mae and Department of Housing and Urban Development*	*Energy efficient mortgage: Lower downpayment requirement; closing costs can be financed; higher loan amount* http://www.hud.gov/offices/hsg/sfh/eem/energy-r.cfm
US	*Indigo Financial Group*	*Higher Loan Amount; the costs for the energy efficiency improvements are added onto the appraised value of the home.* http://www.energyefficientmortgages.com/
UK	*Norwich and Peterborough Building Society*	*Green Mortgage: offered is a discount of 0.25% off the interest rates of the bank's standard products for the first two years of the mortgage term.* http://www.npbs-commercial-mortgages.co.uk/products.html
UK	*Co-operative Bank*	*Green Mortgage: lower interest rates; in addition the bank uses a share of the mortgage payments to financially support the organisation Climate Care, an organisation dedicated to helping solve global warming problems.* http://www.co-operativebank.co.uk/

3.2.5 Insurance practices

Already in 1994, Franklin Nutter[60] stated that 'the insurance business is first in line to be affected by climate change. It is clear that global warming could bankrupt the industry' (cited in Mills et al., 2002, p. 16). During the last decades, adverse weather-related events increased dramatically in both frequency and extent (IPCC, 2001a and Munich Re, 2006a). The insured losses caused by large natural events only increased more than 100-fold from 1.6 US$ billion in the 1950s to US$ 176 billion during the last ten years. Munich Re's Geo Risk Research (2006a) estimated that during 1980 and 2005 alone, the world's economies have endured over US$ 1.2 trillion in economic losses (not including fatalities). Figure 17 depicts long term trends in overall and insured losses between 1950 and 2005. According to Munich Re (2006a, p. 12) the year 2005 broke all records: 'As in the previous year, great natural catastrophes set new records again in 2005, and the trend towards higher and higher losses continues.' Weather-related natural catastrophes have never been so expensive, either for the world's economies or for the insurance industry. It was also one of the deadliest years of the last decade. Overall losses exceeded US$ 210 billion (the most expensive year before was 1995 with

---

[60] At that time president of the Reinsurance Association of America

US$ 175 billion, in original values) and insured losses reached unprecedented dimensions: the year's overall balance for the global insurance industry was US$ 94 billion.

Figure 17: *Overall losses and insured losses caused by large natural catastrophes in US$ – Absolute values and long-term trends 1950-2005 (adopted from Munich Re, 2006a, p. 13)*

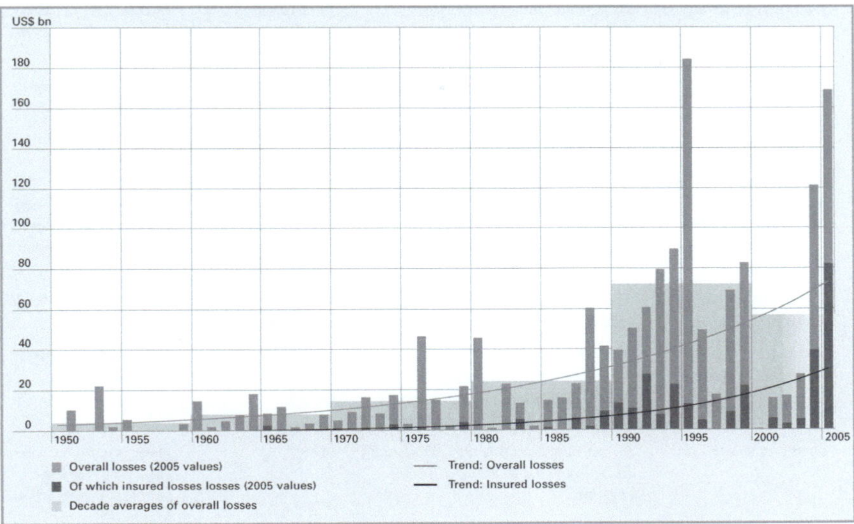

According to IPCC (2001a) there is new and stronger evidence that most of the global warming observed over the last 50 years is attributable to human activities. Furthermore, the trend of global warming and associated adverse natural events continues to expand and leads to increased vulnerability of social and economic systems. 'Recent history has shown that weather-related losses can stress insurance companies to the point of impaired profitability, consumer price increases, withdrawal of coverage, and elevated demand for publicly funded compensation and relief' (IPCC, 2001b, p. 40). Obviously, buildings and infrastructure works – and thus property insurers – are most vulnerable to extreme weather-related events, with exposures ranging from physical damage to disruption of business operations to adverse health and safety consequences for building occupants. This argument can be supported with two different sources of strong evidence: (1) In 2001 the IPCC projected changes in extreme climate-related phenomena during the 21st century and identified their effects on the insurance industry. Some of IPCC's findings are summarized in Table 15 which reveal that the property sector can and will be hit by *all* identified climate-related phenomena. (2) Of the 50 most severe natural catastrophes in 2005, 46 hit the property sector and resulted, amongst other adverse effects, in millions of houses being damaged or destroyed (Munich Re, 2006b).

Table 15: *Extreme climate-related phenomena and their effects on the insurance industry – Projected changes during the 21st century (based on IPCC, 2001b, pp. 39-41)*

Type of Event	Expected changes in extreme climate phenomena	Likelihood[61] (projected changes)	Sensitive sectors / Insurance branches
Temperature Extremes *- Heat waves, droughts*	*Higher maximum temperatures, more hot days and heat waves over nearly all land areas*	*Very likely*	*Health, life,* **property**, *crop, business interruption*
- Frost, frost heave	*Higher (increasing) minimum temperatures, fewer cold days, frost days, and cold waves over nearly all land areas*	*Very likely*	*Health, crop,* **property**, *business interruption, vehicle*
Precipitation Extremes *- Flash flood, flood, inundation, mudslide*	*More intense precipitation events*	*Very likely over many areas*	**Property**, *flood, vehicle, crop, business interruption, marine, life, health*
- Summer drought, land subsidence, wildfire	*Increased summer drying and associated risk of drought*	*Likely in a few areas*	*Crop,* **property**, *health*
- Snowstorm, ice storm, avalanche, hailstorm	*Increased intensity of mid-latitude storms (changes in regional distribution of tropical cyclones are possible but have not been examined)*	*Little agreement among current models*	*Crop, vehicle,* **property**, *aviation*
- Drought and flood	*Intensified droughts and floods with El Niňo events in many different regions*	*Likely*	**Property**, *flood, vehicle, crop, marine, business interruption, life, health*
Wind extremes *- Mid-latitude windstorms, tornadoes*	*Increased intensity of mid-latitude storms*	*Little agreement among current models*	**Property**, *vehicle, aviation, marine, life, business interruption*
- Tropical storms, including cyclones, hurricanes, and typhoons	*Increase in tropical cyclone peak wind intensities, mean and peak precipitation intensities (changes in regional distribution of tropical cyclones are possible but have not been examined)*	*Likely over some areas*	**Property**, *vehicle, aviation, marine, business interruption, life*
Other extremes *- Lightning*	*Refer to entries above for higher temperatures, increased tropical and mid-latitude storms*	*Refer to relevant entries above*	*Life,* **property**, *vehicle, aviation, marine, business interruption*
- Tidal surge (associated with onshore gales), coastal inundation	*Refer to entries above for increased tropical cyclones, Asian summer monsoon, and intensity of mid-latitude storms*	*Refer to relevant entries above*	*Life, marine,* **property**, *crop*
- Flood and drought	*Increased Asian summer monsoon precipitation variability*	*Likely*	*Crop,* **property**, *health, life*

---

[61] Likelihood refers to judgemental estimates of confidence: very likely (90-99% chance); likely (60-90% chance)

Insurance companies' exposure to major financial losses through damaged or destroyed buildings and infrastructure works is highest in megacities such as Tokyo, New York, Seoul, or Mexico City. Today, there are 15 cities with more than 10 million inhabitants, 3 cities with more than 20 million, and 1 city, Tokyo, with more than 35 million. Rural-to-urban migration is a megatrend, particularly in developing countries. This development presents major opportunities for the insurance industry because

> *'For every high-rise building, every underground railway system and every manufacturing company – and of course also for the people who live and work in the cities – there is a need for insurance. [...] The risks that go hand in hand with global urbanisation are also large, however. Owing to the high concentration of people, values and infrastructure in a very confined area, the loss potentials in megacities are very much higher than in rural areas. Consequently, even small occurrences can cause severe losses. [...] The long-term risks are much more serious though, with many megacities being virtually predestined to suffer major natural disasters' (Munich Re, 2005, p. 4).*

The insurance and risk management industry's responses to increasing threats imposed by climate change have been identified by Mills (2003a and 2003b). He argues that while a number of insurers have given some attention to the issue, the vast majority has not publicly indicated an opinion. 'Some have taken definitive positions that there is a threat, while others have adopted equally strong views to the contrary. Some have elected to pursue research while promoting disaster preparedness. Others have adopted a strictly 'wait-and-see' stance' (Mills, 2003b, pp. 262-263). These findings are based on a review of actions undertaken by 52 insurers and reinsurers, 5 brokers, 7 insurance organisations and 13 non-insurance organisations in this arena. The actions undertaken can be grouped into the categories of: information, education and demonstration; financial incentives; specialised policies and products; direct investment to promote energy efficiency and renewables; value-added customer service and inspections; efficient codes, standards and policies; research and development; and in-house energy management in insurer-owned properties. But only few insurers have yet taken a more long-term approach, focusing on the roots of climate change rather than simply preparing for it (see Mills, 2003b, p. 268-271).

Climate change, however, is not the only issue representing a serious threat to insurers. The other big threat is represented by unsafe or unhealthy working conditions for building occupants and construction workers. This argument can be backed up by referring to the increasing losses for insurers caused by compensation claims of construction workers who suffer health damages from asbestos as well as by increasing cost for the reparation of occupational diseases. For example, Tillinghast - Towers Perrin (an actuarial consulting firm) has estimated that cumulative global losses from asbestos claims will reach US$ 200 billion. Insurers will be liable for 61% of this amount while the remaining 39% will come from defendant companies that have exhausted their insurance coverage (Angelina and Biggs, 2001). Such claims do not only have direct impact in terms of compensations costs but can also result in share price losses of the companies involved: the German newsmagazine Der Spiegel (2002) reported substantial share price losses (up to 50 %) of companies like ABB, Bayer, DaimlerChrysler, Fresenius Medical Care and Saint-Gobain during July and October 2002 caused by expected asbestos compensation claims. As a consequence, insurers are hit twice since they are major investors in financial markets.

The reparation costs for occupational diseases in several European countries have been calculated by Eurogip (2004) and are displayed in Table 16 [62]. It has to be noted that the large differences in the displayed figures are due to several reasons such as number of insured people, nature and quantity of occupational diseases in each country and great diversity of compensation system. For example, in Belgium, Denmark and Italy, most costs are covered by the health insurance system or the national health services; the occupational disease insurers pay only the co-payment rate or a few specific treatments not otherwise covered (for a detailed explanation see Eurogip, 2004). Figure 18 depicts most commonly recognised occupational diseases and their share in total costs of compensation.

Table 16: *Insurance organisations' total costs for the reparation of occupational diseases in 2000 (Eurogip, 2004, p. 6)*

Country	Costs (in million €)	Insured population (in million	Ratio per 100,000 insured persons (in million €)
Austria	*29.3*	*4.24*	*0.69*
Belgium	*334*	*2.66*	*12.57*
Denmark	*67*	*2.53*	*2.65*
Germany	*1,223*	*34*	*3.59*
Italy	*1,069*	*18.3*	*5.84*
Portugal	*36.7*	*5.11*	*0.72*
Switzerland	*46.5*	*3.44*	*2.11*

---

[62] The amounts indicated exclude the administrative costs of the insurance organisations (wages, operating expenses, etc.) and expenses entailed in the collective prevention of occupational diseases, such as financial support for preventive measures or the production of informative materials designed for a sector of activity or a geographic region.

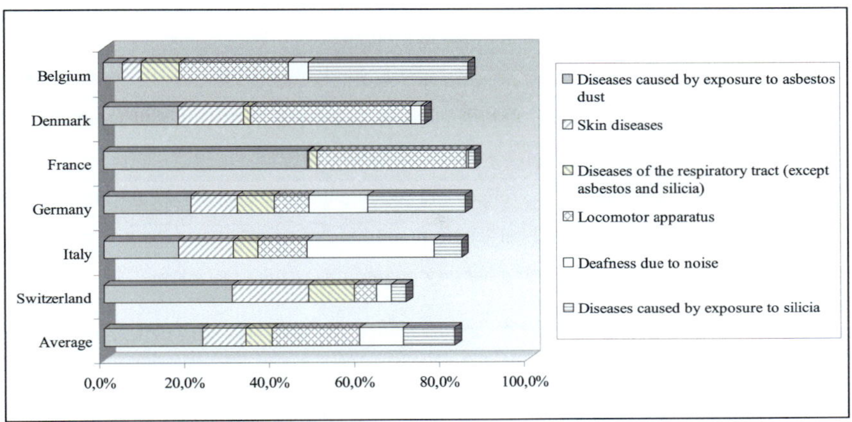

The circumstance that losses from litigation and compensation can be expected to rise dramatically in future years – for the insurance industry but also for various actors of all other business sectors – can best be explained by referring to the so-called 'changing landscape of liability'. According to the strategy consultancy SustainAbility (2004), companies across all business sectors are at growing risk from litigation and liability more generally as a result of a well funded litigation industry. The landscape of liability – and therefore the risks for companies and to shareholder value – is changing rapidly: legal liability is deepening while moral liability is hardening; i.e. they are converging (see Figure 19). This viewpoint is based on six key assumptions put forward by SustainAbility (2004); these are:

- The causes of action, standards of evidence and procedural rules that courts either tolerate or require are all shifting to describe a new legal landscape in which business must operate.
- Business is vulnerable to new forms of 'legal activism'; e.g. actions undertaken by NGOs are shifting from attacking to exploiting legislation, and a new generation of lawyers is arriving, many of whom put correcting social and environmental injustice ahead of salary and career development.
- A shift in societal values and expectations towards more morally acceptable behaviour as well as a corresponding mistrust of industry can be observed; this feeds a demand for greater corporate accountability through new standards of governance, new disclosure requirements and accounting rules.

- The requirement to internalise social and environmental costs is bringing business into the firing line of liability for its past and future impacts resulting from corporate actions which are perceived to be 'irresponsible'.

- Technical innocence or escaping accountability through legal expertise and subtle arguments on points of legal interpretation are becoming increasingly unacceptable in a society which expects sound behaviour standards.

- Laws and regulations often reflect and follow changing societal values and expectations; i.e. an emerging and hardening moral liability affects a company commercially before it is felt as a accounting liability imposed by regulation or law.

Figure 19: *The changing landscape of liability (based on SustainAbility, 2004, pp. 4-6)*

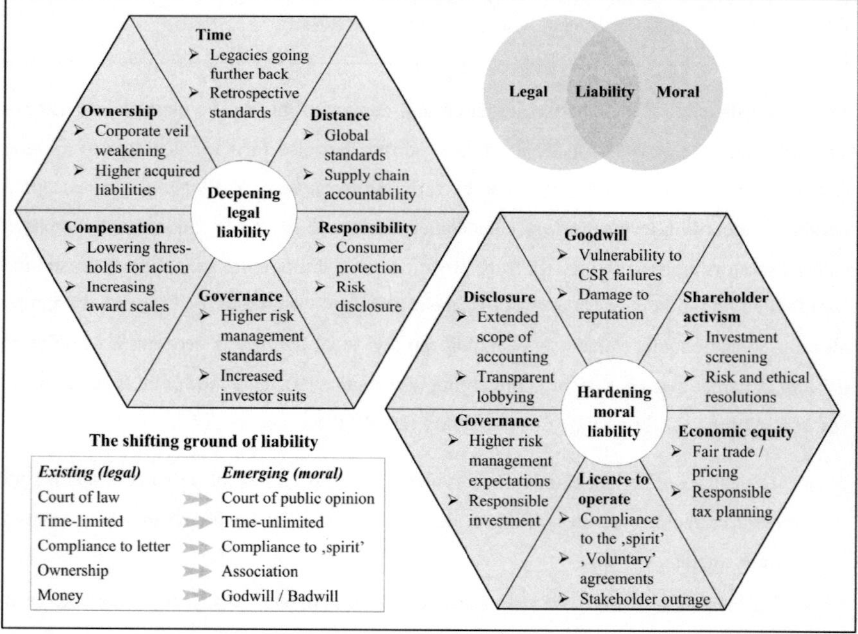

In summary, there is now a series of strong arguments for the insurance industry to support and incentivise sustainable building: on the one hand, the built environment is responsible for a large extent of global resource use and pollution; and thus, for climate change which is in return responsible for increasing natural catastrophes which clearly have the potential to seriously threaten the industry (e.g. through insured buildings' vulnerability to all types of extreme weather-phenomena). On the other hand, the property sector, and thus, property insurers are equally vulnerable to the threats imposed by the increasing risks from litigation and liability due to buildings' substantial role within socio-economic systems. But research conducted by Drouet (2003) and Mills (2003a and 2003b) revealed that supporting sustainable building through preferential insurance conditions or other measures is far from being a mainstream activity within the insurance industry. For example, Mills (2003a) reported that Hanover Insurance Company, US, offers a 10 % credit on homeowner property insurance rates for energy efficient homes. However, this product is not marketed on the company's website.[63] Indeed, examples for the offering of preferential insurance conditions – arguably the insurance industry's most effective or convincing instrument to promote sustainable building – are even harder to identify than it is the case with preferential credit conditions in the banking business.[64] This finding is contradicted by the fact that the world's largest insurance organisations have issued a Statement of Environmental Commitment already in 1995: 'We will reinforce the attention given to environmental risks in our core activities. These activities include risk management, loss prevention, product design, claims handling and asset management. [...] We support insurance products and services that promote sound environmental practice through measures such as loss prevention and contract terms and conditions' (UNEP, 1995). The absence of widely available preferential insurance conditions for sustainable buildings is even less understandable if one considers the many loss prevention benefits that these buildings have to offer:

- Sustainable design and building practices substantially reduce the risk of being held liable for paying compensations to construction workers and building occupants (Kats et al., 2003).

- Many sustainable design features reduce the likelihood of physical damages and losses in facilities. For example, Mills (2003a) identified a wide a range of energy efficient and renewable energy technologies that offer such loss prevention benefits; e.g. water pipe insulation; this is a simple retrofit that saves energy and reduces the likelihood of freeze damage (frozen water pipes have been identified as an important cause of losses in Europe and North America).

- Business interruption risks (e.g. caused by power outages) can be reduced by facilities that derive their energy from on-site resources and/or have energy efficiency features.

- A subset of energy efficient and renewable energy technologies make buildings less vulnerable to natural disasters, especially heat catastrophes (Mills, 2003b).

---

[63] See: www.hanover.com/thg/personal/home/homeowners.htm
[64] In fact, the author has not been able to identify (through internet research) *a single* insurance company worldwide that promotes (on their website) and offers preferential insurance conditions for sustainable buildings.

A possible reason for this lack of insurer involvement in sustainable building issues may be due to the circumstance that the connection between sustainable design features and reduced risk is not yet well-established within the industry because appropriate assessment schemes and 'convincing' long-term studies are not yet widely available. Nonetheless, it can be expected that this lack of insurer involvement is likely to change in the near future. For example, the Association of British Insurers has recently used catastrophe models to examine the financial implications of climate change through its effects on extreme storms (hurricanes, typhoons, and windstorms). They found that climate change could significantly increase the costs of windstorm damage and of flooding (particularly in Europe) and that increased losses could raise the costs of capital and increase the volatility of insurance markets. The report concludes as follows: 'Many costs of climate change could be avoided by taking action today' (ABI, 2005, p. 5).

3.3   Sustainable development in property and construction

3.3.1   Successes and failures

The idea of environmentally friendly (i.e. 'green') – and later environmentally and socially friendly as well as financially sound (i.e. 'sustainable') – building is not a new concept. It has been discussed, promoted and applied by certain actors of the construction and property sector since decades. Already the ancient Greeks and Romans used solar design features in their houses; the first 'organic' buildings[65] of modern times have been built during the late 1890s and the first solar-heated houses were built during the 1930s and 1940s by George F. Keck and William Keck (Keck & Keck) and other architects in several suburbs of Chicago (Butti, 1980). Sustainable development in property and construction is a story of great success and of great failures, however. As such, the performance of the property and construction sector in contributing to sustainable development is both impressive and disappointing. On the one hand, much more has been achieved than a sceptic might have anticipated but on the other hand, far less has been done than that minimum for which a committed proponent of sustainable building might have hoped. Reviewing all these successful steps and disappointments is elusive and cannot be achieved within the scope of this dissertation. For this reason, two key successes and two key failures will be discussed in the following:

---

[65] See: www.organische-architectuur.org/de/frameset.html or www.greatbuildings.com/types/topics/organic.html

Key successes

(1) The knowledge, the methodologies and the products to build more sustainable (i.e. to squeeze more utility for owners, users and the wider public out of the lowest possible use of land and throughput of energy and raw materials) are available. This information is spread all over the world; notably through the Sustainable Building conferences which resulted from collaborative effort and action undertaken by the International Council for Research and Innovation in Building and Construction (CIB), the International Initiative for a Sustainable Built Environment (iiSBE) and the United Nations Environment Programme (UNEP). Since 1998 a series of both international and regional conferences on sustainable building have taken place. These conferences became the main events for knowledge and experience transfer, for stimulating research in the area of sustainable building as well as for demonstrating the various benefits of sustainable design. Also, the scope of these conferences constantly widened over time. While the first conferences (Vancouver in 1998, Maastricht in 2000, Oslo in 2002) were mainly tailored to the needs of northern climates and developed countries, seven regional conferences took place between 2004 and 2005 in order to feed regional issues into and prepare for the 2005 international conference which was held in Tokyo.[66] Furthermore, information on sustainable building issues is regularly published on various websites[67], by various organisations (see, for example, CIB, n.d, UNEP, 2003 and iiSBE, 2006) as well as within *Building Research & Information,* an international research journal edited by Richard Lorch. As result, there can be no doubt that the information necessary for shaping the built environment in a more sustainable manner is widely available.[68]

(2) The environmental, social and economic benefits of sustainable buildings are extensively researched, documented and illustrated in the literature. It is now generally agreed that sustainable buildings are more cost and energy efficient, effective, profitable and marketable than conventional buildings and that they exhibit increased functionality, serviceability, and adaptability as well as increased comfort and well-being of occupants while at the same time offering loss prevention benefits and reduced negative impacts on the natural environment (see, for example, Wilson et al., 1998; Yates, 2001; Heerwagen, 2002; Mills, 2003a and 2003b; Kats et al., 2003 and RICS, 2004a and 2005).

---

[66] More information on past and forthcoming events as well as the conferences' main outcomes can be accessed through various websites. See for example: www.sb04.org/iisbe/SB04/index5_overview.htm; www.sb05.com or www.greenbuilding.ca

[67] Two examples are: www.advancedbuildings.org and www.wbdg.org

[68] A restriction needs to be made here: the sustainable building solutions discussed at these conferences and in most publications on sustainable building issues do focus on creating buildings 'more' sustainable; i.e. to produce fewer negative impacts. Approaches on how to build 'genuinely' sustainable (i.e. to produce more positive effects) are, however, rarely discussed. This is one of the key failures which will be discussed below.

Kats et al. (2003) produced a comprehensive and well-documented cost benefit analysis of sustainable buildings and investigated the financial gains associated with incorporating sustainable design features into new building projects. They concluded that minimal increases in upfront costs of about 2% to support sustainable design would, on average, result in life cycle savings of 20% of total construction costs. For example, an initial upfront investment of up to €100.000 to incorporate sustainable building features into a €5 million project would result in a saving of €1 million in today's Euros (discounted by a 5% interest rate) over the life of the building, assumed conservatively to be 20 years. 'From a life cycle savings standpoint, savings resulting from investment in sustainable design and construction dramatically exceed any additional upfront costs' (Kats et al., 2003, p. vii).

Other financial benefits such as increases in market value due to improved marketability or occupant productivity gains are more difficult to evidence empirically. However, this evidence exists: One of the first came from an American study. Nevin and Watson (1998) calculated that market values of residential homes increases US$ 20 for every US$ 1 decrease in annual utility cost and that cost-effective energy efficiency investments do appear to be reflected in residential housing market values. Furthermore, extensive research conducted by Kumar and Fisk (2002); Heerwagen (2002); Heerwagen et al. (2004); and Kampschroer and Heerwagen, (2005) identified strong correlations between sustainable design features (e.g. natural lighting, thermal comfort, air quality, worker-controlled temperature and ventilation, etc.) and reduced illness symptoms, reduced absenteeism and significantly increases of measured productivity of workforce. These findings support earlier results of the Probe studies (Bordass et al., 1999) and a resulting statement by Leaman and Bordass (1999) that losses or gains of up to 15% of turnover in a typical office organization might be attributable to the design, management and use of the indoor environment. Similar evidence is also available from the Rocky Mountain Institute which identified productivity gains of six to sixteen percent, including decreased absenteeism and improved quality of work, from energy-efficient design. Since companies spend an average of 70 times as much money (per square foot per year) on employee salaries as on energy, an increase of just one percent in productivity can nearly offset a company's entire annual energy bill (Rocky Mountain Institute, 1998).

In addition, there are now a number of studies available which refute the commonly held misbelief that sustainable buildings cost up to 15% more in terms of capital cost to build from the outset than conventional buildings. For example, Matthiessen and Morris (2003) found that many building projects can achieve sustainable design within (!) their initial budget, or with very small supplemental funding (< 3% of initial budget). Other sources for information on the costs of sustainable construction are: Bartlett and Howard (2000), Bordass (2000) and

Mackley (2002). To conclude, there can be no doubt that sustainable buildings clearly outperform their conventional counterparts. Figure 20 summarizes the links between sustainable design features and economic benefits. Obviously, these features positively impact on a building's worth and market value. First evidence exists that this relationship is also recognized outside research circles and academia. Recently, a report published by the RICS concluded that a clear 'link is beginning to emerge between the market value of a building and its green features and related performance' (RICS, 2005, p. 3).

Figure 20: *The links between sustainable design features and economic benefits*

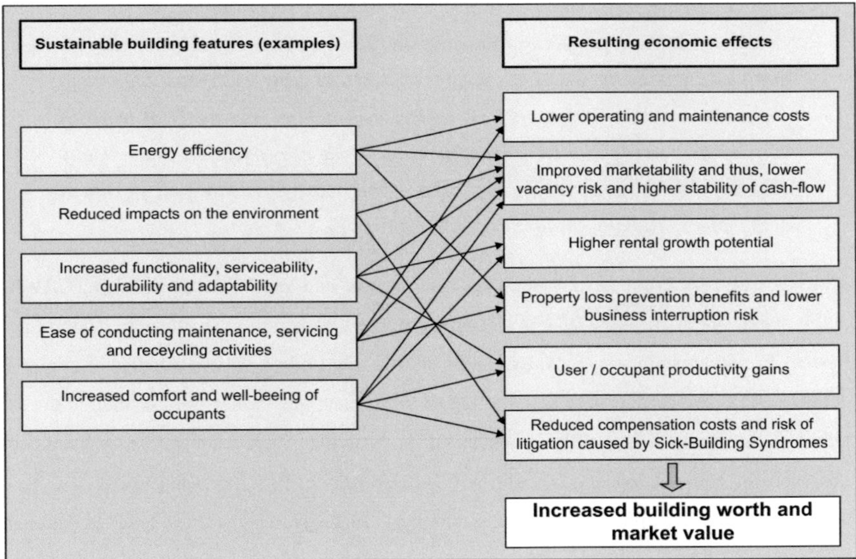

Key failures

(1) Not all, but most approaches to sustainable construction focus on using energy and materials more efficiently; i.e. doing more with less. Of course, eco-efficiency measures[69] are important but they are no longer sufficient. A report published by the World Resources Institute (WRI) in 2000 revealed that between 1975 and 1996 the total quantities of conventional wastes, emissions, and discharges in Austria, Germany, Japan, the Netherlands, and the USA

---

[69] Eco-efficiency can be described as a ratio between two elements: environmental impact (which has to be reduced) and value of production or added value respectively (which has to be increased). According to the World Business Council for Sustainable Development (WBCSD) eco-efficiency is a management strategy that links financial and environmental performance to create more value with less ecological impact. The WBCSD defines eco-efficiency 'as being achieved by the delivery of competitively priced goods and services that satisfy human needs and bring quality of life, while progressively reducing ecological impacts and resource intensity throughout the life cycle, to a level at least in line with the Earth's estimated carrying capacity.'
(See: http://www.wbcsd.org/includes/getTarget.asp?type=p&id=NzA&doOpen=1&ClickMenu=LeftMenu)

have increased by between 16 and 29% – despite the rapid rise of e-commerce and the shift over several decades from heavy industries toward knowledge-based and service industries; i.e. the increasing efficiency in using natural resources.

> *'Over the next 50 years, while the world's population is forecast to increase by 50 percent, global economic activity is expected to increase roughly fivefold. Conventional demand studies suggest that global energy consumption is likely to rise nearly threefold and manufacturing activity at least threefold, driven largely by industrialization and infrastructure growth in developing regions. Global throughput of material is also likely to triple, according to conventional projections. These projections indicate that some measure of "decoupling" is probable: that is, the world economy is expected to grow faster than the rate of resource use. However, a 300 percent rise in energy and material use still represents a substantial increase. Unless economic growth can be dramatically decoupled from resource use and waste generation, environmental pressures will increase rapidly' (Matthews et al., 2000, p. V).*

More recently, the European Topic Centre on Resource and Waste Management (ETCRWM, 2004) stated that total waste quantities remain on the increase in most Western, Central and Eastern European countries, Caucasus and Central Asia. Only a limited number of countries across Europe can demonstrate de-coupling of total waste generation from economic growth although the evidence is mainly inconclusive. In particular, increasing quantities have been observed for construction and demolition (C & D) waste: 'This increasing trend in C & D waste generation is unlikely to change in coming years as growing welfare leads to demands for new and better accommodation, increased renovation and demolition of old buildings' (ETCRWM, 2004, p. 42). Thus, while we are being green-washed by notions of sustainability from governments, industry and the media, in reality the cities are developing much as they always have, with poor planning and design, more and larger buildings consuming more re-sources, energy and water, and little sense of creating real communities (Tidswell, 2005). 'Albert Einstein said that no problem can be solved from the same consciousness that created it. Yet, looking at the current state of sustainable construction, that is exactly what we have been trying to do. The majority of sustainable construction solutions are not focused on fash-ioning a new world model that will be more sustainable because the nature of our relation-ships with the biophysical environment and with each other has actually changed. Instead, these solutions are only trying to keep the old world ticking for as long as possible' (du Plessis, 2003, p. 2). Using less energy to heat and cool high-performance buildings, using less toxic materials to reduce impacts on building occupants, occupying and destroying less land to reduce ecological footprints or sending less building material waste to landfills does not address the roots of the problem; it simply limits the negative impact of poor design (McDonough and Braungart, 2003).

> *'Being less bad is not being good. [...] As long as you're destructive, you can feel guilty and want to be less bad. But if you're actually productive, you can feel good. [...] Imagine a house that makes oxygen, sequesters carbon, fixes nitrogen, distils water, builds soil, creates habitats for hundreds of species, accrues solar energy as fuel, makes complex sugars and food, creates microclimates, changes colours with the seasons, is always beautiful, is always different, and self-replicates' (McDonough, 2005a, p. 40 and 2005b, p. 8).*

Buildings' internal ecosystems need not to be divorced from their surroundings. Buildings that are, indeed, productive and regenerative by design are no utopian dream. It is entirely possible and financially even more advantageous to shift from currently prevailing sustainable construction approaches that focus on *less waste* and *fewer negative impacts* to those approaches that simply reveal *more positive* effects animated by the intelligence of nature. This can be called 'biomimetic', 'cradle-to-cradle' or 'closed-loop' design and does not only apply to buildings and building materials but to all products and manufacturing systems.[70] This design approach takes nature as model, mentor and measure; it is based on studying nature's best ideas and then imitating these designs and processes to solve human problems (Benyus, 1997).

Applied to the construction sector, this approach can lead to breakthroughs in energy efficiency, environmental release, user comfort and cost performance; i.e. to producing genuinely sustainable buildings that can serve as utility providers rather than as energy and resource consumers. According to McDonough et al. (2003), three key design principles can be found in the intelligence of natural systems. These are: (1) Waste equals food; (2) use current solar income; and (3) celebrate diversity. McDonough and Braungart (2002) argue that when designers employ the intelligence of natural systems they can create products, industrial systems, buildings, and even regional plans that allow nature and commerce to fruitfully co-exist.

Applying these approaches in the property and construction sector would mean a shift 'from inanimate, one-size-fits-all structures into which we plug power and largely toxic materials, to buildings as life-support systems embedded in the material and energy flows of particular

---

[70] More information on biomimicry can be found here: www.biomimicry.net; an overview on cradle-to-cradle designed products and certification systems is provided here: www.mbdc.com/

places. The presence of such buildings around the world suggests that human activity can indeed create footprints to delight in rather than lament' (McDonough and Braungart, 2003, p. 14).[71] Imagine a place with buildings designed as organic sculptures, all different, but all invigorating and sustaining the surrounding world. 'If confined to private life, the sphere of [their] activity is narrower; but [their] influence is all benign and gentle. If exalted into a higher station, mankind and prosperity reap the fruit of [their] labours' (Hume, 1751, Section I, Part II). Imagining a better place to live appears a difficult thing to do. For a beautiful vision of such places, see: du Plessis (2003, pp. 10-12).

(2) Sustainable building is a growing market; however, it is still a niche market. Figures on the size of the global sustainable construction market are difficult to obtain. However, one way of approaching the extent and growth of sustainable building activity within the commercial property sector is to refer to the number of buildings certified or rated with one of the numerous 'green' or 'sustainable' building assessment tool. This is because commercial property developers or investors usually aim demonstrating that they actually have considered sustainability issues within their projects. Two popular assessment schemes are LEED from the US and BREEAM from the UK. According to Kibert and Grosskopf (2005), the number of registered buildings using the US Green Building Council's LEED assessment system has increased from 0 in 1998 to almost 1800 in March 2005, representing a total of 22 million square metres.[72] The number of certified buildings has increased from 0 to 180 during the same time period. According to the Building Research Establishment (BRE), 600 office buildings have been assessed by using the BREEAM scheme since its launch in 1990.[73] While these figures are not indicative of the total market size, they show that sustainable construction is taking root but that there is much room for improvement. The number of certified buildings available represents only a small fraction of the overall market. Another possibility to approach the extent of sustainable construction activity is to review major construction companies' attitudes to sustainability. This has been done by Myers (2005) on the basis of publicly available information from websites and the Financial Times Annual Report Service. Myers reviewed 42 major construction firms listed on the UK Stock Exchange and concluded that some of the large companies in the construction sector are *beginning* to acknowledge sustainability. 'They recognise that a business is no longer judged solely on the economic value added by a company's activity; it is also judged on the social and environmental value

---

[71] For more information on living buildings and related technologies see: www.livingmachines.com; www.worldchanging.com; www.mcdonoughpartners.com/projects.shtm and www.eco.barkingcrickets.org
[72] For comparison: Washington, D.C. alone has 23.8 million square metres of office space (DEGI, 2005).
[73] See: http://www.bre.co.uk/service.jsp?id=51

they add (or destroy). Examples of best practice to minimise the negative impacts and develop the obvious business opportunities are stated in their reports. However, it also clear that many companies, particularly the small unlisted ones, have a long way to go, before they can effectively manage the opportunities that emerge from the sustainability agenda. [...] even though the construction industry has been given its own sustainability agenda there is nothing to suggest that it has engaged more efficiently than any other industry. In fact, the little evidence there is would suggest the contrary' (Myers, 2005, p. 784).

Although information on both appropriate design and construction approaches as well as on the various benefits of sustainable buildings is available, this information and awareness is apparently diffusing very slowly through to investors, builders, occupiers and property professionals such as estate agents, valuation professionals and professional advisors. The mainstreaming of sustainable construction and property investment is still constrained by a misalignment between suppliers and those demanding property assets for occupation and/or investment. This misalignment became known as the 'vicious circle of blame' which has been first conceptualized by David Cadman (2000). The vicious circle consists of (1) occupiers who would like to have sustainable buildings but who argue that there are very few available; of (2) constructors who can build sustainable buildings but who argue that the developers do not ask for them; of (3) developers who would ask for sustainable buildings but who argue that the investors will not pay for them; and of (4) investors who would invest in sustainable buildings but who argue that there is no demand for them.

While acknowledging the need for appropriate laws, regulations, incentives and for undertaking the many other measures to promote sustainable building, it is argued that bursting this vicious circle of blame will not be achieved within an acceptable time frame unless actors of property markets are provided with appropriate feedback on both the environmental and social aspects of building performance as well as on its various interrelations with financial performance. One day, even the greatest sceptic might be convinced that sustainable buildings make sense financially because, for example, many competitors might have successfully integrated sustainability issues into property investment and management processes. However, time is running short and much more needs to be done (e.g. developing decision tools for investors and valuation tools for appraisers and advisors) to align environmental and social considerations with economic return in property. In order to achieve this, a framework or performance system is required that allows measuring environmental, social and economic performance along the life cycle of buildings. This will be discussed in the next chapter.

3.3.2 Measuring single building's contribution to sustainable development[74]

3.3.2.1 Constituents of sustainable buildings

As shown earlier, the concept of sustainable development is very broad. As such, it allows many different perceptions of what is actually meant by a sustainable building to be grouped under its roof. As a result of these different perceptions it becomes difficult to measure a building's contribution to sustainable development since there is no agreement yet on what to measure and how. This was also a result of the Central and Eastern European Sustainable Building conference held in Warsaw 2004. It was argued that the definition of sustainable development needs to be 'translated' or operationalised for the following areas:

- cities, urban areas and the national building stock;
- the industry (including construction, housing and commercial property); and
- single buildings and construction works.

Since the focus of this dissertation is more on single buildings and associated plots of land, the other areas will not be addressed in detail. For a discussion on cities' and urban areas' contribution to sustainable development see Fisher (2005) and Downton (n.d.). The construction industry's contribution to sustainable development has been investigated by Pearce (2003 and 2006).

In order to classify sustainable buildings it is possible to start with general areas of protection which can be deduced form the interpretation of sustainable development provided above (see also Rogall, 2004, p. 31). These are as follows:

- Protection and restoration of the natural environment / ecosystem,
- Protection of natural resources,
- Protection of human health and, wherever possible, improvement of well-being,
- Protection and promotion of social values and of public goods,
- Protection of capital and material goods, and
- Protection and extension of people's capabilities.

Transferred to buildings and their associated plots of land, several requirements can be formulated that help to classify sustainable buildings. These are shown in Table 17.

---

[74] This section is partially based on Lützkendorf and Lorenz (2005 and 2006a) and on Lorenz and Lützkendorf (2005b)

Table 17: *Requirements for sustainable buildings (adopted and modified from BMVBW, 2001 and Lützkendorf and Lorenz, 2005)*

• *Minimization of life cycle costs / cost effectiveness from a full financial cost-return perspective,* • *Reduction of land use and use of hard surfaces, i.e. reduction of ecological footprints* • *Reduction of raw material / resource depletion,* • *Closing of material flows; adoption of closed-loop design and construction approaches to the greatest extent which is technically/organically possible and economically feasible,* • *Avoidance of hazardous substances,* • *Reduction of CO_2-emissions and other pollutants,* • *Reduction of impacts on the environment; i.e. integration with natural systems* • *Protection of health and comfort of building occupants / users as well as of neighbours* • *Preservation and promotion of buildings' cultural value*	*Minimising adverse effects*
• *Maximization of the buildings' utility / serviceability* • *Maximization of the buildings' functionality and adaptability*	*Maximizing capability*

In short, a sustainable building squeezes the maximum utility for owners, users and the wider public out of the lowest possible use of land and throughput of energy and raw materials. The measurement of buildings' contribution to sustainable development or their 'sustainability performance' respectively becomes increasingly important for two reasons: (1) Sustainability performance assessments are increasingly required for several reasons, e.g. lending, adherence to performance based building guidelines, reporting, investment analysis and for demonstrating compliance with legal requirements. (2) Performance assessment is the only way to achieve feedback from the built environment's triple bottom line; i.e. to determine if a single building, a property portfolio, a stock of buildings or the property and construction sector as part of the national economy is actually sustainable or at least on a sustainable development path.

3.3.2.2 Performance assessment framework

Property performance is a very broad concept and performance means different things to different people. But in a very general sense, performance can be defined as behaviour in use. Regarding the performance based building approach, performance is understood as the degree of compliance of user/owner requirements with corresponding building characteristics and attributes. This notion of performance has its seeds in the area of describing and assessing the fulfilment of functional requirements (functionality and serviceability) and its development has strongly been influenced and affected by F. Szigeti and G. Davis (see Szigeti and Davis, 2003; Szigeti et al., 2004). Developments in the area of performance based building can be retraced within the literature; see for example Lee and Barrett (2003), Meacham et al. (2005), Bakens et al. (2005) and Huovila (2005). A recent overview and summary can also be found in Lützkendorf et al. (2005). Currently, a variety of efforts are being made on an international and European level to define criteria and indicators that determine several aspects of property performance. These criteria and indicators do no longer relate to aspects of functionality and serviceability only. The updating of performance assessment criteria is currently extending user demands into the realm of societal and environmental requirements.

However, research activities concerning the area of performance based building on the one hand and sustainable building on the other have developed relatively independent from each other in the past. Now they are beginning to merge. Research in the area of 'green' building was focussed on the assessment of environmental and (to some extent) health-related attributes of buildings. The further development towards a 'sustainable building' approach led to the inclusion of economic and social aspects which resulted in a substantially widened scope of assessment criteria. It is increasingly recognised that a building's functionality and serviceability represent major components to be considered in sustainable building assessments. This is because functionality and serviceability are categories required to describe a building's benefits or 'outputs', while costs, energy and mass flows and environmental impacts represent building related expenses or 'inputs'. Concerning sustainable buildings the description of the functional building performance is therefore a precondition for safeguarding comparability of building concepts, and for validating the fulfilment of building users' needs. Also, the assessment of performance must not be restricted to the building itself but must be viewed within a wider context which also involves processes such as commissioning and management. This is because a building designed with strong emphasis on sustainability issues may not reach its targets because of poor operation and management. Conversely, an 'average' building may perform better due to good operation and management.

Due to different starting points concerning property performance assessment approaches, there is now an unwieldy number of criteria and indicators which introduce various ways of measuring various aspects of performance.[75] As a result, complexity becomes overwhelming and needs to be reduced by concentrating on a set of key performance indicators (KPI's) which can be understood and applied by a wider public (e.g. company boards, households,

---

[75] For example, the European thematic network on construction and city-related sustainability indicators (CRISP) aims to develop and validate harmonised criteria and relevant indicators to measure the sustainability of construction projects. An extensive database of indicators is provided on the CRISP website: http://crisp.cstb.fr

professionals of property and financial markets, the media) and not only by specialised researchers and academics. Lützkendorf and Speer (2005) and Then and Clowes (2004) provide initial proposals in determining so-called overall property performance and in defining property specific KPI's. The transference of the performance approach on questions addressing all dimensions of sustainable development simultaneously is quite new. In this context property performance can be expressed by determining the degree of compliance between sustainability requirements formulated by stakeholders (e.g. awarding authorities, building owners/users, public, government, etc.) and corresponding building characteristics and attributes. In cases where it is not possible or appropriate to formulate stakeholder requirements or thresholds (which can be justified scientifically or by any other means), property performance can then be expressed by solely measuring and reporting relevant building characteristics and attributes in the form of unvalued (e.g. results of an inventory analysis), valued (e.g. results of an impact assessment) or qualitative information which can be used, for example, for benchmarking purposes or for the aggregation of assessment results on other levels (e.g. community, nation, region).

The latter issue is of critical importance since property performance assessments are only useful if they provide appropriate feedback tailored to the needs of the different stakeholders involved; i.e. assessments need to reveal performance aspects relevant for single actors, for certain groups of actors such as participants of different sectors as well as for communities, nations or regions. For example, if governments want to achieve Local Agenda 21 improvements, they need to undertake a variety of actions which includes introducing effective instruments that easily communicate these multi-dimensional policy goals and assess the performance in achieving objectives and targets as well as the effectiveness of certain policy actions ('sustainability controlling'). Therefore, the development of key performance sustain indicators involves the understanding of the networks of relationships between policy actors and the local or sector-specific context in which the indicators are being developed and applied to (see also: Rydin et al., 2003 and Astleithner and Hamedinger, 2003). Consequently, key performance indicators can comprise two different types of indicators. First, 'multi-level indicators' that can be aggregated at different levels (community, sector, region, and nation); examples for such indicators are CO_2-emmissions, depletion of non-renewable resources, share of renewables, waste production, and water and land use. Second, indicators with specific relevance for individual groups of actors; these indicators allow linking overall sustainability goals with existing economic, environmental and social interests and goals of actors. Examples for such indicators are indoor air quality, occupant satisfaction, life cycle or operating costs, and energy demand. The processes of assessing this information on the performance of buildings should be linked to or integrated with instruments and tools that are already in use by different groups of actors in order to save time and to make behaviour change easy (e.g. design and planning tools, controlling, reporting and portfolio analysis instruments, rating and due diligence processes, etc.).

The following Figure 21 shows an overall framework for sustainability assessment in property and construction; it includes examples of indicators, instruments and flows of information among various actors at different operational levels.

Figure 21: *Sustainability assessment framework for property and construction (Lorenz and Lützkendorf, 2005b)*

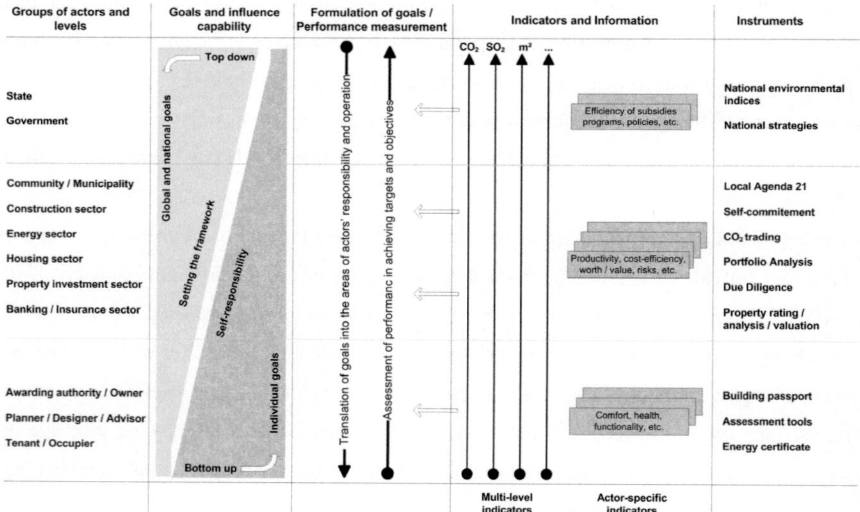

Methodological approaches and frameworks for assessing the performance of single buildings are currently being developed and standardised by the International Standardisation Organisation (ISO) within the scope of ISO TC 59[76] 'Building Construction' (notably SC 14 'Design Life' and SC 17 'Sustainability in building construction') and ISO TC 207[77] 'Environmental Management'. Furthermore, standardisation activities in this area are carried out by CEN (the European Committee for Standardization) within the scope of TC 350 ,Sustainability of Construction Works'. Amongst others, objects of standardisation are:

---

[76] See:
www.iso.org/iso/en/stdsdevelopment/tc/tclist/TechnicalCommitteeDetailPage.TechnicalCommitteeDetail?COMMID=1912
[77] See: www.tc207.org/

- calculation algorithms;

- assessment algorithms and procedures;

- performance aspects within buildings; and

- indicator frameworks.

In summary, current standardisation activities involve technical, functional, social, environmental and economic aspects. These activities and proposals can be arranged into an overall system of building performance. The following Figure 22 depicts different aspects of property performance within a framework of building-related information. It needs to be noted that the activities at ISO and CEN do not cover all aspects portrayed in Figure 22. On the basis of these building performance characteristics, the contribution of single buildings to sustainable development becomes measurable and distinguishable.

Figure 22: *Different aspects of property performance within an overall framework (Lützkendorf and Lorenz, 2006a)*

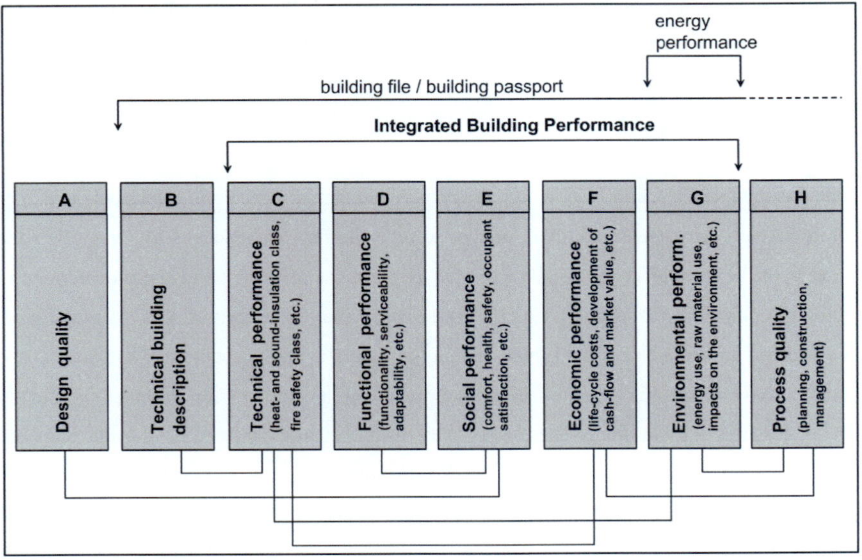

Ideally, this performance information is contained within a so-called building file or building passport. But building files are yet only issued occasionally on a voluntary basis and mainly for residential property. However, in the UK all sellers of dwellings will need to prepare a so called 'Home Information Pack' from 1 June 2007 onwards in order to inform prospective buyers.[78] The Home Information Pack consists of a set of documents providing information about a property such as copies of planning documents, warranties, deeds and a new document called the Home Condition Report, which assesses the condition of a property and its energy efficiency.

A good example for the commercial property sector is the electronic data exchange standard called PISCES which is currently being developed by major UK property market players (PISCES, 2004). The standard (which could be interpreted as an electronic building file for commercial property assets) does not yet contain references to sustainability performance aspects; however, since the standard is flexible and intended to evolve over time, these issues could and should be integrated.

3.3.2.3   Assessment methodologies and indicators

Besides essential technical and functional information, the description and assessment of a building's economic and environmental performance is usually established on the basis of life cycle costing (LCC) and life cycle assessment (LCA). For the description and assessment of a building's social performance, the methodological basics are not yet agreed upon or are still under discussion respectively. This will be discussed in more detail in the following:

The concepts of LCA and LCC within the construction and property industry have developed independently in response to either economic or environmental issues. LCC was originally developed in the mid-1960s to assist the US Department of Defence in the procurement of military equipment (Cole and Sterner, 2000). Today the application of LCC is much more widespread and encompasses all those techniques that take into account both initial costs and future costs and benefits (savings) of an investment over a certain period of time (e.g. the projected lifetime of a building). These techniques systematically consider all relevant costs and revenues associated with the acquisition and ownership of an asset and they are used to facilitate the effective choice between different project or building alternatives; e.g. to asses which design and construction technology choices have the greatest influence over the life cycle of a building, and by focusing on these areas, to evaluate if and how significant improvements can be made (Kishk and Al-Hajj, 1999). LCC calculations usually consist of the following elements:

---

[78] See: http://www.homeinformationpacks.gov.uk

- initial capital cost for design and construction or acquisition;
- management and operating costs;
- costs for maintenance and renovation, and;
- the costs incurred or benefited from the building's disposal.

Recently, however, attempts are being made to also include the income generated by the property within the calculation. An ISO standard under development currently investigates these issues (ISO DIS 15686-5). With LCC techniques it is possible to demonstrate economic benefits of sustainable design because less or smaller plant and equipment is required and buildings also consume fewer resources for their construction and during operation. But LCC techniques have several limitations, which have to be understood in order to interpret the results. For example, it is very difficult to estimate future maintenance and operation costs. Observation and longitudinal evidence are also needed to determine the life of building materials and components. Furthermore, very few owners pay all the costs of the acquisition and ownership of a building and therefore regard some costs more important than others. There is an ongoing discussion about the appropriate form of representation of LCC results depending on its application (e.g. capital value for general comparison, investment plans for the scheduling of payment flows, etc.). But despite these limitations, the well founded prognosis of life cycle costs is now seen as indispensable for the purpose of investment decisions and will continue to gain significance with the rising prevalence of BOT-models (built – operate – transfer).

Investment appraisal using cost data is relatively straightforward, compared to appraisal and comparison on the basis of environmental information, due to the wide range of data available and imprecise and diverging perceptions of good environmental performance (Edwards et al. 2000). LCA has been developed as a result of a more responsible attitude towards the environment. The basic framework and principles for conducting LCA are contained within ISO standard 14040. 'LCA methodologies have emerged as a means to profile the environmental performance of materials, components and buildings through time and have been generally accepted within the environmental research community as the only legitimate basis to compare competing alternatives' (Cole and Sterner 2000 p. 368). Usually LCA examines energy and mass flows in order to provide information on resource consumption and determine the origin of harmful environmental loads which have potential impacts on global warming, acidification, ozone depletion, biodiversity, eco-toxicity, human toxicity and on occupational and living health. A detailed description of LCA can be found in Guineé (2002) and in CLARINET (2002b). Due to the complexity of combining LCC- and LCA-based approaches, only few examples for a combination of economic and environmental issues in building assessments exist. The methodical basics for an 'integrated life cycle analysis' as well as a practical example are described in Kohler and Luetzkendorf (2002). While current assessment schemes take the issue of occupant health into consideration, there is less focus on occupant satisfaction, functional fit and productivity. LCA's do not provide information on what kind of building solutions work best in practice and why. This is the goal of post occupancy evaluation (POE). Zimring and Reizenstein (1980) defined POE's as 'examinations of the effectiveness for human users of occupied design environments.' The methodology, development and benefits of POEs are explicitly described in Preiser (2002), Derbyshire (2001) and Zimmermann and Martin (2001). POE can be characterized (at least in theory) as:

- a design aid – as a means of improving building procurement, particularly through 'feed-forward' into briefing
- a management aid – as a 'feed-back' method for measuring building performance, particularly in relation to organizational efficiency and business productivity
- a benchmarking aid for sustainable development – for measuring progress in the transition towards sustainable production and consumption of the built environment (Cooper, 2001).

Although the use of POEs is widely advocated as best practice in guides to construction and facility management, POEs are far from being a 'mainstream' activity within the construction and property sector. The Probe studies are one of the first systematic and rigorous attempts to investigate the performance of buildings, modern workplace environments and their occupant's responses (Bordass et al., 1999). The Probe studies gave valuable insights into the functioning and performance of buildings and lead to the identification of four 'killer variables' that positively correlate with occupant's comfort, satisfaction and perceived productivity (Leaman and Bordass, 1999). The variables are:

- Personal control: occupants perception of control over their workplace environment (i.e. heating, cooling, lighting, ventilation and noise),
- Responsiveness: the building's capability to meet occupants needs very rapidly either in anticipation or as they arise (e.g. adaptability of spaces to accommodate change, speed of response to complaints by the facilities management, etc.)
- Building depth: the building's depth of space (a depth of about 12 m across the building seems optimal for human performance; the deeper the building gets, overall satisfaction and productivity tend to go down),

- Workgroups: relates to room size and workspace organisation; productivity is higher in smaller (less then four people) and more integrated workgroups.

Derbyshire (2001, p.81) summarized the significance of the results of the Probe studies:

'If we take the Probe findings seriously we must rigorously prune unnecessary complexity and acknowledge that users will be more tolerant of their internal environment if they can control some aspect of it themselves by throwing a switch or opening a window. Users like buildings that like them!'

Despite these achievements, uncertainties and substantial gaps still prevail for the assessment of social aspects. Although a variety of studies deal with indicators for the description and assessment of social aspects, a consensus on appropriate indicators which are *directly applicable for single buildings* has not been reached (see for example Bentivegna et al., 2002; Brindley, 2003; Baines and Morgan, 2004; and WHO, 2004). The description and assessment of *single* building's contribution to sustainable development should focus on the social aspects of the characteristics and attributes of the building itself. Within the scope of standardisation activities at ISO and CEN, aspects of health, comfort, safety, and user satisfaction are assigned to the social dimension of sustainable development for single buildings.

The following indicators seem appropriate for assessing social aspects of single buildings (Lützkendorf and Lorenz, 2006a):

- thermal comfort during winter and summer (e.g. predicted percentage dissatisfied (PPD) and predicted mean vote (PMV));
- visual comfort (e.g. daylight ingress, quality of artificial light, glare);
- acoustic comfort (e.g. reverberation time);
- indoor air quality, (e.g. total volatile organic compound, olfactory freshness, CO_2);
- accessibility (e.g. barrier free access);
- number accidents within the building;
- building-related illnesses; and
- appearance of black mould;
- concentration of radon;
- intensity of electromagnetic fields;
- quality of drinking water; and
- cultural value (of existing buildings).

Regarding existing buildings it is desirable to assess occupants' satisfaction through POEs as described earlier. The indicator 'occupant satisfaction' represents a key performance indicator which may replace some other partial indicators mentioned above (Leaman and Bordass, 1999; Bordass et al. 2001). This indicator reveals a very close relationship between the social aspects of sustainable development (in terms of health, comfort and well-being) and economic or financial considerations. There is a close correlation between occupant satisfaction and occupant productivity (Heerwagen et al. 2004; Kampschroer and Heerwagen, 2005).

Occupant satisfaction has an impact on the risk of losing the tenants, on the cash flow generated by the building, and thus on the building's market value. Furthermore, aspects of occupational health and safety feed into the 'labour practice' and 'decent work' criteria, which are applicable within the framework of the Global Reporting Guidelines. In summary, the adoption of the social dimension to the assessment of single buildings is one of the most controversially discussed issues in the literature and it is still far from being satisfactorily solved. There exists an urgent need for further research and debate. Nonetheless, it is necessary to focus more clearly on those social indicators that are directly applicable for single buildings.

Based on a synthesis of research reviewed above as well as by taking into account the current stage of discussion at the roundtable on 'sustainable building' at the German Federal Ministry for Transport, Building and Urban Development (Bundesministerium für Verkehr, Bau- und Stadtentwicklung, BMVBS), the following list (Table 18) of sustainability key performance indicators for buildings has been identified in Lützkendorf and Lorenz (2005).

Table 18: *Sustainability Key Performance Indicators (Lützkendorf and Lorenz, 2005)*

Criteria	Indicators for the design stage	Indicators for the assessment of existing buildings
Object characteristics / Object performance		
Technical performance	Planned heat insulation class	Realised heat insulation class
	Planned sound insulation class	Realised sound insulation class
	Planned fire safety class	Realised fire safety class
	Planned load carrying capacity	Realised load carrying capacity
	Ease of conducting maintenance, servicing and recycling activities	Ease of conducting maintenance, servicing and recycling activities
Functional performance	Functionality and serviceability	Functionality and serviceability
	Adaptability and responsiveness	Adaptability and responsiveness
	Suitability for planned service life	Suitability for remaining service life
	Accessibility	Accessibility
Environmental performance		
Energy use	Primary energy demand during occupation (calculated)	Primary energy demand during occupation (measured)
Raw material depletion	Use of fossil fuels	Use of fossil fuels
	Use of mineral resources	
	Use of biotic / renewable resources	

Land use	Planned degree of sealing of the lot	Current degree of sealing of the lot
	Ecological value of the lot / change of ground quality	
	Planned land use per unit (e.g. number of workstations)	Current land use per unit (e.g. number of workstations)
Impacts on the environment	Global warming potential, GWP 100 (CO_2-equivalent)	Global warming potential, GWP 100 (CO_2-equivalent)
	Ozone depletion potential, ODP	Ozone depletion potential, ODP
	Acidification potential, AP (SO_2-equivalent)	Acidification potential, AP (SO_2-equivalent)
	Eutrophication potential, EP	Eutrophication potential, EP
	Photo-oxidant formation potential	Photo-oxidant formation potential
Waste production	Waste production during construction processes	Waste production during occupation and use
	Total waste accumulation (by categories)	Total waste accumulation (by categories)
Impacts on soil and ground water of lot	Material selection subject to separate checklist	Impacts on soil and ground water of lot
Economic performance		
Life cycle costs	Construction costs	Costs for refurbishment and modification
	Projected maintenance and operating costs	Effective maintenance and operating costs
	Projected disposal costs	Effective / projected disposal costs
Development of income, value and/or worth		Income stream / current market value / current calculation of worth
Social performance		
Health of occupants / users		Appearance of Sick Building Syndrome / Building Related Illness
		Appearance of black mould
Comfort and well-being of occupants / users	e.g. thermal comfort measured as PPD / PMV	Occupant / user satisfaction measured through post occupancy evaluations
Safety of occupants / users		Number of building related accidents
Indoor air quality		Olfactory freshness
	Material selection subject to separate checklist	Concentration of selected substances (total volatile organic compound)
		Concentration of radon
Comfort and well-being of neighbours		Disturbance through building / use and occupation of building
Cultural value		Existing monumental protection

These indicators and the information derived from their use fit into a system of building related information that allows for an integrated assessment of property assets (see Figure 22 above). The idea is to have a 'building information system' which contains building related information of every aspect and in great detail. Then, depending on the purpose and on the viewpoint of the user (e.g. asset and facility managers, valuers, tenants, etc.) information can be retrieved at different levels of aggregation. This idea has been conceptualised in Lorenz et al. (2004) and in Lützkendorf and Speer (2005).

Within the scope of further work it is necessary to find a balance between quantitative and qualitative measures and to develop rules and guidelines concerning inquiry and assessment of each indicator, including a determination of system boundaries. In order to assure comparability of different assessment approaches and to assure a certain degree of quality and amount of required information it is essential to reach agreement on a 'minimal list' of indicators within an international or European framework respectively. Furthermore, it is necessary to develop appropriate schemes and software tools that allow for a simultaneous assessment of these indicators.

3.3.2.4   Assessment tools and instruments

Existing performance assessment tools for single buildings have been frequently described, evaluated and comparatively analysed in the literature; for example in IEA Annex31 (2001); in Todd et al. (2001); in Kats et al. (2003) and recently in Cole (2005) and in Peuportier and Putzeys (2005); furthermore, assessment tools are under continuous review of the European Thematic Network on Practical Recommendations for Sustainable Construction (PRESCO)[79]. Examples for tools are: BREEAM and ENVEST (UK); GBTool; LEED (US); Eco-Quantum (NL); Okoprofil (NOR); ESCALE (FR); and LEGEP (D), to mention only a few.

But most of these tools assess buildings after they are designed and do not account for future life cycle costs of the building. Due to the complexity involved, only a few tools exist that allow for a combined determination and assessment of cost, environmental and (to some extent) occupational health and other social issues in the planning phase. The basic goal of these combined assessment approaches is to allow professionals to appreciate a design or building solution simultaneously from different points of view and within different life cycle scenarios. First examples of combined tools are LEGEP (Germany) and OGIP (Switzerland). One major problem, however, associated with combined or/and mere LCA-based assessment approaches is the lack of standardisation in terms of scope, definition of performance indicators and weighting of different aspects (Todd et al., 2001).

Given the variety of existing assessment tools available in the marketplace, it seems reasonable to provide a classification of assessment tools. They can be classified according to the following aspects:

- Dimensions of sustainable development (i.e. does the tool solely focus on environmental aspects, or does it additionally assess economic, social, technical and functional aspects?
- Phases of the building life cycle (i.e. does the tool cover all phases of the building life cycle, or is it focused on single parts or time-frames respectively?)
- Integration of design and assessment issues (i.e. does the tool focus on the assessment process only, or is it linked to CAD-software and therefore capable of internally calculating assessment inputs?)

---

[79] See: www.etn-presco.net

- Nature of the assessment (i.e. does the tool predominantly use qualitative, quantitative information or a balanced combination of the two?)

- Level of detail or extent of aggregation respectively (i.e. to what extent does the tool summarise or aggregate assessment results?)

- Nature and breadth of assessment results (i.e. does the tool deliver an energy certificate, building file, and/or an assessment report and does it additionally provide any label for building products or construction works?)

- Applicability for the assessment of existing buildings (i.e. is it possible to use the tool to assess already existing building and/or does it even allow for an application accompanying the entire building life cycle?)

A more detailed description and explanation of different tools can be found in IEA Annex31 (2004). In addition to assessment tools, a number of supporting instruments for safeguarding good sustainability performance are available and frequently applied in practice. These include: Positive and negative lists of building products and construction materials; recommendations and exclusion criteria for tendering purposes; element catalogues including assessment results for building components; labels for building products and construction works; checklists, guidelines and case studies; codes, regulations and standards; and energy certificates and building files.[80] The main problem associated with existing assessment tools is that they are not yet applied within a consistent framework of tools and instruments and that the tools themselves are not integrated; i.e. they are not able to address questions and assessment tasks concerning the interrelationship between environmental, social and economic aspects. This can be exemplified by referring to the evolution of building assessment scenarios (see Figure 23). The evolution of building assessment scenarios can be sub-divided into four main stages of development: Stage 1: Initially, buildings and building concepts were assessed and compared entirely on the basis of construction costs. Stage 2: In the 1970s or 80s, the approaches of LCC and LCA emerged. However, both approaches have been applied for different purposes and completely separated from each other. Stage 3: In recent years, there was a shift from 'green building' to 'sustainable building' approaches which increased information demand for combined building assessment results. Multidimensional optimization and comparison of building concepts are, however, still not achievable since existing building assessment tools do not take into account mutual interdependencies and interrelations between different building performance aspects. Stage 4: Integrated assessment tasks will require a multidimensional optimization and comparison of building concepts. These will have to address

---

integrated considerations such as: To what extent does a change of technical parameters (e.g. u-values, air renewal rate) lead to a change in occupants' satisfaction and productivity? To what extent does a higher degree of occupants' satisfaction reduce the risk of losing the tenant and, as a consequence, improve the building's cash flow and market value? To what extent does the incorporation of sustainable design features reduce external costs for society or the risk of property default for banks and insurance companies?

Figure 23: *Evolution of assessment scenarios (Lützkendorf and Lorenz, 2006a)*

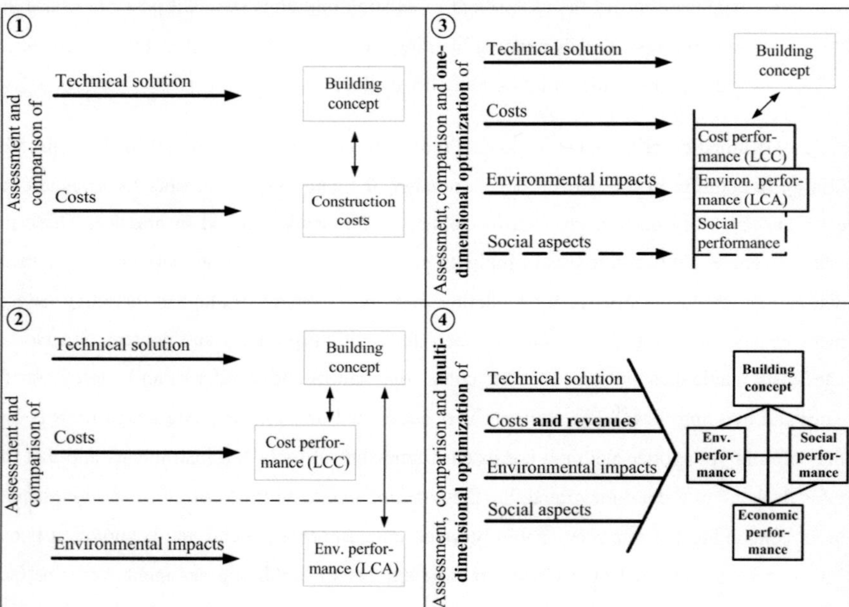

By addressing these questions mentioned above, a new and desirable quality of support would be provided for design, assessment and decision making processes. At the moment, this is hampered by both, methodological and technical problems as well as a lack of appropriate data, particularly concerning economic performance aspects. For a more detailed investigation of integrated building assessment tools, see Lützkendorf and Lorenz (2006a).

3.4 Sustainable property investment framework and the role of property valuation

Sustainable property investing is based on a vision of sustainability and on finding out how to best get there. It can encompass four main investment strategies and can be applied for direct investment as well as for indirect property investment. In the latter case, it would mean investing into such property investment products only, that are committed to one ore more these four main strategies which are: (1) Purchase and/or disposal of property assets that meet / don't meet predefined environmental and social performance requirements; (2) Investments into new building projects that are designed, constructed and subsequently managed according to the requirements of sustainable buildings as outlined above; (3) Investments into the existing building stock in order to systematically improve sustainability performance; and (4) Investments into community projects such as affordable housing and urban revitalisation in order to foster sustainability at large.

Currently, three different approaches to property investment can be observed and sustainable property investing is the least practiced among the three: (1) *Defensive property investing* which can be defined as investment practices that adhere to written law only; i.e. conventional mainstream property investment practice. (2) *Responsible property investing* which has been defined as 'maximising the positive effects and minimizing the negative effects of property ownership, management and development on society and the natural environment in a way that is consistent with investor goals and fiduciary responsibilities' (Pivo and McNamara, 2005, p. 129). This definition of property investing would, however, allow that an investment strategy can be considered responsible even if the maximisation of positive effects and the minimization of negative effects take place within the tight boundaries set by prevailing, financially oriented, short-term investor goals. (3) *Sustainable property investing* encompasses the goal of maximising positive and minimising negative effects but it goes one significant step further since the investor lays down appropriate preconditions so that all his (or her) actions are aimed to be sustainable. A respective proposal for possible adjustments to current practice in property investing is portrayed in Figure 24.

Sustainable property investing can therefore be described as property investing in pursuit of sustainability. This requires considering the entire building life cycle including upstream and downstream as well as construction, acquisition, use, management and maintenance in-between. Sustainable property investing requires that actions are undertaken which are entirely different from current 'best practice' in property investment, e.g. integrated sustainability assessment of property assets; true sustainability accounting and reporting (which means no 'creative writing exercises'); and promoting next-generation construction approaches such as closed-loop design and the use of organic materials in order to reach breakthroughs in energy efficiency and to create buildings that serve as utility providers rather than acting as utility consumers. This does, of course, not mean that sustainable property investors cannot operate highly profitable. In fact, current experience suggests that these innovative or 'radical' approaches to construction are the most profitable ones (see McDonough and Braungart, 2003, p. 16) and that those investors or companies who take the most proactive approach are the most successful ones (see Murphy, 2002). Sustainable property investing involves adjusting or 'fine-tuning' actions at the following levels or areas: strategy, business processes, building/portfolio level, and stakeholder level (see Figure 24).

Figure 24: *Sustainable property investment framework*

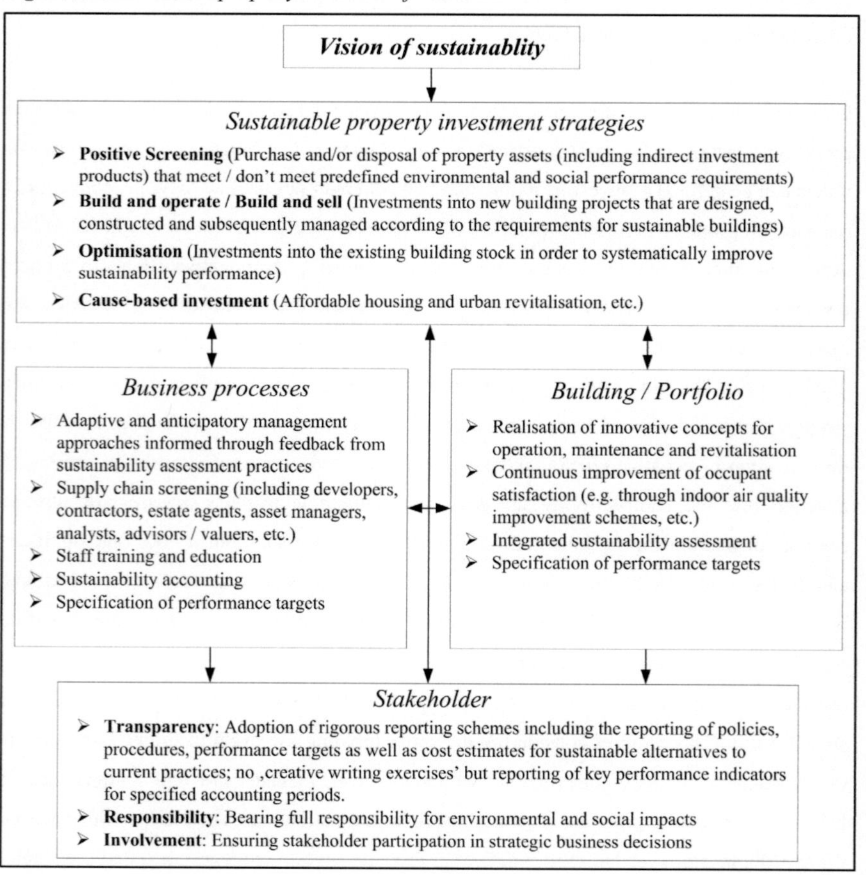

All indirect property investment forms could be used to offer private and institutional investors the opportunity to invest in sustainable buildings. Figure 25 gives an overview on possible investment products and strategies. In addition, the preconditions for assessing the environmental, economic and social advantageousness of such products are listed. In general, however, conventional approaches to property investment (including expenditure on the purchase of existing assets and expenditure on the creation new assets) neglect sustainability issues. The discussion on sustainability assessments of buildings and the struggle towards more sustainable development in property and construction mainly takes place without any involvement of the property investment industry. Of course, there are certain exceptions; some have already been mentioned, some others will be mentioned in the following; however, these exceptions cover fractions of the market only.

Figure 25: *Sustainable property investment strategies and indirect investment vehicles*

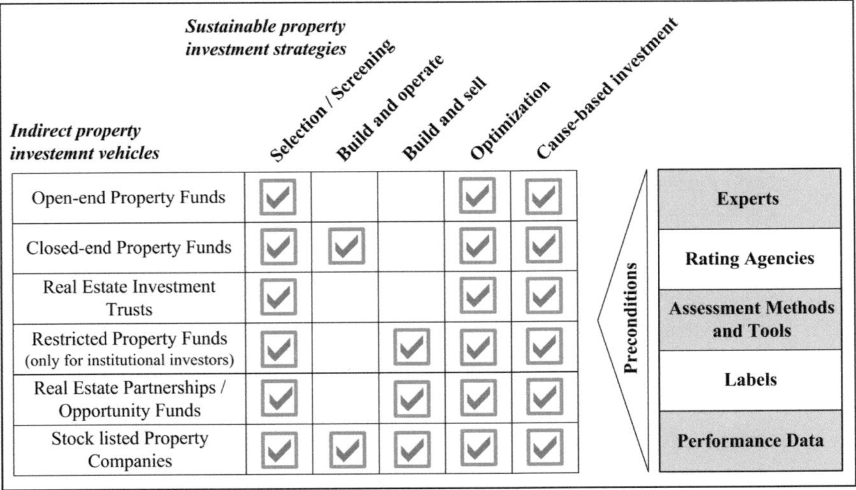

Indirect property investemnt vehicles	Selection / Screening	Build and operate	Build and sell	Optimization	Cause-based investment		Preconditions
Open-end Property Funds	✓			✓	✓		Experts
Closed-end Property Funds	✓	✓		✓	✓		Rating Agencies
Real Estate Investment Trusts	✓			✓	✓		Assessment Methods and Tools
Restricted Property Funds (only for institutional investors)	✓		✓	✓	✓		Labels
Real Estate Partnerships / Opportunity Funds	✓		✓	✓	✓		
Stock listed Property Companies	✓	✓	✓	✓	✓		Performance Data

A lack of sustainable practices in property investment bears the great risk for society that property (and other) values are in fact being destroyed through irresponsible or unsustainable behaviour among property investors and others. As a consequence, the property investment industry as a whole or certain actors of it may be held liable – first, morally and later, financially (see the changing landscape of liability, Figure 19) – by the court of public opinion for violating the principles of sustainable development and for all the adverse side effects of such behaviour; e.g. hostile public spaces[81], social conflicts, occupational diseases, contaminated

---

[81] See a recent RICS publication titled *What kind of world are we building? – The privatisation of public space* (Minton, 2006).

land[82]; contribution to climate change, brownfield sites[83] within cities and throughout the countryside.

As a consequence of neglecting sustainability issues, conventional approaches to property investment and analysis fail to assess the full range of factors that create or destroy value. This is of critical importance since, the 'most pervasive problem of economic life is of course that of value …' (Stiegler, 1965, p. 22, cited in: Canonne and Macdonald, 2003, p. 116). Value can be defined as the relationship recognized by human judgment that a thing can be a means to the fulfilment of some desired end (provided that the end desired is the satisfaction of a human need or an end that is causally connected with the satisfaction of a human need):

> *'If the requirements for a good are larger than the quantity of it available, and some part of the needs involved must remain unsatisfied in any case, the available quantity of the good can be diminished by no part of the whole amount, in any way practically worthy of notice, without causing some need, previously provided for, to be satisfied either not at all or only less completely than would otherwise have been the case. The satisfaction of some one human need is therefore dependent on the availability of each concrete, practically significant, quantity of all goods subject to this quantitative relationship. If economizing men become aware of this circumstance (that is, if they perceive that the satisfaction of one of their needs, or the greater or less completeness of its satisfaction, is dependent on their command of each portion of a quantity of goods or on each individual good subject to the above quantitative relationship) these goods attain for them the significance we call value. Value is thus the importance that individual goods or quantities of goods attain for us because we are conscious of being dependent on command of them for the satisfaction of our needs.' (Menger, [1871] 2004, pp. 114-115)*

Expressed in other words, the value of a thing consists in its recognized fitness for attaining an end, or in its recognized utility[84] (see Menger, [1871] 2004, Appendix C). Thus, property value can be defined as the *perceived benefits* that accrue to the one who has ownership- or

---

[82] Contaminated land can have adverse effects on human health; quality of surface and groundwater; viability of ecosystems; condition of buildings and archaeological artefacts within the ground; and on the visual amenity of an area (CLARINET, 2002a, p. 4).

[83] Brownfield sites have been affected by the former uses of the site and surrounding land; are derelict or under-used; have real or perceived contamination problems; are mainly in developed urban areas; and require intervention to bring them back to beneficial use (Bardos, 2003, p. 5).

[84] Utility can be defined as 'the capacity of a thing to serve for the satisfaction of human needs, and hence (provided the utility is *recognized*) it is a general prerequisite of goods-character. Non-economic goods have utility as well as economic goods, since they are just as capable of satisfying our needs' (Menger, 1871, p. 119).

use-rights in a particular property asset. As stated earlier, major sustainability-related benefits (and vice versa risks) associated with the ownership and use of property are simply not accounted for within the scope of property valuations. As a consequence, this bears the great risk for investors that property valuations are being distorted; and as a result, that uninformed and harmful decisions are made on the basis of these valuations. In contrast to many other goods and services, the price of a property cannot be observed in the marketplace until the property is actually sold. For this reason, property valuations are among the key sources of information within property investment decisions. If property valuations do not attempt to account for major factors that actually determine or destroy value, these valuations are misleading since they fail to reflect the full range of benefits and risks that accrue to the one who has ownership- or use-rights in a particular property asset. This may be the deeper cause for harmful decision making and unsustainable behaviour in property investment.

Property valuation represents the major mechanism to align economic return with environmental and social performance of property assets. Thus, valuation and valuers play a crucial role within the struggle towards sustainability in property and construction. Since the material impact of sustainability issues on the financial performance of residential and commercial property investments has not yet been fully captured within the financial world, mainstream financial professionals will not account for sustainability issues in property investment and financing decisions unless sustainable building features and related performance are integrated into property valuations; i.e. unless 'the financial sector understands the benefits of green to the net value of an asset' (RICS, 2005, p. 17).

If conducted appropriately, a property valuation (i.e. the attempt to provide a monetary measure of the utility derived through ownership and/or use of property) should be understood by everyone; irregardless if the end-user of a valuation is committed to sustainable building or even aware of its benefits. This does, however, not mean that property valuation has to account for sustainability issues in any case and to the widest possible extent. Since one form of property valuation – market valuation – requires estimating the most likely sale price, these valuations need to account for sustainability issues only to the extent to which these issues impact on the competitive position of property assets in the marketplace. As there already is growing awareness of the benefits of sustainable building – and market valuations need to reflect this circumstance since they would produce misleading price estimates otherwise – valuers need to find effective measures to monitor and account for the increasing change in market participant's preferences for certain building features. This in return, can lead to a positive feedback-loop: as market participants see certain benefits of sustainable building (e.g.

energy efficiency) reflected in the price estimates produced by property valuers, they are encouraged to become more sustainable in order to achieve higher price estimates for the buildings they own or aim to sell.

Regarding another form of property valuation which is equally important as a basis for investment decision making – calculation of worth[85] – the case is, however, entirely different. Here, the extent of integrating sustainability issues into property valuation depends on subjective investment objectives. As shown above, subjective investment objectives can well be shaped by strict sustainability requirements. As a consequence and in order to avoid producing misleading calculations of worth, valuers need to find measures to account for a wider range of benefits of sustainable buildings (such as environmental release, occupant productivity, loss prevention or image gains). This, however, requires a deeper understanding of the differences between conventional and sustainable buildings, on how sustainable building features affect property risk and returns, and on how the utility derived from these buildings adds value for individuals or groups of individuals.

In any case, property valuation has the potential to significantly contribute to bursting the 'vicious circle of blame' and to turning it into a 'circle of fate' (see Figure 26 and Figure 27).

Figure 26: *The 'vicious circle of blame' (Cadman, 2000)*

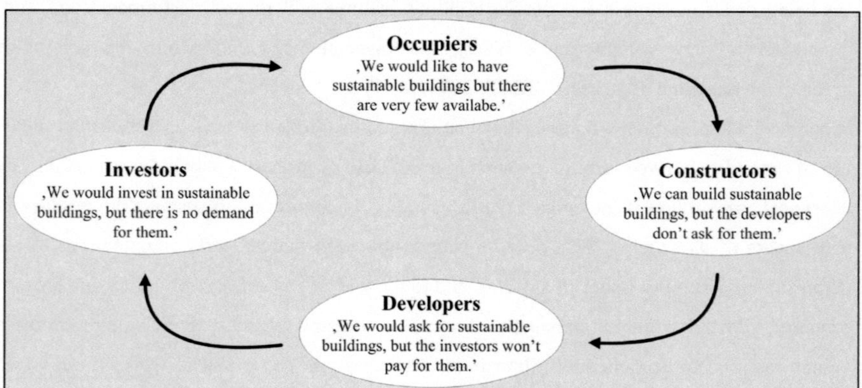

---

[85] Worth is defined as the value of the property to a particular investor, or class of investors, for identified investment objectives. In this context an investor includes an owner-occupier. (RICS, 2003b)

Figure 27: *Turning the 'vicious circle of blame' into a 'circle of fate'*

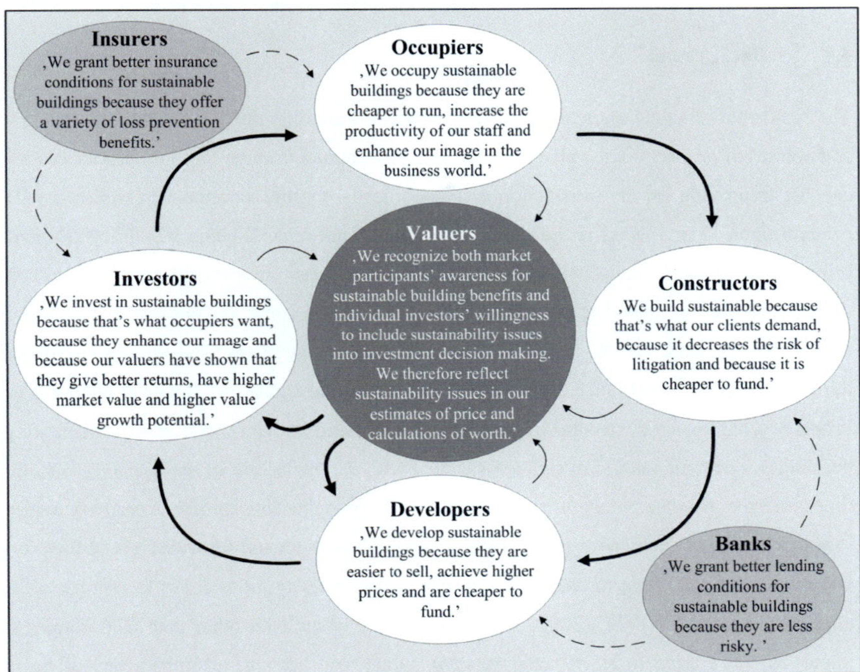

Nonetheless, integrating sustainability issues into property valuation practice represents a great challenge for valuers. Appropriately adjusting discount or capitalisation rates as well as rental estimates to account for sustainability issues in property valuation is currently very difficult due to a lack of comparative financial data, associated information on building performance and guidance and tools for valuers and professional advisors to link a building's environmental and social performance with its investment performance. Possibilities and suggestions to overcome these constraints will be discussed in the next chapter.

4. Sustainability in property valuation

4.1 Background

The basic goal of valuation is to provide a measure of the utility derived through the access to and control of property. The value of property is determined through the flow of services it is capable to provide for the satisfaction of human needs; i.e. the increment in well-being dependent upon it, or – what is the same – the impairment of well-being which its loss must bring about (see von Mises, 1949, p. 120). In general, the term property describes a legal concept; it refers to the rules that govern people's access to and control of physical things (tangible assets) like land, natural resources, and manufactured goods as well as of non-physical things (intangible assets) such as inventions or contractual rights and financial claims. Real Property refers to the ownership of land (see Box 11) and its man-made improvements (e.g. buildings). The combination of rights associated with the ownership of real property is sometimes referred to as the bundle of rights. 'The bundle-of-rights concept likens property ownership to a bundle of sticks with each stick representing a distinct and separate right of the property owner, e.g., the right to use, to sell, to lease, to give away, or to chose to exercise all or none of these rights' (IVSC, 2005, p. 22). Ownership of an asset other than land (vacant or improved) is referred to as personal property which can be generally characterised by its moveability. Thus, the term property, used without further specification, can either refer to real property or to personal property. However, whenever the term property is used in the following it is meant to refer to real property.

Box 11: *What is land? (Lou Scott, cited in Harvey, 2000, p. v)*

> *I am the basis of all wealth, the heritage of the wise, the thrifty and prudent.*
> *I am the poor man's joy and comfort, the rich man's prize, the right hand of capital, the silent partner of many thousands of successful men.*
> *I am the solace of the widow, the comfort of old age, the cornerstone of security against misfortune and want.*
> *I am handed down to children, through generations, as a thing of greatest worth.*
> *I am the choicest fruit of toil. Credit respects me. Yet I am humble. I stand before every man, bidding him know me for what I am and possess me.*
> *I grow and increase in value through countless days. Though I seem dormant, my worth increases, never failing, never ceasing, time is my aid and population heaps up my gain. Fire and elements I defy, for they cannot destroy me.*
> *My possessors learn to believe in me; invariably they become envied. While all things wither and decay, I survive. The centuries find me younger, increasing with strength.*
> *The thriftless speak ill of me. The charlatans of finance attack me. I am trustworthy. I am sound. Unfailingly I triumph and detractors are disproved.*
> *Minerals and oils come from me. I am producer of food, the basis for ships and factories, the foundation of banks.*
> *Yet I am so common that thousands, unthinking and unknowingly, pass by me. I am land.*

Property valuation, also referred to as appraisal[86], is carried out for many different purposes (see Table 19) and the services that property valuers provide are critical for the functioning of property markets, interconnected financial markets as well as of national economies. Poor property valuation has a domino effect and can lead to corporate financial crises first which can in return result in severe crisis within national economies. This could be observed during the 1970s property crash in the UK, the 'savings and loan' crisis of the late 1980s in the US as well as during the banking and property crisis in Asia that started with the collapse of the Bangkok Bank of Commerce (Gilbertson and Preston, 2005). Property valuers are 'the independent axis around which property information flows. They touch every aspect of development from feasibility studies in the beginning of a project to the determination of value when an asset is to be taken by the government or destroyed to make way for new growth' (Motta and Endsley, 2003, p. 8).

Table 19: *Main purposes of property valuation (based on Adair et al., 1996, pp. 6-7)*

Valuation for	Examples
Purchase and sale	*Occupation, investment, (re)development*
Accounting and financial reporting	*Annual accounts, stock market flotation, pricing of investment bonds, performance measurement*
Lending	*Calculation of loan amount / loan security*
Insurance	*Calculation of insurance coverage*
Taxation	*Inheritance tax, accessions tax, taxation on capital gains on disposal, taxation on transfer*
Statutory purposes	*Compulsory acquisition by a public body, compensation for planning restrictions or gains*
Courts of law	*Divorce, inheritance, compulsory auction*

The history of property valuation goes back over three thousand years. There are valuation anecdotes from biblical times, the Persian, Greek, Asian, and Roman Empires. However, the first book on property valuation, entitled *Book of Surveying* was published in 1523 in England by John Fitzherbert[87]. An overview on the history of property valuation is provided in Yovino-Young (1997) who described the development form the Middle Ages until today and in Miller and Markosyan (2003) who cover the past 100 years of property valuation in the US. The professional guild of property valuers was created during the mid-nineteenth century along with the expansion of railroads and other agents of urban settlement. The first professional body of surveyors was formed in 1834 in London as a precursor of the Royal Institu-

---

[86] Similarly to the use of the terms (real) property and real estate, the terms valuation and appraisal can be used interchangeably. While the term valuation is more common in a UK context, the term appraisal is used in the US. Within this dissertation the term valuation is used unless a direct quote contains the term appraisal.

[87] See Yovino-Young (1997) and the Cambridge History of English and American Literature, Volume IV, Chapter XVII: www.bartleby.com/214/1702.html

tion of Chartered Surveyors which was founded in 1868. During this time, towns and urban areas grew and developed rapidly and the property professionals helped to draw boundaries, subdivide parcels, plan for town centres and determine property values for taxation; they also helped to decide if the right buildings were being built for the needs of the population and what kind of public infrastructure was required. During the time of continuing urbanisation in Europe and in North America, property valuers were part of a vision for the future (Motta and Endsley, 2003). Today, the property valuation profession stands at a crossroads and has to reconsider the role it plays within the society.

> *'For every profession, it is useful to pause and reflect on developments over the past hundred years or so and who influenced these changes. Without taking the time to reflect on "change", it becomes easy to believe that current practices are sufficient and that we can simply become more experienced at doing the same thing we did last month or last year. But viewed from a longer perspective, we see that business practices have changed dramatically and will likely continue to change. "Business as usual" will never last more than part of a single generation' (Miller and Markosyan, 2003, p. 172).*

Gilbertson and Preston (2005) have formulated a vision for valuation by investigating the actions that need to be taken in order to ensure the provision of valuation services that the modern economy requires. They find that there is a bright future for those valuers who understand the dynamics in the marketplace and who are willing to anticipate or respond to change. However, whatever the drivers of change in the property marketplace are, 'it is fundamental for the survival of professional valuation services that the public interest is protected' (Gilbertson and Preston, 2005, p. 123).

Contemporary property valuation practice is being shaped by a combination of strong forces within and external the profession. Among the external forces are the adoption of new capital adequacy rules for international banks called Basle II, the introduction of International Financial Reporting Standards (IFRS) within the European Union, a general shift in accounting conventions from depreciated historical costs to market value reporting of property assets as well as the growing acceptance of International Valuation Standards (IVS) which is closely interconnected with developments in the accounting arena. For a more detailed investigation of these issues see Mansfield and Lorenz (2004), Dorchester (2004) and Gilbertson and Preston (2005). In addition, the continuing globalisation of property investment requires valuers to significantly extend the scope investigations to include aspects of the national or regional 'rule regimes' in order to produce useful valuation services for international clients (see Seabrook et al., 2004). Furthermore, valuation services will be influenced through developments within the sustainability accounting and performance reporting arena. Figure 28 provides an overview.

Figure 28: *Property valuation within a global economy*

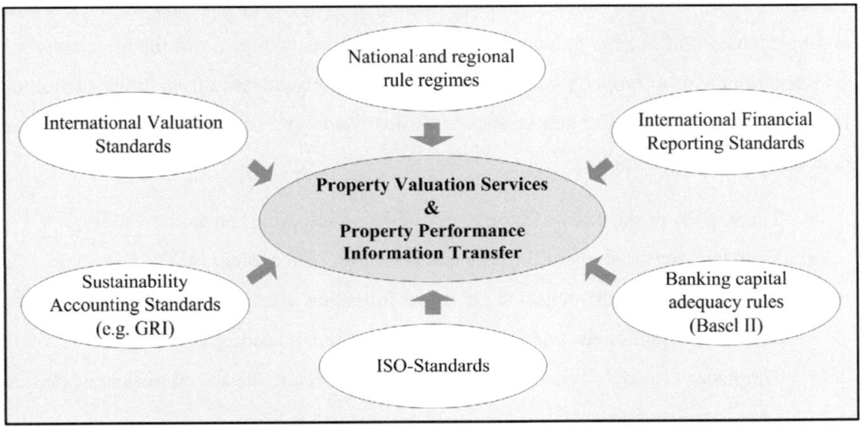

Among the internal forces that currently shape valuation practice is the growing awareness of academics and practitioners that an urgent need to increase the transparency of valuation services exists by adopting procedures to systematically assess and report property risks as well as to account for the uncertainties associated with any property valuation (see Adair and Hutchison, 2005 and French and Gabrielli, 2005).

In addition, there is an emerging concern that property valuations are conducted without appropriate value theory in place; i.e. a lack of professional foundation. For example, Canonne and Macdonald (2003) investigated in detail the extent to which over 100 major North American textbooks on property valuation as well as a wide number of property valuation manuals, treaties and anthologies cover the theory of economic value and its history. They come to a sobering conclusion: 'the theory of value [...] is systematically neglected' (Canonne and Macdonald, 2003, p. 113). The reason for this state of affairs is seen in the circumstance that economists in the twentieth century have turned away from the analytical study of value to concentrate on the apparently more tangible econometrical analysis of prices. 'It is much more comfortable to technically concentrate on prices and price models than to go into the domain of deductive speculation and intellectual conceptualization, which is prerequisite to the study of the nature of value, and this is quite contrary to the usual inductive nature of economics' (Canonne and Macdonald, 2003, p. 116). Thus, it is not surprising that the fundamental notion of value has not become an integral part of professional valuers' education: the concept finds little or no foundation in the literature, with blatant errors in the theory of value and the history of value thought (Canonne and Macdonald, 2003). This is a critical issue because future progress in the field of valuation 'is not on further development of mathematical process; it will be in the discovery and applications between man and his environment' (Schmutz, 1948, cited in Canonne and Macdonald, 2003, p. 151). For this reason, Canonne and Macdonald (2003) have proposed a new science in order to lay down the basic concepts, laws and principles of property valuation so that the field can advance from art to science and from trade to profession. The new science is termed *Timology*[88] or *The Doctrine of Value* and is divided into five disciplines:

- Timography or the study of the concept of economic value and its derivatives;
- Timonomy or the study of the laws and principles of economic value;
- Timotistics or the theoretical study of the formation of any particular economic value due to the action of law and principles of value upon its concept;
- Timometry, (today's appraisal), or formulation of the monetary equivalent of particular economic values; and
- Epistomology or the critical analysis (origin, value, range and rank) of Timology.

Now, the pressing need for more sustainable development in general and in property markets in particular represents another force that will significantly impact on the practice of property valuation. Even more, the challenges imposed by sustainable development represent a landmark for the valuation profession. If the profession fails to meet these challenges – i.e. if it fails to protect public interest and to provide clients with real feedback – the profession will not prosper, it will decline. If property valuers adopt a 'wait and see' strategy, others (e.g. accountants and consultants) will use this opportunity and offer those services that are increasingly valued by clients. On the other hand, 'if the valuation profession can once again become part of the vision for the future, by analyzing the status of entire markets and helping corporations, governments, and individuals shape real property markets into sustainable, rational assets for the people of the world, then the vitality of the profession will be unquestioned' (Motta and Endsley, 2003, p. 8).

For this reason, the effort is undertaken in the following to bring sustainability issues on the property valuation agenda. After a review of theoretical and methodological basics of property valuation, it is investigated how sustainability issues can be integrated into existing property valuation practice.

---

[88] The term timology is derived from the ancient Greek expression *timi*: value

4.2 Theoretical and methodological basics

4.2.1 The theory of value

Economic value thought has its roots in the works of Xenophon (427-355 B.C.), Plato (427-347 B.C) and Aristotle (384-324 B.C.).[89] For example, Xenophon discovered in *Economics*[90] that the same goods can be both valuable (i.e. wealth-generating) and useless, depending on ones understanding of how to use them:

> *'Some men spend large sums in building houses that are useless, while others build houses perfect in all respects for much less [...] [and] some possess many costly belongings and cannot use them at need, [...] whereas others, though they possess not more, but even less, have whatever they want ready for use.'*
> *(Xenophon, Economics, Chapter II and III)*

Xenophon found that to people who do not understand how to use a particular good, the good is not valuable if they keep it instead of selling it (provided that they know how to sell). He also argues that money is not valuable or wealth to one who doesn't know how to use it (Xenophon, Economics, Chapter I): 'wealth is that from which a man can derive profit. At any rate, if a man uses his money to buy a mistress who makes him worse off in body and soul and estate, how can his money be profitable to him then?' Thus, Xenophon addressed a fundamental concern of economic value thought; i.e. the distinction between objective value and subjective value and between value in use and value in exchange.

The distinction between value in use and value in exchange has first been examined by Aristotle in *Politics*. 'Of everything which we possess there are two uses: both belong to the thing as such, but not in the same manner, for one is the proper, and the other the improper or secondary use of it. For example, a shoe is used for wear, and is used for exchange; both are uses of the shoe' (Aristotle, Politics, Book I). According to Aristotle, the value of a good consists in its usefulness for satisfying the necessities of life. The use value of a good, however, depends upon the good's capability to satisfy individual human's wants; as such, use value of a particular good can vary significantly among different individuals. Aristotle observed that exchange of goods arises 'from what is natural, from the circumstance that some have too little, others too much' (Aristotle, Politics, Book I).

---

[89] An overview on the history of economic value thought can be found in Canonne and Macdonald (2003, pp. 145-150)

[90] Full text translations of the works of the ancients can be accessed through The Perseus Digital Library: www.perseus.tufts.edu or through The Internet's Classics Archive: http://classics.mit.edu/index.html

Following Aristotle, exchange value is derived from use value as communicated through market demand. However, use value begins diminishing at some threshold point (i.e. at the point where someone has enough) and exchange value and demand are affected by the circumstances of rarity or scarcity. A more detailed analysis of Aristotle's views on value and economics is provided by Younkins (2005) who argued that Aristotle understood the role of diminishing marginal utility in price formation and recognized that the value of a something could be determined by examining what its addition to (or subtraction from) a group of commodities did to the total value of the group. In doing so, Aristotle anticipated major elements of the value theory put forward by the representatives of the so-called Austrian School of economics[91], notably be Carl Menger (1840-1921) who is recognized as the founder of the Austrian School.

In 1871 Menger's *Principles of Economics* (Grundsätze) and William Jevons' (1835-1881) *Theory of Political Economy* were published. This year is now generally regarded as the beginning of the modern period in the development of economics. Until that time, economic analysis in the tradition of Adam Smith (1723-1790) – which is still prevailing today[92] – struggled with apparently irresolvable contradictions that stemmed from Smith's labour theory of value: 'Labour [...] is the real measure of the exchangeable value of all commodities. [...] What is bought with money or with goods is purchased by labour, as much as what we acquire by the toil of our own body. They contain the value of a certain quantity of labour which we exchange for what is supposed at the time to contain the value of an equal quantity. Labour was the first price, the original purchase-money that was paid for all things. It was not by gold or by silver, but by labour, that all the wealth of the world was originally purchased; and its value, to those who possess it, and who want to exchange it for some new productions, is precisely equal to the quantity of labour which it can enable them to purchase or command' (Smith, 1776, Book I, Chapter 5). Smith and his followers believed that the costs of a good's production (i.e. the labour contained within it) fully determine its economic value. Following this logic, a good's economic value is intrinsic to it and is determined externally through the considerations, valuations, and expectations of economically acting subjects: purchasers and sellers (Stolyarov II, 2006). A view of value as intrinsic led classical economists into a paradox in their attempt to answer the question why diamonds are more valuable than water. 'The things which have the greatest value in use have frequently little or no value in exchange; and

---

[91] See: www.mises.org/etexts/austrian.asp
[92] See, for example, the speech of Alan Greenspan held at the Adam Smith Memorial Lecture, Kirkcaldy, Scotland, February 6, 2005: www.federalreserve.gov/boarddocs/Speeches/2005/20050206/default.htm

on the contrary, those which have the greatest value in exchange have frequently little or no value in use. Nothing is more useful than water: but it will purchase scarce any thing; scarce any thing can be had in exchange for it. A diamond, on the contrary, has scarce any value in use; but a very great quantity of other goods may frequently be had in exchange for it' (Smith, 1776, Book I, Chapter 4). The observation that things with higher utility can be valued less than things with far smaller utility and the inability to solve this paradox lead classical economists to abandon a theory of value and prices that is based on the concepts of utility and use value; instead they tried to explain the phenomena of value by other theories (von Mises, 1949). The paradox was, however, solved by Menger, Jevons and Leon Walras (1834-1910) who developed independent from each other and almost simultaneously a the theory of economic value based on the concept of marginal utility. Menger's work distinguishes itself from the other formulations by its greater adherence to reality, theoretical precision, and concern with the valuations of the individual actor (Stolyarov II, 2006).

Menger refuted the labour theory of value. He argued that quantities of labour or cost of production cannot be the determining factor in the value of a good. 'In general, no one in practical life asks for the history of the origin of a good in estimating its value, but considers solely the services that the good will render him and which he would have to forgo if he did not have it at his command' (Menger, 1871, p. 146). Nonetheless, Menger acknowledged that comparing the value of a good with the costs of its production reveals whether and to what extent its *past* production was appropriate or economic.

> *According to Menger the value of goods is always 'the necessary consequence of human knowledge that the maintenance of life, of well-being, or of some ever so insignificant part of them, depends upon control of a good or a quantity of goods. [...] The value of goods arises from their relationship to our needs, and is not inherent in the goods themselves. With changes in this relationship, value arises and disappears' (Menger, 1871, p. 120).*

Menger resolved the water-diamond paradox by explaining that this paradox was only the outcome of a malicious formulation of the problem involved. People's valuations and choices that result in the exchange ratios of the market do *not* decide between *all* the diamonds and *all* the water. People do not express any academic or philosophical judgement concerning the 'absolute' value of water or diamonds simply because they are usually not in a position to choose between all the water and all the diamonds. Instead, an individual chooses at a definite time and place under definite conditions between a strictly limited quantity of water and a strictly limited quantity of diamonds. As such, an individual's decision on the desirability of a quantity of water and a quantity of diamonds is entirely contextual and does focus on the margin rather than on grand totalities. And this decision does in no way depend on the decision the individual would make if it were in the position to decide between all the diamonds and all the water (von Mises, 1949). This explains why concrete quantities of water usually have no value to economizing individuals while concrete quantities of diamonds or gold a high value. However, this also explains that this relationship only holds for the ordinary circumstance of life when water is available in copious quantities and diamonds or gold in very small quantities. 'In the desert, however, where the life of a traveller is often dependent on a drink of water, it can by all means be imagined that more important satisfactions depend, for an individual, on a pound of water than on even a pound of gold. In such a case, the value of a pound of water would consequently be greater, for the individual concerned, than the value of a pound of gold. And experience teaches us that such a relationship, or one that is similar, actually develops where the economic situation is as I have just described' (Menger, 1871, p. 141). Although, Menger did never use the terms marginal utility or law of diminishing marginal utility[93], he explained that up to a certain degree of completeness, the satisfaction of any specific intense need or want has relatively the highest importance. After consuming a unit, quantity or amount of a particular good, however, an individual's need or want will be less intense until eventually, after having consumed more, a state is reached at which the satisfaction of a specific need or want is a matter of indifference. Finally, 'a stage occurs at which every act having the external appearance of a satisfaction of this need not only has no further importance to the consumer but is rather a burden and a pain' (Menger, 1871, p. 125).

Following Menger, the magnitude of value of a particular good for an individual is therefore equal to the importance attached to the least important satisfaction assured by a single unit of the available quantity of the good. Thus, it becomes clear that the law of marginal utility does not refer to objective use value or value in exchange but only to subjective use value. 'It does not deal primarily with the value of things, but with the value of services a man expects to get from them' (von Mises, 1949, p. 125). According to Menger (1871, p. 228), use value and exchange value are two concepts subordinate to the general concept of value and coordinate in their relations to each other: 'Use value [...] is the importance that goods acquire for us because they *directly* assure us the satisfaction of needs that would not be provided for if we did not have the goods at our command. Exchange value is the importance that goods acquire for us because their possession assures the same result *indirectly*.' It is, however, very often

---

[93] See also Hermann Heinrich Gossen's (1810-1858) work on *The Laws of Human Relations and the Rules of Human Action Derived Therefrom* (1854) which introduced the concept of diminishing marginal utility.

the case that when economic goods have exchange value and use value simultaneously to the individual possessing them, that the two forms of value are of different magnitudes.

Offering a more detailed investigation of the relationship between exchange value and use value is not feasible here since this would lead beyond scope and intent of this dissertation; for a more thorough treatment of this issue see also Marshall (1890), von Wieser (1891-92 and 1893) and Böhm-Bawerk (1894-95). It needs, however, to be pointed out that the concept of exchange value and its measurement is a controversially discussed and unsolved economic problem. For example, Alexander Gersch (1969, p. v) noted that the theory of exchange value is by nature a most ungrateful topic to be dealt with. 'Yet, being of essential importance to economics and a problem which was not solved, it invites adventurous minds to attempt its solution.' Furthermore, Canonne and Macdonald (2003) pointed out that up to the present, no hidden passage form use value to value in exchange has been found.

According to Gossen (1854), a good has exchange value only when the demand for it exceeds supply; furthermore, Gossen stated that the exchange ratio of goods is equal to the ratio of marginal utilities of the traders. However, the measurement of this exchange ratio is a delicate issue. For example, Menger (1871) and von Mises (1949) explained in detail why the measurement of value is a vain endeavour. For Menger (1871, p. 273), the entire theory that presents money as the measure of exchange value of goods 'disintegrates into nothingness, since the basis of the theory is a fiction, an error.' Similarly, von Mises (1949, p. 204) explained that everything that can be measured is that of two things one is valued higher. Valuing means preferring *a* to *b*: 'Preferring always means to love or to desire *a* more than *b*. Just as there is no standard and no measurement of sexual love, of friendship and sympathy, and of aesthetic enjoyment, so there is no measure of the value of commodities.' In addition, the measurement of exchange ratios is further complicated by the fact that preferences for the same goods can be entirely different among different individuals.

> *'There is no reason why a good may not have value to one economizing individual but no value to another individual under different circumstances. The measure of value is entirely subjective in nature, and for this reason a good can have great value to one economizing individual, little value to another, and no value to a third, depending on the differences in the their requirements and available amounts. [...] Hence not only the nature but also the measure of value is subjective.' (Menger, 1871, p. 146)*

This insight is of critical importance for the practice of property valuation since it pinpoints the limitations of any attempt to assign 'objective exchange values' or market values to property assets. Market valuation involves a comparison of observed money prices (i.e. exchange ratios between money and property). But whenever property valuers compare prices they need to bear in mind that prices are social phenomena brought about by the interplay of market participant's valuations preferring *a* to *b*. And there is nothing constant and invariable in these prices or exchange ratios. They are permanently fluctuating and defy any attempt to measure them:

> *'[Money prices] are not facts in the sense in which a physicist calls the estab-lishment of the weight of a quantity of copper a fact. They are historical events, expressive of what happened once at a definite instant and under definite cir-cumstances. The same numerical exchange ratio may appear again, but it is by no means certain whether this will really happen and, if it happens, the ques-tion is open whether this identical result was the outcome of preservation of the same circumstances or of a return to them rather than the outcome of the inter-play of a very different constellation of price-determining factors.' (von Mises, 1949, p. 210)*

Assigning market value to property is therefore always the attempt to anticipate the price which the market will determine. As such, its major tool is *market analysis* and its result is an *estimate* of an *expected* outcome of the interplay of a constellation of price-determining factors. It is – usually a well-founded – guess! And it will be shown later that whenever property valuers fail to acknowledge and account for the subjective and uncertain nature of their task – which simply stems from the subjective and fluctuating nature of the underlying concept – they clearly face the risk of putting the credibility of the valuation profession into question.

So far, the subjective nature of value and of its measure has been explained. In general, how-ever, it can be concluded that four factors must be present for a property to have economic value. These factors are: (1) utility – the ability to satisfy human needs and wants, (2) scarcity – the present or anticipated supply relative to demand, (3) desire – the purchaser's wish to have command over an asset, and (4) effective purchasing power – the ability of an individual or group to participate in a market (AI, 2001, pp. 28-31). Following AI (2001) and Gaddy and Hart (2003) property value is affected by the interaction of four basic forces:

- *Physical forces* including man-made and environmental externalities. Examples are: climate; topography and characteristics of the land; natural barriers to future development such as rivers, mountains, lakes, and oceans; primary transportation systems and public service amenities; and the nature and desirability of the immediate area surrounding a property (i.e. time-distance relationships between a property or neighbourhood and all other possible origins and destinations of people going to or coming from the property or neighbourhood).

- *Economic forces* including the fundamental relationship between supply and demand and the economic ability of the population to satisfy its wants, needs and demands through its purchasing power. Examples are availability of employment; wage and salary levels; the economic base of the region and the community; cost and availability of mortgage credit; the existing stock of vacant properties; new developments under construction; rental and sale price patterns of existing properties; and construction costs.

- *Political and governmental forces* which can overshadow the market forces of supply and demand. Examples are government controls over money and credit; local zoning, building codes and regulations, health and safety codes; rent controls and fiscal policy; environmental legislation; and restrictions on forms of ownership.

- *Social forces* including not only population changes and characteristics but also the entire spectrum of human activity. Examples are: population age and gender; birth rates and death rates; attitudes towards marriage and family size; current lifestyle, lifestyle changes and options; attitudes towards education, law and order as well as other moral attitudes.

An understanding of these value-influencing forces is fundamental to the valuation of property assets. It becomes evident that the issues related to the growing awareness of and need for more sustainable development are driving all four basic forces mentioned above. For example, political and governmental actions are currently changing to emphasise the need for more sustainable development in nearly all areas of human economic activity. Furthermore, environmental forces increasingly impact on property value through adverse weather-related phenomena. Also, peoples' moral attitudes – particularly in mature economies – impact on buy and sell decisions and the awareness of sustainable design benefits is likely to change the nature of housing and commercial property demand. As a result, property valuers are well-advised to take the full spectrum of issues surrounding the sustainable development discourse into account when forming an opinion on the value of a property.

*'To develop an opinion of value, an appraiser investigates how the market
views a particular property, and the scope of this investigation is not limited to
static, current conditions. Rather, the appraiser analyzes trends in the forces
that influence value to determine the direction, speed, duration, strength, and
limits of these trends' (AI, 2001, p. 44).*

This process – i.e. market analysis – has two basic functions: First, market analysis provides
the data input to determine the competitive position of a particular building in the marketplace. Second, market analysis provides the data input and identifies the key factors of value
that are to be measured by applying one of the property valuation methods (Fanning, 2006).
Thus, rigorous market analysis is the essential precondition to derive at a buildings current
market value.

4.2.2 Main concepts of value in property valuation

There are many different concepts of value that can serve as an underlying basis of property
valuation. Depending on the purpose of the valuation as well as on the historical background
of countries, concepts of value used in property valuation can differ from each other (see
Adair et al., 1996; McParland et al., 2000 and VDP, 2004). The two fundamental concepts of
value used in property valuation, however, are *market value* (i.e. exchange value) and *worth*
(i.e. use value). Most property valuation methods are designed to determine market value. In
this case, valuation input parameters are based on market derived information. In contrast,
whenever the intention is on calculating worth, valuation input parameters depend on both
market information and individual specific inputs. For example, if an individual investor believes that most market participants overestimate the risk associated with sustainable construction, then the yield figure used within the calculation of worth is changed in order to calculate the worth of a particular sustainable building based on that new assumption.
The internationally accepted definition of market value can be found in International Valuation Standards and reads as follows:

*'Market Value is the estimated amount for which a property should exchange
on the date of valuation between a willing buyer and a willing seller in an
arm's-length transaction after proper marketing wherein the parties had each
acted knowledgeably, prudently and without compulsion' (IVSC, 2005, p. 82).*

Almost every word of that definition is explained in detail within International Valuation Standards and will therefore not be repeated here. It seems, however, appropriate to stress once again that market value needs to be clearly distinguished from price and worth. Price is the observable exchange amount paid for a particular property, whereas market value is an estimation of the most likely price achievable if the property were to be sold in the open market. It is important to bear in mind that the price paid for goods or services by an individual with particular motivations or special interests 'may or may not have any relation to the value which might be ascribed to the goods or services by others' (IVSC, 2005, p. 25). Any observed price from a comparable sale is not indicative of market value since prices from particular transactions depend on the negotiating strengths of the buyer and seller as well as on their perceptions of worth (Fisher, 2002).

Worth can be defined as the value of the property to a particular investor, or class of investors, for identified investment objectives. In this context an investor includes an owner-occupier (RICS, 2003b). Or expressed in other words, worth is the maximum/minimum capital sum an individual would be prepared to pay/accept for an asset. However, whether the individual is considering investment or occupation will have consequences for the calculation of worth. An investor's view of worth can be described as the discounted value of the cash flows generated by the property whereas the owner-occupier regards the property as a factor of production. Thus, the owner-occupier's view of worth depends on the property's contribution to the profits of the business and, and thus also on issues such as image, identity and other personal preferences. Irrespective of possible methodological difficulties in calculating worth to the occupier, the intention of the concept should be clear; i.e. the calculation of subjective use values. However, regarding the definition of worth, there exists some confusion in the literature which is mainly due to two reasons:

(1) Sometimes a distinction is made between individual worth and market worth (see Baum et al., 1996; Hutchison and Nanthakumaran, 2000; Crosby et al., 2000; and Mackmin and Emary, 2000). Market worth has been defined as 'the price at which an asset would trade on a market where sellers and buyers were using all available information in an efficient manner' (Crosby et al., 2000, p. 37). The intention of this notion of worth is to find something that is more justified than the current market value by investigating what the price would have been if the market had been efficient. The idea is to find out whether there are mispricing and speculation on the market. However, Lind (2005) explained very convincingly that the concept of market worth should be put aside since there is no way for valuers to determine this

figure in an objective way. Estimating market worth is an impossible ambition since 'it is never possible to show that the market is wrong. The reason is not that the market is always right, but because the words right and wrong are meaningless when we look at asset prices' (Lind, 2005, p. 146).

(2) Sometimes a distinction is made between value in use and worth which is also referred to as investment value. Notably the International Valuation Standards (IVSC, 2005) draw this distinction: value in use is defined here as the value a specific property has for a specific use to a specific user. While in contrast, worth or investment value refers to the value of a property to particular investor, or a class of investors, for identified investment objectives (IVSC, 2005, p. 94). This distinction, however, is unnecessary and unhelpful. It is confusing since worth to an individual user and worth to a particular investor are both concepts of worth and could be included in one definition (French, 2004).

Similarly, regarding the concept of market value there is also some confusion in the property valuation literature (at least from a German valuer's perspective). This may sound strange since the definition provided above is now generally accepted and elusively explained (see TEGoVA, 2003b; RICS, 2003b and IVSC, 2005). However, it appears that the intention of market valuation is unclear. This can be pinpointed by comparing German valuation theory with internationally accepted theory. The German definition of market value ('Verkehrswert') is contained with Federal legislation (§ 194 Baugesetzbuch) and reads as follows: 'The Verkehrswert (Market Value) is the price which, at the time to which the valuation refers, would be attainable in normal business dealings, in accordance with the legal circumstances and actual characteristics, the particular state and situation of the property or other object of valuation, and without regard to unusual or personal circumstances.' On a casual glance, it could be argued that the Verkehrswert is identical to the definition of market value provided above. Yet on closer inspection, it is clear that this is not the case.

The commentary and interpretation of German valuation definitions and guidelines is provided by Kleiber et al. (2002) who state that the Verkehrswert is estimated on the basis of all characteristics of the property which are value-determining for *all bidders* (within a particular submarket). Thus, market valuation in Germany is clearly intended to produce an average price estimate based on market consensus (see Kleiber et al., 2002, pp. 430-431). Expressed in other words, German valuation theory intents producing 'conservative' or 'safe' property price estimates.[94] Furthermore, German valuation theory implies that there exists something as 'market consensus' or 'average view'. But an interpretation of Market Value as an average price clearly conflicts with valuation theory put forward by the International Valuation Standards Committee (IVSC, 2005), the Appraisal Institute (AI, 2001), TEGoVA (2003b), and the RICS (2003b). Here the concept of *highest and best use* is a 'fundamental and integral part of Market Value estimates (IVSC. 2005, p. 29). According to the Appraisal Institute's flagship publication *The Appraisal of Real Estate*, the concept of highest and best use 'can be described as the foundation on which market value rests' (AI, 2001, p. 305). Furthermore, Lennhoff and Parli (2004, p. 45) recently noted that 'it is hard to overstate the importance of highest and best use to the valuation process. The concept serves as the focus of market analysis as well as the springboard for the application of all three of the traditional approaches.' The concept, or to be more precise its proper definition is currently discussed in the US (see Lennhoff and Parli, 2001 and 2004; and Wolverton, 2004) but it is not at the forefront of contemporary UK valuation literature. The RICS Appraisal and Valuation Manual (RICS, 2003b) does not refer to the highest and best use concept directly but the definitions of value that have been put forward by the RICS (e.g. the definition of open market value) have always encompassed the highest and best use concept implicitly. Today, the RICS Appraisal and Valuation Manual states that 'valuations based on Market Value (MV) shall adopt the definition, and the conceptual framework, settled by the International Valuation Standards Committee' (RICS, 2003b, PS 3.2). Highest and best use is defined in international standards as follows:

> *'The most probable use of a property which is physically possible, appropriately justified, legally permissible, financially feasible, and which results in the highest value of the property being valued.' (IVSC, 2005, p. 29)*

---

[94] A 'safe' or extremely 'conservative' approach to valuation is also inherent in valuations for lending purposes based on mortgage lending value (MLV). This German valuation concept – which is applied in day-to-day banking practice – has found its way into European valuation standards (TEGoVA, 2003b) as well as into International Valuation Standards (IVSC, 2005). Mortgage lending valuations shall produce price estimates that retain its validity as long as possible into the future (see Rüchardt, 2001). Many academics and practitioners are more than sceptical regarding this concept of value (see Crosby et al., 2000, Craig, 2003 or Lind, 2005). For example, John Edge (2002), past Chairman of the IVSC commented on MLV as follows: 'Its usefulness is questioned, as is its relevance. Many valuers prefer to explain the context of the property market in the text body of the valuation report. These comments may be fairly subjective in nature, but that is the value (and limitations) of a professional's opinion. The bankers would prefer to see a specific figure to represent MLV rather than have to make a judgement themselves as to loan risk based upon their reading of the valuer's valuation report.' Also the RICS (2004c) has clearly rejected the concept MLV because it is regarded not as a robust concept of valuation. Given this and the explanations contained within the previous chapter on the theory of value it should be clear that a 'long-term value' of anything simply does not exist. Thus, the concept of MLV should be put aside since it is a fiction, an error.

The concept of highest and best use can be traced back to the land rent theory of von Thünen (1826) and its underlying premise is that the maximally productive use must be the winner in a hypothetical auction of a given site.

> *'The maximally productive use outbids all other uses because it generates the greatest surplus productivity to the land and therefore generates more purchasing power.' (Wolverton, 2004, p. 323)*

Since market valuation always means estimating the most likely price attainable within a hypothetical transaction, highest and best use analysis must always be the first step within the valuation process because this analysis forms the basis for identifying comparable properties and it identifies the most profitable or competitive use to which the property can be put. It is this use of a property which determines its utility for a potential purchaser. Highest and best use is shaped by the competitive forces within the market where the property is located. Analysing these forces means setting 'the foundation for a thorough investigation of the competitive position of the property in the minds of the market participants' (AI, 2001, p. 306).

Market valuation is therefore not an issue of identifying 'market consensus' or 'average view' but of identifying what is likely to be the highest and best bid. It is this highest bid that will determine market value and not the average view! Thus, the property valuer has to view the transaction through the eyes of a hypothetical buyer; i.e. to replicate the hypothetical buyer's calculation of worth. Furthermore, the valuer must consider all possible buyers in the market in order to identify what is likely to be the highest and best bid. Without any question, this is a difficult task since the valuer has not only to identify the best bidder in the market but also the level of this bid. But just because analysing the market is difficult, property valuers must not take a conservative view and simply calculate the market value estimate on the average of past prices. This may be much more comfortable but in doings so, property valuers are abdicating their responsibility since they are hired to provide a professional expert opinion which includes an interpretation of the market at the date of the valuation (French, 2004).

However, this approach to property valuation has not yet found its way into German as well as into some other European countries' valuation theory (see also Adair et al., 1996 and VDP, 2004). Given that international standards will be the platform upon which international valuations will be undertaken, the time may be right to adjust valuation theory to comply with internationally accepted best practice. Otherwise, valuers relying on national definitions and methodology are to be marginalized by those operating internationally and those exclusively applying the international definitional bases and methodology (Mansfield and Lorenz, 2004).

In addition, it is indeed questionable if something like 'market consensus' or 'average view' exists at all since this would imply that there is something than can be called rational expectations within property investment markets; the existence of rational expectations would imply that if people use best available theories and all available information they should come to about the same expectations about the future if they act rationally (Lind, 2005). In order to refute the notion of rational expectations it may be appropriate to refer to the work of De Bondt (e.g. 1995 and 1998) who argued that market participants often react in repeating patterns and that these patterns are not always rational. In order to describe these phenomena the term 'bounded rationality' has been created. Bounded rationality perspective looks on people as reasonable beings, but it accepts the limitations of human intelligence (quality of judgement) and crowd psychology (animal spirits). Phases of boom and bust as well as many other phenomena of property markets do not comply with theories based on the assumption that people act always rational. Furthermore, it can be argued that different market participants see different opportunities and risks in the same situation. From the perspective of the Austrian School of economics there is never any market consensus. In contrast a lack of consensus is regarded as a major force that drives transactions. Individual value judgements which result in the determination of definite prices are different by nature: 'Each party attaches a higher value to the good he receives than to the good he gives away. The exchange ratio, the price, is not the product of an equality of valuation, but, on the contrary, the product of a discrepancy in valuation' (von Mises, 1949, p. 332). Lind (2005, p. 143) explained it this way:

> *'A market is a place where there are countless "experiments": different people trying to do different things based on different beliefs about the future. All have different expectations about the future because there is seldom information enough to show that one expectation is more rational than a number of other expectations. Some people that act on the market make profits and others losses, but no one really knows whether those who make profits have skill or luck.'*

Two conclusions from this are: (1) The single value opinion at a single point in time is a shrinking market. Without doubt, reporting single value estimates is important when it comes to providing values for performance measurement, for the courts of law, or for protecting the public from unscrupulous developers, predatory lenders or fraudulent financial reporting (Motta and Endsley, 2003). However, the various uncertainties involved in determining the most likely sale price reveal that property valuation cannot be an exact science. Therefore, providing clients with detailed market and risk analysis as well as with an indication of the range of likely sale prices in addition to the single value opinion is regarded to be more appropriate since this better reflects the nature of the valuation process (see Motta and Endsley, 2003; French, 2004; French and Gabrielli, 2005 and Adair and Hutchison, 2005). (2) Market valuations can never be based on an average of past prices. This argument also counts if one assumes that market participants' future expectations are contained within the prices paid in the past. Estimating property values on the basis of average past prices paid for comparable properties (i.e. current German valuation practice) cannot lead to market value as defined in international standards since an average of past prices is in no way indicative of the highest bid attainable for the property under investigation simply because this average does not reveal the property's *current* competitive position. This does, however, not mean that past prices are unimportant. In contrast, it is necessary to be familiar with these prices because 'if more is known about the past development of the market, the smaller is the risk of at least making similar mistakes' and because whenever 'we make an empirical statement saying that "A leads to B", this must be based on something, and this base is primarily observed relations in the past' (Lind, 2005, p. 146 and p. 143).

As it was said before, identifying what is likely to be the highest bid for the property under investigation involves studying market forces in order to determine the competitive position of the property in the marketplace. If valuers take this task seriously, the importance of accounting for sustainability issues cannot be overstated. As explained in the previous chapters, sustainability issues are major, if not the most influential market forces currently observable and this is likely to have tremendous impact on the competitive position of properties in the marketplace.

4.2.3   Property valuation methods

Property valuation methods are described within a plethora of textbooks, manuals and journal papers. Examples include Scarret (1998), White et al. (1999), Johnson et al. (2000), AI (2001), Gaddy and Hart (2003), and Ling and Archer (2005). A good overview on North American textbooks is offered by Canonne and Macdonald (2003). An overview and concise description of valuation methods can be found in Pagourtzi et al. (2003). All property valuation methods rely on some form of comparison and they can be subdivided into traditional and advanced methods (see Table 20); while the former are usually applied to estimate the value of single properties the latter ones are mainly applied for mass valuation purposes. Advanced valuation methods are described, for example, in Linne et al. (2000); Curry et al.

(2002); d'Amato (2002); Kauko (2003a; 2003b and 2004); Kane et al. (2004a and 2004b); Chin and Fan (2005): and in Kauko and d'Amato (2004). Although these methods are termed *valuation methods* they might be better termed *data analysis methods* or *decision support tools* for valuers. This is because many of the advanced valuation methods are used for the construction of automated valuation models (AVM) and because these AVMs can be described as black boxes with a funnel on top. 'You put data in the funnel, the box whirrs and clanks, and out comes the "estimate", which is not an appraisal' (Dell, 2004, p. 13). The problem with some of the advanced methods is that they cannot observe the subject, its conditions, safety hazards, site utility, traffic conditions, and so on. They cannot tell if it is really a house that is being valued. They work poorly for unique properties and for mixed neighbourhoods and they can be in deep error in either direction (Dell, 2004). Nonetheless, advanced valuation methods can greatly improve the valuer's informational data basis through the quantification of particular relationships between value-determining factors and property prices. And this, in return, helps valuers to adjust the valuation input parameters when applying one of the more traditional valuation approaches (see Figure 29).

Figure 29: *The valuation process*

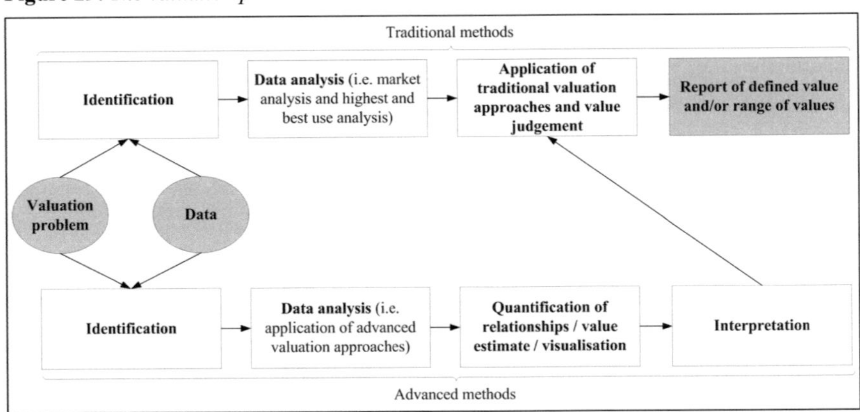

In order to test the usefulness of advanced valuation methods, Kauko and d'Amato (2004) have proposed a general protocol that involves investigating the following seven issues: (1) accuracy of independent valuations; (2) conceptual soundness; (3) valuation variation; (4) internal consistency; (5) nature of adjustments; (6) reliability and robustness of the model; and (7) feasibility. From a practitioner's perspective the latter point is of particular importance; i.e. the method should not be too esoteric in comparison with existing practices.

Table 20: *Property valuation methods*

Traditional valuation methods	Advanced valuation / data analysis methods
Sales comparison method	*Hedonic pricing methods*
Investment / income method	*Artificial neural networks*
Cost method	*Spatial analysis methods*
Profits method	*Fuzzy logic*
Residual method	*Autoregressive integrated moving average*
	Real options method
	Rough set method

A brief description of each property valuation method will be provided in the following:

4.2.3.1 Traditional property valuation methods

Sales comparison method: The sales comparison method considers the sales of similar substitute properties and related market data and establishes a value estimate on that basis. Sales comparison is the preferred method of valuation. In fact, valuers turn to alternative methods of valuation only when available sales data is insufficient (which is very often the case, however). The sale prices of the properties that are judged to be the most comparable ones tend to indicate the range in which the estimated value for the subject property will fall. The degree of similarity or difference between the subject property and the comparable sales is usually established on the following elements of comparison: property rights conveyed, financing terms, conditions of sale, expenditures made immediately after purchase, market conditions (time), location, physical characteristics, economic characteristics, use (zoning), and non-realty components of value (AI, 2001). Then adjustments are made to the known sale prices to derive at an indication of the value of the subject property. These adjustments are either Euro or percentage adjustments; the former are summed while the latter are multiplied (Williams, 2004).

Investment / income method: This valuation method is usually applied for property that is capable of generating rental income and for which and investor is the most likely purchaser. The property's expected benefits (cash flow and resale value upon reversion) are converted into an expression of value either through the application of an overall capitalisation rate in direct capitalisation or through the application of a discount rate and in yield capitalisation. Direct capitalisation converts an estimate of a single year's income into an indication of value in one direct step. In yield capitalisation, the relationship between several year's stabilized income and a reversionary value at the end of the designated period (usually 5 to 10 years) is reflected in a discount rate. The most common form of yield capitalisation is discounted cash flow analysis. The valuation input parameters are extracted through an analysis of comparable sales, comparable properties and of supply and demand relationships. Comparable properties should have similar income-expense ratios, land value-to-building ratios, risk characteristics, and future expectations of income and value changes over a typical holding period (Svelka, 2004).

Cost method: The cost method (sometimes referred to as depreciated replacement costs method) approximates the value of a property by estimating the construction costs associated with replacing or reproducing the property under investigation. The valuer will assess the market value of the raw land (by applying the sales comparison approach), add to this value the cost of rebuilding a new building which could perform the function of the existing structure and make adjustments to allow for obsolescence and depreciation of the existing building relative to the new hypothetical unit. This method of valuation must be used only if the property is so specialized that there are no comparables (e.g. oil refineries and nuclear power stations).

Profits method: In some special cases, where the factors that determine the value of the property are so unique that comparison with other properties is impracticable, the value can be determined by looking at the actual level of business (level of sales, etc.) achieved in the property or achievable form it. This is called the profits approach. For example, if a property is producing € 50,000 profit per year and a purchaser will invest capital at 6 times the level of profits, the value of the property is € 300,000. Alternatively, if an occupier is prepared to pay a rent of € 20,000 per year out of the profits to be able to earn the € 50,000 and a purchaser will invest capital at 15 times the rent, then again the value is € 300,000. Even here there is a need to obtain comparable evidence, in this instance the ratio of profits or rent to capital. Furthermore, the application of this approach requires knowledge of the type of business performed in the property as well as the ability to interpret financial accounts and to analyse the profits (Johnson et al., 2000).

Residual method: If a valuer needs to give a valuation of land or buildings which are to be developed or re-developed the residual method is used when the nature of the subject property or the development proposed is so unique that comparables cannot be found. This approach is can best be described by an example: If it is intended to develop some land with new warehouses in an area where no warehouses have been built in recent years it is possible to predict the rent which will be obtained from an occupier, and thus the capital sum which an investor would pay for the warehouses when built by adopting the income method. Further, it is possible to predict the cost of building the warehouses and the profits which someone would require to carry out such an operation. Given the value of the finished product and the cost of producing it (including required profits), it is clear that any difference represents the sum which can be paid for the land. So, if the value of the finished warehouses is € 1,000,000, the cost of producing them is € 600,000 and the required profit is € 100,000, then someone can afford to spend 300,000 on the land. Consequently, the land value is € 300,000. Since great uncertainty is associated with the determination of input parameters such as construction cost or rental values, scenario analyses are usually carried out to accompany the residual method's results.

4.2.3.2   Advanced property valuation / data analysis methods

Hedonic pricing methods: The theory of hedonic price functions provides a framework for the estimation of prices based on an analysis of the price formation process of differentiated products like housing units, office buildings, etc., whose individual features or quantitative and qualitative characteristics do not have observable market prices. It is assumed that the different quality characteristics have particular relationships to the price of the product that are defined in a hypothesised formal model. The analysis is conducted by using multiple regression techniques on large transaction data sets whereby the basic idea is to compare different products and to assess the value of their differences, so called 'shadow prices', with respect to all the factors determining the price. The hedonic pricing method aims measuring the value market participants place on these different quantitative and qualitative characteristics (Kauko, 2003b).

Artificial neural networks: An extension to hedonic pricing methods is the artificial neural network approach that is applied because of its greater flexibility and in order to better handle potential non-linearities in the hedonic functions. Neural networks are artificial intelligence models which have been designed to replicate the human brain's learning processes; in order to use a neural network to estimate property values it must first be trained with a set of property data (transaction prices or rent levels and data on the associated building characteristics) from the same market. Neural networks consist of three basic components: the input data layer (information on different building characteristics), the hidden layer(s) and the output layer (the estimated property value).The hidden layer(s) contain two processes: the weighted summation functions and the weighted transformation functions (Pagourtzi et al., 2003). Both of these functions relate the values from the input data to the output measures. The weights in the functions determine the strength of the impulses between the layers, i.e. they provide information about the importance of different value-determining factors. The training of the neural network leads to an adjustment of the weights until the observed values and the values estimated by the network are at the minimum. However, the neural network approach is plagued by a certain lack of transparency, i.e. it is unclear how to explain the computations behind the results ('black box problem') because there is no straightforward functional relationship between input and output values. Consequently, neural network approaches provide *a posteriori* support for a certain loosely formulated theory (Kauko, 2003a).

Spatial analysis methods: These methods are concerned with the investigation of geo-referenced information. They combine spatial statistics[95] and Geographic Information Systems (GIS) technology[96]. GIS handle raster and vector data and are made up of two types of databases: (1) the spatial database which describes the location, the shape of geographic features, and their spatial relationship to other features; and (2) the attribute database which contains data on the characteristics or qualities of the spatial features (i.e. descriptive information). GIS offer a variety of applications that can assist valuers when analysing markets and locations; two of these applications are of particular interest: proximity analysis (e.g. how many houses lie within 1km of a hazardous waste site?) and overly analysis (e.g. how many people live within 1km of a hazardous waste site and which of them live in areas with the greatest risk of exposure?). Spatial analysis methods can be used to account for and detect locational attributes and neighbourhood factors that are usually not considered explicitly within hedonic and other price models (Pagourtzi et al., 2003). Often the distance to the central business district or few sub-market indicators (e.g. distance to schools, recreation area, and shopping facilities) are included in hedonic price models, but it is questionable if this takes care of the entire spatial dimension in property data. If variables concerning geographic and neighbourhood attributes and/or interactions are missing in hedonic regression equations, the regression results may be biased, inefficient and inconsistent. Therefore spatial analysis methods are used to consider a wider range of spatial attributes such as quality of view, the effect of vegetation, traffic noise, distance and travel times to a variety of amenities, etc. Various studies have shown that doing so improves the usefulness and explanatory power of property price models (see for example Pace et al., 1998; Wilhelmsson, 2002; Lee and Pace,

---

[95] See: www.statistical.org
[96] Good sources for GIS-related information are: www.geo.ed.ac.uk/home/giswww.html; www.ec-gis.org; http://vega.soi.city.ac.uk/~dk708/part_2.htm; and www.clarklabs.org

2005). An impressive example of spatial hedonic modelling is provided by Thériault et al. (2003).

Fuzzy logic: This method represents the application of fuzzy set theory which was introduced by Lotfi Zadeh in 1965. Fuzzy logic deals with the imprecision of the present; it is a method of processing data by allowing partial set memberships rather than crisp set membership and non-membership; i.e. instead of assuming that something is either true or false or that an object either belongs to a set or not, fuzzy logic allows the notion of nuance. Fuzzy logic works with linguistic or 'fuzzy' variables that are used to construct a series of rules that define the desired system output response for given system input conditions. For example, two rules could be 'if accessibility to public service amenities is limited then value is low' and 'if accessibility to public service amenities is great then value is high'. Thus, fuzzy logic can be described as *computing with words* (Kauko and d'Amato, 2004). The method allows gradations in the extent to which qualitative characteristics and numerically scaled measures belong to the relevant sets of evaluation. This degree of membership of each element is a measure of the element's belonging to the set, and thus provides an indication of the precision with which it explains the phenomenon being evaluated (Bagnoli and Smith, 1998). In doing so, the method provides a way to arrive at a definite conclusion based upon vague, ambiguous, imprecise, noisy, or missing input information (Kaehler, 1998). As such, the method is well-suited for solving property valuation problems since it is more flexible and can be more powerful than its formal regression based counterparts. For an overview on the application of fuzzy logic to the valuation of property see Bagnoli and Smith (1998). A recent example for the combination of fuzzy logic, spatial analysis and GIS technology is provided by Pagourtzi et al. (2006).

Autoregressive integrated moving average (ARIMA): ARIMA models are univariate time series models which are essentially used for economic forecasting based on the direct modelling of the lagged relationships between a data series and its past. They have been proved to be reliable for the short-term forecast of property prices. ARIMA models are also used to identify cyclical patterns and cyclical turning points of economic time series as well as to analyze the efficiency and behaviour of property markets (see McGough and Tsalacos, 1995; Tse, 1997; Chin and Fan, 2005). These models consist of a combination of: (1) Autoregressive models (AR) whose purpose is to study the dynamics or temporal structure of time-series data; and (2) moving average (MA) models which are employed to capture the impact of past shocks (i.e. significant, important events). This is then called an autoregressive moving average (ARMA) process. But the method can only be applied if the time-series data is stationary[97], which is seldom the case. If the observed time series is actually non-stationary then it is often possible to transform the series into a stationary ARMA process by differencing the time series one or more times; i.e. an ARIMA process (Chin and Fan, 2005). ARIMA models are useful applications to better understand how property prices change in relation to the national economic climate.

Real options method: This approach represents the mathematical application of financial options pricing theory to property investment. It can be seen as an extension to the residual method described above since it is mainly used within the context of valuing either vacant land or existing structures with development and/or re-development potential. While the conventional residual method assumes that land value is simply the difference between the market value of the completed project and the gross development costs, the standard land option model assumes that land is a call option[98] on its underlying asset and should therefore reflect a premium for the options to select an optimal time and scale of a development (Sing and Patel, 2001). Whenever an investor is particularly concerned with entrepreneurial flexibility and sees property as a product of miscellaneous decisions that are to be taken out of a range of options, the real options method can be useful since 'the standard methods undervalue investment opportunities and myopic decisions result because they ignore or do not properly value important alternative decisions' (Lucius, 2001, p. 75). Theoretical real option models and their practical application can, for example, be found in Sing and Patel (2001); Cauley and Pavlov (2002); and in Leung and Hui (2002). The real options method, however, is plagued by a variety of theoretical difficulties and conceptional problems that mainly arise from the difference between financial and real options. As a consequence, applying the method in practice is a complex exercise and the mathematical requirements can be quite high. An understandable explanation of the real options method is offered by Greden and Glicksman (2005) who apply the method for valuing flexible office space.

Rough set method: This method is based on rough set theory and derives Boolean rules from actual market data and not from expert knowledge; it offers a clear and logical multi-criteria method to the valuation and price modelling community (Kauko and d'Amato, 2004). Rough set theory has been applied in many areas (e.g. systems theory, bankruptcy risk evaluation,

---

[97] In the statistical sense the stationary assumption means that the mean, variance, skew and kurtosis of the underlying population distribution are taken to be stable over time. In the dynamical sense the stationary assumption means that the forms of equations that describe a system's dynamic are assumed to be constant through time. If one translates this assumption into the real world one must assume that market participants do not learn from experience, do not change their behaviour and are mindless automata with infinitely long time horizons (Hoppe, 1999). In most instances this is not the case; therefore most time-series data are non-stationary.

[98] The term call option is used in finance to describe a complex derivative security.

data mining) but its first application to the property valuation field can be found in d'Amato (2002). Rough set theory is not based on prior model assumptions as fuzzy logic or conventional hedonic pricing methods; instead it estimates and explains property prices from 'the knowledge of the data and from their organisation without any interpretative model' (d'Amato, 2002, p. 406). The intention is to define deterministic rules between the property features and their price. The property valuation is then a consequence of these rules. According to Kauko and d'Amato (2004) this method can overcome two different fundamental problems with standard rule-based expert systems: (1) using actual market data avoids interviewing of and relying on experts, and (2) using fuzzy class boundaries avoids a too 'straightjacketing' model structure. Furthermore, the method can be superior to artificial neural networks since it is surely more transparent and more qualitative. Besides mass appraisal applications this method could be applied to explain property market cycles. Coupled with GIS technology, rough set theory and its application represent (from the author's viewpoint) the most promising valuation approach among the advanced methods. However, as many of the other valuation approaches described above, the method is in an experimental phase and not yet applied by practitioners.

Within the next Sections 4.3.1 and 4.3.2 the suitability of the traditional and advanced valuation methods in reflecting sustainability issues in property valuation practice will be reviewed.

4.3 Reflecting sustainability issues in property valuation practice

4.3.1 General options for valuers

Given the variety of valuation methods available there are also a number of options for valuers to do both reflect sustainability issues within estimates of market value and calculations of worth as well as to better understand the relationships between certain building characteristics and property prices. While the former task would be typically performed by using the traditional valuation methods, the advanced methods of valuation lend itself to address the latter issue:

4.3.1.1 The application of traditional valuation methods

Among the traditional methods there are mainly two – sales comparison and investment method – that can be particularly useful for reflecting sustainability issues when estimating market value. The other three traditional methods are considered inappropriate in this regard and will not be investigated any further for the following reasons: the cost method is ruled out simply because 'the market value of anything may be much above or much below the normal cost of production' (Marshall, 1890, Book V, Ch. VIII). The residual method is not considered further because it relies on an estimation of construction and/or development cost and because there are too many uncertainties associated with predicting the other valuation input parameters. The profits method is regarded inappropriate since it is much more concerned with evaluating the profitability of the tenant's businesses than with the subject property itself. In summary, these three methods can be considered as substitute methods of property valuation. They shall be used to estimate market value only if the sales comparison or the investment method cannot be applied for whatever reason. How these two methods can be used to reflect sustainability issues will be discussed in the following. In addition, it will be discussed how sustainability issues can be reflected within calculations worth which also rely on traditional methods but which focus on estimating investor specific values instead of market values.

(1) When using the sales comparison method the primary task of the valuer is to carry out a process termed comparative analysis which involves quantitative and/or qualitative techniques in order to derive appropriate adjustments to the comparable sales observed in the marketplace. This subsequently leads to a value indication for the property under investigation. The valuation process involves the following general steps (AI, 2001, p. 429):

- Identifying the elements of comparison that affect the value of the type of property being valued.
- Comparing the characteristics and attributes of each comparable sale with those of the subject property; and then measuring the difference in each element of comparison in order to justify and support the reasonableness of the adjustment.
- Deriving at a net adjustment (either in a Euro or in a percentage figure) for each comparable and applying it to the sale price or unit price of the comparable to arrive at a range of adjusted sale or unit prices for the subject property. This allows the valuer to determine the most probable position of the subject property within the range of adjusted sale or unit prices.
- Reconciling the range of adjusted sale or unit prices to the subject property by using qualitative analysis if appropriate. This is usually done by dividing the adjusted comparables into two groups: those that are qualitatively superior and those that are qualitatively inferior to the subject property. The adjusted prices of these two groups then frame the value indication for the property under investigation.

It is clear that this method works best when a sufficient amount of comparable sale prices is available *and* when the characteristics and attributes of these sales prices and of the subject property can be appropriately specified in order to avoid comparing 'apples with oranges'. As a consequence, the valuer usually faces two problems when trying to reflect sustainability issues. The first one is the difficulty of finding comparable sale prices of properties that exhibit sustainable design features. However, 'in some markets, especially those with municipally sponsored programs, it will be relatively easy to find comparable properties and the sales comparison approach can be applied with a great deal of reliability (Guidry, 2004, p. 64). The second difficulty lies in identifying the physical characteristics and attributes of the subject property as well as of the comparable sales that are indicative of their degree of sustainability or sustainability performance respectively. In order to do this, the valuer can rely either on building descriptions, building files, and energy certificates or, if these sources of information are unavailable, on personal judgement. Within some markets, particularly within European housing markets, building files and energy certificates are already available to a certain extent (see Table 21) or will be available on a wider basis in the near future. This information can then be used by the valuer to form an opinion on the superiority or inferiority of the subject property in comparison to the observed comparable sales.

Table 21: *Examples of national building files and passports for residential property*

Country	Name	Source
Austria	*, Gebäudezertifikat nach dem Total Quality Assessment'*	*Österreichisches Ökologie-Institut, Wien, http://www.argetq.at/*
Germany	*, Hausakte für den Neubau von Einfamilienhäusern'*	*Bundesministerium für Verkehr, Bau- und Wohnungswesen, Berlin, http://www.bmvbw.de/*
Italy	*, Fascicolo del fabricato'*	*Various sources*
Netherlands	*, Gebouwdossier / Woningprofiel'*	*Ministerie van VROM (Ministry of Housing), Den Haag, http://www.vrom.nl/pagina.html*
Scotland	*, Purchaser's Information Pack'*	*Scottish Executive, Edinburgh, http://www.scotland.gov.uk/library5/ housing/pfph-00.asp*
Spain	*, Libro del Edificio'*	*Various sources*
UK	*'Home Information Pack'*	*Office of The Deputy Prime Minister, London www.housing.odpm.gov.uk*

However, if building files or energy certificates are not available or only in part, the valuer has to rely on personal judgement which requires that the valuer knows which building features render a building superior or inferior in terms of sustainability performance. This pinpoints the need to integrate the topics of sustainability and sustainable building into education and training of valuers and professional advisors (see Lützkendorf and Lorenz, 2006b). In order to demonstrate how a valuer can reflect sustainability issues through the application of the sales comparison approach in practice, the following hypothetical situation is constructed: Assume that the valuer is equipped with the knowledge on the benefits of sustainable design;

assume further that the valuer has been assigned to provide a value estimate for a single-family house that exhibits certain energy efficiency features and that has been built by using environmentally friendly construction materials. Assume also, that the valuer has been able to identify sales of comparable properties only which do not exhibit energy efficiency features and which have been built with conventional construction materials. In this case the sales comparison approach is still valid since energy efficiency and building materials relate to only one of the elements of comparison; i.e. physical characteristics.

> *'If the physical characteristics of a comparable property and the subject property differ in many ways, each of these differences may require comparison and adjustment.' (AI, 2001, p. 436)*

However, the valuer has not been able to identify enough sales to provide a basis for all adjustment calculations; notably for those relating to energy efficiency and environmentally friendly building materials. Four consequences will result from this circumstance: First, the valuer has to explain within the valuation report that a lack of supporting data has eliminated the possibility of applying a direct sales adjustment process for certain elements of comparison.[99] Second, the adjustments made in order to reflect the subject property's energy efficiency features and environmentally friendly building materials will depend on the valuer's judgement. Third, the valuer will have to back up this judgement through indirect market support; i.e. through investigating a wider array of market sales and/or through analysing the competitive position of energy efficient single-family houses that have been built by using environmentally friendly materials from a broader perspective. Fourth, if the valuer finally decides that energy efficiency and environmentally friendly materials render the subject property superior to the comparable properties and if he decides to assign a 'valuation bonus' on that basis, then, the validity of this judgement solely depends on the valuer's capability to explain and justify his or her assumptions within the valuation report. In summary, it is perfectly possible for valuers to reflect sustainability issue through the application of the sales comparison method even if there are not enough comparable sales available to calculate price adjustments directly.

(2) When using the investment or income method the major valuation input parameters are market rent, operating costs and capitalisation or discount rate. Sustainable design features can affect all three input parameters. Sustainable design can significantly reduce operating

---

[99] This applies for most valuation assignments since there are very seldom enough comparable sales to justify all adjustments through direct sales adjustment processes.

expenses which results in higher net operating income. But most sustainable design features affect operating expenses that are usually attributable to the tenant (such as costs for heating, cooling, electricity and water) and are therefore not considered when calculating net operating income. Nonetheless, sustainable design can reduce the costs for maintenance, repair, and management as well; and these costs are often attributable to the property owner (at least in Germany). Thus, valuers can try taking these cost reductions into account when calculation net operating income. However, German valuation theory and practice intents not to estimate property-specific operating costs but uses average figures instead. These figures mainly depend on property type and age of the building; they can be found in valuation literature and guidelines. This valuation practice can be considered inappropriate for reflecting sustainability issues because when the same average figures are used for all valuation assignments, then sustainable buildings are punished and conventional ones are rewarded. Other countries' valuation theory and guidelines advises valuers to take a close look at property-specific expenses. For example, in the US a comprehensive analysis of annual property operating expenses of the subject property is considered an essential element of the income method (see AI, 2001, p. 486).

Sustainable design can also affect market rent. But it may be difficult for valuers to justify a higher market rent for sustainable buildings when they are unable to find comparable properties.[100] This is particularly true if one considers that sustainable design features may not yet be fully reflected in the building's current rental and market value. For example, McNamara (2005b) recently stated that 'environmentally friendly buildings will become more desirable property assets in future years even if it is not reflected in their current value.' As a consequence, the main valuation input parameter that allows valuers to reflect sustainability issues when using the investment method is the capitalisation or the discount rate. These rates are used to convert future benefits (i.e. income) into and indication of the overall property value. Under certain conditions, the capitalisation rate for a property may be numerically equivalent to the corresponding discount rate; but the rates and their underlying concepts are not the same, nor are they interchangeable (AI, 2001). The capitalisation rate reflects the relationship between a single year's net operating income and property value. In contrast, the discount rate is applied to a series of periodic incomes to obtain their present value. The discount rate reflects the assumption that benefits received in the future are worth less than the same benefits

---

[100] In this regard, the German town Darmstadt offers valuers and landlords the first 'ecological rental index' for residential properties which shows that energy efficiency does appear to be reflected in rental values. The index can be used to justify higher rents for energy efficient buildings. The rental index has been developed by the Institute for Housing and Environment (Institut für Wohnen und Umwelt, IWU), see: http://www.iwu.de/aktuell/mietspiegel-darmstadt.htm

received now.[101] In property valuation practice a variety of different capitalisation and discount rates are applied and a range of different terms can be found in the literature to describe them. An overview on different rates as well as concise definitions is contained in AI (2001 and 2002); whereas the relationship between capitalisation and discount rates is explored in Sevelka (2004). Whether it is a capitalisation rate (which is called all risks yield (ARY) in the UK) or a discount rate, both rates shall reflect the risks associated with the property under investigation.[102] Although the basis for deriving these rates usually is an analysis of comparable properties, the suitability of a particular rate 'cannot be proved with market evidence, but the rate estimated should be consistent with the data available. Rate estimation requires appraisal judgement and knowledge of prevailing market attitudes and economic indicators' (AI, 2001, p. 491). Expressed in other words, the valuer makes a judgement on the future when finally determining capitalisation or discount rates. As a consequence, it is this process of rate estimation that allows the valuer to account for a range of sustainability issues indirectly; e.g. for lower operating costs and increased occupant comfort which makes the building more attractive in the marketplace and which finally results in lower vacancy rates, lower risks of losing the tenant(s)[103], and thus, in more stable cash flows; or for the use of environmentally friendly building materials which results in lower risk of litigation and of facing penalties and burdens imposed by regulation and public authorities. The problem for valuers, however, is that they do not know how to exactly adjust capitalisation and/or discount rates in order to reflect the superiority of buildings that exhibit certain sustainable design features. As a result, the process of rate estimation is subjective and highly uncertain. On the one hand, this is due to a lack of detailed property performance data which could be analysed by making use of advanced valuation methodology in order to provide a more scientific basis for these rate adjustments. But on the other hand, subjectivity and uncertainty are inherent parts of the valuation process. Therefore, the valuer has to explain and account for subjective elements and uncertainty within the valuation report. And again, the validity of the final decision to assign a

---

[101] A detailed explanation of discounting practices and a critical examination of the discounting concept's underlying assumptions is offered by Colin Price (1993).

[102] The capitalisation rate shall reflect *all* the risks whereas the discount rate shall reflect those risks that are not explicitly treated through other valuation input parameters within a discounted cash flow analysis.

[103] Regarding the risk of losing the tenant(s) German valuation practice exhibits another deviation from internationally accepted practice: the risk of losing the tenant(s) is not expressed within the capitalisation rate but as a percentage amount of the annual income generated by the property which reduces the property's net operating income. The percentage figures usually applied do not depend on property specific factors since these figures are predetermined in German valuation guidelines (Wertermittlungsrichtlinien, WertR). It is stated within the WertR that valuers can use 2% for residential and mixed-use properties, and 4% for commercial properties. Again, this valuation practice can be considered inappropriate for reflecting sustainability issues because when the same percentage figures are used for all valuation assignments, then the increased attractiveness or superiority of sustainable buildings cannot be accounted for. As a consequence sustainable buildings are punished and conventional ones are rewarded.

'valuation bonus' (i.e. a lower rate) to a sustainable building depends on the valuer's capability to explain and justify the underlying assumptions within the valuation report.

(3) When calculating worth, valuers typically apply discounted cash flow (DCF) techniques as this is also the norm in calculating worth of the equity and fixed interest asset classes. As said before, valuation input parameters in calculating worth depend on both market derived information as well as investor specific inputs. As a consequence, the valuer is not facing the same (but similar) difficulties when determining valuation input parameters and when trying to reflect sustainability issues as this is the case in market valuations. This is because, 'in the majority of circumstance, investors will already have set appropriate discount rates (target rates) for a calculation of worth. However, it is not uncommon for a valuer to be asked to contribute an opinion in the selection process. At the very least, the valuer should be conversant with the client's thinking in determining the discount rate as this my affect his treatment of other elements of the cash flow' (RICS, 1997, p. 29). Thus, the valuer takes an advisory role and helps investors to find an appropriate discount rate which compensates the investor for the risks taken and which reflects the investor's interests and risk preferences. As a result, the valuer should be fully aware of the risk-reduction potential of sustainable buildings and vice versa of the higher risks associated with conventional or unsustainable buildings. In addition, the valuer should be able to advise clients on that basis in order to derive a discount rate and other input parameters that truly reflect investor specific interests and risk preferences. The discount rate applied is usually calculated on a risk-free basis; i.e. the rate of long-term government bonds is taken as a baseline to which premia for *perceived* property-specific and property-market-specific risks are added. Figure 30 depicts the salient factors in deriving a risk premium for property. These risk factors are not entirely separable or mutually exclusive; i.e. they cannot by clearly assigned to either market- or property-specific-risks. For example, the failure to meet market yield expectations could be a function of any one of, or a combination of these factors. Furthermore, the accepted norm is that certain elements of risk are best incorporated through adjustments of the discount rate while others are best incorporate into the estimate of the cash flow itself. The more market-risk related factors (b-g) are typically reflected through the discount rate while the more property-specific factors (h-k) are built into the cash flow estimate (RICS, 1997).

Figure 30: *Risk factors in calculating property worth (based on RICS, 1997, pp. 25-26)*

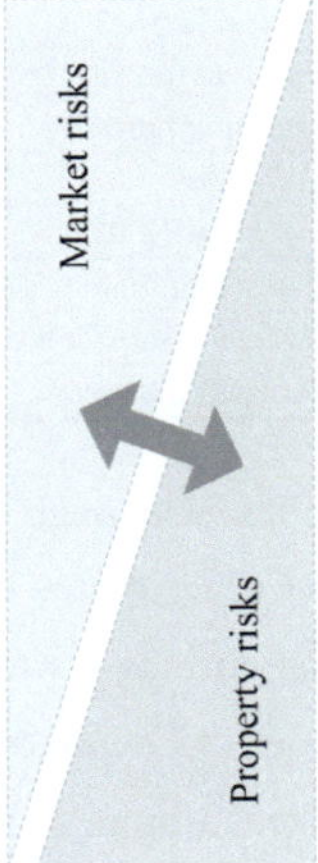

(a) Risk-free rate of investment

(b) Inflation expectations (if the real-return of index-linked government bonds is taken as the risk-free rate)

(c) Illiquidity upon sale (e.g. lot size, transaction time, availability of finance)

(d) Failure to meet market rental expectations (forecast rental growth)

(e) Failure to meet market yield expectations (forecast yield shift)

(f) Risk of locational, economic, physical and functional depreciation through structural change

(g) Risks associated with legislative change (e.g. planning / privity of contract, changes in fiscal policy)

(h) Tenant default on rental payment (covenant risk)

(i) Risk of failure to relet (void risks)

(j) Costs of ownership and management

(k) Differing lease structures

The explanations provided above indicate that sustainability issues can and will affect the majority of risk factors considered within calculation of worth. Thus, valuers can either try to ascribe a risk premium to each of these factors or to group risk factors and to adjust the other calculation input parameters accordingly.

The latter approach has been put forward through a recent research project which was funded by the UK Department of Trade and Industry and a consortium of UK commercial property industry representatives. This project developed an appraisal model that allows incorporating sustainability issues into calculations of property worth (Sayce et al., 2004b). For reasons of simplification, the proposed model assumes that all the characteristics of a property investment can be reflected through four key variables: rental growth, depreciation, risk premium and cash flow. It is further assumed that specific sustainability criteria impact on one or more of these key variables. Selection, classification and weighting of the sustainability criteria were based on consultations with property professionals, investors and occupiers who participated in the research project. A total of nine sustainability criteria (see Table 22) have been selected and integrated into the appraisal model.

Table 22: *Sustainability criteria linking through to worth (Sayce et al., 2004a, p. 4)*

Sustainability criteria	Weighting	Conduit
Building Adaptability	*0.8*	*Risk premium, cash flow, rental growth, depreciation*
Accessibility	*1*	*Rental growth, depreciation*
Building Quality	*0.9*	*Rental growth, cash flow, depreciation*
Energy Efficiency	*0.4*	*Rental growth, risk premium, cash flow, depreciation*
Pollutants	*0.6*	*Rental growth, risk premium, cash flow, depreciation*
Contextual Fit	*0.5*	*Rental growth*
Waste and Water	*0.3*	*Rental growth, cash flow, depreciation*
Occupier Satisfaction	*0.7*	*Risk premium*
Occupier Impact	*0.2*	*Risk premium*

In the next stage of the research project appraisals of selected properties have been carried out. Once on the basis of the RICS standard method for calculating worth (see RICS, 1997) and once as a weighted sustainability appraisal with adjusted figures for the four key variables. As expected, the application of the standard appraisal method to 'average' properties resulted in an over-valuation in comparison to the results of the sustainability appraisal. In contrast, the application of the standard method to a building performing particularly well under the sustainability criteria would lead to an under-valuation in comparison to the results of the sustainability appraisal. The concluding remark of the study that summarized the research project outcomes is of major interest: 'What is clear, however, is that a deeper analysis of property characteristics is necessary if appraisals are to keep pace with the investment risk implications of changing occupier demands' (Sayce et al., 2004a, p. 20).

This research project is unique because it is the first time that major property market players are making substantive efforts to introduce sustainability issues into their investment decision processes and its value for increasing sustainable development in the property sector is recognized. However, with respect to sustainability criteria selection and weighting, the project represents the assumptions of a particular group of investors. This is perfectly fine for the purpose of calculating worth which has been defined as the value of the property to a particular investor, or class of investors, for identified investment objectives. However, whenever the purpose is to estimate market value (which is an estimation of the most likely price achievable if the property were to be sold in the open market), then sustainability criteria (and their relative importance) to base valuations on should be derived from market evidence. This can be accomplished (at least in theory) by using advanced valuation methods in order to monitor relationships between property characteristics and observed market prices.

4.3.1.2 The application of advanced valuation methods

Advanced valuation methods offer a variety of possibilities for valuers to account for sustainability issues. Given the variety of methods available, the manifold of opportunities for valuers appears to be overwhelming. Almost all of the advanced valuation methods can be used in one way or another to account for and to reflect sustainability issues in property valuations. Probably only ARIMA models are inappropriate in this regard since they are designed to better understand the property price formation process in relation to the national economic climate. Furthermore, the real options method takes a particular position among the advanced methods of valuation; i.e. while the other methods are designed to analyse property prices observed in the past and to draw conclusions from this analytical process for current and future valuation problems, the real options methods looks almost exclusively into the future; it is designed to value future opportunities that may arise from a particular parcel of land or building. As such, the real options method can be particularly useful in order to account for the increased flexibility and adaptability that sustainable buildings have to offer. The other advanced methods can be used to better understand the relationships between particular building or locational features and observed property prices and therefore can assist valuers in justifying their assumptions when trying to account for sustainability issues by using one of the traditional methods of valuation. However, advanced valuation methods can only be effectively used in this regard if the property transaction data sets that are to be analysed contain information on the properties' degree of sustainability or sustainability performance. The absence of such information within property transaction databases and within building descriptions in general is currently the main obstacle the hampers the application of advanced valuation methodology to address issues of sustainability in property valuation. This will be explained in more detail within the next chapter. Hereby, the hedonic pricing method will be used because this method is currently the most widespread and readily understood among the advanced valuation methods and because this method is particularly useful in measuring the value market participants place on different qualitative and quantitative property characteristics. Thus, the method can be used to explain the relationship between the sustainability of construction and observed property prices in order to offer a more scientific basis for the value adjustments that have to be made to account for sustainability issue in property valuation. The applicability of the method is tested by applying it to a sample of over 20,000 transactions of flats and apartments that occurred in Suttgart, Germany, during 1995 and 2005.

4.3.2   Testing the applicability of hedonic pricing methods – a case study

4.3.2.1   Hedonic pricing and index construction techniques

The basic idea of the hedonic pricing approach goes back to the late 1930s when Court (1939) established the first hedonic price model for the automobile industry. Since then the method expanded to a variety of other goods like washing machines, computers, and housing units. The theoretical foundations of the hedonic price model were set by Lancaster (1966) and Rosen (1974). Lancaster was the first to put forward a new approach expanding the consumer theory of classical economics. He argued that demand for a product is not based on the product itself but on the product's utility-generating characteristics. That explains why the method is termed 'hedonic'. Rosen (1974) established the modelling foundation for the hedonic price theory by putting forward the equilibrium model of market supply and demand based on product characteristics.

The hedonic model relates the property price P to a vector x of structural and locational variables or other building characteristics. Then the marginal cost of an additional unit of a given characteristic x_i is calculated as the partial derivative of $P(x)$ with respect to that characteristic, i.e.,

$$dP_{x_i} = \frac{dP}{dx_i} \qquad (1)$$

Parameter estimation is usually based on a multiple regression model and results in the marginal value that the consumer is willing to pay for each of the considered characteristics. In general the regression model takes the form:

$$P = f(x, \beta) + \varepsilon \qquad (2)$$

where P denotes the vector of observed transaction prices, x the matrix of exogenous variables, β the vector of coefficients and ε the error term that is assumed to be 'white noise'. In such a model the regression parameters β_i reflect the price of the attribute x_i and are called hedonic prices. Apart from the identification and selection of appropriate variables that are hypothesized to have an influence on the price of property within a given region or market, an adequate functional form for the explanation of the relationship between these variables and property price has to be chosen. The literature shows the use of various functional forms in hedonic pricing studies, including linear, log-linear, logged or non-linear form; (see for example Sirmans et al., 2005). A discussion of major issues regarding the functional form of hedonic pricing models can be found in Milton et al. (1984) or in Cassel and Mendelsohn (1985). Janssen et al. (2001), however, argue that there is no agreement in the literature as to what is an appropriate functional form for the effect of property attributes. There appears to be conflict between an optimal fit of the model on the one hand and the determination of useful hedonic prices for property characteristics on the other hand. But since the objective of this analysis was not the comparison of different model specifications, in the sequel a standard log-linear model is chosen.[104] Because the regression results did not give cause to refute the model, appeared reasonable and logical, and were in agreement with accepted beliefs, the model was regarded as appropriate. Also, Flemming and Nellis (1997) considered the log-linear form most appropriate for the construction of the Halifax Bank House Price Index.

The log-linear regression model has the following form:

$$\ln(P) = \beta_0 + \beta_1 x_1 + \beta_2 x_2 + ... + \beta_k x_k + u \qquad (3)$$

with

P	= the price of the property;
β_0	= intercept term;
$\beta_1, \beta_2, ..., \beta_k$	= coefficients of variables, including dummy variables;
$x_1, x_2, ..., x_k$	= value-determining characteristics; and
u	= residual unexplained by the independent variables.

While in a strictly linear model, the coefficients of a variable are equal to absolute prices for the unit of the respective property characteristic, in a log-linear model, the parameters give the percentage effect of the exogenous variable to the variable being explained, i.e. property price. Thus, the coefficients in the log-linear model can be interpreted as the approximate percentage change in the property price relative to a per-unit change in the given variable.

Over the last decades hedonic pricing models have been applied widely to property for three reasons: (1) to explain the price formation of (mainly residential) property assets by identifying the main determinants of property prices, (2) to isolate and quantify the impact of different physical and locational characteristics on property prices, and (3) to account for changes in the price formation process across regions or over time. Today, the literature dealing with hedonic pricing applications to property is abundant but there seems to be a lack of studies that try examining the price effect of the property's structural condition, the quality (and not mere availability) of equipment and fittings, the degree of modernisation or (most interestingly) of sustainable design. For the central business district (CBD) office sector this view is

---

[104] The comparison of different model specifications has been investigated in various studies, among others in Bowen et al. (2001) or in Fletcher et al. (2004).

also supported by Ho et al. (2005, p. 425) who argue that 'the role of property-specific attributes that are intrinsic features to CBD office building quality has been a neglected area of CBD office property research.' Early and exceptional examples for the office sector are, however, two hedonic pricing studies carried out in the 1980s that measured the positive impact of 'good' architecture on rental rates for commercial offices (Hough and Kratz, 1983 and Vandell and Lane, 1989). In addition, the research of Baum (1993 and 1994) and of Bottom et al. (1999) shows that high office building quality leads to higher returns or improved investment performance respectively.

In order to explore property price movements in dependency of certain qualitative building or locational characteristics, the hedonic regression function can be used to construct hedonic price indexes. Usually, hedonic price indexes are used to adjust for quality change in consumer price indexes; several European countries, the US and Japan are using a hedonic pricing methodology to account for quality change of certain goods (like cars, computers, household equipment, and recently owner-occupied residential property) within the determination of their national consumer price indexes (Behrmann and Kathe, 2004).

Triplett (2004) provides a detailed explanation of hedonic indexes and distinguishes between four major methods for the calculation of hedonic price indexes. These are: the time dummy variable method, the characteristics price index method, the hedonic price imputation method and the hedonic quality adjustment method. The time-dummy variable method and the characteristics price index method are also sometimes describes as "direct" methods. For these methods all the price information comes directly from the hedonic regression function. Direct methods also require a hedonic function to be estimated for each period for which a price index is needed. The hedonic price imputation method and the hedonic quality adjustment method have often been referred to as "indirect" or "composite" methods. Since in these methods the hedonic function is used only to impute prices or to adjust for quality changes in the sample, they are often also called "imputation" methods. Indirect methods assume that the hedonic function can be estimated also from a data source being different from the one used for calculating the price index.

For the purpose of this analysis the characteristics price index method has been considered most appropriate since it is a direct method (i.e. no price information is used from alternative sources) and because it has several advantages over the other direct method, the time dummy variable method (Triplett, 2004). The characteristics price index method uses the implicit characteristics prices (i.e. the regression coefficients from the hedonic function) in a conventional weighted index number formula. It is assumed that the coefficients estimate implicit prices for the characteristics such that the quantity weights are quantities of the characteristics rather than quantities of the goods. Recent applications of this index method include television sets (Moulton et al. 1999), computer prices (Moch and Triplett, 2004) and various aspects of cost-of living (Schultze and Mackie, 2002).

The index is calculated as follows: a hedonic regression function is estimated for property prices in period t. Then the estimated price of $\hat{p}_{t,i}$ property i with the characteristics $(x_{1,i}, x_{2,i}, \ldots, x_{k,i})$ that was sold in period t according to the model is:

$$\hat{p}_{t,i} = \beta_{0,t} + \beta_{1,t} x_{1,i} + \beta_{2,t} x_{2,i} + \ldots + \beta_{k,t} x_{k,i} \qquad (4)$$

where $(\beta_{0,t}, \beta_{1,t}, \beta_{2,t}, \ldots, \beta_{k,t})$ are the estimated regression coefficients in period t. Furthermore, another hedonic regression function with the coefficients $(\beta_{0,t+1}, \beta_{1,t+1}, \beta_{2,t+1}, \ldots, \beta_{k,t+1})$ is estimated for the period $t+1$. The estimated price of the same property in period t+1 would then equal

$$\hat{p}_{t+1,i} = \beta_{0,t+1} + \beta_{1,t+1} x_{1,i} + \beta_{2,t+1} x_{2,i} + \ldots + \beta_{k,t+1} x_{k,i} \qquad (5)$$

The characteristics price index method now uses the estimated coefficients of both periods t and $t+1$ as well as specified weights $(w_1, w_2, \ldots, w_k)$ to determine a price index by comparing W_t with W_{t+1} according to

$$I = \frac{W_{t+1}}{W_t} = \frac{\beta_{0,t+1} + \beta_{1,t+1} w_1 + \beta_{2,t+1} w_2 + \ldots + \beta_{k,t+1} w_k}{\beta_{0,t} + \beta_{1,t} w_1 + \beta_{2,t} w_2 + \ldots + \beta_{k,t} w_k} \qquad (6)$$

It becomes apparent that to construct any price index, adequate weights $(w_1, w_2, \ldots, w_k)$ are needed. In general, weights for a characteristics price index are quantities of characteristics, for property assets the weights represent the characteristics of the property. To determine the change in the characteristics price index from period t to t+1, therefore, the mean characteristics are chosen as weights:

$$(w_1, w_2, \ldots, w_k) = (\bar{x}_{1,t}, \bar{x}_{2,t}, \ldots, \bar{x}_{k,t}) \qquad (7)$$

Then, the numerator of equation (6) is constructed by using the prices of the initial-period's mean characteristics, estimated with the second period's hedonic function. The denominator is calculated by using the prices of the initial period's mean characteristics, estimated with the initial period's hedonic function, which is simply the mean property price in the initial period.

4.3.2.2   The data

During the author's search for transaction data in Germany it turned out that the valuation expert committee of the city of Stuttgart was able and willing to provide the largest and most comprehensive set of property transaction data appropriate for performing a hedonic pricing analysis. The valuation expert committees ('Gutachterausschüsse') are the main sources for property transaction data in Germany. The valuation expert committees constitute independent institutions or collegiate bodies at the states or cities level; the committees' members are appointed by public authorities on an honorary basis for a time period of between four and five years. The main function and duty of these committees is improving market transparency by collecting and publishing property sales and market-related data. Every property transaction in Germany must be attested by a notary and is recorded within the land registry; this information (i.e. the sales contract) is passed on to the valuation expert committees and forms their primary source of information. In addition, valuation expert committees gather further information (e.g. on qualitative and quantitative characteristics of traded property assets, rent levels or on the quality of location) by using questionnaire surveys or by conducting personal investigations. However, rules or guidelines on the extent and depth of these additional investigations do not exist; thus, the quality and coverage of property transaction data that can be provided by the German valuation expert committees varies significantly depending on the committees' size and resources.

The original data set provided by the expert valuation committee of the city of Stuttgart for this analysis contained 28,789 observations of property transactions within the city of Stuttgart during the time period between January 1995 and March 2005; the sales data was preselected by the Stuttgart valuation expert committee (i.e. only sales that have taken place under normal circumstances were included) and covered flats and apartments only that were not occupied by a tenant at the date of transaction. The mean price for a flat in Stuttgart during this time period was € 153,614 and the size of the flats ranged from 15 to 412 m² with a mean close to 73.5 m².

Some of the variables used by the Stuttgart valuation expert committee to specify the property transactions were rather different from the variables typically appearing in hedonic pricing studies: besides essential information on size and age, most hedonic pricing studies use variables that focus on structural, internal and external features (e.g. number of rooms, bathrooms and garages) as well as on variables reflecting particular aspects of location and neighbourhood (e.g. distance to the city centre or to public service amenities). Sirmans et al. (2005) reviewed a wide range of US studies published during the last decade and compiled a list of top twenty characteristics appearing most often in hedonic pricing studies (see Table 23).

Table 23: *Top twenty characteristics appearing most often in hedonic pricing studies (based on Sirmans et al., 2005)*

Rank	Variable	Rank	Variable
1	*lot size*	*11*	*number of full baths*
2	*natural logarithm of lot size*	*12*	*fireplace*
3	*square feet*	*13*	*air conditioning*
4	*natural logarithm of square feet*	*14*	*basement*
5	*brick-built*	*15*	*garage spaces*
6	*age*	*16*	*deck*
7	*number of stories*	*17*	*pool*
8	*number of bathrooms*	*18*	*distance*
9	*number of rooms*	*19*	*time on market*
10	*number of bedrooms*	*20*	*time trend*

Similar characteristics are used in European hedonic pricing studies (see for example Maurer et al., 2004 and Bover and Velilla, 2002) and it appears that – as it was said before – there is a lack of variables that are indicative of the property's structural condition, quality (and not mere availability) of equipment and fittings or of the degree of modernisation. Given the huge efforts necessary to obtain such property-related information this circumstance is not surprising; however, the Stuttgart valuation expert committee undertook efforts in gathering information on these latter property characteristics by using a two page questionnaire with more than 20 questions addressing the properties' overall condition, the flats' quality of equipment, fittings and installations as well as the extent of modernisation and maintenance activities. The questionnaire was sent out either to the private buyers of the flats or to the commercial property developers, construction companies or housing corporations that sold the flats. Unfortunately, the returned questionnaires did not feed into the transaction database directly but only in a highly aggregated format; i.e. members of the Stuttgart valuation expert committee analyzed the returned questionnaires and assigned score points for the *flats' quality* and *degree of modernization* to each observed property transaction. Similarly, the flats' *quality of location* was assessed by the members of the Stuttgart valuation expert committee by using score points based on the committee's locational classification system as well as on the members' individual experience. The other property characteristics used to specify the transactions were *floor area, year of construction, number of flats*, and *storey*. The variables and their expected signs in the regression function are described in more detail within Table 24. Of course, the information contained with this property transaction dataset does not refer to a flat's degree of sustainability or sustainability performance directly; however, the variables *flat quality* and *degree of modernization* can be considered as indirect indicators that partially relate to the flat's ability to contribute to sustainable development.

Table 24: *Explanation of hedonic regression variables used in this case study*

Variable	Type	Variable meanings and measurement methods	Sign
Floor area	*Scale*	*Total floor area of the flat in square metres*	+
Quality of location	*Scale*	*The quality of location is expressed by score points ranging from 0 (poor quality of location; e.g. compact and dense design with very limited open space, green areas and sunlight combined with impacts (emission, noise, smell) through industry, trade and/or transport) to 40 (best quality of location, e.g. very quiet and green living areas with aerate design and with no impacts through emissions; highly preferred areas with good image, infrastructure and easy access to leisure and recreation facilities)*	+
Flat's quality	*Scale*	*The quality of the flat is expressed by score points ranging from 0 (poor quality; e.g. no heat and sound insulation, no central heating, single glazed windows, no carpet or wooden floors, poor quality of sanitary and electronic installations, simple and cheap internal fittings like doors or panelling, restricted durability of construction and fitting materials, unfavourable layout) to 40 (best quality; e.g. good heat and sound insulation, double glazed windows, central heating, wooden floors, highest quality of sanitary and electronic installations, high durability of construction and fitting materials, favourable layout)*	+
Degree of modernization	*Scale*	*The degree of modernization is expressed by score points ranging from 1 to 6: 1 indicates that the building has not been modernized; 2 indicates that the façade has been restored; 3 indicates that the building has been partially modernized; 4 indicates that the building has been predominantly modernized; 5 indicates that the building has been fully modernized; 6 indicates that the building is newly built*	+
Year of construction	*Scale*	*Year of construction (ranges from 1773 to 2005)*	+
Number of flats	*Scale*	*Number of flats within the building or building complex (ranges from 2 to 1137)*	-
Ground floor	*Dummy*	*If the flat is located at the ground floor the dummy is set 1, otherwise 0*	-
1. floor	*Dummy*	*If the flat is located at the 1. floor the dummy is set 1, otherwise 0*	+
>1. floor	*Dummy*	*If the flat is located at above the 1. floor and below the attic floor the dummy is set 1, otherwise 0*	-
Attic floor	*Dummy*	*If the flat is located at the attic floor the dummy is set 1, otherwise 0*	+
Basement	*Dummy*	*If the flat is located at the basement the dummy is set 1, otherwise 0*	-

The problem of missing, exceptional or obviously incorrect data within the data set has been addressed as follows:

- all cases where selling price was obviously incorrect have been removed;
- all cases where the flat's quality, the building's degree of modernization or the quality of location were not specified have been removed;
- all cases with floor areas below 20 or above 245 square metres have been removed since these transactions have been considered exceptional.

After removing these observations from the original data set the remaining sample consisted of 20,697 observations.

4.3.2.3   The regression model

Based on the transaction data and the variables described in the previous section, a hedonic regression model according to equation (3) was estimated. The model summary is displayed in Table 25 and Table 26. An R-square of 0.850 was obtained indicating that more than 80% of the variance of the considered prices could be explained by the specified model. These results are comparable with other studies on hedonic price indexes; see for example Palmquist (1980), Milton et al. (1984) or Maurer et al. (2004). Also the F statistic of 11694.38 giving a p-value of 0.000 indicates that the model is statistically significant.

Table 25: *Regression Model Summary*

Model	R	R Square	Adjusted R Square	Std. Error of the Estimate
1	.922	.850	.850	.20115

Table 26: *ANOVA Table for the hedonic regression function*

Model		Sum of Squares	df	Mean Square	F	Sig.
1	Regression	4731.595	10	473.159	11694.380	0.000
	Residual	836.964	20686	.040		
	Total	5568.559	20696			

Table 27 shows the value, standard error, t-statistics and p-values for the regression coefficients. The signs of all coefficients are economically plausible. Except for one variable, all coefficients were highly significant at the 1%-level. Only the coefficient for the 'number of apartments' has a p-value of 0.043 which can still be considered significant at the 5%-level. The dummy variable '1. Floor' has been excluded from the model since the first floor has been taken as the reference storey.

Table 27: *Regression Coefficients*

Variable	Coefficient	Std. Error	Std. Coefficient	t-statistics	Sig.	VIF
(Constant)	9.10470	.143		63.525	.000	
Floor Area	.01390	.000	.704	251.272	.000	1.081
Quality of Location	.00774	.000	.080	27.982	.000	1.130
Flat's Quality	.02189	.000	.311	58.723	.000	3.871
Degree of Modernisation	.04243	.001	.164	43.462	.000	1.970
Year of construction	.00037	.000	.024	4.560	.000	3.335
Number of Flats	-.00002	.000	-.006	-2.020	.043	1.129
Ground Floor	-.02209	.004	-.018	-5.453	.000	1.489
Attic Floor	.03309	.004	.024	7.565	.000	1.413
Basement	-.07336	.009	-.024	-8.515	.000	1.100
>1. Floor	-.01155	.004	-.010	-3.004	.003	1.640

In order to test for multicollinearity between the independent variables, the variance inflation factor (*VIF*) was considered. VIF is the factor by which the variance of the estimated linear regression coefficient increases due to multicollinearity. Typically, a factor of 10 is considered a critical value, in some references also 7 (Neter et al., 1996). Among *VIF* values of the considered variables, the minimum was 1.081 for the variable 'Floor Area' while the maximum was 3.871 for the variable 'Flat's Quality'. Thus, all values were far smaller than the critical value, indicating that the multicollinearity degree between the independent variables was not significant. In summary, it can be argued that an appropriate overall fit of the model to the data has been achieved.

As an interim result, the regression coefficients indicate the approximate percentage change in the mean property price relative to a per-unit change in the given variable (for example, an increase of the Flat's Quality by one score point increases the property price by 2.2 %). Furthermore, given the standardized coefficients of the regression function, it can be concluded that particularly Floor Area, the Flat's Quality, the Quality of Location and the Degree of Modernization have the most substantial impact on the price of flats in Stuttgart. In addition it can be seen that a large number of flats within a building has a negative effect on price and that the attic floor is the most preferred storey while the basement is the least. These results are not surprising; they are in agreement with accepted beliefs and confirm and quantify the major determinants of a flat's price or market value respectively. Thus, the hedonic pricing approach can be considered useful and is likely to work for quantifying the impacts of sustainable design as well.

4.3.2.4   Conditional hedonic price indexes

In order to explore the behaviour of property prices over time in dependence of different qualities of location, different qualities of a flat or of different degrees of modernisation, conditional hedonic price indexes were calculated by making use of the hedonic regression model estimated above. Initially, a hedonic price index based on the complete sample for the considered time period from 1995 to 2005 was calculated. Secondly, the complete sample was divided into sub-samples subject to the three flat's characteristics mentioned before. In doing so, all changes in the other property characteristics were adjusted for and the effect of the variable under consideration was isolated. This, for example, enables the demonstration of whether high-quality flats are able to outperform the complete sample or sub-samples of flats with average or low quality.

As described above, the characteristics price index method was used to determine a hedonic price index for all flats in the sample; this index is displayed in Figure 31(a). Note that the index was fixed to a value of 1 for the initial period 1995. It can be seen that there was quite a dramatic decline in price levels for the period between 1995 and 2000 where the index reaches it lowest value of 0.88. Within the period 2001 to 2005 the index stabilised and remains in the range of 0.89 and 0.91. Overall, in 2005 the calculated value of the index is 0.89, indicating an average decrease of the property prices for flats in Stuttgart by more than 10% during the last ten years.

In order to investigate the performance of subgroups of different qualities of location the complete sample has been divided into three groups: Score points 0 – 20: 'simple location'; score points 21 – 29: 'average location'; score points 30 – 40: 'preferred location'. Each of these groups contains a similar number of observations (i.e. roughly 6,900); for each group, a separate regression model was estimated and a hedonic index calculated subsequently. The results are displayed in Figure 31(b). The results reveal that flats within preferred locations clearly outperform their competitors in terms of price stability. There is also a decline in prices, however, and index value of 0.914 in 2005 indicates a loss of approximately 8.6 % only; while in contrast, prices for flats situated in average or simple locations decreased by approximately 11 % during 1995 to 2005.

With regard to the variable 'Flat's Quality', a similar classification has been chosen to form the subgroups: score points 0 – 20: 'low quality'; score points 21 – 30: 'average quality' and score points 30 – 40: 'high quality'. Again, a regression model as well as a respective hedonic price index was calculated for each group. The results are displayed in Figure 31(c); and again, high quality flats tend to outperform their competitors. The index indicates that prices for high quality flats decreased by 9.5 % only, while flats with low quality lost 12 % and flats with average quality lost 13 % during the time period under consideration.

The same procedure has been repeated for different degrees of modernisation. The results for this variable are displayed in Figure 31(d) and are even more striking. Flats within fully modernized or new buildings lost only 6.5 % during the 10 year period while prices for flats within partially or unmodernized buildings decreased by 12 % and 13.5 % respectively.

Figure 31: *Hedonic Price Indexes: (a) hedonic index for the complete sample 1995-2005, (b) indexes for divided subsample according to the quality of location, (c) indexes for divided subsample according to the flat's quality, (d) indexes for divided subsample according to the degree of modernisation.*

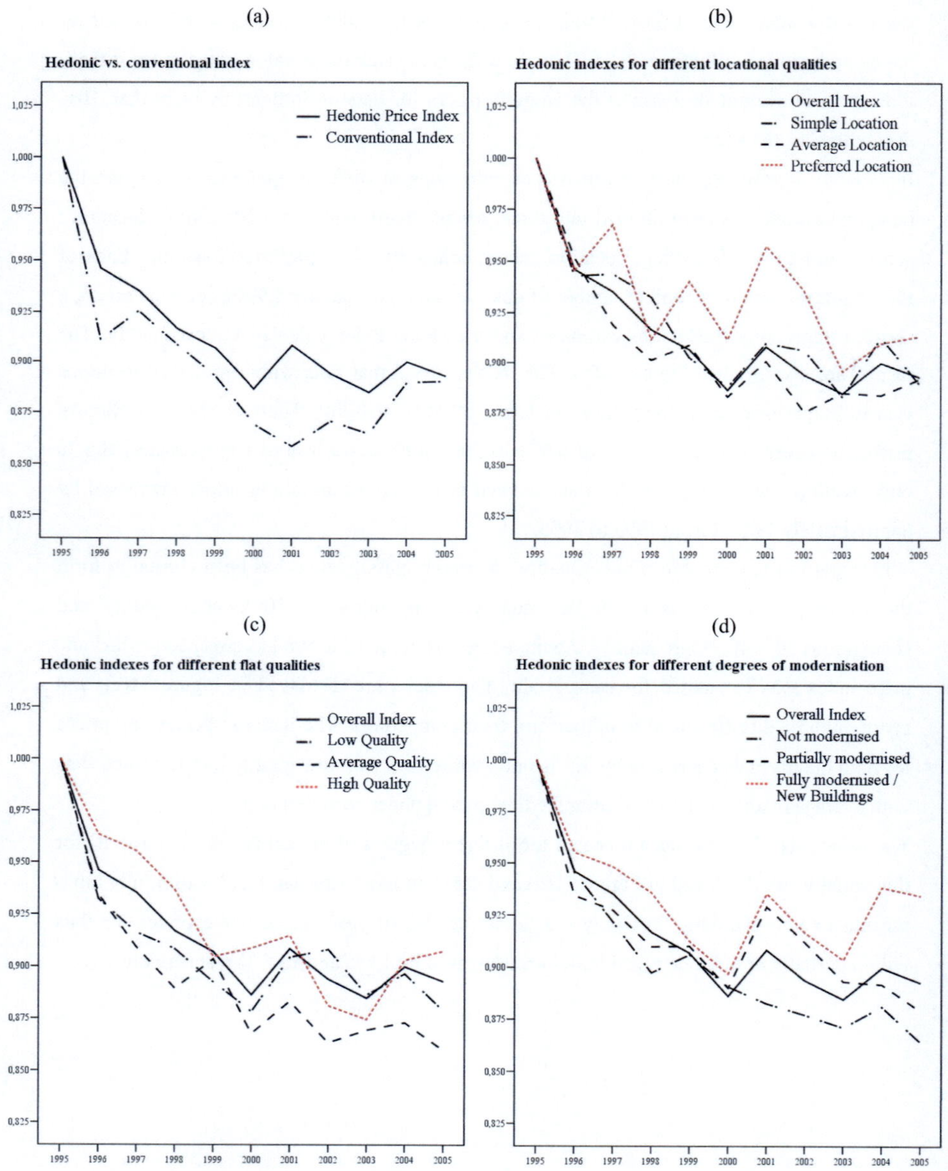

In summary, the results confirm that investing in properly maintained or high-quality flats and/or in flats within preferred locations does pay. It is, however, very interesting to see that both low quality flats and flats within simple locations tend to outperform the average. A possible explanation of this circumstance lies within the nature of the Stuttgart residential property market. Although selling prices for flats decreased in Stuttgart over the last years, the rental prices for residential property (particularly within the city centre) increased dramatically. Thus, many market participants who formerly lived in rented premises decided on buying a flat. Since prices for flats in Stuttgart are still relatively high compared to other cities in Germany, this demand concentrated on the cheaper market segment, i.e. lower quality flats with simple locations. As a consequence, prices for these flats were more stable compared to the more expensive flats of average quality and within average locations.

Although, the transaction data used for this study represents one of the most detailed property transaction databases publicly available in Germany, the nature of the data or the variable structure respectively did not allow accounting for differences in building quality in more detail. For example, conclusions on price differences according to the availability of particular building features (e.g. the availability of particular energy efficiency features such as heat insulation or of double-glazed windows) or more interestingly, on the flats' environmental performance (e.g. primary energy demand) could not be drawn. In order to illustrate this central point Table 28 classifies different levels of building descriptions.

Table 28: *Different levels of building descriptions*

	Type	**Brief Explanation**	**Examples**
1	*Characteristics based description*	*Statement on the availability, number, age or size of particular building features or components*	*Pool, central heating, green roof, number of rooms, flexible walls, suspended ceiling, etc.*
2	*Experience based description*	*Subjective and mainly qualitative judgement mainly based on implicit assumptions*	*Building quality is considered 'good' because of sound structural condition, favourable layout, equipment, etc.*
3	*Attribute based description*	*Judgement or classification based on quantifiable technical and/or physical building characteristics*	*Heat and sound insulation class, degree of efficiency of heating system, share of renewable materials, etc.*
4	*Performance based description*	*Measurement of direct impacts that result from the building's technical and physical characteristics*	*Primary energy demand, CO₂-emissions, life-cycle-costs, annual maintenance costs, etc.*

To a certain extent buildings and building quality can be characterised by using quantifiable descriptions based on clear criteria or performance indicators. The problem with the database used for this study – and with most transaction datasets used for other hedonic studies as well – is that buildings are described by using rather crude statements on the availability, number, age or size of particular building features and/or by making use of subjective and mainly qualitative judgements based on implicit assumptions. Very few advanced valuation studies rely on building descriptions of levels 3 or 4 as indicated in Table 28 above. This is the main reasons why it is so difficult at the moment to explore the functional relationship between sustainable design and property prices.

Also, it is likely that there are diverging perceptions of what constitutes 'quality' across regions, between different groups of property market participants or over time. All this restricts the accuracy and transferability of the results achieved from the analysis described above. Nonetheless, it has been shown that the methodology to account for differences in quality in far greater detail is available and that the usefulness of results of applications of hedonic pricing techniques mainly depends on the quality and accuracy of the data used to describe the property assets under investigation. Thus, in order to account for the price differences between sustainable buildings and conventional ones, the description of property assets needs to be improved by using clear criteria and performance indicators.

4.3.2.5   Future data availability

Ideally, the performance information necessary to describe buildings appropriately (which covers all quality-levels of building descriptions as defined in Table 28 above) is contained within a building file or building passport. However, building files are yet only issued occasionally on a voluntary basis and only for residential property (see Table 21 above). In addition, building files are not yet standardised. Respective standardisation activities at the international and European level have already been mentioned but these standards are still under development. Thus, a time frame of approximately five years needs to be bridged. Therefore, the author recommends following a three-stage plan with increasing informational requirements for assessing the building's contribution to sustainable development. Of course, describing and assessing buildings in such great detail may seem a very ambitious exercise but even today a variety of information that is indicative of a building's sustainability performance is available already within planning documents or will soon be available on a wide basis due to the introduction of energy certificates within Europe. This information can form the starting point for describing a building's contribution to sustainable development:

Phase 1 – Use of information that is (in principle) available already

a) Information related to lot and location:

    * Information on potential contaminations on site;

    * Information on the degree of sealing of the lot;

    * Information on potential environmental influences and risks that can impact on the building (e.g. flooding or storms, or pollution and vibration caused by traffic);

    * Information on potential influences and risks that result from the building and its use and that can impact on the lot and/or on the environment (e.g. contamination of soil and ground water).

b) Building related information:

    * Energy certificate with

        - References to the degree of fulfilment of legal requirements (i.e. primary energy demand which indicates the use on non-renewable resources for energetic utilization);

        - references to the demand for end-energy (information on the demand for end-energy according to single energy sources form the basis for both calculating expected energy costs for heating, warm-water supply and electricity as well as for estimating resulting impacts on the environment, particularly CO_2-emissions);

        - References to the quality of the building's mechanical services (expressed through their degree of efficiency);

        - References to the quality of building's external envelope (expressed through transmission heat losses);

        - References to the quality of the planning/design (expressed by referencing the manner of treating heat bridges);

        - References to the quality of the workmanship (expressed by referencing the manner of safeguarding and portraying the hermetic sealing of the building's external envelope).

    * Estimation of the building's thermal comfort (expressed through PPD (predicted percentage dissatisfied) or PMV (predicted mean vote));

    * Estimation of the building's acoustic comfort (i.e. sound insulation and room acoustics);

    * Estimation of the building's longevity, adaptability and appropriateness for third-party use;

    * Estimation of the ease of conducting maintenance, servicing and recycling activities.

In addition, information on the indoor air quality (expressed for example through TVOC (total volatile organic compound) or through olfactory freshness), on the quality of drinking water, on the appearance of black mould or on electro-magnetic fields as well as on potential strains through radon can be given for existing buildings.

c) Facility management-related information on the existence (and implementation) of:

> * a concept to safeguard the quality of the planning and construction phase;
>
> * energy management and consumption controlling systems;
>
> * occupancy cost management and benchmarking systems;
>
> * maintenance and servicing plans;
>
> * a plan to ensure health, safety and environmental protection during the occupancy phase and during maintenance activities; and
>
> * a concept to measure, monitor and improve occupant satisfaction

Phase 2 – Full declaration

In addition to the information and documents that form the basis for assessing the building's contribution to sustainable development during phase 1, a list of employed building products and materials can be compiled for new buildings. The aim of this documentation (which goes beyond a conventional building specification) is to provide a basis for estimating risks for the environment and for occupants' health, as well as for estimating potential problems (and costs) of the building products' subsequent disposal. One possibility of describing the share of renewable, mineral and fossil resources employed within buildings has been developed by the German working group on declared resources ('Arbeitsgemeinschaft kontrolliert deklarierter Rohstoffe e.V. - ARGE kdR'). The working group developed a label – called 'Ressource-R' – which portrays the share of renewable, mineral and fossil resources on a scale between 0 and 10 (for more information on this label see: ARGE kdR, n.d.).

Phase 3 – Implementation of international standards

It is likely that within approximately five years applicable international and European standards will be available on life cycle assessment, on life cycle costing as well as on the assessment of certain health and comfort related aspects. In the future, these standards can form the precondition and starting point for compiling building files or reports on the 'integrated building performance' respectively. For example, in Germany an integrated design and building assessment tool called LEGEP that follows these standards under development is already available (LEGEP, 2005). An overview on other building assessment tools that also follow these standards to a lesser or greater extent can be found in IEA Annex31 (2001); in Kats et al. (2003) or in Cole (2005). For more information on building assessment tools, see also Section 3.3.2 above.

4.3.2.6 Practical implications

This analysis shows that the application of hedonic pricing techniques leads to plausible and useful results. Major factors that determine property price formation for flats in Stuttgart have been identified and explained. Also, conditional price indexes based on the quality of location, different degrees of modernisation and the overall quality of the flats were calculated. The outcome was that prices for high quality flats, within preferred locations and/or within properly maintained buildings tend to be more stable or to decrease less during an overall market downturn. This has one practical implication: With respect to value retention or investment safety, the empirical analysis confirms that investments into high quality (residential) property assets should be given priority since their market value is more stable within an overall market downturn.

However, this empirical analysis also shows that the usefulness of results obtained through hedonic pricing techniques (or through any other advanced valuation method) is strongly restricted by the quality of the transaction data. In summary, the informational data basis available to date does not allow for a satisfactory explanation of the relationship between property prices and the sustainability of construction. Two practical consequences result from this:

(1) Efforts need to be undertaken by the property profession in combining and transferring financial performance data along with information that is indicative of buildings' contribution to sustainable development. However, in this regard a conflict exists between the potential for a large number of information components to be used when assessing buildings' contribution to sustainable development (see Section 3.3.2 above) and the contradictory need of property professionals for selecting only a few key indicators to base valuations on. The problem is that these few key indicators – which should be capable of satisfactorily explaining the relationship between property prices and the sustainability of construction – can only be identified by using empirical evidence if property transaction databases or property indexes respectively would contain far more detailed building descriptions (ideally on the integrated building performance as explained above). In addition, these few key indicators and their relative importance are can be different between regions and are likely to change over time as value perceptions change and as the knowledge on the benefits of sustainable design becomes more

widespread among market participants. As a consequence, solving this conflict requires starting a collaborative and continuos research effort involving property professionals, researchers, and providers of property indexes and/or transaction databases.

(2) As long as advanced valuation methods are not capable of robustly underpinning a valuer's decision to assign 'valuation bonuses' for sustainable buildings due to data limitations, property valuers can account for sustainability issues on a rather uncertain and subjective basis only. However, this is not a major obstacle since all property valuations are, by nature, subjective and uncertain. The difficulty lies in explaining subjective elements and uncertainty to the end-user of the valuation. For this reason, measures need to be applied that allow valuers to explain their assumptions to clients and to express the uncertainties associated with rather subjective value judgements. Concerning the investment method – the most widespread valuation technique – this will be discussed in the following chapter. The intention is not to offer a valuation approach entirely different from day-to-day practice of most property valuers. By contrast, the intention is to help making current practice change easy by offering valuers a framework that allows responding to the urgent need for more transparency in valuation *and* to account for sustainability issues in an understandable manner at the same time.

4.3.3   Sustainability *and* transparency in property investment valuation

4.3.3.1   The transparency rationale – a 'case study' from Germany

While issues of risk and uncertainty in property valuation are rarely discussed within the German valuation community (the focus is rather on defending the notion of valuation precision), the need to identify and express risk *and* uncertainty within the scope of property valuations is currently one of the key concerns in contemporary UK valuation literature. It is argued that risk and uncertainty are inherent parts of the valuation process because the valuer is 'unable to specify and price accurately all current and future influences on the value of the asset' (Adair and Hutchison, 2005, p. 254).

The debate started in 1994 with the publication of the Mallinson Report that outlined a number of initiatives which the Royal Institution of Chartered Surveyors (RICS) should undertake to help improve the quality of valuations and the standing of the valuation profession in the business world. Among other issues this report argued that all valuations are uncertain and that a single valuation figure is an individual valuer's estimate of the exchange price of a certain property in the marketplace; i.e. an expert *opinion* (RICS, 1994). Therefore, one recommendation (Nr. 34) of the Mallinson Report was that common professional standards and methods should be developed for measuring and expressing valuation uncertainty. This recommendation was addressed by Mallinson and French (2000, p. 28) who proposed a statistical method to account for uncertainty in valuation reports and argued that 'the solution must lie in the creation of some format description, accepted as a norm, which conveys the essence with simplicity, but is capable of expansion and interpretation. This would need to be presented in a prescribed professional standard, and would always be appended to a valuation figure.' Finally, the RICS Carsberg Report (RICS, 2002, p. 3) re-addressed the issue within recommendation Nr. 15 where it is stated that 'RICS should commission work to establish an acceptable method by which uncertainty could be expressed in a manner which will be helpful and will not confuse users of the valuation.'

Around the same time the UK Investment Property Forum (IPF, 2000 and 2002) stressed the need for more advanced and rigorous risk assessment measures within the property investment industry and argued that 'we need a much tighter measurement framework that is designed to operate initially at least at the level of the individual asset rather than one drawn from conventional theory which operates primarily at the portfolio level.' (IPF, 2000, p. 15)

However, to date the decision if and how risk and uncertainty are expressed and reported within property valuations is left to the judgement and experience of the individual valuer alone. More precisely, the latest edition of the RICS Red Book (RICS, 2003) does not provide guidance on how to report risk and uncertainty in a comprehensible and appropriate manner. As a consequence, 'individual valuers must take the issue into their own hands and offer the client what they feel is their best price estimate.' (Joslin, 2005, p. 270)

The situation is pinpointed by the following – admittedly very extreme but real – example:

In 1973 a German bank issued a closed-end property fund consisting of one mixed-use property asset with more than 20.000 square metres of rentable floor area located in the city centre of a major town in the northern part of the country. In August 2004 the rental contract with the major tenant (occupying more than 60 % of available floor space) expired. Since a new tenant has not been found until today the fund is facing serious financial difficulties. However, a sale of the property is not a feasible option for the investors because the expected selling price is below outstanding loans. A particularity of this closed-end fund was that the property asset's market value was estimated by a group of German valuation experts on an annual basis (this procedure is usually required for German open-end property funds). At 31 October 2003 the valuation experts estimated the property's market value at € 17,6 Million (DGA, 2004). One year later, however, the valuation experts' estimate was € 6,3 Million only, which is a correction of the previous year's figure by considerable 64 % (DGA, 2005). The valuation experts argued that this correction was due in order to reflect increased expenses necessary for the revitalisation of the property asset (since it no longer complied with today's office user requirements) as well as a longer time span required for finding a new tenant. However, the circumstance that the major tenant would not renew the rental contract was already well-known at the date of the 2003 valuation. Sadly, this is not the end of the story; today the fund management expects that a 'realistic' selling price ranges between € 2 - 3 million which would represent a correction of the 2004 valuation by another 60 %. In total, this amounts up to a deviation from the 2003 valuation figure by more than 80 % within slightly more than 2 years only (DGA, 2005 and Loipfinger, 2006). That the group of valuers was not able (or wiling) to detect and account for this risk of obsolescence as well as for associated uncertainties with regard to finding a new tenant gives cause for serious concern.

Unfortunately, this is not the only recent example for considerable 'over-valuation' of property assets in Germany: At the end of 2005 German 'HypoVereinsbank' (HVB) – now owned by the Italian 'Unicredit' – had to buy a portfolio consisting of 20 properties from their related property fund company ('iii-investments') because the fund company was facing financial difficulties due to the circumstance that the properties' market values could not have been realised in the open market; the selling price was on the order of € 500 million but immediately after the transaction HVB revalued the portfolio for their balance sheet at approximately € 290 million (FTD, 2005; SZ, 2005 and Jumpertz, 2005). Also, 'Deutsche Bank' has refused to re-buy shares of their open-end property fund ('Fonds-Grundbesitz-Invest') in December 2005 because all 130 fund properties needed to be revalued (Reichel, 2005); and German 'Deka-Immobilien' is facing pressure to revalue their fund's ('Deka-Immobilienfonds') property assets as well: at the end of 2004 the auditors of Deloitte & Touche (mandated by the fund company themselves) and KPMG (mandated by the German financial supervisory authority, BaFin) detected a difference of € 700 million between the market values estimated by the group of valuers responsible for valuing the fund's assets and the auditors' own estimate (Hönighaus, 2004 and Börsen-Zeitung, 2005); in November 2005 the fund company's CEO stated that within the next 4 years downward-adjustments in market value of the fund's assets are likely to be on the order of € 1.1 billion (Haimann, 2005).

As a consequence, the German open-end fund industry is criticised heavily for the quality of valuation reports issued by the group of 'sworn' valuation experts which are syndicated within the association of property-investment-experts ('Bundesverband der Immobilien-Investment-Sachverständigen', BIIS) and which are usually mandated to value the open-end funds' property assets. This has lead to an intense debate among German valuation experts about the usefulness of particular valuation methodologies and practices. In essence, it is a debate on the superiority of valuation approaches between those who stick to traditional German valuation practice (i.e. a practice that distinguishes between a land element and an element for the building when estimating market value and therefore exhibits a range of particularities that are usually termed 'not understandable' by the international valuation and investment community) and those that favour internationally accepted (mainly UK based) methodology. Recent examples of diverging statements can be found in Stroh (2004), in Immobilien Zeitung (2005) and in Engel and Kieffer (2005). Particularly one statement of a German valuer is astonishing given the valuation 'problem' outlined above: The valuer was asked in an interview with Frankfurter Allgemeine Zeitung (2005, p. 25) if there can be precision in property valuations at all and answered that 'the results of valuations conducted by professional valuers can deviate from the correct figures by a maximum of 5 % only.'

It appears that most of the current debate in Germany is entirely misleading because it neither captures nor reflects the nature of the problem. Even worse, the debate facilitates the illusion that property values can be estimated precisely and that one only needs to apply the 'right' methodology for doing so.

> *'The illusion of precision is a milestone for the valuation profession. Valuers and the valuation profession are acting against their own interest by allowing this misconception to continue. The idea that a valuer can precisely estimate price in all instances is sophistry.' (French and Gabrielli, 2005, p. 86)*

There is no such thing as the best or right property valuation method. French (2005, p. 184) argues that 'readers may have been told that some methods are better than others – but this is not necessarily the case. Certain methods can sometimes be more appropriate than others, but mathematical precision does not necessarily equate with superiority.' It is, without doubt, not the valuation methods that cause the problem. Rather, at the core of the problem lies the issue of transparency and traceability of the valuation results (regardless of the valuation method applied); i.e. the manner in which valuers express their assumptions, account for risk and uncertainties and communicate the results of the estimation process to the end user of the valuation report.

4.3.3.2   Risk and uncertainty

Some confusion exists within valuation literature regarding the terms risk and uncertainty because they are often used interchangeably and because one can often be found within the description of the other. Therefore, a brief discussion of what is meant by both terms as well as a description of the interpretations adopted within this paper seems appropriate:

The Royal Society (1983) views risk as the probability that a particular adverse event occurs during a stated period of time, or results from a particular challenge; and that as a probability in the sense of statistical theory risk obeys all the formal laws of combining probabilities. French and Gabrielli (2004, p. 485) define risk as 'the measurement of a loss identified as a possible outcome of the decision' and uncertainty as 'anything that is not known about the outcome of a venture at the time when the decision is made.' With a focus on (property) investments Adair and Hutchison (2005, p. 255-256) define risk 'as the probability that a target rate of return will not be realised' and argue that the concept of risk supposes that all outcomes together with their probabilities of occurrence are known. In addition, they state that uncertainty 'denotes situations where outcomes and their probabilities are not known.'

In conventional investment and finance theory the risk associated with an asset is usually defined as the volatility (quantified through the variance or standard deviation) of its returns. Other literature, however, suggests that both terms risk and uncertainty cannot be defined operationally but only intuitively. For example, Holton (2004) argues that uncertainty that is not perceived cannot be defined operationally and that all one can hope to define operationally is the *perception* of uncertainty. In order to clarify how one can be uncertain but not realize it, he provides the following example: 'Suppose you are in a casino. A man is about to roll a die. If the result is a six, you are going to lose $100. What is your risk? What, in your subjective opinion, is the probability that you will lose $100? If you say it is one chance in six, you may want to reconsider. I neglected to mention that the die is 10-sided.' (Holton, 2004, p. 22)

Similarly, definitions of risk are likely to carry an element of subjectivity depending on the nature of the risk and to what it applies to. Adams (2005a and 2005b, p.1) argues that 'risk is a word that refers to the future. It has no objective existence. The future exists only in the imagination.' Thus, risk is all in the mind. In order to acknowledge this subjective element of risk no definition of the term is adopted for this dissertation. As an alternative, the *interpretation* of risk provided by Chicken and Posner (1999) is used which also better reflects the idea behind the property rating approach introduced below. Instead of defining risk, they define the constituents of risk:

$$Risk = Hazard * Exposure$$

Whereby hazard is the way in which a thing or situation can cause harm while exposure is the extent to which the likely recipient of the harm can be influenced by the hazard. With a focus on property, harm is meant to be damage or loss of performance and finances while exposure involves the notions of frequency and probability. Because probability is often used as a metric of uncertainty, it is important to acknowledge Holton's (2004) point that, at best, probability quantifies *perceived* uncertainty as well.

Accounting for uncertainty

Uncertainty arises due to a lack of knowledge or imperfect information about all the inputs that can be used in an analysis and it is likely that eliminating uncertainty will not be possible since no one will have perfect knowledge about all the circumstances that can impact on the outcome of a property investment. 'Unless a property is actually sold to determine market price, any estimate is uncertain. The role of the valuer is to assess current market conditions and from a "sea of uncertainty" produce a single judgement.' (Joslin, 2005, p. 269 and RICS, 1994, p. 14) As a consequence, uncertainty needs to be dealt with. According to Enever and Isaac (2002) the individual valuer has got three possible options of doing so: (1) ignore it, (2) express it verbally, and (3) express it numerically.

French and Gabrielli (2004) suggest that the latter option is most appropriate and adopt a statistical approach commonly referred to as Monte Carlo simulation. Monte Carlo simulation was named for Monte Carlo, Monaco, where the primary attractions are casinos containing games of chance. Games of chance such as roulette wheels and slot machines exhibit random behaviour. The basic idea of Monte Carlo simulation is to carry out a calculation process (i.e. property valuation) a large number of times. Instead of using a single point estimate for each input variable Monte Carlo simulation allows ascribing a probability distribution to each input. Depending on the 'view' of the valuer how certain he is about a particular input a smaller or greater range of possible input figures will be allowed. Probability distributions are usually ascribed to the variables market rent and capitalisation rate (ARY) which affect market value most significantly within implicit valuation models; however distributions can also be ascribed to a multiple of inputs depending on the valuation methodology adopted and on the complexity of the property to be valued.[105] Possible distribution types include for example, normal distribution, uniform, lognormal or triangular distribution; the triangular form is assumed to mirror the valuer's thought process most appropriately since it requires defining three absolute figures for each input variable: the most likely, the maximum and the minimum. The Monte Carlo technique (e.g. applied by making use of an Excel-spreadsheet-plug-

---

[105] In the following, the focus lies more on capitalisation rates than on discount rates. However, when using discount rates similar procedures may apply. But looking also at discount rates in detail would require discussing the concepts of the 'time value of money' and of the 'social discount rate'. This will not be done here, but the topic is considered an important area of further research.

in like @RISK or Crystal Ball) then selects random figures for each variable and produces a valuation figure before selecting another random input from within the set range and repeating the exercise (e.g. 50.000 times). In doing so, a multiple of possible outcomes is produced that can be statistically analysed to provide an average outcome, a probability distribution, a range, a standard deviation, and skewness, etc. The information on the assumptions and results of the simulation process, reported to the client in an organised and comprehensive manner and accompanying the single figure estimate, enables the end user to understand the valuer's uncertainties and may, for example, give a key insight into the desirability of proceeding with a transaction (French and Gabrielli, 2005).

But the procedure described by French and Gabrielli (2004; 2005) is based on the supposition that the valuer was able to analyse comparables of the sales of similar properties in order to determine and justify (to the client) an appropriate yield (and/or market rent) as well as a range or probability distribution subsequently. 'The valuer will have taken a view on the appropriate [or most likely] yield by an analysis of comparables of the sale of similar properties' (French and Gabrielli, 2004, p. 491). But if there is insufficient market evidence deriving at an appropriate ARY by analysing comparable sales is not feasible; in this case valuation literature suggests the valuer to take another approach; i.e. to explain and build up the ARY from a risk free rate and adding risk premia for all the risks associated with the property to be valued. Also, the valuer is advised to bear in mind that the valuation must not reflect the nuances applied by specific investors; otherwise the valuation becomes a calculation of worth which is not necessarily representative of market value (Scarret, 1996; Estates Gazette, 2000). This is an extremely difficult exercise and requires the valuer to be very explicit with regard to the assumptions made because he or she should explain these assumptions (including the underlying fundamentals) and the derived ARY figure to the client in order to comply, for example, with RICS core value Nr. 3 'Transparency' (RICS, 2004b). Also, deriving at the ARY by adding up risk premia requires the valuer – in order to express uncertainty – to ascribe a probability distribution to each single risk premium he or she feels uncertain of; instead of ascribing a probability distribution to the ARY figure.

Due to the variety of buildings and contractual arrangements in the marketplace, finding comparables or to be more precise, finding information to make observed transactions comparable becomes more and more difficult. As a consequence, valuers need to deal with insufficient market evidence for particular valuation assignments quite regularly. This is specifically true for valuers operating within the context of the Germany property market:[106] although informa-

---

[106] Germany ranks at 10 on Jones Lang LaSalle's (2004) real estate transparency index after a list of countries that include Australia, US, UK, Canada and Sweden.

tion on average rent levels and selling prices as well as on general market conditions in Germany are now more readily accessible through various sources (for an overview on reliable sources see VDP, 2005, p. 41) it is usually the yields of comparable sales and other performance information from comparable properties that are not observable. This particularly applies to the valuation of properties that are not located in one of the top-five property towns (i.e. Berlin, Düsseldorf, Hamburg, Frankfurt, and Munich). In addition, the average yields of other sales ('Liegenschaftszinssätze') which are (sometimes) made available by the German valuation expert committees ('Gutachterausschüsse') are not equivalent to ARY since the 'Liegenschaftszinssätze' are calculated in a different manner. This difference is, amongst other issues, due to the German valuation practice of separating the land element from the element for the improvements (i.e. the building) when calculating market value. The underlying assumption for this practice is that the land does not deteriorate over time whereas the building will deteriorate and therefore needs a different treatment. As a side issue, it may be interesting to note that German valuers have been criticised for this valuation practice by the international valuation community for many years. However, the current adoption of International Financial Reporting Standards (IFRS) within the European Union has recently introduced a strong need to 'separate the inseparable' (Hendriks, 2005); i.e. to apportion the reported values, allocating value separately to the land element and to the improvements.

Returning to the problem of insufficient market evidence, it can be concluded that the appropriate determination of ARY and the explanation of this judgement to a client can be very difficult and highly uncertain. This problem does not only apply to the German property market. Nonetheless, in the absence of sufficient comparable sales data the composition of the ARY (i.e. its risk components) should be made explicit in order to provide a transparent valuation service.

Addressing risk

In order to report risk within property valuations Adair and Hutchison (2005) and Hutchison et al. (2005) have argued that the use of a risk scoring system represents an appropriate way of addressing the issue because a risk scoring system can be easily understood and communicated to third parties, is applicable to all property types, and the results enhance the decision-making process and do not confuse end users.

Adair and Hutchison (2005) apply a standard credit rating technique, based on the rating model of a UK commercial rating company called D&B, to the determination of risk within property pricing. They introduce a property risk scoring (PRS) that involves the analysis of the risks associated with the property asset under for key headings: (1) market transparency risk, (2) investment quality risk, (3) covenant strength risk; and (4) depreciation and obsolescence risk. In order to assess the risk of each of these groups or of sub-groups a scoring system is used that ranges from 1 (minimal risk) to 5 (high risk). Hutchison et al. (2005, p. 150) define that the aim of PRS is 'to record the current risk perception of the investment attributes of the investment property, on the date of valuation, based on its specific characteristics and current state of the market. ... PRS asks the valuers to form an opinion on the current state of the market and the likely future direction of the key variables in the valuation, but it is not a forecasting tool.' Although, Adair and Hutchison (2005, p. 266-267) state that the property risk scoring needs further research in order to calibrate the model, they argue that 'if risk cannot be eliminated the valuer is required to manage the analysis of risk within the valuation process so that the impact is minimised and the end user of the valuation can have confidence in the value estimate.' They go on arguing that 'the property risk score represents a potential method of applying a business risk indicator which is simple for end user to understand thereby fulfilling part of the objectives of the Investment Property Forum and Carsberg report.'

The author fully agrees with this statement; however, it is argued that the application of another risk scoring model (i.e. an approach based on the European Group of Valuers Associations' (TEGoVA) property and market rating) may be more appropriate for valuers operating in Germany or within other European countries that heavily rely on financing property through banks for the following reason: The introduction of new banking capital adequacy rules entitled Basel II requires banks to adopt a much more sophisticated approach with regard to the risks they take in lending. As a consequence, so called property ratings will increasingly be conducted for lending purposes. Recently, TEGoVA has developed and published a property and market rating system which is likely to become influential for other rating systems within European property lending practice (e.g. the German Association of Public Banks ('Bundesverband öffentlicher Banken Deutschlands', VÖB) has adopted and further developed TEGoVA's rating system, see VÖB, 2005; in addition, the mortgage bank HypoVereinsbank has already implemented a rating system which is in accordance with TEGoVA's proposal). This may not be so much an issue in the UK or in the US because corporations are financed through the capital market to a very large extent and bank financing does not play such an important role. However, the situation is different in Germany: the share of bank financing among corporations is 71 % while in contrast this share is only 10 % in the UK and 18 % in the United States (Holter, 2005, p. 12). For this reason, Basel II and the resulting banking practice is far more influential for the German property market and for the manner property assets will be treated for lending purposes than this may be the case in the

UK. Thus, by using a rating approach based on TEGoVA's proposal, valuers can address risk (in a very similar way as described by Adair and Hutchison, 2005) *and* provide their clients with information in communication formats that banks require within the scope of lending decisions anyway. This can speed up transaction processes and thereby create a synergetic effect; i.e. saving time and money for the valuer's client. However, the valuer should be aware of potential consequences with regard to liability and responsibility caused by possible third-party reliance on the valuer's judgements. This reinforces the need to address and account for the uncertainties the valuer is facing when preparing valuation reports.

4.3.3.3 Identifying and expressing risk through property rating

In today's banking practice, ratings are used, amongst other issues, to predict the probability of default of granted loans based on historical credit data. Banks have developed sophisticated rating instruments which enable them to predict the probability of default of individual or corporate borrowers subject to a wide range of rating criteria and/or performance information. However, similar and equally sophisticated instruments that allow predicting the probability of default as well as the bank's loss in the event of the default of loans secured by property assets do not (yet) exist; this is mainly due to a lack of information on property characteristics and attributes associated with historical credit data. Nonetheless, Basel II requires banks to develop such property rating systems[107] as a precondition for the application of the so-called 'advanced internal rating based approach'. This approach for determining the bank's equity capital is perceived to be beneficial since it allows banks to calculate the required amount of equity capital by themselves (BCBS, 2004). As a consequence, banks and banking associations in Germany are keen on developing appropriate property rating systems and a number of different initiatives are currently ongoing. For example, German mortgage banks have pooled their data in order to achieve more robust time series of property related credit data, see VDP, 2005). A wide range of different rating systems are also being tested, under further development or are already applied in practice. This was done initially to enhance the bank valuers' estimates of mortgage lending or market value by visualising the risks associated with granting a property loan in more detail. In addition, consulting agencies are offering property rating services to the public. Table 29 shows selected property rating systems.

---

[107] However, the required property rating systems will need to be tested and approved by the national banking supervisory authorities.

Table 29: *Overview on different Property Rating Systems*

Name	Developer	Property types	Stage of development / Application	Further information
European Property and Market Rating (PaM)	TEGoVA (The European Group of Valuers Associations)	Retail, residential, office, warehousing, distribution and production, projects	Guideline for Valuers and Advisors	www.tegova.org
MoriX Immobilien-Markt- und Objektrating	HVB Expertise GmbH (member of the HVB Group, HypoVereinsbank)	Retail, residential, office, warehousing, distribution and production, projects	Applied by more than 100 valuers of HypoVereinsbank; permanent 'evolutionary' development of the rating system is aspired	www.hvbexpertise.de (the rating system was developd in accordance with TEGoVA's guideline)
VÖB-Immobilienanalyse	German Association of Public Banks (VÖB), Expert commission for property valuation	Office and retail	Rating for residential, warehousing and logistics currently under development; ratings for office and retail are currently implemented in associated public banks	www.voeb.de (the rating system represents a possible further development of TEGoVA's guideline)
Sparkassen-Immobiliengeschäfts-Rating (DSGV-Rating)	S-Rating und Risikosysteme GmbH (spin-off from German Savings Bank Association, DSGV)	Office, retail, residential, others (also covers property management aspects)	Applied by nearly all savings banks (Sparkassen) and state banks (Landesbanken) in Germany	www.dsgv.de (only limited information publicly available)
Feri Immobilien Rating	Feri Research GmbH	All property types and property portfolios	Rating service offered to the public in cooperation with TÜV-Süddeutschland	www.feri-research.de (only limited information publicly available)
TRX-Immorating	Bank Austria Creditanstalt AG	Office, retail and residential	Applied within the scope of rating the bank's commercial property clients	www.ba-ca.com (only limited information publicly available)

The author has reviewed these rating systems on the basis of publicly available information and information provided by some of the rating systems' developers. All these systems briefly portrayed above have their benefits and shortcomings and it is difficult to judge one system as superior over the others. Nonetheless, for the purpose of addressing risk in individual valuers' reports the approaches of TEGoVA and VÖB were considered most appropriate mainly for three reasons: (1) Information on the functioning of these rating systems is publicly available to a very large extent and thus, valuers can re-build the systems by making use of Excel-spreadsheets. (2) Both rating approaches already contain the rating criteria ecological sustainability. (3) The selection of criteria classes and rating indicators as well as the calibration of both rating systems was based on in-depth expert surveys and tests with concrete samples. As a consequence, individual valuers can cite reliable sources when referencing the rating system within their valuation reports.

The rating system originally proposed by TEGoVA and further developed by VÖB contains four main criteria classes and up to 4 levels of sub-criteria classes that are weighted according to their influence on the medium-term sales prospects of the individual property in its relevant market. The rating system employs a rating scale that ranges from 1 (excellent) to 10 (disastrous). The average rating is set at 5 because the 'disastrous' rating is designated for specific circumstances only. In order to refer to the interpretation of risk outlined above, the rating criteria or indicators represent potential hazards which can cause harm while the rating scale represents the perceived level of exposure to which the property investment can be influenced by the hazards. Table 30 provides an overview on the rating for office buildings.

Table 30: *Main criteria classes, rating scale, weightings and sample result (TEGoVA, 2003a)*

Rating Scale	Excellent	Very good	Good	Slightly above Ø	Ø	Slightly below Ø	Mediocre	Poor	Very poor	Disastrous	
Criteria Classes	1	2	3	4	5	6	7	8	9	10	**Weighting**
Market					5						20%
Location						6					30%
Property						6					20%
Quality of the property cash flow				4							30%
Overall Rating Result					5						100%

It needs to be mentioned that the rating system introduced in the following is neither the exact TEGoVA rating nor the exact VÖB approach; it rather is a combination of the two. For example, a detailed specification of rating criteria for the sub-category *national market* can only be found within TEGoVA's country ratings[108]; in contrast the VÖB approach does contain more detailed rating criteria for the rating classes *regional market, location, property* and *quality of the property cash flow* than TEGoVA's publications. In addition, the author has modified the rating approach with regard to the following issues: (1) Weighting factors needed to be introduced for the indicators that specify the rating of the regional market at the fourth level because these weighting factors have not been published by VÖB. As an initial solution equal weighting factors have been assigned to these indicators. (2) In order to achieve a higher sensitivity of the model and to avoid rounding errors the calculation of the rating results for the sub-criteria classes as well as their subsequent aggregation to the overall result is conducted at an accuracy of one decimal place. In contrast, the TEGoVA and VÖB approaches work with whole numbers only.

Table 31 shows the full list of criteria classes, indicators and weightings for the rating of office buildings. In order to state explicitly which parts of the rating system represent a modification of TEGoVA's original approach, the indicators introduced by VÖB are marked with *; furthermore, the weighting factors introduced by the author are marked with **.

---

[108] See: www.tegova.org/en/4291ed80f067d

Table 31: *Full rating criteria list and weightings (adopted from TEGoVA, 2003a and VÖB, 2005)*

Property and Market Rating for office buildings			2. Level	3. Level	4. Level
Criteria Class 1 'Market'				**20,0%**	
1.1	**National Market**		30,0%		
	1.1.1	**Acts of God**		5,0%	
		1.1.1.1 Natural disasters			70,0%
		1.1.1.2 Emissions			20,0%
		1.1.1.3 Man-made disasters			10,0%
	1.1.2	**Socio-demographic development**		10,0%	
		1.1.2.1 Population Growth			33,3%
		1.1.2.2 Gross Domestic Product (GDP) per capita			33,3%
		1.1.2.3 Unemployment rate			33,3%
	1.1.3	**Overall economic development**		30,0%	
		1.1.3.1 GDP growth			20,0%
		1.1.3.2 Inflation			20,0%
		1.1.3.3 Exchange rate volatility			10,0%
		1.1.3.4 Economic structure			10,0%
		1.1.3.5 Infrastructure			20,0%
		1.1.3.6 International competitiveness			20,0%
	1.1.4	**Political, legal, taxation and monetary conditions**		15,0%	
	1.1.5	**Property market: office**		40,0%	
1.2	**Regional Market**		70,0%		
	1.2.1	**Socio-demographic development**		30,0%	
		1.2.1.1 Number of children per woman *			16,7% **
		1.2.1.2 Population movements over district boundaries (per 1.000 inhabitants) *			16,7% **
		1.2.1.3 Ratio of employable people (over 20 - below 65 in % of inhabitants) *			16,7% **
		1.2.1.4 Population density (inhabitants / km²) *			16,7% **
		1.2.1.5 Highly qualified employable people (in % of inhabitants) *			16,7% **
		1.2.1.6 Unemployed people and those that receive social welfare (per 1.000 inhabitants) *			16,7% **
	1.2.2	**Economic situation and attractiveness**		30,0%	
		1.2.2.1 Economic concentration (GDP per capita) *			20% **
		1.2.2.2 Earnings from business taxes (in € per branch) *			20% **
		1.2.2.3 Public investments (investments per household) *			20% **
		1.2.2.4 Debt service (debt service / administration expenses) *			20% **
		1.2.2.5 Economic success (regional GDP growth, insolvency ratio, new businesses) *			20% **
	1.2.3	**Property Market: Office**		40,0%	
		1.2.3.1 Rent level (in € per m²) *			50% **
		1.2.3.2 Market fluctuation / volatility *			50% **
Criteria Class 2 'Location'				**30,0%**	
2.1	**Image of the quarter (office district) and of the location**		15%		
	2.1.1	**Centrality ***		20,0%	
	2.1.2	**Quarter quality / Centrality and settlement of particular branches ***		40,0%	
	2.1.3	**Address quality / Image ***		40,0%	
2.2	**Suitability of the micro location for the property type and for target occupiers**		25%		
2.3	**Quality of transportation infrastructure of the plot and quarter**		25%		
	2.3.1	**Airport ***		10,0%	
	2.3.2	**Train ***		25,0%	
	2.3.3	**Public transport services ***		25,0%	
	2.3.4	**Road access ***		25,0%	
	2.3.5	**Parking space situation ***		15,0%	
2.4	**Quality of local supply facilities of the plot and quarter for target occupiers**		15%		
	2.4.1	**Shopping facilities, services offered, social and medical facilities, public authorities ***		70,0%	
	2.4.2	**Restaurants and catering facilities ***		30,0%	
2.5	**Acts of God**		20%		
	2.5.1	**Natural disasters ***		10,0%	
	2.5.2	**Environmental burdens / brownfields (micro location – regional assessment) ***		10,0%	
	2.5.3	**Technical / man-made disasters ***		25,0%	
	2.5.4	**Safety of location ***		30,0%	
	2.5.5	**Immissions (pollution, noise, etc.) ***		25,0%	

Table 30 (cont.): *Full rating criteria list and weightings (adopted from TEGoVA, 2003a and VÖB, 2005)*

Property and Market Rating for office buildings		Weightings		
		2. Level	3. Level	4. Level
Criteria Class 3 'Property'			**20,0%**	
3.1	**Architecture / Type of construction**	20,0%		
	3.1.1 Design Quality *		25,0%	
	3.1.2 Illumination / Shading *		15,0%	
	3.1.3 Quality of the layout / Functionality *		60,0%	
3.2	**Fitout**	10,0%		
	3.2.1 Quality of the building's technical and security equipment *		25,0%	
	3.2.2 Quality of information and communication technology *		25,0%	
	3.2.3 Internal fixtures and fittings *		35,0%	
	3.2.4 Social facilities *		15,0%	
3.3	**Structural condition**	15,0%		
	3.3.1 Age / year of construction / construction era *		20,0%	
	3.3.2 Degree of modernisation / Revitalisation *		40,0%	
	3.3.3 Maintenance situation / Maintenance backlog *		40,0%	
3.4	**Plot situation**	25,0%		
	3.4.1 Plot layout / Topography *		25,0%	
	3.4.2 Geological condition and archaeological aspects *		20,0%	
	3.4.3 Contaminations *		20,0%	
	3.4.4 Internal and external accessibility / infrastructure *		20,0%	
	3.4.5 Appurtenant structures / External facilities *		15,0%	
3.5	**Ecological sustainability**	10,0%		
	3.5.1 Building materials *		40,0%	
	3.5.2 Energetic performance / energy demand / energy consumption *		35,0%	
	3.5.3 Emissions *		25,0%	
3.6	**Profitability of the building concept**	20,0%		
	3.6.1 Space efficiency (rentable floor area / gross floor space) *		30,0%	
	3.6.2 Operating costs (in € per m² of gross floor space) *		50,0%	
	3.6.3 Public burdens (planning regulations, fire safety requirements, historical interest, etc.) *		20,0%	
Criteria Class 4 'Quality of the property cash flow'			**30,0%**	
4.1	**Tenant and occupier situation**	20,0%		
	4.1.1 Number of tenants, tenants' solvency and image, appropriate mix of tenants *		60,0%	
	4.1.2 Duration and structure of rental contracts *		40,0%	
4.2	**Rental growth potential / Value growth potential**	30,0%		
	4.2.1 Rental growth potential *		50,0%	
	4.2.2 Value growth potential (estimated change of re-selling price) *		50,0%	
4.3	**Letting prospects**	20,0%		
4.4	**Vacancy / Letting situation**	10,0%		
4.5	**Recoverable and non-recoverable operating expenses**	10,0%		
	4.5.1 Level of operating costs *		65,0%	
	4.5.2 Possibility of attributing management and operating costs to the tenants *		35,0%	
4.6	**Usability by third parties and/or alternative use**	10,0%		

This rating criteria list shows that the rating criterion ecological sustainability as well as three sub-criteria (building materials, energy performance and emissions) are already included within the property rating system and thus, are recognized as risk factors that can impact on the outcome of a property investment. However, other sustainability key performance indicators such as those discussed in Section 3.2.2.3 are not yet fully included. Nonetheless, it is clear that aspects of a building's sustainability performance can have an impact on a range of other property rating criteria (such as architecture, fitout, rental / value growth potential, letting prospects and usability by third parties) and can therefore be taken into account indirectly when expressing the perceived risk associated with the property under investigation. This, however, requires (1) that the valuer undertaking the rating knows about the risk reduction potential of sustainable design or of its benefits respectively and (2) that information on the building's sustainability key performance indicators are available or can be evaluated by the valuer.

As already mentioned in Section 3.2.4, the rating system exhibits an interesting peculiarity; i.e. that the basic weighting assigned to each indicator or sub-criteria class is not fixed. The more the rating score deviates from the average, the more significantly changes its impact on the overall rating results; i.e. a dynamic risk weighting function is applied. The dynamic risk weight functions proposed by TEGoVA and VÖB differ from each other: within TEGoVA's approach the rating 'disastrous' for one sub-criterion or indicator leads to the entire criteria class being rated 'disastrous'. In contrast the VÖB approach assigns a very high secondary weighting factor to each sub-criterion or indicator rated 'disastrous'; this also leads to an adjustment of the whole system's weights but does not result in a 'disastrous' rating of the entire criteria class. For the purpose of expressing risk in valuation reports the latter dynamic risk weight approach is regarded superior since it reflects the risk-profile of the property under investigation in more detail and points the end user's attention to the most critical risk factors which deserve (if possible) measures to improve the property's risk-profile (see Figure 32).

Figure 32: *Secondary risk weight function (VÖB, 2005)*

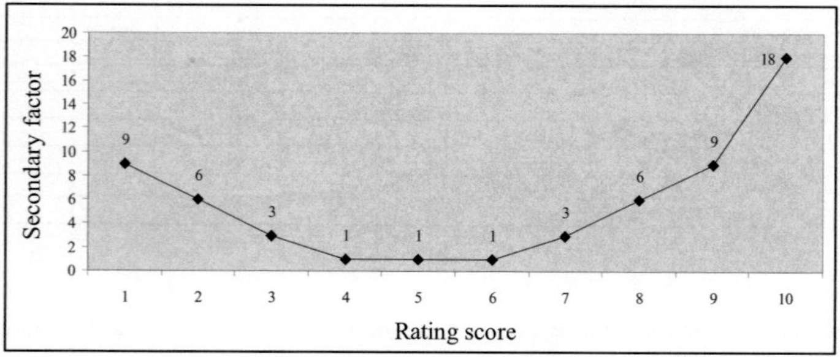

In order to communicate the results of the rating process to the client the valuer has several options. Depending on the level of detail required the results can either be reported for the main criteria classes and/or for selected sub-criteria class individually. Furthermore, Excel-spreadsheets offer a number of possibilities that allow graphically displaying the rating results (see Figure 33).

Figure 33: *Overview on sample rating results for an office building, criteria class 'Property'*

Rating Results Criteria Class 'Property'

Rating Scale	Excellent	Very good	Good	Slightly above Ø	Ø	Slightly below Ø	Mediocre	Poor	Very poor	Disastrous	
Criteria Classes	**1**	**2**	**3**	**4**	**5**	**6**	**7**	**8**	**9**	**10**	**Weighting**
Architecture / type of construction					5,2						16,7%
Fitout					4,5						8,3%
Structural condition						5,6					12,5%
Plot situation					5,0						20,8%
Ecological sustainability							7,2				25,0%
Profitability of the building concept					4,8						16,7%
Result						**5,6**					100,0%

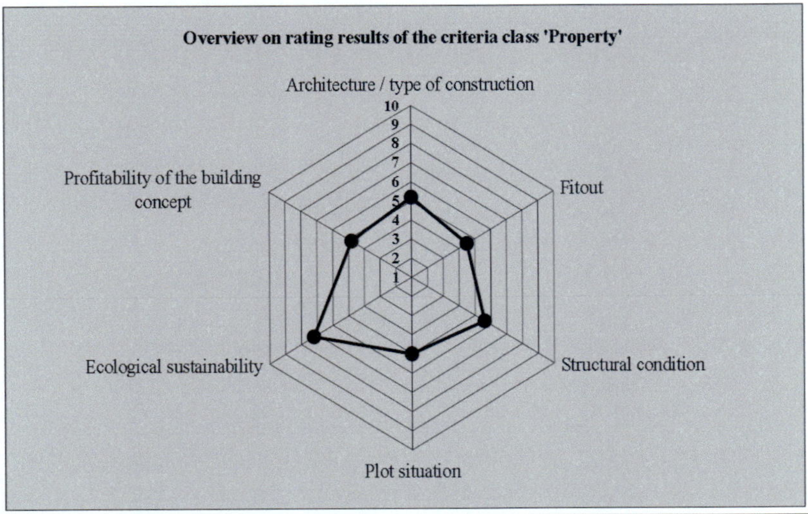

Making use of the rating system portrayed above obviously results in a win-win situation for valuers and clients. On the one hand, clients learn more about the risks associated with the subject property. This can, amongst other issues, greatly enhance decision making processes by enabling a better understanding of the nature of the investment. On the other hand, valuers are forced to think about and account for risks they probably would not have addressed in the valuation report without using the rating system. Critics may now argue that the rating system needs further improvement with regard to its components, calibration, empirical validation and measurement standards. This is certainly true and particularly counts for the definition and agreement upon the latter which has not been addressed here in detail and which represents an ambitious arena for further research. However, it can also be argued that the rating system has already deserved considerable expert-involvement through TEGoVA and VÖB, that the use of the rating system addresses the major activities necessary for the management and control of risk – i.e. 'identification, measurement, management and reporting' (Adair and Hutchison, 2005, p. 263) – and, that it is sufficient if the rating system improves over time. Indeed, at the current stage of development it is likely that the rating system can only improve if widely applied in practice.

4.3.3.4 Reflecting sustainability issues and increasing transparency in valuation through yield pricing

In order to offer a practical solution how sustainability issues can be reflected within the most widespread valuation technique, the income approach, and how the transparency of the valuation process can be increased at the same time, the author suggests (1) to explicitly state the risk components contained within the applied capitalisation rate or ARY (in the following the 'yield'), (2) to treat sustainability issues as additional factors that either increase or decrease the risk associated with the property under investigation, and (3) to use simulation techniques in order to account for valuation uncertainty that arises due to a lack of imperfect knowledge and comparable property data.

For this reason, a yield pricing scheme is introduced that builds upon the property rating system portrayed above. This is done because it can be assumed that the rating system captures all (major) risk factors that can impact on the outcome of a property investment and because this allows a consistent approach of identifying and assessing property risk first and subsequently determining the risk components contained within the applied yield figure. In addition, the rating system already contains the rating criteria ecological sustainability as well as other rating criteria (such as *architecture, fitout, growth potential, letting prospects* and *usability by third parties*) that are affected through the subject property's sustainability performance. The following Figure 34 shows the blank yield pricing scheme including a brief description of its components.

Figure 34: *Blank yield pricing scheme*

Composition and calculation of the All Risks Yield	Maximum Risk Score	Maximum Risk Premium	Assigned Risk Score	Risk Premium	Calculation
Risk Free Rate					
Risk Premia for:					
Market (national and regional)	In accordance with the property rating, the maximum risk score is 10 for all criteria	Valuer's judgements (backed up with comparable sales data and/or evidence from the wider market)	Rating results adopted from the property rating	Function of maximum risk premium and assigned risk score	Summation of individual risk premia
Location					
Property					
Architecture / Type of construction					
Fitout					
Structural condition					
Plot situation					
Ecological sustainability					
Profitability of the building concept					
Quality of the property cash flow					
Tenant and occupier situation					
Rental growth potential / Value growth potential					
Letting prospects					
Vacancy / Letting situation					
Recoverable and non-recoverable operating expenses					
Usability by third parties and/or alternative use					
Exceptional circumstances					
All Risks Yield					

Following the valuation literature, the yield can be built up by adding risk premia for property specific factors and for the market risk to a risk free rate. Property valuation literature offers some figures for risk premia that are either based on general views and experiences, anecdotal evidence, or on surveys among valuers. These figures can serve for general orientation and are displayed in the following Table 32.

Table 32: *Risk premia and yields in valuation literature*

Risk premium (market and sector)	Risk premium (property specific / idiosyncratic)	Yields	Source
2 %	varying premium depending on the risks attached to the cash flows		Adair and Huchison, 2005, p. 257
		6 % to 12 % (Normal range of yields for office buildings including market and property specific risk premium)	Johnson, 2000, p. 85
0 % to >6 % (depending on office or reail sector, risk premium can vary heavily over time and region)			Tansens et al., 2005
2 %	0 % to 3 %	10 % or more for secondary (i.e. less than prime but still reasonable quality) properties	Estates Gazette, 2000, p. 136
0 % to 1 %	0 % to 4% (or more for exceptional circumstances)		Münchehofe and Springer, 2004, p. 10
0,3 % to 2 % (for basic property markt risk) + 0 % to 2 % (for sector specific risk)			Hordijk and van de Ridder, 2005, p. 174

However, little guidance can be found in the valuation literature on which property specific factors are to be included as risk components as well as on the impact of these property specific factors on the applied yield figure. Due to a great lack of property performance data (including returns on property investment *and* property specific information) it is not yet possible for valuers to determine property risk premia (and thus capitalisation or discount rates) on a statistically robust basis. For this reason, Adair and Hutchison (2005, p. 257) have recently stated that these 'rates for property will continue to be estimated subjectively.'

If detailed property performance databases were more readily available, it would be possible by using multiple regression techniques to derive at an indication of the most decisive property specific risk factors and on their influence on the yields that would have to be applied in individual property valuation practice. An approach may be to assign maximum risk premia according to a multiple regression model and relative importance of the determined factors for idiosyncratic risk of a property. However, existing property databases and indexes in Europe (such as the Investment Property Databank[109]) only allow for an analysis of average yearly excess returns for different property classes over risk-free investments; and thus to derive at an indication for the market risk premium that can be applied when estimating the yield (Lorenz et al., 2006). Due to this general lack of property performance data, valuers typically express the yield as one single figure without explicitly stating individual risk premia for

---

[109] See: http://www.ipdindex.co.uk/

property specific risk factors. However, this valuation practice does not allow clients tracing the thought process of the individual valuer.

In order to make the thought process of the valuer explicit and to offer a transparent (yet subjective) valuation service, the yield's components can be made explicit by using the yield pricing scheme introduced above. In order to demonstrate how this can be done in property valuation practice, the following hypothetical valuation example is constructed:

Assume that the valuer has been engaged to estimate market value of an office building located in Germany. The building is fully let to one tenant only and the rental contract has a remaining length of 5 years. Assume further that the valuer has obtained sufficient price information from reliable sources to determine the most likely, maximum and minimum figure for the input variable market rent. The office building is let at market rent; in this the valuer has to determine the yield as the second key input. Assume further that the valuer knows about the benefits of sustainable design but that the property under investigation does *not* exhibit sustainable design features. Assume also that the valuer was not able to observe a sufficient number of yields from comparable sales and that the valuer was also not able to collect enough performance information to adjust the observed yields in order to make them actually comparable. Therefore, the yields of observed sales from the wider marketplace can be used as a general indication for the range within the yield applied to the subject property is likely to fall. Assume that yields collected from the wider marketplace range from 6.5 to 8.5%.

In order to derive at an indication for the property market risk premium it is possible to investigate the yearly excess returns of office property in Germany over risk-free investments. The data is taken from the DIX (German Property Index, provided through Investment Property Databank) and comprises a history of yearly income returns from 1996 to 2004 for different market sectors (i.e. retail, office and residential) and for the market as a whole. Figure 35 displays the spreads of yearly returns for the subclasses of office, retail, residential property and the index for all properties. Following the literature (e.g. Ling and Naranjo, 1997; Brooks and Tsolacos, 2001; and Chen et al., 2004) the spread was calculated as the difference of the property income return and the risk-less yield, measured by a 10-year government bond. The spread can be interpreted as the risk premium compensating investors for additional risk associated with an investment into the asset class property. Note that only for the office sector a positive yield spread for the whole time period could be observed. For all other sectors including the overall market also negative spreads could be observed, indicating that the return of a 10-year government bond was higher than the income return from the property during these years. This particularly counts for residential properties where (except for 1999) the yield spread was negative for the whole period. The average spread for income returns of residential property was -30 basis points which would indicate a negative risk premium for this type of property. Spreads for office property and for the overall market behave very similar and are negative for the initial years 1996-1997 and for 2000. They are clearly positive for the years 2001-2004 where the spread lies between 50 and 100 basis points. These risk premia are very low compared to the situation in other countries during the same time period; see Lorenz and Trück (2006) for a comparative study on income returns in property markets across Europe. For example, for the same time period average spreads were 160 basis points in France, 188 in the UK and 289 basis points in the Netherlands. The average market risk premium for office buildings in 2004 in Germany was about 80 basis points.

Figure 35: *Spreads over 10-year Government Bond for property investments in Germany (Data source: Eurostat and Investment Property Databank)*

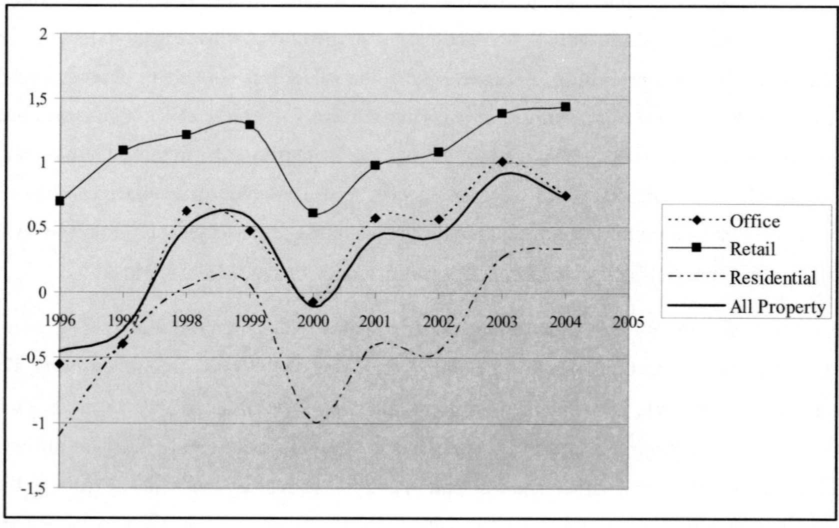

Due to the lack of data, idiosyncratic risk premia for property specific factors need to be estimated subjectively and can only be based on the individual valuer's experience and judgement. The yield pricing scheme for the hypothetical valuation example is calibrated as follows: if the risk score for each individual criteria contained within the rating system is set at the average level of 5, then the overall risk premium is set at 4 %. In combination with the current risk free rate of roughly 3.5 % this assumption would result in a yield of 7.5 % which is ca. 2.1 % above the current average rate of return for *prime* office buildings across the major property towns in Germany which was at 5.4 % in 2005 (Source: CB Richard Ellis, Germany). Furthermore, an additional component is introduced that allows accounting for exceptional circumstances in individual cases. Initially, the maximum risk premium for this component is set at 1 %. Thus, the maximum yield obtainable through the use of the provisional pricing model is 12.5 %. This coincides with the figures found in valuation literature as well as with the author's personal experience. It is assumed that higher yields are only used for liquidation purposes, for property assets that are perceived to require unusually long marketing periods or for forced sale valuations, etc.

The maximum risk premium assigned to the rating criteria market is set at 2 % since the average premium for office property market risk in Germany was ca. 80 basis points in 2004 (as shown above) and has increased in 2005 (assuming that the development within the major property towns is indicative for the rest of market). The remaining risk premia are assigned to the other rating criteria on the basis of the author's assumptions and personal experiences (see Table 33). The criterion location is assigned most attention since location is of paramount importance. Also, the criterion 'ecological sustainability' receives a relatively high maximum risk premium for all the reasons explained above.

A consequence of referring to the risk score (which ranges from 1 to 10) used in the property rating system is that the risk premium ascribed to an individual property characteristic or to the property investment as whole can never be zero. That the risk premium can only tend towards zero (not including the premium assigned for exceptional circumstances) is a reasonable assumption because there will always be risk associated with any property investment; i.e. the yield applied for valuing the property can never be equal to or below the risk free rate. That yields for property can, indeed, fall below the risk free rate has been termed the 'reverse yield gap phenomenon' because this circumstance appears to contradict with the stated belief that yields for riskier investments should be higher than those for safer ones. However, this circumstance is not really a phenomenon. It is not as surprising as one would first imagine if the difference between property investments and government bonds is taken into account. Opposed to government bonds, there is the potential in property for both rental and capital growth which can more than compensate for the lower initial yield. Although, in the past this assumption of growth potential was in most instances valid for longer time horizons (except, for example, during the last 15 years within many regions of central and eastern Germany), this must not necessarily be the case in the future. The author believes that valuers should not value property assets below the risk free rate unless there is valid comparable transaction evidence available to justify this assumption of value growth. Therefore, the yield pricing scheme introduced here does not allow the yield to fall below the risk free rate. In contrast, the absence of value growth potential is treated as an investment risk. If the valuer assumes that the property exhibits high value growth potential than only a marginal risk premium is added for this yield component. The following Table 33 shows the yield pricing example.

Table 33: *Yield pricing example*

Composition and calculation of the All Risks Yield	Maximum Risk Score	Maximum Risk Premium	Assigned Risk Score	Risk Premium	Calculation
Risk Free Rate					**3,50%**
Risk Premia for:					
Market (national and regional)	10	2,00%	5,0	1,00%	1,00%
Location	10	2,50%	5,0	1,25%	1,25%
Property					
Architecture / Type of construction	10	0,25%	5,2	0,13%	0,13%
Fitout	10	0,20%	4,5	0,09%	0,09%
Structural condition	10	0,35%	5,5	0,19%	0,19%
Plot situation	10	0,25%	5,0	0,13%	0,13%
Ecological sustainability	10	0,50%	7,1	0,35%	0,35%
Profitability of the building concept	10	0,25%	4,9	0,12%	0,12%
Quality of the property cash flow					
Tenant and occupier situation	10	0,50%	5,5	0,28%	0,28%
Rental growth potential / Value growth potential	10	0,30%	3,5	0,11%	0,11%
Letting prospects	10	0,25%	5,0	0,13%	0,13%
Vacancy / Letting situation	10	0,25%	1,0	0,03%	0,03%
Recoverable and non-recoverable operating expenses	10	0,20%	3,0	0,06%	0,06%
Usability by third parties and/or alternative use	10	0,20%	2,0	0,04%	0,04%
Exceptional circumstances	10	1,00%	0,0	0,00%	0,00%
		9,00%		3,90%	
All Risks Yield					**7,40**

For simplicity, the hypothetical valuer is expected to be relatively certain regarding the assumptions made for the criteria classes *market* and *location* because the valuer can rely on TEGoVA's country ratings or on freely available data from Eurostat or from the Organisation for Economic Co-operation and Development (OECD) in order to assign a rating score to the national market. In addition, the valuer can rely on publicly offered data form official sources in order to assign a rating score to the regional market (in this instance, the extent and quality of data available in Germany for comparatively low cost is very good).[110] Also, the valuer can achieve a high level of certainty with regard to the criteria of location through personal investigation and by making use of data obtained from geographical information systems that are now available for most parts of the country.[111] For these reasons, the criteria classes market and location exhibit no further level of detail within the sample portrayed in Table 33. In contrast, the valuer may feel very uncertain regarding particular assumptions made for the rating of the criteria classes *property* and *quality of the property cash flow*. Thus, in order to derive at an appropriate yield the valuer will have to mix empirical data with judgement. This judgement element can be vaguely specified within our hypothetical valuation example; it is a maximum risk premium of 3.5% (i.e. the cumulated maximum risk premia for the criteria classes *property* and *quality of the property cash flow*. How and why the valuer decides

---

[110] See, for example, the publications of the Federal Office for Building and Regional Planning ('Bundesamt für Bauwesen und Raumordnung', BBR): www.bbr.bund.de/english/index.htm

[111] See, for example: www.on-geo.de

within this maximum range of 3.5% is probably the most interesting and useful part of the valuation report. And it is this range of 3.5% which allows the valuer to explicitly account for sustainability issues. Those rating criteria that are affected through the subject property's sustainability performance are *architecture, fitout, ecological sustainability, growth potential, letting prospects* and *usability by third parties*; in total these rating criteria make up for a maximum risk premium of 1.7%. Given that (1) property valuation is a fairly subjective exercise because of data limitations but also because both the concept of value and its measure are subjective; and that (2) most of the time valuers do not have enough comparable sales data available to empirically validate all the yield adjustments made, it is now relatively easy for valuers to justify a valuation bonus of, let's say, 0.5% for sustainable buildings or a valuation reduction of the same magnitude for unsustainable ones. A change of 0.5% in the yield applied to value the subject property can have a tremendous effect on the valuation figure reported (see Table 34).

Table 34: *Percentage change in income multiplier[112] caused by a 0.5% change in ARY*

ARY	4.5%	5.0%	5.5%	6.0%	6.5%	7.0%	7.5%	8.0%	8.5%	9.0%	9.5%	10.0%
Multiplier (rounded)	22.22	20	18.18	16.67	15.38	14.29	13.33	12.5	11.76	11.11	10.53	10
Percentage change (upward)		-10.0%	-9.1%	-8.3%	-7.7%	-7.1%	-6.7%	-6.3%	-5.9%	-5.6%	-5.3%	-5.0%
Percentage change (downward)	11.1%	10.0%	9.1%	8.3%	7.7%	7.1%	6.7%	6.3%	5.9%	5.6%	5.3%	

In order to express uncertainty the valuer now proceeds as follows: Instead of ascribing a probability distribution to the single ARY figure (see Section 4.3.3.2 above), the valuer ascribes triangular probability distributions[113] to each single risk score he or she feels uncertain of. For example, the letting prospects of the property under investigation have initially been rated average. However, the valuer feels that letting prospects could also be slightly below or above average. Similarly, the valuer is uncertain with regard to other indicators of the rating classes property and cash flow. In addition, the valuer puts his or her initial assessment of location into question and allows for range of 1 score point up- and downwards. The valuer ascribes asymmetric probability distributions to some of the indicators because he or she prefers taking rather a more pessimistic than a too optimistic approach. Table 35 provides an overview on the assumptions made.

---

[112] The income multiplier is the reciprocal figure of ARY. Within implicit valuation models this figure is multiplied by the income generated with the property under investigation in order to produce an estimate of value.
[113] The triangular form is assumed to mirror the valuer's thought process most appropriately since it requires defining three absolute figures for each input variable: the most likely, the maximum and the minimum (see also French and Gabrielli, 2004 and 2005).

Table 35: *Valuer's assumptions made explicit (triangular probability distributions)*

Rating indicators	Risk Score			Assumed correlations	
	Minimum	Most likely	Maximum	Correlated with	Cor. coefficient(s)
Location	4	5	6		
Structural condition	4	5,6	7		
Ecological sustainability	5	7,2	9	Structural condition	0,5
Profitability of building conept	4	4,8	6		
Tenant and occupier situation	4	5,5	7		
Letting prospects	3	5	7	Usability by third parties / Ecological sustainability	0,7
Usability by third parties	1	2	3		

In the next step the valuer performs a Monte Carlo simulation (run for 50.000 trials) by using, for example, Palisade @Risk Decision Tool. The results are as follows:

Figure 36: *Frequency chart for All Risks Yield*

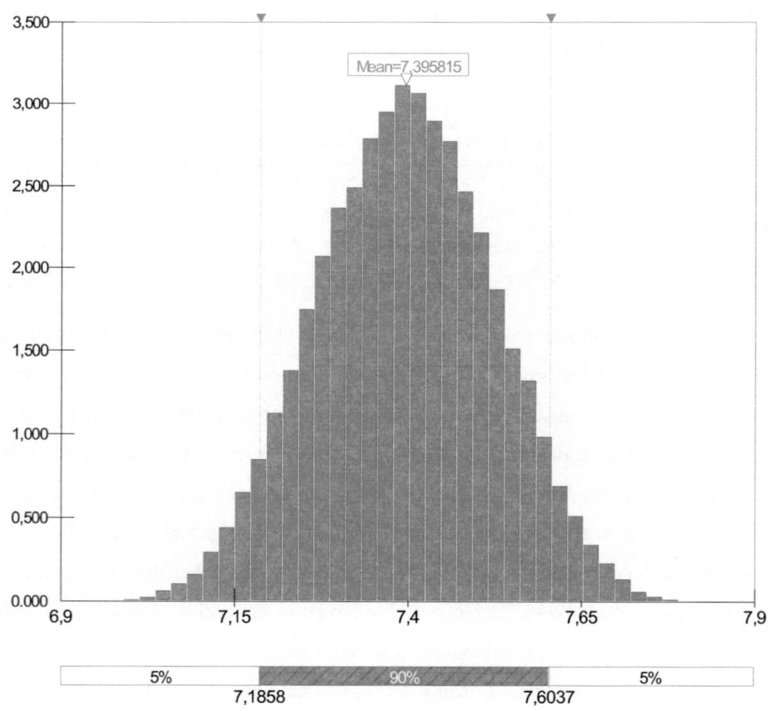

Output range: 6.95 to 7.86
Range of the most likely observations (90 %): 7.19 to 7.6
Mean: 7.4
Standard deviation: 0.13
Variance: 0.016
Skewness: -0.016

Now the valuer would use the mean ARY figure of 7.4 % for calculating the single point valuation estimate. In addition, the valuer would proceed simulating the overall valuation result by using the ARY's probability distribution portrayed above and by assuming further probability distribution(s) (and, if applicable, correlations) for the other input variable(s); e.g. market rent. The result of this procedure would be a range of possible market values and the valuer would be able to indicate, for example, that there is a probability of 90 % that the expected market value falls within a particular range based on the assumptions made. In addition, the standard deviation gives a representation of the uncertainty involved and measures how widely values are dispersed from the average value (the mean); the greater the uncertainty the higher the standard deviation. The skewness represents the degree of asymmetry of the distribution around the mean. A positive skewness indicates a distribution with an asymmetric tail extending toward more positive values. In contrast a negative skewness would indicate a distribution with an asymmetric tail extending toward more negative values. Thus, by applying Monte-Carlo simulation within property valuations, additional information about the certainty of the valuation result is provided for the client and particular circumstances of a valuation which are usually not explicitly expressed or which are described by the valuer in words can be quantified and accounted for in more detail.

Of course, the main shortcoming of the yield pricing scheme presented above is that the maximum risk premium assigned to each rating criterion is largely based on the authors' (or valuer's) assumptions and experiences. Thus, determining the yield is still a fairly subjective exercise. As pointed out before, if more data on individual property performance and ratings were available, risk premia could be assigned within a multiple regression model based on relative importance and variability of the determined factors for idiosyncratic risk. With the current scheme, the valuer has, at least, attempted to explain to the client how he or she arrived at the ARY figure applied and which factors may cause a deviation from the reported figure. Yield pricing also explicitly reveals which factors (and their relative importance) have been considered at all in order to derive a value estimate (which is usually unclear for clients when all property specific factors are 'hided' within one single ARY figure). As a consequence, the value estimation process becomes traceable. In addition, this approach pinpoints the difficulties of 'correctly' determining property values in the absence of appropriate comparable sales and property performance data. The valuer openly admits that he or she has delivered a subjective price estimate and that he or she does not pretend to know exactly the 'correct' property value.

4.3.3.5   Summary and practical implications

The above sections 4.3.3.1 and 4.3.3.2 have shown that there is currently a serious concern within international valuation literature that the traditional investment valuation process is not as transparent as it should be. This is due to the circumstance that the traditional valuation process (as depict in Figure 29 above) does not contain procedures to report property risks to clients in a clear and understandable manner as well as to account for valuation uncertainty which is an inherent part of the valuation process. Furthermore, it has been argued that the benefits of sustainable buildings (or vice versa the risk of unsustainable ones) are usually not accounted for when estimating market value. For this reason the author suggests including three additional components into the traditional valuation process. These components are property rating, yield pricing and simulation (see Figure 37). This represents an extension to the income approach – the most widely used valuation technique.

Figure 37: *Additional property valuation components*

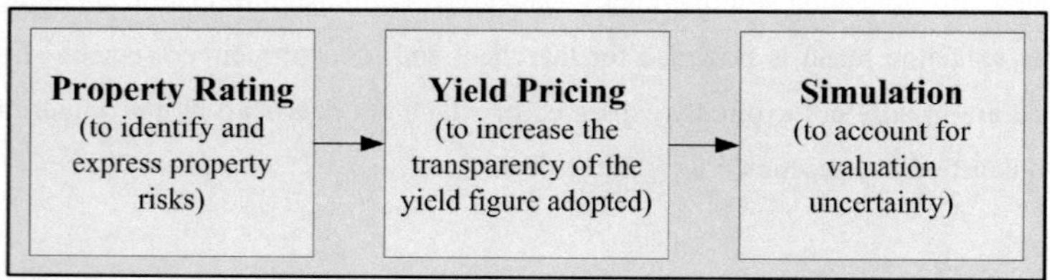

By using these additional components valuers can: (1) address risk and uncertainty within their valuation reports; (2) create added-value for their clients by providing them with information in communication formats banks require within the scope of financing decisions anyway; (3) reflect sustainability issues as additional risk factors in a transparent and understandable manner; and (4) increase the reputation and credibility of the valuation profession within the business world and among the wider public.

How these components fit into the overall process of property valuation is shown in the following Figure 38. The figure also shows that advanced methods of valuation such as hedonic pricing based on multiple regression techniques can be used (provided that appropriate property performance databases will be available in the future) to underpin the valuer's assumptions when assigning risk premia to property specific factors.

Figure 38: *Extended valuation process*

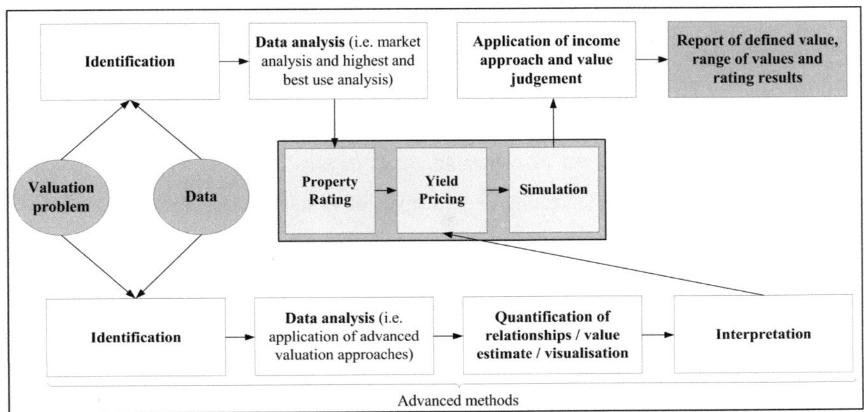

Despite considerable need for further research activities, the additional valuation components introduced above can, indeed, be applied in practice already today. Using this components is considered superior of providing the client with a single point estimate of market value only and stating in a valuation report (without further explanation) that 'after detailed analysis of the market conditions the valuer estimates that the ARY is 7 %' (anonymous valuer, 2005). Even more controversially, it can be said that there are very few (if any) rational reasons for valuers not to use available approaches for addressing uncertainty and risk, and thus issues of sustainability as additional risk factors within their reports. In summary and despite the un-questioned necessity for reporting a single point estimate of market value for particular valua-tion assignments (e.g. financial reporting, financial performance measurement, court valua-tions, etc.) valuers should not proceed in reporting this figure only and in ignoring elements of risk and uncertainty. Valuers cannot be expected to predict the future but they can be expected to be transparent with regard to their assumptions even if these are (by nature) subjective, highly uncertain and maybe wrong from an omniscient observers' perspective.

4.4 The way ahead – real feedback and education

Property valuation is the major mechanism for aligning economic return with environmental and social performance. Valuation clearly has a huge potential for pushing the property market on more sustainable grounds. Imagine the reputation and standing of the valuation profession in a business environment of hardening moral liability and powerful courts of public opinion if it would start implementing the principles of sustainable development and help realising the vision of a more sustainable future. But for the valuation profession to become part of this vision of the future, two issues play decisive roles: real feedback and education.

Real Feedback

Why feedback obtained through sustainability assessment is important has already been explained above. In summary, feedback from the triple bottom line is essential to reduce or correct for delay or mistake in the perceptions and the responses that strive to keep the system within its limits (see Meadows et al., 2004). To express this with a focus on property: if building owners and investors know nothing or very little about the real performance of the buildings they buy, use and operate, (i.e. if they are cut off from feedback), then these buildings cannot be improved systematically in pursuit of both individual and collective well-being. In addition, uninformed decision-making leads to adverse selection and finally to a loss in the quality of buildings that are offered in the marketplace (Lützkendorf and Speer, 2005).

Unfortunately, however, current property valuation practice provides clients with little feedback. The only form of feedback offered is based on cash flows and consists in an estimate of money prices. Critics may argue that performing sustainability assessments of property assets is not within the remit of valuers' business and that clients will not pay more for this 'extra service'. In contrast, the notion put forward in this dissertation is that performing sustainability assessments should become one of the valuers' activities. Two arguments are used to back up this assumption:

(1) Property valuers are hired to estimate property values and they express value in monetary terms. But are subjective estimates expressed in monetary terms (prices) adequate and sufficient measurement units to express property values? Remember, a market value figure is only an estimate, it is only ever a guess, it is not a real price. Is it reasonable to assume that expressing all factors that determine the competitive position of an asset in the marketplace through a money figure estimate is, after all, impossible? Carl Menger's (1871) and Ludwig von Mises' (1949) position regarding the measurement of exchange value have already been mentioned. They explained why the measurement of exchange value in money prices is a vain

endeavour. Von Mises (1949, p. 204) stated that everything that can be measured is, that of two things one is valued higher. This would lead to the argument that additional measures of property performance or of their behaviour in use respectively (which includes environmental, social and economic performance) are better suited to express property value than a mere estimate of money prices because these performance measures give a more transparent and detailed indication of why someone prefers *property a* to *property b* or why the possessions of *property a* is more desirable than the possession of *property b*.

(2) Whatever performance measurement of property assets is considered to be – an extra service that complements the value estimate or an integral part of the valuation process – it is likely that clients will sooner or later pay for and request it:

> *'By providing the client with advice that goes beyond the scope of the original information requested, the valuer may actually be providing something of greater benefit than what was requested. This is about valuers helping their clients make the best possible property decisions. The more clients are aware that this service is available, the more they will be willing to pay a fair price for it.'*
> *(Gilbertson and Preston, 2005, p. 135)*

Property performance assessment adds a new and desirable quality to the services the valuation profession has to offer. And simply because valuers do not *yet* offer such services and clients do not *yet* pay for them, does not mean that this will not change in future years. This is because 'quality in a product or service is not what the supplier puts in. It is what the customer gets out [...] Customers pay only for what is of use to them and gives them value' (Peter Drucker, cited in Gilbertson and Preston, 2005, p. 135). What gives clients value is not fixed, it depends, amongst other issues, on the business environment. Given that the business environment is currently changing to favour more sustainable products and services, it is likely that information on the sustainability performance of property assets will become highly valuable for clients.

Education

The importance of *education for sustainable development* has often been emphasized in the literature (Ahlberg, 2005; Marshall and Harry, 2005; and Haigh, 2005). Also the United Nations Decade of Education for Sustainable Development (2005-2014) was launched on 1 March 2005.[114] There is no universal model or educational strategy but this concept of educa-

---

[114] See: http://portal.unesco.org/education/en/ev.php-
URL_ID=27234&URL_DO=DO_TOPIC&URL_SECTION=201.html

tion emphasises a holistic, interdisciplinary approach to developing the knowledge and skills needed for a sustainable future as well as changes in values, behaviour, and lifestyles. According to the UN Educational, Scientific and Cultural Organization (UNESCO)

> *'there can be few more pressing and critical goals for the future of humankind than to ensure steady improvement in the quality of life for this and future generations in a way that respects our common heritage – the planet we live on. As people we seek positive change for ourselves, our children and grandchildren; we must do it in ways that respect the right of all to do so. To do this we must learn constantly – about ourselves, our potential, our limitations, our relationships, our society, our environment, our world. Education for sustainable development is a life-wide and lifelong endeavour which challenges individuals, institutions and societies to view tomorrow as a day that belongs to all of us, or it will not belong to anyone.' (UNESCO, n.d.)*

Education for sustainable development is particularly important within the property and construction sectors. However, respective efforts and debates are usually focused on the development of educational programs tailored to the needs of architects, engineers and construction managers (see Graham, 2000; Myers, 2003; Tetior, 2004; and Lourdel et al., 2005). Also, many of these programs lack focus on issues of cost efficient construction, of planning and construction within the existing building stock as well as of systematic maintenance and management of construction works. Furthermore, educational programs and teaching materials tailored to the needs of property professionals such as valuers and estate agents apparently do not yet exist.

A possible educational strategy to overcome these shortcomings is currently pursued at the Chair of Sustainable Management of Housing and Real Estate, School of Economics, University of Karlsruhe. The chair's concept of combining economic, environmental and social aspects in order to offer a complex teaching profile is (so far) unique in Germany. Starting from the basic principles of sustainable development (overall concept, areas of protection, management rules and guidelines) the teaching profile involves introducing aspects of describing and assessing buildings' contribution to sustainable development into both the design-oriented as well as into the assessment-oriented areas. A more detailed description of this educational strategy is contained in Lützkendorf and Lorenz (2006b); an overview of contents offered to students is provided in Figure 39.

Figure 39: *Building blocks of education for sustainable development in property and construction (Lützkendorf and Lorenz, 2006b)*

Design related contents	**Basics / Assessment methods**
Energy efficient design *Design for environment* *Low energy house / Passive house* *Solar energy use (active/passive)* *Rainwater use* *Green roof* *Selection of building materials* *Selection of heating systems* *Design for deconstruction* *User-oriented design* *Design for senior citizens*	*Sustainability basics* *Energy demand calculation* *Life-cycle assessment (LCA)* *Assessment of surface areas /* *Ecological footprint* *Assessment of environmental risks* *Assessment of health risks* *Analysis of user requirements* *Assessment of user satisfaction /* *Post occupancy evaluation (POE)* *Life-cycle costing (LCC)* *Property valuation*

The actors of property and construction markets need to be sensitised for their role, responsibility and options in contributing to sustainable development. One possible option to achieve this quickly among property professionals would be to include elements of education for sustainable development into the Assessment of Professional Competence (APC) procedures of the large valuation organisation such as the RICS[115] and the Appraisal Institute[116]. At the moment, APC procedures do not yet cover the topic at all, but this can change in future years. Introducing elements of education for sustainable development into these procedures would mean that one can only become a 'valuer' or 'appraiser' if one has understood the importance of sustainable development and knows what to do to achieve more of it.

---

[115] See: http://www.rics.org/Careerseducationandtraining/Assessmentofprofessionalcompetence/apc_guides.htm
[116] See: http://www.appraisalinstitute.org/join/Mai_Sra_sum.asp

5.   Conclusion

This dissertation has presented evidence and constructed a case for the following conclusion: The perception of property as a commodity is changing to emphasize sustainable design features and performance characteristics as important determinants of a property's value, thereby requiring new ways of assessing value. Private and corporate market participants are becoming more aware and informed of the quality and performance of the space they use and occupy. Furthermore, poor environmental and social performance is increasingly being seen as an investment risk and a change in investment paradigms can be observed. Certain investors no longer see a conflict between acting sustainable and making profit (see Figure 40). Even more, sustainable behaviour and responsible business practices are increasingly seen as a precondition for achieving better investment returns.

Figure 40: *Changing investment paradigm*

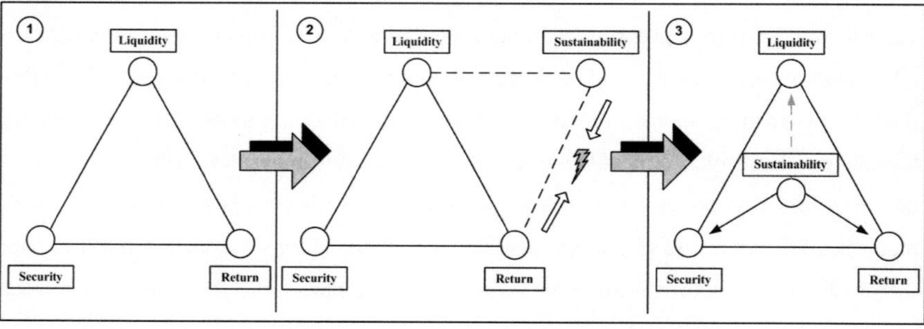

All this affects the way property will be treated for valuation purposes since valuation represents the major mechanism that allows environmental and social considerations to be more closely aligned with economic return. Thus, the valuation profession's contribution to drive change in investment and construction markets could be immense.

This dissertation project had two primary research objectives:

First, to explore the rationale for immediately and rigorously integrating sustainability issues into property investment strategies as well its integration into property valuation theory and practice. This research objective has been accomplished since it has been shown that (1) more sustainable patterns of behaviour are urgently necessary to reach a more symbiotic relationship between human economic activity and nature in order to sustain the viability of the Earth's ecosystems, (2) a huge untapped market potential exists for sustainable property investment products and consulting services, (3) sustainable buildings clearly outperform their conventional competitors in all relevant areas (i.e. environmentally, socially, and financially);

and (4) neglecting the benefits of sustainable design (and vice versa the risk of conventional design) leads to distorted price estimates.

The second research objective was to offer a property valuation framework that would allow valuers to simultaneously respond to the need of expressing property risk and valuation uncertainty more explicitly within valuation reports *and* to account for sustainability issues when estimating market value. This objective could, however, only be accomplished in part. It has been shown that (1) property valuation can be a fairly subjective exercise (or, to be more precise, a process based on rather subjective value judgments); that (2) both the concept of value and its measure are subjective; and that (3) most of the time valuers do not have enough comparable sales data available to empirically validate all the necessary price adjustments. Therefore, accounting for sustainability issues (i.e. assigning a valuation bonus for a sustainable building or a reduction for a conventional one) in valuation assignments becomes relatively easy since the validity of this judgemental decision solely depends on the valuer's capability and level of sophistication to explain and justify his or her assumptions within the valuation report by using evidence from the wider market environment. Furthermore, the methodology for expressing valuation uncertainty associated with this and other valuer's judgements through simulation is relatively straightforward and sound, but the same cannot be said of the methodologies to express risk through rating and to accurately reflect sustainability issues through yield pricing. These are in a provisional stage only and their further development is mainly hampered by the lack of appropriate property performance and transaction data available. Much more research is necessary to put the valuation of property on more solid and sustainable grounds. Key areas for further research and activity are summarized below:

- Providing a more robust informational basis for determining property specific risk premia by obtaining more detailed information on the sustainability performance of individual property assets; this requires the use of building files for property information transfer and the creation of new and the extension of existing property transaction databases and indexes;

- Development of and agreement upon measurement standards for evaluating the risks associated with property investments. For example, measurement standards for single rating criteria are not completely published by TEGoVA or VÖB. Those measurement standards that are published by these two bodies or by other rating system developers diverge from each other and are predominantly qualitative in nature. This represents a continuous research task since these risk measurement standards (particularly those relating to the property itself and the quality of the property cash flow) need to be adjusted whenever a change in market forces alters the competitive position of buildings in the marketplace.

- Adjusting and re-calibrating both property rating systems and yield pricing schemes (over time, for different sectors of the property market as well as for different countries or regions). Valuers are by no way bound to the property rating system and interlinked yield pricing scheme introduced in Section 4.3.3.3 and 4.3.3.4 above; they can develop other ones, including other variables as the knowledge on and the availability of building performance information progresses;

- Raising awareness among valuers, clients and the public that risk and uncertainty are inherent parts of any property valuation and that property prices cannot be estimated precisely,

- Providing more guidance for valuers (preferably published by the large valuation bodies such as the RICS or the Appraisal Institute) on how to deal with and account for sustainability issues within valuation reports.

- Investigating more thoroughly the nature of property values and the laws and principles of value creation.

Despite this need for further research, the additional valuation components proposed above can be used (already today) to try aligning prevailing short-term interest with long-term value drivers in property investment markets. If valuers focus on and report value creation through sustainable design, they can incentivise change and more sustainable behaviour in property and construction markets. This will create a positive, self-perpetuating loop encouraging more change and sustainable behaviour.

However, focussing on value creation through sustainable design – and in doing so, accepting the property professions' huge responsibility for society at large – requires a better understanding of the concept of sustainable development and of its implications for the property and construction sector. Distinguishing more clearly between conventional buildings and sustainable ones creates a large challenge for property professionals, their professional bodies and their educational institutions. Making these distinctions by quantifying the positive impacts of sustainable design will not only move sustainable construction quickly into the mainstream; it will also apply greater pressure on investors and investment managers (who traditionally relied only on financial performance information) to include sustainability issues in their decisions in order to boost property returns.

Bibliography

ABI, 2005, *Financial Risks of Climate Change* [online], Published by: The Association of British Insurers, Available at: <URL: http://www.abi.org.uk/climatechange>, [Accessed at: 22 April 2006]

AccountAbility, 2006, *AA1000 Series* [online], Published by: The Institute of Social and Ethical AccountAbility, Available at: <URL: http://www.accountability.org.uk/aa1000/default.asp>, [Accessed at: 14 April 2006]

Adair, A., Downie M.L, McGreal, S. and Vos, G. (Eds.), 1996, *European Valuation Practice - Theory and Techniques*, E & FN Spon, London

Adair, A. and Hutchison, N., 2005, *The reporting of risk in real estate appraisal property risk scoring*, Journal of Property Investment & Finance, Vol. 23, No. 3, 2005, pp. 254-268

Adams, C.A., 2004, *The ethical, social and environmental reporting-performance portrayal gap*, Accounting, Auditing & Accountability Journal, Vol. 17, No. 5, 2004, pp. 731-757

Adams, J., 2005b, *Risk Management: it's not rocket science - it's much more complicated* [online], Available at: <URL: http://www.socialaffairsunit.org.uk/blog/archives/000318.php>, [Accessed at: 29 January 2006]

Adams, J., 2005b, *Big ideas: Risk* [online], From New Scientist Print Edition, 17 September 2005, Available at: <URL: http://www.geog.ucl.ac.uk/~jadams/publish.htm>, [Accessed at: 29 January 2006]

ADGC, 2001, *The Amsterdam Declaration on Global Change* [online], declared at the Global Change Open Science Conference, 13 July 2001, Amsterdam, The Netherlands, Available at: <URL: http://www.sciconf.igbp.kva.se/fr.html>, [Accessed at: 15 March 2006]

Ahlberg, M., 2005, *Integrating Education for Sustainable Development*, In: Filho, W.L. (ed.), Handbook of Sustainability Research, Peter Lang Verlag, Frankfurt

AI, 2001, *The Appraisal of Real Estate*, 12th edition, Published by: The Appraisal Institute, Chicago

AI, 2002, *The Dictionary of Real Estate Appraisal*, 4th edition, Published by: The Appraisal Institute, Chicago

Ambachtsheer, J., 2005, *Socially Responsible Investing – Moving into the Mainstream* [online], Published by: Mercer Investment Consulting, Available at: <URL: http://www.merceric.com/summary.jhtml/dynamic/idContent/1181715>, [Accessed at: 08 December 2005]

Anand, S. and Sen, A., 2000, *Human development and economic sustainability*, World Development, Vol. 28, No. 12, 2000, pp. 2029-2049

Angelina, M.E. and Biggs, J.L., 2001, *Sizing Up Asbestos Exposure* [online], Published by: Tillinghast - Towers Perrin, Available at:<URL: http://www.towersperrin.com/tillinghast/publications/publications/emphasis/Emphasis_2001_3 /2002041814.pdf>, [Accessed at: 22 April 2006]

ARGE kdR, n.d., *Das Ressourcen-R – Produkte für Generationen* [online], Available at: <URL: http://www.argekdr.de/>, [Accessed at: 30 March 2006]

Astleithner, F. and Hamedinger, A., 2003, *The Analysis of Sustainability Indicators as Socially Constructed Policy Instruments: benefits and challenges of 'interactive research'*, Local Environment, Vol. 8, No. 6, 2003, pp. 627–640

Axelrod, R., 1981, *The Emergence of Cooperation Among Egoists*, The American Political Science Review, Vol. 75, pp. 306-318
Bagnoli, C. and Smith, H.C., 1998, *The Theory of Fuzzy Logic and its Application to Real Estate Valuation*, Journal of Real Estate Research, Vol. 16, No. 2, pp. 169-199

Baines, J. and Morgan, B., 2004, *Sustainability Appraisal: A Social Perspective*, In: Dalal-Clayton, B. and Sadler, B. (Eds.), Sustainability Appraisal – A Review of International Experience and Practice [online], Published by: International Institute for Environment and Development, Available at: <URL: http://www.iied.org/Gov/spa/docs.html>, [Accessed at: 01 March 2006], pp. 95-111

Bakan, J., 2004, *The Corporation*, Constable, London

Bakens, W., Foliente, G., Jasuja, M., 2005, *Engaging stakeholders in performance-based building: lessons form the Performance-Based Building (PeBBu) Network*, Building Research & Information, Vol. 33 No. 2, 2005, pp. 149-158

Baum A., Crosby, N. and MacGregor, B.D., 1996, *Price formation, mispricing and investment analysis in the property market*, Journal of Property Valuation & Investment, Vol. 14, pp. 36-49

Bardos, P., 2003, *The Contaminated Land Rehabilitation Network for Environmental Technologies – Managing and Developing the UK Interface with CLARINET* [online], Published by: The Department for Environment, Food and Rural Affairs, Available at: <URL: http://www.defra.gov.uk/ENVIRONMENT/land/contaminated/pdf/clarinet-report.pdf>, [Accessed at: 22 March 2006]

Barrett, S., 2005, *Obituary: Professor David Pearce; Economist who priced the environment* [online], Available at: <URL: http://www.ucl.ac.uk/news/news-articles/05092101>, [Accessed at: 01 March 2006]

Bartlett, E. and Howard, N., 2000, *Informing the decision makers on the cost and value of green building*, Building Research & Information, Vol. 28 No. 5/6, 2000, pp. 315-324

Batten Briefings, 2006, *A Conversation with William McDonough* [online], Published by: The Darden Graduate School of Business Administration, University of Virginia, Available at: <URL: http://www.darden.virginia.edu/batten/batten_briefings/Articles/ battenbrf_spring_06_mcdonough.pdf>, [Accessed at: 22 April 2006]

Baum, A., 1993, *Quality, depreciation and property performance*, Journal of Real Estate Research, Vol. 8, No. 4, pp. 541-565

Baum, A., 1994, *Quality and property performance*, Journal of Property Valuation and Investment, Vol. 12, No. 1, pp. 31-46

BCBS, 2004, *International Convergence of Capital Measurement and Capital Standards – A Revised Framework* [online], Published by: Bank for International Settlements, Available at: <URL: http://www.bis.org/publ/bcbs107.htm>, [Accessed at: 25 July 2004]

Becker, C. and Manstetten, R., 2004, *Nature as a You: Novalis' Philosophical Thought and the Modern Ecological Crisis*, Environmental Values, Vol. 13, 2004, pp. 101-118

Becker, C., Faber, M., Hertel, K. and Manstetten, R., 2005, *Malthus vs. Wordsworth: Perspectives on humankind, nature and economy. A contribution to the history and the foundations of ecological economics*, Ecological Economics, Vol. 53, 2005, pp. 299-310

Behrmann, T. and Kathe, A., 2004, *Zur Anwendung hedonischer Methoden beim Häuserpreisindex*, Published by: Statistisches Bundesamt (German Statistical Agency), Wirtschaft und Statistik 5/2004, pp. 525-529

Bentivegna, V., Curwell. S., Deakin, M., Lombardi, P., Mitchell, G., Nijkamp, P., 2002, *A vision and methodology for integrated sustainable urban development: BEQUEST*, Building Research & Information, Vol. 30, No. 2, pp. 83-94

Benyus, J., 1997, *Biomimicry: Innovation Inspired by Nature*, William Morrow and Company, New York

Berg, J., 2006, *'Green' Loans Touted as Profit Opportunity* [online], Amerikan Banker, 9 May 2006, Available at: <URL: http://www.americanbanker.com/article.html?id=20060508UYJJN8U8&from=mortgages>, [Accessed at: 16 May 2006]

Beyer, D., 2002, *Sustainable Building and Construction – Initiatives and Regulatory Options towards a Sustainable Planning, Building, Design and Construction Sector in Western Australia* [online], Background Paper for the State Sustainability Strategy, Western Australia, Available at: <URL: http://www.sustainability.dpc.wa.gov.au/docs/BGPapers/DavidBeyer.pdf>, [Accessed at: 12 Mai 2004]

BMU, 2004, *Umweltbewusstsein in Deutschland 2004 - Ergebnisse einer repräsentativen Bevölkerungsumfrage* [online], Published by: Bundesministerium für Umwelt, Naturschutz und Reaktorsicherheit (BMU), Available at: <URL: http://www.bmu.de/files/umweltbewusstsein2004.pdf>, [Accessed at: 18 January 2005]

BMVBW, 2001, *Guideline for sustainable building* [online], Published by: Bundesministerium für Verkehr, Bau- und Wohnungswesen (BMVBW), Available at: <URL: http://www.bbr.bund.de/bauwesen/nachhaltigbauen/download/leitfaden_engl.pdf>, [Accessed at: 22 November 2003]

Bordass, B., Leaman, A., Ruyssevelt, P., 1999, *Probe Strategic Review 1999 – Report 4: Strategic conclusions* [online], Available at: <URL: http://www.usablebuildings.co.uk>, [Accessed at: 12 Mai 2003]

Bordass, B., 2000, *Cost and value: fact and fiction*, Building Research & Information, Vol. 28 No. 5/6, 2000, pp. 338-352

Bordass, B., Leaman, A. and Ruysevelt, P., 2001, *Assessing building performance in use 5: conclusions and implications*, Building Research & Information, Vol. 29, No. 2, pp. 144-157

Bottom, C., McGreal, S. and Heaney, G., 1999, *Appraising the functional performance characteristics of office buildings*, Journal of Property Research, Vol. 16, No. 4, pp. 339-358

Bover, O. and Velilla, P., 2002, *Hedonic house prices without characteristics: The case of new multiunit housing* [online], Published by: European Central Bank, Available at: <URL: http://www.ecb.int/pub/pdf/scpwps/ecbwp117.pdf> [Accessed at: 18 April 2004]

Brooks, C. and Tsolacos, S., 2001, *Forecasting real estate returns using financial spreads*, Journal of Property Research, 2001, Vol. 18, No. 3, pp. 235-248

Bowen, W. M., Mikelbank, B. A. and Prestegaard, D. M. , 2001, *Theoretical and empirical considerations regarding space in hedonic house price estimation*, Growth and Change, Vol. 32, No. 4, pp. 466-490

Böhm-Bawerk, E., 1894-95, *The Ultimate Standard of Value* [online], Annals of the American Academy of Political and Social Science, Vol. 5, pp. 149-208, Available at: <URL: http://www.ecn.bris.ac.uk/het/bawerk/value.txt>, [Accessed at: 8 Mai 2006]

Börsen-Zeitung, 2005, *Deka eilt ihrem Immobilienfonds zu Hilfe*, Börsen-Zeitung, 21. Dezember 2005, Nr. 247, S. 4

Brekke, K.A., and Howarth, R.B., 2002, *Status, Growth and the Environment: Goods as Symbols in Applied Welfare Economics*, Edward Elgar Publishing, Cheltenham

Brindley, T., 2003, *The social dimension of the urban village: A comparison of models for sustainable urban development*, Urban Design International, Vol. 8, No. 1-2, pp. 53-65

Bruhns, H., 2003, *The role of information in a sustainable property market* [online], published by RICS Foundation, Available at: <URL: http://www.rics-foundation.org/publish/download.aspx?did=3160>, [Accessed at: 13 June 2004]

Brulator, M.M., 1999, *Henry David Thoreau: Walking – Study text* [online], Published by: Virginia Commonwealth University, Available at: <URL: http://www.vcu.edu/engweb/transcendentalism/authors/thoreau/walking/>, [Accessed at: 01 March 2006]

Butti, K., 1980, *A golden thread: 2500 years of solar architecture and technology*, Van Nostrand Reinhold, New York

Cadman, D., 2000, *The vicious circle of blame*, Cited in: Keeping, M., 2000, What about demand? Do investors want 'sustainable buildings'? [online], Published by: The RICS Research Foundation, Available at: <URL: http://www.rics-foundation.org/publish/download.aspx?did=1955> [Accessed at: 14 May 2003]

Canonne, J. and Macdonald, R.J., 2003, *Valuation without Value Theory: A North American "Appraisal"*, Journal of Real Estate Practice and Education, Vol. 6, No. 1, pp. 113-162

Carlowitz, H.C. von, [1713] 2000, *Sylvicultura Oeconomica – Hausswirthliche Nachricht und Naturmäßige Anweisung zur Wilden-Baum-Zucht*, Hrsg. Irmer, K., TU Bergakademie Freiberg, Freiberg

Carnoules Appeal, 2000, *Carnoules Appeal For Global Welfare - International Initiatives For Operational Progress Toward Sustainability* [online], Meeting at the Factor 10 Institute, Provence, June 2000, Available at: <URL: http://www.factor10-institute.org/pdf/CarnoulesAppeal.pdf>, [Accessed at: 01 March 2006]

Carter, N., 2001, *The Politics of the Environment – Ideas, Activism, Policy*, Cambridge University Press, Cambridge

Cassel, E. and Mendelsohn, R., 1985, *The choice of functional forms for hedonic price equations: comment*, Journal of Urban Economics, Vol. 18, 1985, pp. 135-42

Castells, M., 1996, *The Rise of the Network Society, The Information Age: Economy, Society and Culture, Vol. I*, Blackwell Publishing, Cambridge

Castells, M., 1997a, *The Power of Identity, The Information Age: Economy, Society and Culture, Vol. II*, Blackwell Publishing, Cambridge

Castells, M., 1997b, *The End of the Millennium, The Information Age: Economy, Society and Culture, Vol. III,* Blackwell Publishing, Cambridge

Cauley, S.D. and Pavlov, A.D., 2002, *Rational Delays: The Case of Real Estate*, Journal of Real Estate Finance and Economics, Vol. 24, No. ½, pp. 143-165

Chen, J., Hudson-Wilson, S. and Nordby, H. 2004, *Real Estate Pricing: Spreads & Sensibilities: Why Real Estate Pricing is Rational*, Journal of Real Estate Portfolio Management, 2004, Vol. 10, No. 1, pp. 1-21

Chen, L. and Mills, T., 2004, *Global real estate investment – Going Mainstream* [online], Published by: UBS Global Asset Management, Available at: <URL: http://www.ubs.com/1/e/globalam/gre.html>, [Accessed at: 29 March 2006]

Chen, L. and Mills, T., 2006, *Global real estate investment – vol. II, The world is becoming flatter* [online], Published by: UBS Global Asset Management, Available at: <URL: http://www.ubs.com/1/e/globalam/gre.html>, [Accessed at: 29 March 2006]

Chicken, J. C. and Posner, T., 1999, *The Philosophy of Risk*, Thomas Telford Ltd, London

Chin, L. and Fan, G.Z., 2005, *Autoregressive analysis of Singapore's private residential prices*, Property Management, Vol. 23, No. 4, pp. 257-270

Chiu, R., 2004, *Socio-cultural sustainability of housing: a conceptual exploration*, Housing, Theory and Society, Vol. 21, No. 2, 2004, pp. 65-76

Chomsky, N., 2002, *Media Control: The Spectacular Achievements of Propaganda*, 2nd edition, Seven Stories Press, New York

Chomsky, N., 2003, *Understanding Power: The Indispensable Chomsky*, Vintage, New York

CIB, n.d, *Overview on recent CIB Publications* [online], International Council for Research and Innovation in Building and Construction, Available at: <URL: http://www.cibworld.nl/website>, [Accessed at: 29 April 2006]

CLARINET, 2002a, *Sustainable Management of Contaminated Land: An Overview* [online], Published by: Contaminated Land Rehabilitation Network for Environmental Technologies, Available at: <URL: http://www.clarinet.at/library/rblm_report.pdf>, [Accessed at: 19 April 2006]

CLARINET, 2002b, *Review of Decision Support Tools for Contaminated Land Management, and their Use in Europe* [online], Published by: Contaminated Land Rehabilitation Network for Environmental Technologies, Available at: <URL: http://www.clarinet.at/library/final_report_1102.pdf>, [Accessed at: 19 April 2006]

CLARINET, 2002c, *Brownfields and Redevelopment of Urban Areas* [online], Published by: Contaminated Land Rehabilitation Network for Environmental Technologies, Available at: <URL: http://www.clarinet.at/library/brownfields.pdf>, [Accessed at: 19 April 2006]

Cohen, R., 2004, *Hume's Moral Philosophy* [online], Stanford Encyclopaedia of Philosophy Available at: <URL: http://plato.stanford.edu/entries/hume-moral/>, [Accessed at: 01 March 2006]

Cole, R.J. and Sterner, E., 2000, *Reconciling theory and practice of life-cycle costing*, Building Research & Information, Vol. 28 No. 5/6, 2000, pp. 368-375

Cole, R. J., 2005, *Building environmental assessment methods: redefining intentions and roles,* Building Research and Information, Vol. 33 No. 5, pp. 455-467

Cooper, I., 2001, *Post-occupancy evaluation – where are you?*, Building Research & Information, Vol. 29 No. 2, 2001, pp. 158-163

Co-operative Bank, 2005, *The Ethical Consumerism Report 2005* [online], Available at: <URL: http://www.co-operativebank.co.uk/images/pdf/coopEthicalConsumerismReport2005.pdf>, [Accessed at: 28 March 2006]

CORE, 2005, *A Big Deal? Corporate Social Responsibility and the Finance Sector in Europe* [online], Published by: The Corporate Responsibility Coalitions, Available at: <URL: http://www.corporate-responsibility.org/module_images/A_Big_Deal_CSR_&_the_Finance_ Sector_in_Europe_Report_(Dec2005).pdf>, [Accessed at: 18 April 2006]

Costanza, R., 2003, *A vision of the future of science: reintegrating the study of humans and the rest of nature*, Futures, Vol. 35, pp. 651-671

Costanza, R., d'Arge, R., Groot, R., Farber, S., Grasso, M., Hannon, B., Limburg, K., Naeem, S., O'Neill, R.V., Paruelo, J., Raskin, R.G., Sutton, P. and van den Belt, M., 1997, *The value of the world's ecosystem services and natural capital,* Nature, Vol. 387, 1997, pp. 253–260

Court, A. T., 1939, *Hedonic Price Indexes with Automotive Examples,* The Dynamics of Automobile Demand, pp. 99-117, New York

Craig, J, 2003, Interview with Financial Times, In: *Capital plans bang on for big banks: Basel II: New accord is less onerous for lenders, says Jack Ozanne. But what do borrowers think?*, Financial Times, London, 1 October 2003, p. 8

Crosby, N., French, N. and Oughton, M., 2000, *Bank lending valuations on commercial property – Does European mortgage lending value add anything to the process?,* Journal of Property Investment & Finance, Vol. 18, No. 1, 2000, pp. 68-83

Curry, B., 2002, *Neural networks and non-linear statistical methods: an application to the modelling of price quality relationships*, Computers and Operations Research, Vol. 29, No. 8, pp. 951-969

d'Amato, M., 2002, *Appraising property with rough set theory*, Journal of Property Investment & Finance, Vol. 20, No. 4, pp. 406-418

Dalal-Clayton, B. and Sadler, B. (Eds.), 2004, *Sustainability Appraisal – A Review of International Experience and Practice* [online], Published by: International Institute for Environment and Development, Available at: <URL: http://www.iied.org/Gov/spa/docs.html>, [Accessed at: 01 March 2006]

Daly, H.E., 1993, *The Steady-State Economy,* In: Daly, H.E. and Townsend, K.N., (Eds.), Valuing the Earth: Economics, Ecology, Ethics, MIT Press, Cambridge, pp. 325-363

Damodaran, A., 2002, *Investment Valuation: Tools and Techniques for Determining the Value of Any Asset*, Second Edition, John Wiley and Sons

Dasgupta, P. and Heal, G.M., 1974, *The optimal depletion of exhaustible resources*, Symposium on the economics of exhaustible resources, Review of Economic Studies, Vol. 41, pp. 3-28

DCAT, 2001, *Public and Private Initiatives in Sustainable Building and Development* [online], Published by: Development Center for Appropriate Technology, Available at: <URL: http://www.dcat.net>, [Accessed at: 22 November 2003]

De Bondt, W.F.M., 1995, *Real Estate Cycles and Animal Spirits,* In: Pagliari, J. (Ed.), 1995, The Handbook of Real Estate Portfolio Management, McGraw-Hill, New York

De Bondt, W.F.M., 1998, *Behavioural Economics – A portrait of the individual investor,* European Economic Review, Vol. 42, pp. 831-844

DEGI, 2005, *Global Values – Immobilieninvestments 2005* [online], Published by: Deutsche Gesellschaft für Immobilienfonds, Available at:
<URL: http://www.degi.de/pdf/research/marktreport/DEGI_Global_Values2005.pdft>, [Accessed at: 16 March 2006]

Dell, G., 2004, *AVMs: The Myth and the Reality; the Problem and the Solution,* Valuation Insights & Perspectives, Third Quarter 2004, pp. 12-17 and 50-52

Dena, 2005, *Der Energiepass für Gebäude,* Published by: Deutsche Energie-Agentur, Berlin

Der Spiegel, 2002, *Kurseinbrüche durch Asbest-Klagen,* Ausgabe Nr. 46, 2002, p. 199

Derbyshire, A., 2001, *Editorial - Probe in the UK context,* Building Research & Information, Vol. 29 No. 2, 2001, pp. 79-84

DGA, 2004, *Rechenschaftsbericht 2003 – Deutsche Grundbesitz-Anlagegesellschaft* [online], Available at: <URL: https://www.rreef.com/GER_de/bin/03_RB_HannoverLT.pdf >, [Accessed at: 29 January 2006]

DGA, 2005, *Rechenschaftsbericht 2004 – Deutsche Grundbesitz-Anlagegesellschaft,* [online], Available at: <URL: https://www.rreef.com/GER_de/bin/04_RB_HannoverLT.pdf >, [Accessed at: 29 January 2006]

Donovan, N. and Halpern, D., 2002, *Life satisfaction: The state of knowledge and implications for government* [online], UK Cabinet Office, London, Available at: <URL: http://www.strategy.gov.uk/downloads/seminars/ls/paper.pdf >, [Accessed at: 27 May 2006]

Dorchester, J.D., 2004, *Market Value for Financial Reporting: The Premise,* The Appraisal Journal, Winter 2004, pp. 20-34

Doughty, M. and Hammond, P., 2004, *Sustainability and the built environment at and beyond the city scale,* Building and Environment, Vol. 39, 2004, pp. 1223-1233

Downton, P.F., n.d., *Ecopolis Development Principles*, [online], Published by: Ecopolis Architects, Available at: <URL: http://www.ecopolis.com.au/theory/principles.html>, [Accessed at: 23 March 2006]

Dresner, S., 2002, *The principles of Sustainability*, Earthscan, London, 2002

Drouet, D., 2003, *Economic Instruments for Sustainable Construction – A survey for the Paris Regional Agency for Environment and New Energies*, Published by: Recherche Développement International, Paris, 2003, Available through: <URL: http://rdi-consultant.com>

du Plessis, C., 2003, *Boiling Frogs, Bursting Dykes, Sinking Ships and the End of the World as We Know It* [online], International Electronic Journal of Construction, Special Issue article in: The Future of Sustainable Construction, Available at: <URL: http://www.bcn.ufl.edu/iejc/pindex/64/du_plessis.pdf>, [Accessed at: 29 March 2006]

Dupree, C., 2001, *Purse Strings of the Heart* [online], Harvard Magazine, September-October 2001, Available at: <URL: http://www.harvardmagazine.com/on-line/0901212.html>, [Accessed at: 29 March 2006]

Edge, J., 2002, *Personal interview*, London, 20 March 2002

Edwards, S., Bartlett, E. and Dickie, I., 2000, *Whole life costing and life-cycle assessment for sustainable building design* [online], Published by: The Building Research Establishment, Available at: <URL: http://www.brebookshop.com/details.jsp?id=32991>, [Accessed at: 26 Mai 2002]

Ekins, P., 2000, *Economic Growth and Environmental Sustainability*, Routledge, London

Ekins, P., Simon, S., Deutsch, L., Folke, C. and De Groot, R., 2003, *A framework for the practical application of the concepts of critical natural capital and strong sustainability*, Ecological Economics, Vol. 44, pp. 165-185

Encyclopaedia Britannica, 2004, *Encyclopaedia Britannica 2004 – Ultimate Reference Suite DVD*, Encyclopaedia Britannica Inc., Chicago

Energeia, 2005, *Energeia – Newsletter des Bundesamtes für Energie (BFE)*, Ausgabe 5, November 2005, Bern

Enever, N. and Isaac, D., 2002, *The Valuation of Property Investments*, 6th ed., Estates Gazette, London

Engel, R. and Kieffer, H., 2005, *Nutzungsdauer bei der Wertermittlung: "Hartnäckiger Autismus"*, in: Immobilien Zeitung, Nr. 9, 21. April 2005, S. 16

Enquete-Kommission, 1998, *Abschlußbericht der Enquete-Kommission "Schutz des Menschen und der Umwelt - Ziele und Rahmenbedingungen einer nachhaltig zukunftsverträglichen Entwicklung" des 13. Deutschen Bundestages: Konzept Nachhaltigkeit - Vom Leitbild zur Umsetzung*, Hrsg.: Deutscher Bundestag, Referat Öffentlichkeitsarbeit, Berlin

Escobar, A., 1996, *Constructing Nature: elements for a poststructural political ecology*, In: Peet, R. and Watts, M. (Eds.), Liberation Ecologies: Environment, Development, Social Movements, Routledge, London, pp. 46-68

Estates Gazette, 2000, *Times of Change*, Estates Gazette, 15 July 2000, p. 136

ETCRWM, 2004 *Waste and material flows 2004 - Current situation for Europe, Caucasus and Central Asia* [online], Published by: European Topic Centre on Resource and Waste Management, Available at: <URL: http://waste.eionet.eu.int/publications/wp2_2004>, [Accessed at: 23 April 2006]

EU Expert Working Group Sustainable Construction Methods & Techniques, 2004, *Final Report – January 2004* [online], Brussels, 2004, Available at: <URL: http://europa.eu.int/comm/environment/urban/sustainable_urban_construction.htm>, [Accessed at: 18 November 2004]

Eurogip, 2004, *Costs and funding of occupational diseases in Europe* [online], Published by: Groupement de l'Institution Prévention de la Sécurité sociale pour l'Europe, Available at: <URL: http://www.europeanforum.org/pdf/Eurogip-08_E-cost.pdf>, [Accessed at: 18 November 2004]

European Commission, 2001, *Directive on the assessment of the effects of certain plans and programmes on the environment* [online], 2001/42/EC, Available at: <URL: http://europa.eu.int/comm/environment/eia/full-legal-text/0142_en.pdf>, [Accessed at: 05 March 2006]

European Commission, 2002, *Directive of the European Parliament and of the Council on the energy performance of buildings*, 2002/91/EC, Official Journal of the European Communities, December, 2002, L1 pp. 65-71

European Commission, 2003, *Directive on the annual and consolidated accounts of certain types of companies, banks and other financial institutions and insurance undertakings* [online], 2003/51/EC, Brussels, 2003, Available at: <URL: http://europa.eu.int/eur-lex/lex/LexUriServ/LexUriServ.do?uri=OJ:L:2003:178:0016:0022:EN:PDF>, [Accessed at: 05 December 2004]

European Commission, 2004a, *Construction sector overview* [online], Available at: <URL: http://europa.eu.int/comm/enterprise/construction/index_en.htm>, [Accessed at: 05 January 2005]

European Commission, 2004b, *Towards a thematic strategy on the urban Environment* [online], COM(2004)60, Brussels, 2004, Available at: <URL: http://europa.eu.int/comm/environment/urban/thematic_strategy.htm>, [Accessed at: 05 September 2004]

European Commission, 2004c, *Mandate on the development of horizontal standardised methods for the assessment of the integrated environmental performance of buildings*, Europeans Commission's standardisation mandate to CEN M/350, Brussels, 2004

European Commission, 2005, *Draft Declaration on Guiding Principles for Sustainable Development* [online], COM(2005) 218 final, Available at: <URL: http://www.eu.int/comm/sustainable/docs/COM_2005_0218_F_EN_ACTE.pdf>, [Accessed at: 05 March 2006]

Eurosif, 2003, *Socially Responsible Investment among European Institutional Investors* [online], Published by: European Sustainable and Responsible Investment Forum, Available at: <URL: http://www.eurosif.org/pub2/lib/2003/10/srirept/index.shtml>, [Accessed at: 12 May 2004]

Equator Principles, 2003, *The "Equator Principles" - An industry approach for financial institutions in determining, assessing and managing environmental & social risk in project financing* [online], Available at: <URL: http://www.equator-principles.com/principles.shtml>, [Accessed at: 30 March 2006]

Fanning, S.F., 2006, *Market Analysis for Real Estate – Concepts and Applications in Valuation and Highest and Best Use*, Published by: Appraisal Institute, Chicago

Federal Ministry of Transport, Housing and Building, 2001, *Guideline for Sustainable Building* [online], Available at: <URL: http://www.bbr.bund.de/bauwesen/nachhaltigbauen/download/leitfaden_engl.pdf>, [Accessed at: 10 March 2003]

Fichte, J.G., [1794] 1997, *Grundlage der gesamten Wissenschaftslehre, als Handschrift für seine Zuhörer*, Hrsg. Medicus, F. und Jacobs, W.G, 4. Auflage, Meiner Verlag, Hamburg

Fichte, J.G., [1795] 1966, *'Von der Sprachfähigkeit und dem Ursprung der Sprache'*, in *J. G. Fichte-Gesamtausgabe der Bayerischen Akademie der Wissenschaften*, Hrsg. Lauth, R. und Jacob, H., Bd. I, 3, Stuttgart, Cited in: Becker and Manstetten (2004)

Filliou, R., 1996, *Robert Filliou - From Political to Poetical Economy*, Catalogue of an exhibition at the Morris and Helen Belkin Art Gallery, Vancouver, Available through: <URL: http://www.belkin-gallery.ubc.ca/webpage/editions/filliou.html>, [Accessed at: 01 March 2006]

Filose, J., 2005, *Do corporate occupiers place a premium on energy efficient premises*, Presentation held at the RICS Valuation conference 2005, 29 December 2005, London, Available at: <URL: http://www.rics.org/NR/rdonlyres/9498BB8A-7D74-4C2D-9506-B9D03F574894/0/JulietFilose.pdf>, [Accessed at: 01 February 2006]

Financial Times, 2005, *Designing our way out of trouble*, Financial Times, 15 October 2005, p. 8

Fisher, J.D., 2002, *Real time valuation*, Journal of Property Investment and Finance, Vol. 20 No. 3, 2002, pp. 213-221

Fisher, M., 2005, *Sustainable Cities Publication, Project Proposal on: What is a Sustainable City, and how do we get there from here?* [online], Published by: Urban Ecology Australia, Available at: <URL: http://www.urbanecology.org.au/projects/sustainablecities.html>, [Accessed at: 15 April 2006]

Flemming, M. C. and Nellis, J. G., 1997, *The Halifax house price index technical details*, Halifax PLC, UK, Cited in: Booth, P. M. and Marcato, G., 2004, *The measurement and modelling of commercial real estate performance*, British Actuarial Journal, Vol. 10, No. 1, 2004, pp. 5-73

Fletcher, M., Mangan, J. and Raeburn, E., 2004, *Comparing hedonic models for estimating and forecasting house prices*, Property Management, Vol. 22, No. 3, 2004, pp. 189-200

Forsyth, T., 2003, *Critical political ecology: the politics of environmental science*, Routledge, London

Forum for the Future, 2002, *Sustainability Pays* [online], Available at: <URL: http://www.forumforthefuture.org.uk/publications/Sustainabilitypays_page712.aspx>, [Accessed at: 01 March 2006]

Forum for the Future, n.d, *The Five Capitals Model*, [online], Available at: <URL: http://www.forumforthefuture.org.uk/aboutus/fivecapitalsmodel_page814.aspx>, [Accessed at: 01 March 2006]

Frank, R., 1988, *Passions within Reason: The Strategic Role of the Emotions*, W. W. Norton, New York

Frankfurter Allgemeine Zeitung, 2005, *"Es wird nicht nur um Abwertungen gehen"*, 19. Dezember 2005, S. 25

French, N., 2004, *A Question of Value: A Discussion of Definitions and the Property Pricing Process*, In: Sirmans, C.F. and Worzala, E. (Eds.), Essays in Honor of William N. Kinnard, Jr., Research Issues in Real Estate Volume 9, Kluwer Academic Publishers, London, pp. 45 - 54.

French, N., 2005, *Comparing Notes*, Estates Gazette, 29 October 2005, p. 184

French, N. and Gabrielli, L., 2004, *The uncertainty of valuation*, Journal of Property Investment & Finance, Vol. 22, No. 6, pp. 484-500

French, N. and Gabrielli, L., 2005, *Discounted cash flow: accounting for uncertainty*, Journal of Property Investment & Finance, Vol. 23, No. 1, pp. 76-89

French, N. and Gabrielli, L., 2006, *Uncertainty and feasibility studies: an Italian case study*, Journal of Property Investment & Finance, Vol. 24, No. 1, pp. 49-67

FTD, 2005, *Fondsgutachter unter Beschuss*, Financial Times Deutschland, 16. Dezember 2005, Nr. 245, S. 22

FTSE, 2006, *FTSE4Good Index Series Inclusion Criteria* [online], Published by: FTSE – The Index Company, Available at: <URL: http://www.ftse.com/Indices/FTSE4Good_Index_Series/index.jsp>, [Accessed at: 30 March 2006]

Furtak, R.A., 2005, *Henry David Thoreau* [online], Stanford Encyclopaedia of Philosophy Available at: <URL: http://plato.stanford.edu/entries/thoreau/>, [Accessed at: 01 March 2006]

Gaddy, W.E. and Hart, R.E., 2003, *Real Estate Fundamentals*, 6th edition, Dearborn Financial Publishing, Chicago

Gersch, A., 1969, *On the Theory of Exchange Value,* Universität Druckerei H. Stürtz, Würzburg

Gilbertson, B. and Preston, D., 2005, *A vision for valuation*, Journal of Property Investment & Finance, Vol. 23, No. 2, pp. 123-140

Gossen, H.H. [1854] 1983, *The Laws of Human Relations and the Rules of Human Action Derived Therefrom*, The MIT Press, Cambridge

Gowdy, J. and Erickson, J.D., 2005, *The approach of ecological economics*, Cambridge Journal of Economics, Vol. 29, 2005, pp. 207-222

GRI, 2005, *G3 – Global Reporting Guidelines* [online], Published by: Global Reporting Initiative, Available at: <URL: http://www.grig3.org/index.html>, [Accessed at: 30 March 2006]

Graham, P., 2000, *Building education for the next industrial revolution: teaching and learning environmental literacy for the building professions*, Construction Management and Economics, Vol. 18, pp. 917-925

Gray R., Owen D. and Maunders K., 1988, *Corporate Social Reporting: Emerging Trends in Accountability and the Social Contract*, Accounting, Auditing & Accountability Journal, Vol. 1, No. 1, pp. 6-20

Gray, R., 1992, *Accounting and environmentalism: An exploration of the challenge of gently accounting for accountability, transparency and sustainability*, Accounting, Organizations and Society, Vol. 17, No. 5, pp. 399-425

Gray, R., 2002, *Of Messiness, Systems and Sustainability: Towards a more Social and Environmental Finance and Accounting*, British Accounting Review, Vol. 34, pp. 357-386

Greden, L. and Glicksam, L., 2005, *A real options model for valuing flexible spaces*, Journal of Corporate Real Estate, Vol. 7, No. 1, pp. 34–48

Grieg-Gran, M. and Dufey, A., 2004, *Sustainability Appraisal: Economics-Based Approaches*, In: Dalal-Clayton, B. and Sadler, B. (Eds.), Sustainability Appraisal – A Review of International Experience and Practice [online], Published by: International Institute for Environment and Development, Available at: <URL: http://www.iied.org/Gov/spa/docs.html>, [Accessed at: 01 March 2006], pp. 67-94

Guidry, K., 2004, *How Green Is Your Building? An Appraiser's Guide to Sustainable Design*, The Appraisal Journal, Winter 2004, pp. 57-68

Guinée, J.B., (Ed.), 2002, *Handbook on Life Cycle Assessment - Operational Guide to the ISO Standards*, Springer, Heidelberg

Haigh, M., 2005, *Greening the University Curriculum: Appraising an International Movement*, Journal of Geography in Higher Education, Vol. 29, No. 1, pp. 31-48

Haimann, R., 2005, *Sanierung des Deka-Fonds zeigt erste Erfolge*, Die Welt, 23. November 2005, Heft 274, S. 23

Hamilton, C., 2003, *Growth Fetish*, Allen and Unwin, Sydney

Harris, J.M., 2000, *Basic Principles of Sustainable Development* [online], Published by: Global Development and Environment Institute, Working Paper 00-04, Available at: <URL: http://ase.tufts.edu/gdae/publications/working_papers/Sustainable%20Development.PDF>, [Accessed at: 05 March 2006]

Harvey, J., 2000, *Urban Land Economics*, 5th edition, Macmillan Press, London

Hausman, D., 2003, *Philosophy of Economics* [online], Stanford Encyclopaedia of Philosophy Available at: <URL: http://plato.stanford.edu/entries/economics/>, [Accessed at: 01 March 2006]

Hawken, P., Lovins, A. and Lovins, L.H., 1999, *Natural Capitalism – Creating the next industrial revolution*, Little, Brown and Company, London

Heerwagen, J., 2002, *Sustainable Design Can Be an Asset to the Bottom Line - expanded internet edition* [online], Environmental Design & Construction, Available at: <URL: http://www.edcmag.com/CDA/ArticleInformation/features/BNP__Features__Item/0,4120,807 24,00.html> [Accessed at: 10 April 2004]

Heerwagen, J.H., Kampschroer, K., Powell, K.M., and Loftness, V., 2004, *Collaborative knowledge work environments*, Building Research & Information, Vol. 32, No. 6, pp. 510-528

Hendriks, D., 2005, *Apportionment in property valuation: should we separate the inseparable?*, Journal of Property Investment & Finance, Vol. 23, No. 5, 2005, pp. 455-470

Hermes, 2006, *Responsible Property Investment – defining the challenge* [online], Available at: <URL: http://www.hermes.co.uk/real_estate/real_estate_rpi_challenges.htm>, [Accessed at: 13 April 2006]

Ho, D., Newell, G. and Walker, A., 2005, *The importance of property-specific attributes in assessing CBD office building quality*, Journal of Property Investment & Finance, Vol. 23, No. 5, 2005, pp. 424-444

Hodgson, G., 1997, *Economics, Environmental Policy and Transcendence of Utilitarianism*, In: Foster, J. (Ed.), Valuing Nature? Economics, Ethics and Environment, Routledge, London, pp. 47-63

Holling, C.S., 2001, *Understanding the Complexity of Economic, Ecological and Social Systems*, Ecosystems, Vol. 4, 2001, pp. 390-405

Holter, R., 2005, *Die Bewertung von Immobilien vor dem Hintergrund von Basel II* [online], Published by: Verband deutscher Hypothekenbanken (VDH), Available at: <URL: http://www.fntev.de/SITE/UPLOAD/DOCUMENT/040518CEFS.pdf>, [Accessed at: 25 January 2006]

Holton, G. A., 2004, *Defining Risk*, Financial Analysts Journal, Vol. 60, Nr. 6, 2004, pp. 19-25

Hoppe, R., 1999, *It's time we buried Value-at-Risk* [online], Risk Professional, July/August 1999, p. 14, Available at: <URL: http://www.itrac.com/paper/BURYVAR.DOC>, [Accessed at: 13 Mai 2006]

Hordijk, A. and van de Ridder, W., 2005, *Valuation model uniformity and consistency in real estate indices - The case of The Netherlands*, Journal of Property Investment & Finance, Vol. 23, No. 2, 2005, pp. 165-181

Hough, D. and Kratz, C., 1983, *Can 'good' architecture meet the market test?*, Journal of Urban Economics, Vol. 14, 1983, pp. 40–54

Hönighaus, R., 2004, *Deka-Fonds stößt Risiko-Immobilien ab*, Financial Times Deutschland, 21. Dezember 2004, S. 17

Huber, J., 1995, *Nachhaltige Entwicklung. Strategien für eine ökologische und soziale Erdpolitik*, Edition Sigma, Berlin

Huber, J., 2000, *Konsistenz, Effizienz und Suffizienz in zyklusanalytischer Betrachtung*, In: Kreibich, R. und Simonis, U.E. (Eds.), Global Change, Berlin Verlag Arno Spitz, Berlin, pp. 109-126

Hume, D., [1751] 1898, *An Enquiry Concerning the Principles of Morals*, In: Green, T.H. and Grose, T.H. (Eds.), Essays: Moral, Political and Literary, Longmans, Green & Co., London, Available at: <URL: http://www.anselm.edu/homepage/dbanach/Hume-Enquiry%20Concerning%20Morals.htm>, [Accessed at: 02 February 2006]

Hummels, H. and Timmer, D., 2004, *Investors in Need of Social, Ethical, and Environmental Information*, Journal of Business Ethics, Vol. 52, 2004, pp. 73–84

Hutchison, N. and Nanthakumaran, N., 2000, *The calculation of worth – Issues of market efficiency, variable estimation and risk analysis*, Journal of Property Investment & Finance, Vol. 18, No. 1, pp. 33-51

Huovila, P. (Ed.), 2005, *Performance Based Building*, Advancing Facilities Management & Construction through Innovation Series, Published by: Technical Research Centre Finland (VTT) and Association of Finnish Civil Engineers (RIL), Helsinki

Hutchison, N., Adair, A. and Leheny, I., 2005, *Communicating Investment Risk to Clients: Property Risk Scoring*, Journal of Property Research, June–September 2005, Vol. 22, No. 2-33, pp. 137-161

IEA Annex31, 2001, *Directory of Tools – A survey of LCA Tools, Assessment Frameworks, Rating Systems, Technical Guidelines, Catalogues, Checklists and Certificates* [online], Available at: <URL: http://annex31.wiwi.uni-karlsruhe.de/INDEX.HTM>, [Accessed at: 15 January 2005]

IEA Annex31, 2004, *Types of Tools* [online], Available at:
<URL: http://www.iisbe.org/annex31/pdf/D_types_tools.pdf>, [Accessed at: 15 December 2004]

IFC, 2005, *'Who Cares Wins': One Year On – A Review of the Integration of Environmental, Social and Governance Value Drivers in Asset Management, Financial Research and Investment Processes* [online], Published by: International Finance Corporation, Available at:
<URL: http://www.ifc.org/ifcext/home.nsf/Content/Who_Care_Wins>, [Accessed at: 11 March 2006]

iiSBE, 2006, *Advanced Building News – iiSBE Newsletter* [online], Nr. 9, January 2006, Published by: International Initiative for a Sustainable Built Environment, Available at: <URL: http://greenbuilding.ca/iisbe/start/iisbe.htm>, [Accessed at: 22 April 2006]

IISD, 1997, *Assessing Sustainable Development: Principles in Practice* [online], Hardi, P. and Zdan, T. (Eds.), Published by: International Institute for Sustainable Development, Available at: <URL: http://www.iisd.org/pdf/bellagio.pdf>, [Accessed at: 13 March 2006]

Immobilien Zeitung, 2005, *Problemkind Ertragswert*, Immobilien Zeitung, 10. Februar 2005, S. 1-5

IPCC, 2001a, *Climate Change 2001: Synthesis Report – Summary for Policymakers* [online], Published by: Intergovernmental Panel on Climate Change, Available at: <URL: http://www.ipcc.ch/pub/un/syreng/spm.pdf>, [Accessed at: 28 December 2005]

IPCC, 2001b, *Climate Change 2001: Impacts, Adaptation and Vulnerability – Technical Summary* [online], Published by: Intergovernmental Panel on Climate Change, Available at: <URL: http://www.ipcc.ch/pub/wg2TARtechsum.pdf>, [Accessed at: 28 December 2005]

IPF, 2000, *The Assessment and Management of Risk in the Property Investment Industry* [online], Published by: Investment Property Forum, Available at:
<URL: http://www.ipf.org.uk/resources/pdf/research/research_reports/RiskReport.pdf>, [Accessed at: 26 January 2006]

IPF, 2002, *Risk Measurement and Management for Real Estate Investment Portfolios – Summary Report* [online], Published by: Investment Property Forum, Available at:
<URL: http://www.ipf.org.uk/servlet.cgi?page_id=336>, [Accessed at: 26 January 2006]

IVSC, 2005, *International Valuation Standards 2005*, International Valuation Standards Committee, London

Jacobs, M., 1997, *Environmental Valuation, Deliberative Democracy and Public Decision-Making Institutions*, In: Foster, J. (Ed.), Valuing Nature? Economics, Ethics and Environment, Routledge, London, pp. 211-231

Jackson, T., 2005, *Motivating Sustainable Consumption* [online], Published by: Sustainable Development Research Network, Available at: <URL: http://www.sd-research.org.uk/documents/MotivatingSCfinal.pdf>, [Accessed at: 15 February 2005]

Janssen, C., et al., 2001, *Robust estimation of hedonic models of price and income for investment property*, Journal of Property Investment and Finance, Vol. 19 No. 4. 2001, pp. 342-360

James A.N., Gaston, K.J. and Balmford, A., 1999, *Balancing the Earth's accounts*, Nature, Vol. 401, pp. 323-324

James, W., [1890] 1981, *The Principles of Psychology*, Harvard University Press, Cambridge

Jeucken, M., 2001, *Sustainable Finance and Banking – The Financial Sector and the Future of the Planet*, Earthscan Publishing, London

Jeucken, M., 2002, *Banking and Sustainability: Slow starters are gaining pace*, Ethical Corporation Magazine, Nr 11, November 2002, pp. 44-48

Jeucken, M., 2004, *Sustainability in Finance - Banking on the Planet*, Eburon Academic Publishers, Delft

Johnson, T., Davies, K. and Shapiro, E., 2000, *Modern Methods of Valuation of Land, Houses and Buildings*, Ninth Edition, Estates Gazette, London

Jones Lang LaSalle, 2004, *Global Real Estate Transparency Index 2004* [online], Available at: <URL: http://www.joneslanglasalle.com/en-GB/research/researchabstract?artid=1220>, [Accessed at: 30 January 2006]

Jordan, A. and O'Riordan, T., 2003, *Institutions for global environmental change*, Global Environmental Change, Vol. 13, 2003, p. 223

Joslin, A., 2005, *An investigation into the expression of uncertainty in property valuations*, Journal of Property Investment & Finance, Vol. 23, No. 3, 2005 pp. 269-285

Jumpertz, N., 2005, *Pikanter Preisabschlag*, in: Immobilienwirtschaft 12/05 – 01/06, S. 24-25

Kaehler, S.D., 1998, *Fuzzy Logic Tutorial* [online], Published by: The Seattle Robotics Society, Available at: <URL: http://www.seattlerobotics.org/encoder/mar98/fuz/flindex.html>, [Accessed at: 13 May 2006]

Kane, M.S., Linné, M.R. and Johnson, J.A., 2004a, *Practical Applications in Appraisal Valuation Modelling – Statistical Methods for Real Estate Practitioners*, Published by: The Appraisal Institute, Chicago

Kane, M.S., Linné, M.R. and Johnson, J.A., 2004b, *Evaluating the Valuers*, The Appraisal Journal, Spring 2004, pp. 147-154

Kampschroer, K. and Heerwagen, J.H., 2005, *The strategic workplace: development and evaluation*, Building Research & Information, Vol. 33, No. 4, pp. 326-337

Kasser, T., 2002, *The High Price of Materialism*, MIT Press, Camebridge

Kats, G., Alevantis, L., Berman, A., Mills, E., Perlman, J., 2003, *The Costs and Financial Benefits of Green Buildings – A Report to California's Sustainable Building Task Force* [online], Available at: <URL: http://www.usgbc.org/Docs/News/News477.pdf>, [Accessed at: 22 January 2004]

Kauko, T., 2003a, *On current neural network applications involving spatial modelling of property prices*, Journal of Housing and the Built Environment, Vol. 18, pp. 159-181

Kauko, T., 2003b, *Residential property value and locational externalities*, Journal of Property Investment and Finance, Vol. 21, No. 3, pp. 250-270

Kauko, T., 2004, *Towards the 4th generation – an essay on innovations in residential property value modelling expertise*, Journal of Property Research, Vol. 21, No. 1, pp. 75-97

Kauko, T. and d'Amato, M., 2004, *Mass Appraisal Valuation Methodologies: Between Orthodoxy and Heresy*, Proceedings of the 11th European Real Estate Society Conference (ERES 2004), Milan, 2004

Kibert, C.J. and Grosskopf, K., 2005, *Radical Sustainable Construction: Envisioning next generation green buildings* [online], Published by: Center for Training, Research and Educationfor Environmental Occupations, University of Florida, Available at: <URL: http://www.treeo.ufl.edu/rsc06/WhitePaper-RSC06.pdf>, [Accessed at: 24 March 2006]

Kimmet, P., 2006, *Theoretical Foundations for Integrating Sustainability Issues in Property Investment Appraisal* [online], Paper presented at the 12th Pacific RIM Real Estate Society Conference, 22 – 25 January 2006, New Zealand, Available at: <URL: http://www.prres.net/papers/Kimmet_Integrating_Sustainability_Property_Investment_Apprai sal.pdf>, [Accessed at: 23 April 2006]

Kishk, M. and Al-Hajj, A., 1999, *An integrated framework for life cycle costing in buildings* [online], Paper for the: RICS COBRA Conference 1999, Available at: <URL: http://www.rics-foundation.org>, [Accessed at: 28 January 2002]

Kiuchi, T., 2003, *What We Learned in the Rainforest: Nature's Lessons for the Green Building Industry* [online], Speech held at the GreenBuilding 2003 conference, Pittsburgh, 12 November, 2003, Available at: <URL: http://www.future500.org/speech/2/>, [Accessed at: 12 March 2006]

Kiuchi, T., 2004, *New Economics for the 21st Century: Natural Economics* [online], Speech held at the APO Forum, Kuala Lumpur, 1 March 2004, Available at: <URL: http://www.future500.org/speech/1/>, [Accessed at: 12 March 2006]

Kiuchi, T., 2005, *What I Learned In The Rainforest: Lessons For World Environment Day* [online], Speech held at the UN Global Compact Symposium, San Francisco, 3 June, 2005, Available at: <URL: http://www.future500.org/speech/12/>, [Accessed at: 12 March 2006]

Kleiber, W., Simon, J. und Weyers, G., 2002, *Verkehrswertermittlung von Grundstücken – Kommentar und Handbuch zur Ermittlung von Verkehrs-, Versicherungs- und Beleihungswerten unter Berücksichtigung von WertV und BauGB*, Bundesanzeiger Verlag, Köln

Klunder, G., 2004, *The search for the most eco-efficient strategies for sustainable housing construction; Dutch lessons*, Journal of Housing and the Built Environment, Vol. 19, No. 1, 2004, pp. 111-126

Kohler, N., and Hassler, U., 2002, *The building stock as a research object*, Building Research & Information, Vol. 30, No. 5, 2002, pp. 226-236

Kohler, N., and Lützkendorf, T., 2002, *Integrated life-cycle analysis*, Building Research & Information, Vol. 30, No. 4, 2002, pp. 338-348

Köhn, J., Gowdy, J., Hinterberger, F. and van der Straaten, J. (Eds.), 1999, *Sustainability in Question: the Search for a Conceptual Framework*, Edward Elgar Publishing, Cheltenham

Kraus, F., 2005, *Der Energiepass – Rahmenbedingungen und Umsetzung* [online], Speech held at: Berliner Energietage, 2-4 Mai, 2005, Published by: Deutsche Energie Agentur (dena), Available at: <URL: http://www.gebaeudeenergiepass.de>, [Accessed at: 22 January 2006]

Kuhn, S., 2003, *Prisoner's Dilemma* [online], Stanford Encyclopaedia of Philosophy, Available at: <URL: http://plato.stanford.edu/entries/prisoner-dilemma/>, [Accessed at: 12 March 2006]

Kumar, S. and Fisk, W., 2002, *The Role of Emerging Energy-Efficient Technology in Promoting Workplace Productivity and Health: Final Report* [online], Available at: <URL: http://www.ihpcental.org>, [Accessed at: 9 March 2004]

Kunstler, J.H., 2001, *The City in Mind: Notes on Urban Condition*, Free Press, New York

Lamberton, G., 2005, *Sustainability accounting – a brief history and conceptual framework*, Accounting Forum, Vol. 29, pp. 7-26

Lancaster, K. J., 1966, *A New Approach to Consumer Theory*, Journal of Political Economy, Vol. 74, pp. 132 - 157

Larsen, V.G., 2004, *Environmental Assessment Directive*, Speech held at the Architects' Council of Europe Taskforce Meeting on Environment and Sustainable Architecture, Strasbourg, 18 October 2004

Leach, M. and Mearns, R., 1996, *The lie of the land: challenging received wisdom on the African environment*, James Currey, London

Leaman, A. and Bordass, B., 1999, *Productivity in buildings: the 'killer' variables,* Building Research & Information, Vol. 27 No. 1, 1999, pp. 4-19

LEGEP, 2005, *LEGEP – An integrated Life Cycle Analysis Tool*, Available through: <URL: http://www.legep.de/index.php?AktivId=1127>, [Accessed at: 30 March 2006]

Lee, A. and Barrett, P., 2003, *Performance Based Building: First International State-of-the-Art Report* [online], Published by: International Council for Research and Innovation in Building and Construction (CIB), Available at: <URL: http://cibworld.xs4all.nl/pebbu_dl/resources/pebbupublications/downloads/01SotaPart1.pdf>, [Accessed at: 15 December 2004]

Lee, M.L. and Pace, R.K., 2005, *Spatial Distribution of Retail Sales,* Journal of Real Estate Finance and Economics, Vol. 31, No. 1, pp. 53-69

Lee, N., 2006, *Bridging the gap between theory and practice in integrated assessment*, Environmental Impact Assessment Review, Vol. 26, pp. 57-78

Lennhoff, D.C. and Parli, R.L., 2004, *A Higher and Better Definition*, The Appraisal Journal, Winter, 2004, pp. 45-49

Leung, B.Y.P. and Hui, E.C.M., 2002, *Option pricing for real estate development: Hong Kong Disneyland*, Journal of Property Investment & Finance, Vol. 20, No. 6, pp. 473-495

Lewis, W. A., 1955, *The Theory of Economic Growth*, Allen & Unwin, London
Li, H. and Shen, Q., 2002, *Supporting the decision-making process for sustainable housing*, Construction Management and Economics, Vol. 20, No. 5, 2002, pp. 387-390

Lind, H., 2005, *Value concepts, value information and cycles on the real estate market – A comment on Crosby, French and Oughton (2000)*, Journal of Property Investment & Finance, Vol. 23, No. 2, pp. 141-147

Ling, D.C. and Archer, W.R., 2005, *Real Estate Principles – A Value Approach*, McGraw-Hill, New York

Ling, D.C. and Naranjo, A., 1997, *Economic Risk Factors and Commercial Real Estate Return*, The Journal of Real Estate Finance and Economics, 1997, Vol. 14, No. 3, pp. 283-307

Linne, M.R., Kane, M.S., Dell, G., 2000, *A Guide to Appraisal Valuation Modelling*, Published by: The Appraisal Institute, Chicago

Lipscomb, R., Maloy, R. and Rogers, C.G., 2006, *Preparing Yourself for New Rules for Environmentally Impaired Property*, Valuation Insights & Perspectives, First Quarter 2006, pp. 18-19

Loew, T., 2002, *Internationale Entwicklung der Regulierungen zur Förderung ökologisch-ethischer Finanzdienstleistungen* [online], Published by: Institut für ökologische Wirtschaftsforschung, Available at: <URL: http://www.ioew.de/home/downloaddateien/DP5602.pdf>, [Accessed at: 10 June 2003]

Loipfinger, S., 2006, *Was taugen Sachverständigengutachten* [online], Available at: <URL: http://www.fondstelegramm.de>, [Accessed at: 23 January 2006]

Lourdel, N., Gondran, N., Laforest, V. and Brodhag, C., 2005, *Introduction of sustainable development in engineers' curricula: Problematic and evaluation methods*, International Journal of Sustainability in Higher Education, Vol. 6, No. 3, pp. 254-264

Lord, C., 2003, *A Citizens' Income: A Foundation for a Sustainable World*, John Carpenter Publishing, Charlbury

Lorenz, D. and Lützkendorf, T., 2004, *The possible use of LCC & LCA for commercial property valuations - Putting a value on 'green' buildings*, Proceedings of the CIB World Building Congress, Toronto, Canada, 2004

Lorenz, D. and Lützkendorf, T., 2005a, *Complexities of operating in foreign property markets: Book review of 'International Real Estate - An Institutional Approach'*, Building Research & Information, Vol. 33, No. 3, pp. 300-307

Lorenz, D. and Lützkendorf, T., 2005b, *Towards sustainable development in property and construction - a survey of drivers, trends, strategies and instruments*, Proceedings of the World Sustainable Building Conference (SB05), Tokyo, Japan, 27-29 September 2005

Lorenz, D., Lützkendorf, T. and Panek, A., 2005, *Sustainable Construction in Central / Eastern Europe: Implications from SB04 in Warsaw*, Building Research & Information, Vol. 33, No. 5, pp. 416-427

Lorenz, D. and Trück, S., 2006, *Risk and Return in European Property Markets – An Empirical Investigation*, Proceedings of the European Real Estate Society Conference 2006, Weimar, Germany

Lorenz, D., Trück, S. and Lützkendorf, T., 2006, *Addressing Risk and Uncertainty in Property Valuations – A viewpoint from Germany*, Journal of Property Investment & Finance, in press

Lovelock, J. 1979, *Gaia: A New Look at Life on Earth*, Oxford University Press, Oxford

Lovelock, J., 2005, *Gaia: Medicine for an Ailing Planet*, Gaia Books, London

Lovelock, J., 2006, *The Revenge of Gaia, Why the earth is fighting back – and how we can still save humanity*, Penguin Books, London

Lundqvist, L., 2004, *'Greening the people's home': the formative power of sustainable development discourse in Swedish housing*, Urban Studies, Vol. 41, No. 7, 2004, pp. 1283-1301

Lucius, D.I., 2001, *Real options in real estate development*, Journal of Property Investment & Finance, Vol. 19, No. 1, pp. 73-78

Lützkendorf, T. and Bachofner, M., 2002, *The consideration of ecological quality in the valuation and funding of buildings – a methodological overview*, Proceedings of the International Sustainable Building Conference, Oslo, 2002

Lützkendorf, T. and Lorenz, D., 2004, *Integrating the concept of "environmental performance" into decision making processes along the life-cycle of buildings*, Proceedings of the Central and Eastern European Conference on Sustainable Building (SB04), Warsaw, Poland, 2004

Lützkendorf, T. and Lorenz, D., 2005, *Sustainable Property Investment: Valuing sustainable buildings through property performance assessment*, Building Research & Information, Vol. 33, No. 3, pp. 212-234

Lützkendorf, T. and Lorenz, D., 2006a, *Using an Integrated Performance Approach in Building Assessment Tools,* Building Research & Information, in press

Lützkendorf, T. and Lorenz, D., 2006b, *The issue of 'Sustainability' in Education and Training of Real Estate Economists*, Proceedings of the International Conference on Building Education and Research, BEAR 2006, Hong Kong, 10-13 April 2006

Lützkendorf, T., Lorenz, D. and Thöne, C., 2006, *Socially Responsible Investment im Immobilienbereich – Wo bleiben nachhaltige Immobilieninvestmentprodukte*, In: Schöller, F. and Witt, M. (Hrsg.), Jahrbuch Geschlossene Fonds 2005/2006, Scope Group, Berlin, pp. 208-218

Lützkendorf, T. and Speer, T., 2005, *Alleviating asymmetric information in property markets: building performance and product quality as signals for consumers*, Building Research & Information, Vol. 33 No. 2, 2005, pp. 182-195

Lützkendorf, T., Speer, T., Szigeti, F., Davis, G., le Roux, P., Kato, A., Tsunekawa, K., 2005, *A comparison of international classifications for performance requirements and building performance categories used in evaluation methods*, Proceedings of the 11th Joint CIB International Symposium; Helsinki, Finland; June 2005

MA, 2005, *Millennium Ecosystem Assessments – Living Beyond our Means, Natural Assets and Human Well-Being, Statement from the Board* [online], Available at: <URL: http://www.millenniumassessment.org/proxy/document.429.aspx>, [Accessed at: 01 February 2006]

MA, 2006, *Millennium Ecosystem Assessments, Our Human Planet: Summary for Decision-Makers* [online], Available at: <URL: http://www.millenniumassessment.org//en/Products.Global.Summary.aspx>, [Accessed at: 24 March 2006]

Mackley, C.J., 2002, *Unlocking the Value in Sustainable Buildings*, Sustainable Building 2002, Summary book of the 3rd International Conference on Sustainable Building, ed. Pettersen, T., EcoBuild, Oslo

Mackmin, D., 1999, *Valuation of real estate in global markets*, Property Management, Vol. 17, No. 4, 1999, pp. 353-367

Mackmin, D. and Emary, R., 2000, *The assessment of worth: the need for standards*, Journal of Property Investment & Finance, Vol. 18, No. 1, pp. 52-65

Mallinson, M. and French, N., 2000, *Uncertainty in property valuation – The nature and relevance of uncertainty and how it might be measured and reported*, Journal of Property Investment & Finance, Vol. 18, No. 1, 2000, pp. 13-32

Mansfield, J.R. and Lorenz, D., 2004, *Shaping the future - The impacts of evolving international accounting standards on valuation practice in the UK and Germany*, Property Management, Vol. 22, No. 4, pp. 289-303

Marshall, A., 1890 [1920], *Principles of Economics*, 8th edition, Macmillan and Co., London

Marshall, A., 1898. *Mechanical and biological analogies in economics*, In: Pigou, A.C. (ed.), 1925, Memorials of Alfred Marshall, Macmillan Press, London

Marshall, R.S. and Harry, S.P., 2005, *Introducing a new business course: "Global business and sustainability"*, International Journal of Sustainability in Higher Education, Vol. 6, No. 2, pp. 179-196

Martinez-Alier, J., Munda, G. and O'Neill, J., 1998, *Weak Comparability of Values as a Foundation for Ecological Economics*, Ecological Economics, Vol. 26, pp. 277-286

Matthiessen, L. and Morris P., 2003, *Costing Green: A Comprehensive Cost Database and Budgeting Methodology* [online], Published by: Davis Langdon Adamson, Available at: <URL: http://www.davislangdon-usa.com/images/pdf_files/costinggreen.pdf>, [Accessed at: 22 June 2004]

Marwell, G. and Ames, R., 1981, *Economists Free Ride. Does Anyone Else? Experiments on the Provision of Public Goods. IV*, Journal of Public Economics Vol. 15, pp. 295-310

Matrosov, Y., Chao, M., Goldstein, D., 2003, *The Fruit has Ripened: Energy Code Implementation and Market Transformation at the Federal and Regional Levels in Russia* [online], Published by: Russian Center for Energy Efficiency, Available at: <URL: http://www.cenef.ru/home-pg/PAPER.92E.pdf>, [Accessed at: 15 Mai 2004]

Matthews, E., Amann, C., Bringezu, S., Fischer-Kowalski, M., Hüttler, W., Kleijn, R., Moriguchi, Y., Ottke, C., Rodenburg, E. Rogich, D., Schandl, H., Schütz, H., Voet, E. and Weisz, H., 2002, *The Weight of Nations – Material Outflows from Industrial Economies*, [online], Published by: World Resources Institute, Available at: <URL: http://pdf.wri.org/weight_of_nations.pdf>, [Accessed at: 22 April 2006]

Maurer, R., Pitzer, M. and Sebastian, S., 2004, *Hedonic Price Indices for the Paris Housing Market*, Journal of the German Statistical Association, Vol. 88, 2004, pp. 303-326

McCarthy, J.P., 2001, *Environmental enclosures and the state of nature in the American West*, In: Watts, M.J. and Peluso, N.L. (Eds.), Violent environments, Cornell University Press, Ithaca

McDonough, W. and Braungart, M., 2002, *Cradle To Cradle – Remaking the Way We Make Things*, North Point Press, New York

McDonough, W. and Braungart, M., 2003, *Towards a sustaining architecture for the 21st century: the promise of cradle-to-cradle design*, In: UNEP, 2003, *Sustainable building and construction*, Industry and Environment, Vol. 26, No. 2-3, Published by: United Nations Environment Programme Division of Technology, Industry and Economics, Paris, pp. 13-16

McDonough, W., Braungart, M., Anastas, P.T. and Zimmerman, J.B., 2003, *Applying the Principles of Green Engineering to Cradle-to-Cradle Design*, Environmental Science & Technology, Special Issue: Principles of Green Engineering, Vol. 37, No. 23, pp. 434A-441A, Available at: <URL: http://www.mcdonough.com/writings/c2c_design.htm>, [Accessed at: 23 April 2006]

McDonough, W., 2005a, Interview with Newsweek, *Designing the Future*, Newsweek, 16 May 2005, p. 40

McDonough, W., 2005b, Interview with Financial Times, *Designing our way out of trouble*, Financial Times, 15 October 2005, p. 8

McGough, T. and Tsolacos, S., 1995, *Forecasting commercial rental values using ARIMA models*, Journal of Property Valuation & Investment, Vol. 13, No. 5, pp. 6-22

McKenzie-Mohr, D., 2000, *Promoting Sustainable Behaviour: an introduction to community-based social marketing*, Journal of Social Issues, Vol. 56, No. 3, pp. 543-554

McNamara, P., 2002, *Towards a research agenda for socially responsible investment in property* [online], Speech held at the European Real Estate Society, August 2002, Available at: <URL: http://www.ishareowner.com/pdf/SRI-in-property.pdf>, [Accessed at: 26 August 2003]

McNamara, P., 2005a, *Sustainable Property Investment – Balancing the Commercial Pressures of Today with the Realities of the Future* [online], Presentation held at the RICS Valuation conference 2005, 29 December 2005, London, Available at: <URL: http://www.rics.org/NR/rdonlyres/DAF0FD53-23F1-4A56-B05A-739A4A41E77B/0/PaulMcNamara.pdf>, [Accessed at: 01 February 2006]

McNamara, P., 2005b, *Interview with Property Week*, Property Week, 14 October 2005, pp. 84-86

McParland, C., McGreal, S. and Adair, A., 2000, *Concepts of price, value and worth in the United Kingdom – Towards a European perspective*, Journal of Property Investment & Finance, Vol. 18, No. 1, pp. 84-102

McWilliams, R., 2002, *History of Dialogue Related to U.S. Government Commitment to Sustainable Forest / Resource Management* [online], Available at: <URL: http://www.fs.fed.us/sustained/history-updated-oct02.rtf>, [Accessed at: 24 March 2006]

Meadows D.H., Meadows D.I., Randers, J., and Behrens III, W.W., 1972, *The Limits to Growth*, Universe Books, New York

Meadows D.H., Randers, J. and Meadows D.I., 2004, *Limits to Growth – The 30-Year Update*, Chelsea Green Publishing, White River Jct.

Meacham, B., Bowen, R., Traw, J., Moore, A., 2005, *Performance-based building regulation: current situation and future needs*, Building Research & Information, Vol. 33 No. 2, 2005, pp. 91-106

Menger, C., [1871] 2004, *Principles of Economics*, Translation of ‚Grundsätze der Volkswirthschaftslehre' [online], Published by: Ludwig von Mises Institute, Available at: <URL: http://www.mises.org/etexts/menger/Mengerprinciples.pdf>, [Accessed at: 24 March 2006]

Miller, N.G. and Markosyan, S., 2003, *The Academic Roots and Evolution of Real Estate Appraisal*, The Appraisal Journal, April 2003, pp. 172-184

Mills, E., Lecomte, E. and Peara, A., 2002, *Insurers in the Greenhouse*, Pre-publication draft [online], Available at: <URL: http://eetd.lbl.gov/emills/PUBS/PDF/Insurers_in_the_Greenhouse.pdf>, [Accessed at: 21 April 2006]

Mills, E., 2003a, *The insurance and risk management industries: new players in the delivery of energy-efficient and renewable energy products and services*, Energy Policy, Vol. 31, 2003, pp. 1257-1272

Mills, E., 2003b, *Climate change, insurance and the buildings sector: technological synergisms between adaptation and mitigation*, Building Research & Information, Vol. 31 No. 3-4, 2003, pp. 257-277

Milner, S.J., Bailey, C., Deans, J. and Pettigrew, D., 2005, *Integrated impact assessment in the UK – use, efficacy and future development*, Environmental Impact Assessment Review, Vol. 25, pp. 47-61

Milton, J.W., Gressel, J. and Mulkey, D., 1984, *Hedonic Amenity and Functional Form Specification*, Land Economics, Vol. 60, 1984, pp. 378-388

Minton, A., 2006, *What kind of world are we building – The privatisation of public space* [online], Published by: The Royal Institution of Chartered Surveyors, Available at: <URL: http://www.rics.org/RICSservices/RICSresearch/privatisation_public230306.html>, [Accessed at: 21 Mai 2006]

Moch, D. and Triplett, J. E., 2004, *PPPs for PCs: Hedonic Comparison of Computer Prices in France and Germany*, Unpublished paper, Center for European Economic Research, University of Mannheim and Brookings Institution

Moore, D.S. 1998, *Subaltern struggles and the politics of place: remapping resistance in Zimbabwe's Eastern Highlands*, Cultural Anthropology, Vol. 13, pp. 344-81

Morris, W.E., 2001, *David Hume* [online], Stanford Encyclopaedia of Philosophy, Available at: <URL: http://plato.stanford.edu/entries/hume/>, [Accessed at: 01 March 2006]

Moulton, B. R., LaFleur, T. J. and Moses, K. E., 1999, *Research on Improved Quality Adjustment in the CPI: The Case of Televisions*, In: Proceedings of the Fourth Meeting of the International Working Group on Price Indices, ed. W. Lane., pp. 77-99

Motta, T.A. and Endsley, W.E., 2003, *The Future of the Valuation Profession: Diagnostic Tools and Prescriptive Practices for Real Estate Markets*, Paper presented at the World Valuation Congress in Cambridge, England, July 2003

Munich Re, 2005, *Megacities – Megarisks: Trends and challenges for insurance and risk management* [online], Published by: Munich Re Group, Available at: <URL: http://www.muenchener-rueck.de/publications/302-04271_en.pdf?rdm=61251>, [Accessed at: 21 April 2006]

Munich Re, 2006a, *Topics Geo – Annual review: Natural catastrophes 2005* [online], Published by: Munich Re Group, Available at: <URL: http://www.muenchener-rueck.de/publications/302-04772_en.pdf?rdm=25801>, [Accessed at: 21 April 2006]

Munich Re, 2006b, *Topics Geo – Significant natural catastrophes in 2005* [online], Published by: Munich Re Group, Available at: <URL: http://www.muenchener-rueck.de/assets/PDF/georisks/04772_significant_natural_catastrophes_en.pdf >, [Accessed at: 21 April 2006]

Murphy, C.J., 2002, *The Profitable Correlation – Between Environmental and Financial Performance: A Review of the Research* [online], Published by: Light Green Advisors, Available at: <URL: http://www.lightgreen.com/files/pc.pdf>, [Accessed at: 28 January 2003]

Münchehofe, M. und Springer, U., 2004, *Die Abbildung des wirtschaftlichen Risikos im Liegenschaftszins,* Grundstücksmarkt und Grundstückswert, Heft 1, 2004, S. 7-10

Myers, N., 1998, *Lifting the veil on perverse subsidies*, Nature, Vol. 392, pp. 327-328

Myers, D., 2003, *The future of construction economics as an academic discipline*, Construction Management and Economics, Vol. 21, pp. 103-106

Myers, D., 2005, *A review of construction companies' attitudes to sustainability*, Construction Management and Economics, Vol. 23, pp. 781-785

Neter, J., Wassermann, W., Nachtsheim, C. and Kuntner, M. H., 1996, *Applied Linear Statistical Models: Regression, Analysis of Variance, and Experimental Designs,* 4th ed., McGraw-Hill, New York

Nevin, R. and Watson, G., 1998, *Evidence of Rational Market Valuations for Home Energy Efficiency* [online], The Appraisal Journal, October 1998, Available at: <URL: http://www.natresnet.org/herseems/appraisal.htm>, [Accessed at: 26 June 2002]

Newman, L., 2005, *Change, uncertainty, and futures of sustainable development* [online], Futures, Article in press, Available at: <URL: http://www.sciencedirect.com>, [Accessed at: 18 March 2006]

Newsweek, 2005, *Designing the Future*, Newsweek, 16 May 2005, p. 40

Noël, J.F. and M. O'Connor, 1998, *Strong Sustainability and Critical Natural Capital*, In: Faucheux, S. and O'Connor, M. (Eds.), Valuation for Sustainable Development: Methods and Policy Indicators, Edward Elgar Publishing, Cheltenham, pp. 75-98

Novalis, [1842] 1964, *Henry Von Ofterdingen*, A novel translated from the German by Palmer Hilty, New York, cited in Becker and Manstetten, 2004

Novalis, 1997, *Philosophical Writings*, edited and translated by Margaret Mahoney Stoljar, New York, cited in Becker and Manstetten, 2004

OECD, 2003, *Environmentally Sustainable Buildings – Challenges and Policies*, OECD Publications, Paris, 2003

Oesten, G., 2004, *Nachhaltige Waldwirtschaft – ein Modell für nachhaltige Entwicklung?* [online], Impulsreferat anlässlich der Konsultation des Rats für Nachhaltige Entwicklung: „200 Jahre danach – Wald und Nachhaltigkeit" am 11.2.2004 in Berlin, Available at: <URL: http://www.ife.uni-freiburg.de/htdoc/Home-20Germann/Impulsvortrag_Gerhard_Oesten_11-02-04.pdf>, [Accessed at: 18 March 2006]

O'Rourke, A., 2003, *The message and methods of ethical investment*, Journal of Cleaner Production, Vol. 11, 2003, pp. 683-693

Özkaynak, B., Devine, P. and Rigby, D., 2004, *Operationalising Strong Sustainability: Definitions, Methodologies and Outcomes*, Environmental Values, Vol. 13, pp. 279-303

Pace, R.K., Barry, R. and Sirmans, C.F., 1998, *Spatial Statistics and Real Estate,* Journal of Real Estate Finance and Economics, Vol. 17, No. 1, pp. 5-13

Pagourtzi, E., Assimakopoulos, V., Hatzichristos, T. and French, N., 2003, *Real estate appraisal: a review of valuation methods*, Journal of Property Investment & Finance, Vol. 21, No. 4, p. 383-401

Pagourtzi, E., Nikolopoulos, K. and Assimakopoulos, V., 2006, *Architecture for a real estate analysis information system using GIS techniques integrated with fuzzy theory*, Journal of Property Investment & Finance, Vol. 24, No. 1, p. 68-78

Palmquist, R., 1980, *Alternative Techniques for Developing Real Estate Price Indexes*, Review of Economics and Statistics, Vol. 62, pp. 442-448

Parkin, S., 2000, *Sustainable development: the concept and the practical challenge*, Proceedings of the Institution of Civil Engineers, Civil Engineering, Vol. 138, 2000, pp. 3-8

Parnell, P., 2005, *Sustainability – A Valuer's Perspective* [online], Presentation held at the RICS Valuation conference 2005, 29 December 2005, London, Available at: <URL: http://www.rics.org/NR/rdonlyres/ABFE4385-9E11-4989-ABC0-2E7783506C68/0/PhilipParnell.pdf>, [Accessed at: 01 February 2006]

Pearce, D., 1993, *Economic Values and the Natural World*, Earthscan, London

Pearce, D., Barbier, E.B. and Markandya, A., 1989, *Blueprint for a Green Economy*, Earthscan, London

Pearce, D. and Barbier, E.B., 2000, *Blueprint for a Sustainable Economy*, Earthscan, London

Pearce, D., 2003, *The Social and Economic Value of Construction – The Construction Industry's Contribution to Sustainable Development 2003* [online], Published by: The Construction Industry Research and Innovations Strategy Panel, Available at: <URL: http://www.crisp-uk.org.uk/reports/SocialandEconomicValue_FR03.pdf>, [Accessed at: 08 November 2004]

Pearce, D., 2005, *Do we understand sustainable development?*, Building Research & Information, Vol. 33, No. 5, pp. 481-483

Pearce, D., 2006, *Is the construction sector sustainable?: definitions and reflections*, Building Research & Information, Vol. 34, No. 3, pp. 201-207

Peuportier, B. and Putzeys, K., 2005, *Inter-Comparison and Benchmarking of LCA-Based Environmental Assessment and Design Tools – Final Report* [online], Published by: The European Thematic Network on Practical Recommendations for Sustainable Construction (PRESCO), Available at: <URL: http://www.etn-presco.net/generalinfo/PRESCO_WP2_Report.pdf>, [Accessed at: 08 August 2005]

Phillips, Hager & North, 2005, *Does Socially Responsible Investing Hurt Investment Returns?* [online], Available at: <URL: http://www.phn.com/pdfs/SRI%20Articles/does_sri_hurt.pdf>, [Accessed at: 01 January 2006]

PISCES, 2004, *PISCES – Property Information Systems Common Exchange Standard, Version 1.6.1* [online], Available at: <URL: http://www.pisces.co.uk/>, [Accessed at: 30 March 2006]

Pivo, G., 2005, *Is There a Future for Socially Responsible Property Investments?*, Real Estate Issues, Fall 2005, pp. 16-26

Pivo, G. and McNamara, P., 2005, *Responsible Property Investing*, International Real Estate Review, Vol. 8, No. 1, 2005, pp. 128-143

Preiser, W., 2002, *Improving Building performance*, Published by: The National Council of Architectural Registration Boards, Washington, DC

Prendergast, R., 2005, *The concept of freedom and its relation to economic development—a critical appreciation of the work of Amartya Sen*, Cambridge Journal of Economics, Vol. 29, 2005, pp. 1145-1170

PRI, 2006, *Principles for Responsible Investment* [online], Published by: UN Environment Programme Finance Initiative in cooperation with UN Global Compact, Available at: <URL: http://www.unpri.org/files/pri.pdf>, [Accessed at: 28 April 2006]

Price, C., 1993, *Time, Discounting & Value*, Blackwell Publishing, Cambridge

Pope, J., Annandale, D. and Morrison-Saunders, A., 2004, *Conceptualising sustainability assessment*, Environmental Impact Assessment Review, Vol. 24, pp. 595-616

Porritt, J., 2000, *Playing safe: science and the environment*, Thames & Hudson, London, 2000

Porritt, J., 2006, *Capitalism as if the World Matters*, Earthscan, London

Princen, T., 2003, *Principles of Sustainability: From Cooperation and Efficiency to Sufficiency*, Global Environmental Politics, Vol. 3, No. 1, 2003, pp. 33-50

RICS, 1994, *Commercial Property Valuations (Mallinson Report)*, Royal Institution of Chartered Surveyors, London

RICS, 1997, *Calculation of Worth – An Information Paper*, Royal Institution of Chartered Surveyors, London

RICS, 2002, *The Carsberg Report* [online], Royal Institution of Chartered Surveyors, London Available at: <URL: http://www.cili.org.uk/library/papers/carsberg_report.pdf>, [Accessed at: 23 December 2005]

RICS, 2003a, *New markets in energy efficient Europe* [online], Environment Faculty news bulletin, February 2003, Available at: <URL: http://www.rics.org/downloads/env_fac_newsletter_0103.pdf>, [Accessed at: 15 April 2003]

RICS, 2003b, *RICS Appraisal and Valuation Standards*, Royal Institution of Chartered Surveyors, London

RICS, 2004a, *Sustainability and the Built Environment – An Agenda for Action* [online], Published by: The Royal Institution of Chartered Surveyors, Available at: <URL:http://www.rics.org/NR/rdonlyres/DE2FC8A1-9600-46F4-9673-D13D6B686023/0/Sustainability_and_built_environment.pdf>, [Accessed at: 10 November 2004]

RICS, 2004b, *RICS Rules of Conduct 2004*, Royal Institution of Chartered Surveyors, London

RICS, 2004c, *The new Capital Adequacy Directive: RICS response* [online], Royal Institution of Chartered Surveyors, London, Available at: <URL: http://www.rics.org/Management/Businessmanagement/Financialmanagement/Accounting/Financialreport-ing/The%20new%20Capital%20Adequacy%20Directive%20CAD%203%20The%20transposition%20of%20the%20new%20Basel%20Accord%20into%20EU%20legislati.html>, [Accessed at: 12 March 2006]

RICS, 2005, *Green Value – Green buildings, growing assets* [online], Published by: The Royal Institution of Chartered Surveyors, Available at: <URL: http://www.rics.org/NR/rdonlyres/93B20864-E89E-4641-AB11-028387737058/0/GreenValueReport.pdf >, [Accessed at: 18 November 2005]

Rifkin, J., 2000, *The Age of Access - The New Culture of Hypercapitalism*, Tarcher/Penguin, New York

Robbins, L. [1932] 1983, *An Essay on the Nature and Significance of Economic Science*, Macmillan, 3rd edition, London

Robbins, P., 2004, *Political Ecology: A Critical Introduction*, Blackwell Publishing, Cambridge

Robertson, J. and Bunzl, J., 2003, *Monetary Reform: Making it Happen*, International Simultaneous Policy Organization, London

Rocky Mountain Institute, 1998, *Greening the Building and the Bottom Line - Increasing productivity through energy-efficient design* [online], Available at: <URL: http://www.rmi.org>, [Accessed at: 28 January 2002]

Rogall, H., 2004, *Ökonomie der Nachhaltigkeit – Handlungsfelder für Politik und Wirtschaft*, VS Verlag für Sozialwissenschaften, Wiesbaden

Rogers, J., 2005, *We have financial fundamentals, so why not sustainability fundamentals?*, In: Ethical Corporation Magazine, No. 2, February 2005, pp. 38-39

Rosen, S., 1974, *Hedonic Prices and Implicit Markets: Product Differentiation in Pure Competition*, Journal of Political Economy, Vol. 82, 1974, pp. 34 - 55

Ruth, M., 2006, *A quest for the economics of sustainability and the sustainability of economics*, Ecological Economics, Vol. 56, 2006, pp. 332-342

Rüchardt, K., 2001, *Der Beleihungswert – Bedeutung, Anforderungen, Ermittlung und Verwendung von Beleihungswerten für Immobilien*, Schriftenreihe des VDH, Fritz Knapp Verlag, Frankfurt

Rydin, Y., 2003, *In pursuit of sustainable development: Rethinking the planning system* [online], published by RICS Foundation, Available at: <URL: http://www.rics-foundation.org/publish/document.aspx?did=3170>, [Accessed at: 13 June 2004]

Rydin, Y., Holman, N., Wolff, E., 2003, *Local Sustainability Indicators*, Local Environment, Vol. 8, No. 6, 2003, pp. 581–589

Sagoff, M., 2004, *Price, Principle, and the Environment*, Cambridge University Press, Cambridge

SAM, 2005, *Sustainability Yearbook 2005*, [online], Published by: SAM Group and PricewaterhouseCoopers, Available at: <URL: http://www.pwcglobal.com/Extweb/ncsurvres.nsf/0cc1191c627d157d8525650600609c03/68b 446882286c7698025711700305703/$FILE/Sustainability%20Yearbook.pdf >, [Accessed at: 17 March 2006]

Sayce, S., Ellison, L., Smith, J., 2004a, *Incorporating Sustainability in Commercial Property Appraisal: Evidence from the UK,* Proceedings of the 11th European Real Estate Society Conference (ERES 2004), Milan, 2004

Sayce, S., Walker, A. and McIntosh, A., 2004b, *Building Sustainability in the Balance: Promoting Stakeholder Dialogue*, Estates Gazette, London

Scarret, D., 1998, *Property Valuation - The five methods*, 4th Edition, E & FN Spoon, London

Schmidt-Bleek, F.B., 1994, *Wieviel Umwelt braucht der Mensch? MIPS, das Maß für ökologisches Wirtschaften*, Birkhäuser, Berlin

Schmidt-Bleek, F.B., 2001, *The Story of Factor10 and MIPS* [online], Available at: <URL: http://www.factor10-institute.org/pdf/Mipsstory.pdf >, [Accessed at: 18 March 2006]

Schmidt-Bleek, F.B., 2004, *Approaching and Measuring Sustainability* [online], Speech held at the International Conference 'Towards Sustainable Futures – Tools and Strategies, Tampere, 14 June 2004, Available at: <URL: http://www.factor10-institute.org/pdf/TURKU%20PAPER.pdf>, [Accessed at: 13 March 2006]

Schmutz, G.L., 1948, *The Evolution of the Interpretation of Appraisal Principles*, The Appraisal Journal, January 1948

Schröder, M., 2003, S*ocially Responsible Investments in Germany, Switzerland and the United States – An Analysis of Investment Funds and Indices* [online], Published by: Zentrum für Europäische Wirtschaftsforschung, Available at: <URL: ftp://ftp.zew.de/pub/zew-docs/dp/dp0310.pdf> [Accessed at: 11 November 2004]

Schultze, C. L. and Mackie, C., eds., 2002, *At What Price? Conceptualizing and Measuring Cost-of-Living and Price Indexes,* National Academy Press, Washington

Scrase, J.I. and Sheate, W.R., 2002, *Integration and Integrated Approaches to Assessment: What do they mean for the environment?,* Journal of Environmental Policy & Planning, Vol. 4, pp. 275-294

Seabrook, W., Kent, P. and Hong How, H.H. (Eds.), 2004, International Real Estate – An Institutional Approach, Blackwell Publishing, Cambridge

Sen, A., 1990, *Development as capability expansion*, In: Griffin, K. and Knight, J. (Eds.), Human Development and International Development Strategy for the 1990s, Macmillan Press, London, in association with the United Nations

Sen, A., 1999, *Development as Freedom*, Anchor Books, New York

Seyfang, G., 2003, *Environmental mega-conferences – from Stockholm to Johannesburg and beyond*, Global Environmental Change, Vol. 13, 2003, pp. 223-228

Serageldin, I. and Steer, A. (Eds.), 1994, *Making Development Sustainable.* Environmentally Sustainable Development Proceedings Series No. 2, World Bank, Washington

Sevelka, T., 2004, *Where the Overall Cap Rate Meets the Discount Rate*, The Appraisal Journal, Spring 2004, pp. 135-146

Seyfang, G. and Jordan, A., 2002, *'Mega' Environmental Conferences: vehicles for effective, long term environmental planning?*, In: Stokke, S. and Thommesen, O. (Eds.), Yearbook of International Cooperation on Environment and Development, Earthscan, London, pp. 19–26

Sing, T.F. and Patel, K., 2001, *Empirical evaluation of the value of waiting to invest*, Journal of Property Investment & Finance, Vol. 19, No. 6, pp. 535-553

Sinner, J., Baines, J., Crengle, H., Salmon, G., Fenemor, A. and Tipa. G., 2004, *Sustainable Development: A summary of key concepts* [online], Available at: <URL: http://www.ecologic.org.nz/content/documents/51.pdf>, [Accessed at: 13 March 2006]

SiRi Group, 2005, *Green, social and ethical funds in Europe 2005* [online], Published by: SiRi Company, Available at: <URL: http://www.siricompany.com/pdf/SRI_Funds_Europe_2005.pdf> [Accessed at: 16 October 2005]

Sirmans, C. F. and Worzala, E., 2003, *International Direct Real Estate Investment: A Review of the Literature,* Urban Studies, Vol. 40, No. 5–6, pp. 1081–1114

Sirmans, G. S., Macpherson, D. A. and Zietz, E., 2005, *The composition of hedonic pricing models*, Journal of Real Estate Literature, Volume 13, No. 1, 2005, pp. 1-44

Smith, A, [1776] 1937, *An Inquiry into the Nature and Causes of the Wealth of Nations*, Random House, New York

Sneddon, C., Howarth, R.B., and Norgaard, R.B., 2005, *Sustainable development in a post-Brundtland world* [online], Ecological Economics, Article in press, Available at: <URL: http://www.sciencedirect.com>, [Accessed at: 18 March 2006]

St. Lawrence, S., 2004, *Review of the UK corporate real estate market with regard to availability of environmentally and socially responsible office buildings,* Journal of Corporate Real Estate, Vol. 6 No. 2, 2004, pp. 149–161

Stolyarov II, G., 2006, *Carl Menger, Individualism, Marginal Utility, and the Revival of Economics* [online], The Rational Argumentator, 30 April 2006, No. 177, Montreal, Available at: <URL: http://www.quebecoislibre.org/06/060430-6.htm>, [Accessed at: 18 Mai 2006]

Stroh, W. T., 2004, *Aktuelle Bewertungsfragen Offener Immobilienfonds*, in: Immobilien & Finanzierung, Nr. 13, 2004, S. 410-413

Sunikka, M. and Boon, C., 2003, *Environmental policies and efforts in social housing: the Netherlands*, Building Research & Information, Vol. 31, No. 1, 2003, pp. 1-12

SustainAbility, 2004, *The Changing Landscape of Liability – A Director's Guide to Trends in Corporate Environmental, Social and Economic Liability* [online], Published by: SustainAbility Ltd., Available at: <URL: http://www.sustainability.com/compass/register.asp?type=download&articleid=23>, [Accessed at: 21 March 2006]

Sustainable Buildings Task Group, 2004, *Better Buildings – Better Lives: the Sustainable Buildings Task Group Report* [online], Available at: <URL: http://www.dti.gov.uk/construction/sustain/EA_Sustainable_Report_41564_2.pdf>, [Accessed at: 10 December 2004]

SZ, 2005, *Erstmals wird Immobilienfonds geschlossen*, Süddeutsche Zeitung, 14. Dezember 2005, S. 19

Szigeti, F. and Davis, G., 2003, *Matching people and their facilities: using the ASTM/ANSI standards on whole building Functionality and serviceability* [online], Published by: Performance Based Building Thematic Network, Available at: <URL: http://www.pebbu.nl/resources/literature/>, [Accessed at: 10 April 2004]

Szigeti, F., Davis, G., Dempsey, J., Hammond, D., Davis, D., Colombard-Prout, M., Catarina, O., 2004, *Defining Performance Requirements to Assess the Suitability of Constructed Assets in Support of the Mission of the Organization*, Proceedings of the CIB World Congress 2004, Toronto, Canada

Tansens, P. R., Van Wouwe, M. and Berkhout, T., *Risk Premiums in Cap Rates of Investment Property,* Proceedings of the 12th European Real Estate Society Conference, Dublin, Ireland, 15-18 June 2005

TEGoVA, 2003a, *European Property and Market Rating* [online], Published by: The European Group of Valuers Associations, Available at: <URL: http://www.tegova.org/reports/EPMR.pdf>, [Accessed at: 10 January 2004]

TEGoVA, 2003b, *European Valuation Standards*, The European Group of Valuers Associations, Brussels

Tetior, A., 2004, *Rethinking Ecological Education for successful Sustainable Building*, Proceedings of the Central and Eastern European Conference on Sustainable Building (SB04), Warsaw, 2004

The Independent, 2005, *Your Plant: Twilight of the Oil Age*, 19 September 2005

The Royal Society, 1983, *Risk assessment: Report of a Royal Society Study Group*, London, Royal Society

Then, D. and Clowes, A., 2004, *Stakeholders' perspectives in defining asset performance*, Proceedings of the CIB World Building Congress 2004, Toronto, Canada

Thériault, M., Des Rosiers, F., Villeneuve, P. and Kestens, Y., 2003, *Modelling interactions of location with specific value of housing attributes*, Property Management, Vol. 21, No. 1, pp. 25-62

Thoreau, H.D., 1849, *Resistance to Civil Government*, Aesthetic Papers, Available at: <URL: http://www.vcu.edu/engweb/transcendentalism/authors/thoreau/civiltext.html>, [Accessed at: 22 April 2005]

Thoreau, H.D., 1854, *Walden; or Life in the Woods*, Ticknor and Fields, Boston, Available at: <URL: http://www.vcu.edu/engweb/transcendentalism/authors/thoreau/walden/index.html>, [Accessed at: 22 April 2005]

Thoreau, H.D., 1862, *Walking*, The Atlantic Monthly, Available at: <URL: http://www.vcu.edu/engweb/transcendentalism/authors/thoreau/walkingtext.html>, [Accessed at: 22 April 2005]

Tidswell, A., 2005, *Help! We need a little help from our friends!* [online], Published by: Urban Ecology Australia, Available at: <URL: http://www.urbanecology.org.au/articles/>, [Accessed at: 18 March 2006]

Todd, J.A., Crawley U., Geissler, S. and Lindsey, G., 2001, *Comparative assessment of environmental performance tools and the role of the Green Building Challenge*, Building Research & Information, Vol. 29 No. 5, 2001, pp. 324-335

Toman, M., 1998, *Why not to calculate the value of the world's ecosystem services and natural capital*, Ecological Economics, Vol. 25, pp. 57-60

Triplett, J. E., 2004, *Handbook on hedonic indexes and quality adjustments in price indexes – Special Application to Information Technology Products* [online], Published by: The Brookings Institution, Available at: <URL: http://www.brookings.edu/views/papers/triplett/200407_book.htm>, [Accessed at: 15 September 2004]

Tse, R.Y.C., 1997, *An application of the ARIMA model to real-estate prices in Hong Kong*, Journal of Property Finance, Vol. 8, No. 2, pp. 152-163

Tungodden, B., 2001, *A Balanced view of Development as Freedom*, Published by: Chr. Michelsen Institute, Development Studies and Human Rights, Bergen

Turner, D. and Hartzell, L., 2004, *The Lack of Clarity in the Precautionary Principle*, Environmental Values, Vol. 13, 2004, pp. 449-460

Turner, M.D., 1993, *Overstocking the range: a critical analysis of the environmental science of Sahelian pastoralism*, Economic Geography, Vol. 69, pp. 402-421

Turner, M.D., 1998, *Long-term effects of daily grazing orbits on nutrient availability in Sahelian West Africa: 1. Gradients in the chemical composition of rangeland soils and vegetation*, Journal of Biogeography, Vol. 25, pp. 669-82

Turner, R.K., 2006a, *Sustainability Auditing and Assessment Challenges*, Building Research & Information, Vol. 34, No. 3, pp. 197-200

Turner, R.K., 2006b, *The 'Blueprint' Legacy*, Environmental Values, in press

Turner, R.K., Adger, W.N. and Brouwer, R., 1998, *Ecosystem value, research needs, and policy relevance: a commentary*, Ecological Economics, Vol. 25, pp. 62-65

Turner, R.K., Paavola, J., Cooper, P., Farber, S., Jessamy, V. and Georgiou, S., 2003, *Valuing nature: lessons learned and future research directions*, Ecological Economics, Vol. 46, 2003, pp. 493-560

UN, 2005a, *2005 World Summit Outcome* [online], Published by: United Nations, Available at: <URL: http://www.un.org/summit2005/documents.html>, [Accessed at: 18 March 2006]

UN, 2005b, *UN Millennium Development Goals Report 2005* [online], Published by: United Nations, Available at: <URL: http://unstats.un.org/unsd/mi/pdf/MDG%20Book.pdf>, [Accessed at: 18 March 2006]

UNEP, 2003, *Sustainable building and construction*, Industry and Environment, Vol. 26, No. 2-3, Published by: United Nations Environment Programme Division of Technology, Industry and Economics, Paris

UNEP, 2004, *Integrated Assessment and Planning for Sustainable Development: Guidelines for Pilot Projects*, [online], Published by: United Nations Environment Programme, Available at: <URL: http://www.unep.ch/etb/areas/inteAsse.php>, [Accessed at: 24 March 2006]

UNEP, 2005, *One Planet Many People: Atlas of our Changing Environment* [online], Published by: United Nations Environment Programme, Available at: <URL: http://www.na.unep.net/OnePlanetManyPeople/index.php>, [Accessed at: 22 March 2006]

UNEP, 2006, *Sustainable Building & Construction Initiative – Information Note* [online], Published by: United Nations Environment Programme Division of Technology, Industry and Economics, Available at: <URL: http://www.unep.fr/pc/pc/SBCI/SBCI_2006_InformationNote.pdf>, [Accessed at: 24 March 2006]

UNEP FI, 1995, *Statement of Environmental Commitment by the insurance industry* [online], Published by: United Nations Environment Programme Finance Initiative, Available at: <URL: http://www.unepfi.org/signatories/statements/ii/index.html>, [Accessed at: 22 April 2006]

UNEP FI, 1997, *Statement by financial institutions on the environment and sustainable development,* Revised Version [online], Published by: United Nations Environment Programme Finance Initiative, Available at: <URL: http://www.unepfi.org/signatories/statements/fi/index.html>, [Accessed at: 22 April 2006]

UNEP FI, 2004, *The Materiality of Social, Environmental and Corporate Governance Issues to Equity Pricing – 11 Sector Studies by Brokerage House Analysts at the Request of the UNEP Finance Initiative Asset Management Working Group* [online], Published by: United Nations Environment Programme Finance Initiative, Available at: <URL: http://www.unepfi.org/work_programme/investment/materiality/mat1/index.html>, [Accessed at: 15 November 2005]

UNEP FI, 2005, *A legal framework for the integration of environmental, social and governance issues into institutional investment,* [online], Published by: United Nations Environment Programme Finance Initiative, Available at: <URL: http://www.unepfi.org/fileadmin/documents/freshfields_legal_resp_20051123.pdf>, [Accessed at: 08 December 2005]

UNESCO, n.d., *UN Decade for Education for Sustainable Development (2005-2014), Background Information* [online], Available at: <URL: http://portal.unesco.org/education/en/ev.php-URL_ID=23279&URL_DO=DO_TOPIC&URL_SECTION=201.html>, [Accessed at: 21 Mai 2006]

UNFPA, 2005, *State of the World Population 2005* [online], Published by: United Nations Population Fund, Available at: <URL: http://www.unfpa.org/swp/swpmain.htm>, [Accessed at: 22 March 2006]

US SIF, 2006, *Report on Socially Responsible Investing Trends in the United States – 10 Year Review* [online], Published by: US Social Investment Forum, Available at: <URL: http://www.socialinvest.org/areas/research/trends/SRI_Trends_Report_2005.pdf>, [Accessed at: 28 February 2006]

Vandell, K. and Lane, J., 1989, *The economics of architecture and urban design: some preliminary findings*, Journal of Urban Economics, Vol. 17, No. 2, 1989, pp 1–10

Vatn, A. and Bromley, W.D., 1995, *Choices without Prices without Apologies*, In: Bromley, W.D. (Ed.), Handbook of Environmental Economics, Blackwell Publishing, Cambridge, pp. 3-26

VDP, 2004, *Europäische Immobilienmärkte und ihre Bewertungsverfahren*, Published by: Verband Deutscher Pfandbriefbanken, Berlin

VDP, 2005, *Fact Book Immobilie 2005* [online], Published by: Verband Deutscher Pfandbriefbanken (VDP), Available at: <URL: http://www.hypverband.de/d/internet.nsf/tindex/de_immobilien.htm>, [Accessed at: 15 January 2006]

VfU, n.d., *Time to act - Environmental Management in Financial Institutions - A survey of recent developments including principles and guidelines for in-house eco-balances of financial services providers* [online], Published by: Association for Environmental Management in Banks, Savings Banks, and Insurance Companies (VfU), Available at: <URL: http://www.vfu.de/download/time-to-act.pdf>, [Accessed at: 22 April 2006]

von Mises, L., 1949, *Human Action – A Treatise On Economics*, 4th edition, Fox & Wilkes, San Francisco

von Thünen, J.H., [1826] 1999, *Der isolierte Staat in Beziehung auf Landwirtschaft und Nationalökonomie*, Scientia Verlag und Antiquariat Schilling, Aalen

von Wieser, F., 1891-92, *The Theory of Value – A Reply to Professor Macvane* [online], Annals of the American Academy of Political and Social Science, Vol. 2, pp. 600-628, Available at: <URL: http://www.ecn.bris.ac.uk/het/wieser/value.txt>, [Accessed at: 8 Mai 2006]

von Wieser, F., 1893, *Natural Value* [online], Available at: <URL: http://www.ecn.bris.ac.uk/het/wieser/natural/index.htm>, [Accessed at: 8 Mai 2006]

VÖB, 2005, *VÖB-Immobilienanalyse - Instrument zur Beurteilung des Chance-Risikoprofils von Immobilien* [online], Published by: Bundesverband Öffentlicher Banken Deutschlands (VÖB), Available at: <URL: http://www.voeb.de/content_frame/downloads/them_fach_immo.pdf>, [Accessed at: 12 November 2005]

Waage, S.A., Geiser, K., Irwin, F., Weissman, A.B., Bertolucci, M.D., Fisk, P., Basile, G., Cowan, S., Cauley, H. and McPherson, A., 2005, *Fitting together the building blocks for sustainability: a revised model for integrating ecological, social, and financial factors into business decision-making*, Journal of Cleaner Production, Vol. 13, 2005, pp. 1145-1163

Wackernagel, M., Schulz, N.B., Deumling, D., Linares, A.C., Jenkins, M., Kapos, V., Monfreda, C., Loh, J., Myers, N., Norgaard, R. and Randers, J., 2002, *Tracking the ecological overshoot of the human economy*, Proceedings of the National Academy of Sciences of the United States of America, Vol. 99, No. 14, pp. 9266-9271

Wackernagel, M., Onisto, L., Linares, A.C., Falfán, I.S.L., García, J.M., Guerrero, A.I.S., Guerrero, M.G.S., n.d., *Ecological Footprints of Nations - How Much Nature Do They Use? - How Much Nature Do They Have?* [online], Available at: <URL: http://www.ecouncil.ac.cr/rio/focus/report/english/footprint/>, [Accessed at: 22 March 2006]

Walker, P.A., 2005, *Political ecology: where is the ecology?*, Progress in Human Geography, Vol. 21, No. 1, 2005, pp. 73-82

Weber, O., 2005, *Sustainability Benchmarking of European Banks and Financial Service Organisations*, Corporate Social Responsibility and Environmental Management, Vol. 12, pp. 73-87

WEF, 2002, *Global Corporate Citizenship – The Leadership Challenge for CEOs and Boards* [online], Published by: World Economic Forum, Available at: <URL: http://www.weforum.org/pdf/GCCI/GCC_CEOstatement.pdf>, [Accessed at: 10 February 2005]

White, D., Turner, J., Jenyon, B. and Lincoln, N., 1999, *Internationale Bewertungsverfahren für das Investment in Immobilien - Praktisch Anwendung internationaler Bewertungsstandards*, 1. Auflage, Immobilien Zeitung Verlagsgesellschaft, Wiesbaden

WHO, 2004, *World Health Organization's technical meeting on Housing-Health Indicators*, Rome, 15-16 January 2004

WI, 2006, *State of the World 2006 – The Challenge of Global Sustainability, A Worldwatch Institute Report on Progress Toward a Sustainable Society*, Earthscan, London

Wilenius, M., 2005, *Towards the age of corporate responsibility? Emerging challenges for the business world*, Futures, Vol. 37, pp. 133-150

Wilhelmsson, M., 2002, *Spatial Models in Real Estate Economics*, Housing, Theory and Society, Vol. 19, pp. 92-101

Williams, T.P., 2004, *Base Adjusting in the Sales Comparison Approach*, The Appraisal Journal, Spring 2004, pp. 155-162

Wilson, A., Uncapher, J., McManigal, L., Hunter Lovins, L., Cureton, M., Browning, W.D., 1998, *Green Development: Integrating Ecology and Real Estate*, John Wiley & Sons, New York

Wijers, L., 2002, *Art meets science and spirituality in a changing economy, collection of quotes* [online], Available at: <URL: http://www.louwrienwijers.nl/amsse.html>, [Accessed at: 18 March 2006]

Wolford, W., 2005, *Book review of Political Ecology: A Critical Introduction*, Annals of the Association of American Geographers, Vol. 95, No. 3, 2005, pp. 692-726

Wolverton, M.L., 2004, *Highest and Best Use: The von Thünen Connection*, The Appraisal Journal, Fall 2004, pp. 318-323

Wordsworth, W. [1814] 1888, *The Prelude, Book IX, Discourse of the Wanderer, and an Evening Visit to the Lake*, In: The Complete Poetical Works, Macmillan and Co., London, Available at: <URL: http://www.bartleby.com/145/ww406.html>, [Accessed at: 18 March 2006]

World Bank, 2006, *Where is the Wealth of Nations? – Measuring Capital for the 21st Century*, [online], Published by: World Bank, Washington, Available at: <URL: http://web.worldbank.org/servlets/ECR?contentMDK=20744819&sitePK=407255>, [Accessed at: 22 March 2006]

Worzala, E. and Sirmans, C. F., 2003, *Investing in International Real Estate Stocks: A Review of the Literature,* Urban Studies, Vol. 40, No. 5–6, pp. 1115–1149

WRI, 2002, *Tomorrow's Markets – Global Trends and Their Implications for Business*, Published by: World Resources Institute, Baltimore, in cooperation with United Nations Environment Programme and World Business Council for Sustainable Development

WWF, 2004, *Living Planet Report 2004* [online], Published by: World-Wide Fund for Nature International, Gland, Available at: <URL: http://www.panda.org/downloads/general/lpr2004.pdf>, [Accessed at: 22 March 2006]

Yates, A., 2001, *Quantifying the Business Benefits of Sustainable Buildings* [online], Published by: The Building Research Establishment, Available at: <URL: http://www.bre.co.uk> [Accessed at: 22 November 2001]

Younkins, E.W., 2005, *Aristotle and Economics* [online], Capitalism & Commerce, 15 September 2005, No. 158, Montreal, Available at: <URL: http://www.quebecoislibre.org/05/050915-11.htm> [Accessed at: 22 April 2006]

Yovino-Young, M.G., 1997, *Appraising - from the Middle Ages to now* [online], Appraisal Today, July 1997, Available at: <URL: http://www.appraisaltoday.com/appraisi.htm> [Accessed at: 10 April 2006]

Zadeh, L.A., 1965, *Fuzzy sets*, Information and Control, Vol. 8, No. 3, pp. 338-353

Zimmerer, K.S., 1991, *Wetland production and smallholder persistence – agricultural change in a highland Peruvian region*, Annals of the Association of American Geographers, Vol. 81, pp. 443-463

Zimmermann, A. and Martin, M., 2001, *Post-occupancy evaluation: benefits and barriers*, Building Research & Information, Vol. 29 No. 2, 2001, pp. 168-174

Zimring, C. and Reizenstein, J.E., 1980, *Post-Occupancy Evaluation: An Overview,* Environment and Behaviour, Vol. 12, 1980, pp. 429-450